Debating Children's Lives

Debating Children's Lives

Current Controversies on Children and Adolescents

edited by
MARY ANN MASON
EILEEN GAMBRILL

SAGE Publications
International Educational and Professional Publisher
Thousand Oaks   London   New Delhi

Copyright © 1994 by Sage Publications, Inc.

All rights reserved. No part of this book may be reproduced or utilized in any form or by any means, electronic or mechanical, including photocopying, recording, or by any information storage and retrieval system, without permission in writing from the publisher.

For information address:

SAGE Publications, Inc.
2455 Teller Road
Thousand Oaks, California 91320

SAGE Publications Ltd.
6 Bonhill Street
London EC2A 4PU
United Kingdom

SAGE Publications India Pvt. Ltd.
M-32 Market
Greater Kailash I
New Delhi 110 048 India

Printed in the United States of America

Library of Congress Cataloging-in-Publication Data

Debating children's lives : current controversies on children and
　adolescents / edited by Mary Ann Mason, Eileen Gambrill.
　　　p. cm.
　　Includes bibliographical references.
　　ISBN 0-8039-5458-1. —ISBN 0-8039-5459-X (pbk.)
　　1. Children—Government policy—United States.　2. Teenagers—
　Government policy—United States.　3. Child welfare—United States.
　　I. Mason, Mary Ann.　II. Gambrill, Eileen D., 1934-
HQ792.U5D43　1994
362.7'0973—dc20　　　　　　　　　　　　　　　　　　　　93-37616
　　　　　　　　　　　　　　　　　　　　　　　　　　　　　　CIP

94　95　96　97　98　10　9　8　7　6　5　4　3　2

Sage Production Editor: Judith L. Hunter

CONTENTS

Preface ix
Introduction xiii

Part I. Children and Family Issues

1. Parental Competency Tests 3
   Should we require all prospective parents to pass competency tests in parenting skills and values?
   Yes: Roger McIntire
   No: Robert P. Hawkins

2. Parent Access After Adoption 18
   Should parents who give up their children for adoption continue to have access to them?
   Yes: Marianne Berry
   No: Mary Beth Seader and William L. Pierce

3. Child Custody and Sexual Orientation 36
   Should sexual orientation be a consideration in custody proceedings?
   Yes: J. Craig Peery
   No: Michael S. Wald

4. Grandparent Access 57
   Should grandparents have the right of access to their grandchildren in intact families and in the event of divorce or adoption?
   Yes: Ethel J. Dunn
   No: Ross A. Thompson

5. Children Divorcing Their Parents   76
   Should children and parents be allowed to divorce one another?
   Yes: Dana F. Castle
   No: Carol Sanger

Part II. Health and Medical Issues

6. Social Costs of an At-Risk Fetus   95
   Should prospective parents be asked to consider the costs to society of giving birth to an offspring when prenatal testing has diagnosed a fetal defect that will produce severe physical and/or mental disabilities?
   Yes: Eileen Gambrill
   No: Rita Beck Black

7. Preventing Teenage Pregnancy   108
   Should public policy be directed toward preventing teenage pregnancy?
   Yes: Jane Mauldon
   No: Kristin Luker

8. Parental Consent for Abortion   130
   Should parental consent to or notification of an adolescent's abortion be required by law?
   Yes: Everett L. Worthington, Jr., David B. Larson, John S. Lyons, Malvin W. Brubaker, Cheryl A. Colecchi, James T. Berry, and David Morrow
   No: Margaret C. Crosby and Abigail English

9. Mainstreaming AIDS Children   153
   Should confidentiality be maintained when children with AIDS are mainstreamed in regular classrooms and nursery schools?
   Yes: Ronald Bayer
   No: David L. Kirp

Part III. Child Abuse and Neglect Issues

10. Mandatory Abuse Prevention Programs in Schools   167
    Should children be required to participate in school programs to prevent molestation?
    Yes: Jon R. Conte
    No: Jill Duerr Berrick and Neil Gilbert

11. Intervening With Drug-Dependent Pregnant Women   182
    Should the state have the right to intervene when a pregnant woman is found to be dependent on drugs or alcohol?
    Yes: John E. B. Meyers
    No: Douglas J. Besharov

12. Corporal Punishment by Parents 195
    Should the use of corporal punishment by parents be
        considered child abuse?
    Yes: Murray A. Straus
    No: Robert E. Larzelere
    No: John K. Rosemond

13. Positive Methods 223
    Should only positive methods be used by professionals who work
        with children and adolescents?
    Yes: Wayne Sailor and Edward G. Carr
    No: James A. Mulick
    No: Jay S. Birnbrauer

Part IV. Children's Legal Issues

14. Discrimination in Juvenile Justice 257
    Does the juvenile justice system discriminate against racial minorities?
    Yes: Jewelle Taylor Gibbs
    No: Mary Ann Mason and Eileen Gambrill

15. Due Process for Adolescents 272
    Should adolescents have the same due process rights as adults when
        they are involuntarily committed to psychiatric hospitals?
    Yes: Mary Ann Mason
    No: James W. Ellis

16. Limiting Abuse Reporting Laws 285
    Should current reporting laws regarding sexual and physical abuse of
        children be sharply limited to discourage overreporting?
    Yes: Douglas J. Besharov
    No: Richard P. Barth

17. Putting Juveniles in Adult Jails 298
    Should there be an absolute prohibition against the placement
        of children and adolescents in adult jails and correctional facilities?
    Yes: Rosemary C. Sarri
    No: William H. McCready

Part V. Work and Family Issues

18. AFDC Mothers and Work 317
    Should AFDC mothers be required to work in order to receive benefits?
    Yes: Ailee Moon
    No: Martha N. Ozawa

19. Parental Leave Policy 340
    Should paid parental leave for family issues such as birth of children or elder care be government mandated?
    Yes: Sheila B. Kamerman
    No: Eileen Gambrill and Mary Ann Mason

About the Editors 355

PREFACE

Social and legal issues relating to children and adolescents are perhaps more volatile today than ever before. There are several reasons accounting for this unsettled state, some relating to significant changes in the lives of adults. The changing family structure, brought about in part by the sharp rise in divorce and the growing incidence of unwed motherhood, has raised a variety of new issues. Child custody arrangements have gained in importance, raising questions concerning such areas as the sexual orientation of parents, visitation rights of parents and grandparents, and access of birth mothers to their children who have been adopted by others. In the changing family, mothers are likely to work outside the home, and this has provoked national debate on the obligations of society to support the family in the form of mandated family leave. Another aspect of this debate is the question of whether mothers of young children should be required to join the workforce or should receive support to stay at home with their children.

Partly as a result of the changing family structure, reports of child neglect and abuse have skyrocketed. An increasing number of these reports contain allegations of sexual abuse. Alcohol- and drug-abusing mothers have become a newly prominent issue also. How can we best protect our children? What constitutes abuse and neglect? Are we defining abuse and neglect so broadly that we are falsely accusing innocent parties? The controversy over the definition of abuse extends to the methods used by teachers and other professionals in charge of children.

The status of adolescence is also changing. Since the lowering of the voting age to 18, and with the gradual lowering of the threshold age of sexual activity, questions are being raised about the decision-making capacity of adolescents. In what circumstances should the law give children the power to decide certain things for themselves, and to be responsible for their own actions? Under what conditions should adolescents be allowed to separate themselves from their families and live alone? The growing birthrate among unwed teenage mothers raises the issue of adolescent competence. A related matter is the issue of requiring parental consent or notification when a minor chooses an abortion. Does medical decision making extend to adolescents whose parents believe that psychiatric hospitalization is their only alternative?

Adolescents sometimes break the law. Does the new emphasis on adolescent competence suggest that adolescents should be treated more as adults in the criminal justice system, or should they be accorded special protection? From the other side of the bench, is the criminal justice system unfairly targeting minority youth for arrest and detention?

Finally, what do we expect from professionals who work with our children and adolescents? What level of competence do we require, and what is the knowledge base we expect them to draw upon? Do we believe that teachers, social workers, and others who work with children must use only positive reinforcement, or does punishment have its place?

In this volume, our contributors address all these timely, controversial issues in a debate format. There are at least two sides to each of these issues, and it is our belief that the best road to understanding begins with an introduction to all points of view. No one discipline can claim expertise in all these complex topics, so our authors are a remarkably diverse group. They are social scientists, social work professors, law professors, public policy professors, and policy makers. One contributor is a judge. Our audience, we hope, will be as diverse as our authors. This book should be valuable to both instructors and students in areas such as education, social work, criminology, and child and adolescent psychology. Policy makers and practitioners will also gain from reading these debates.

We wish to thank our many authors—first of all, for producing statements that will challenge and inform the reader, and second, for their enthusiasm about this project. They believed, as we do, that these are important social issues that often receive only one-sided treatment. They were eager to meet the challenge of addressing opposing pieces. (We should note that, in spite of vigorous efforts, we could not find people willing to prepare opposing statements to three of the questions included in this book. We therefore prepared these arguments ourselves, even though we were sympathetic to the alternative positions or had simply not given much thought to the matters before, as in the debate regarding parents at risk of bearing a child with a severe disability.) We also wish to thank Sharon Ikami for her expert typing and patience.

Preface

Readers will approach this book with already formed opinions on many of the topics. We hope the debates will encourage readers to reexamine their opinions in the light of new information and new arguments. Whether or not their beliefs are changed, we trust that their perspectives will be expanded and enlightened.

Mary Ann Mason
Eileen Gambrill

INTRODUCTION

Children and families deserve our clearest thinking. One of the best ways to consider the beliefs and actions related to any topic, including those concerning children and adolescents, is to listen carefully to both sides of conflicting issues. This is what this book is about. The statement-plus-reply format initiated in *Controversial Issues in Social Work* (Gambrill & Pruger, 1992) is used here for that reason.

Too often we hear only one side of an issue, and too often that one side is presented in a biased way. Information may be omitted or content distorted to "make a point." We have sought input from people who hold different views on topics that affect children and families to increase the likelihood that readers will "get the straight scoop" and therefore be in a position to make "reasoned judgments" about these questions. A reasoned judgment can be defined as "any belief or conclusion reached on the basis of careful thought and reflection, distinguished from mere or unreasoned opinion on the one hand, and from sheer fact on the other" (Paul, 1992, p. 664). A reasoned judgment is arrived at through a careful weighing of the evidence both for and against a position.

The practice of considering both sides of issues has a long history. For example, in the twelfth-century work *Sic et Non* (Yes and No), Abelard analyzed 168 statements from the Bible. He showed that there were inconsistencies in the interpretations of each. Burke (1985) notes that since the time of the early fifth century the method of examining arguments both for and against a position was in general use. It was known as the *quaestio* (the question). Positions both for and against an issue were examined to make a judgment. We assume that the intent was to reach a reasoned judgment. Abelard's rules for argument and investigation include the following:

- Use systematic doubt and question everything.
- Learn the difference between statements of rational proof and those merely of persuasion.
- Be precise in use of words, and expect precision from others.
- Watch for error, even in the Holy Scripture.

As you can imagine, the church was not thrilled with Abelard's views. Burke points out until that time, the word of accepted authority had sufficed as proof. Even though Abelard protested that his aim was to discover the truth, the church was not happy. As Burke notes, when Abelard said, " 'By doubting we come to inquiry; by inquiring we perceive the truth,' Rome heard the voice of a revolutionary" (p. 44). Thus more than 700 years ago the voice of inquiry was not necessarily welcomed. This is true today as well. For example, those who prefer to make pronouncements (simply to assert their positions as accurate) will not appreciate an inquiring, reflective approach. The question is: What is the best way to arrive at reasoned judgments?

As with everything, there are potential disadvantages as well as advantages to the use of a pro/con format. Such a format could encourage a superficial discussion of complex questions in which only polar views are examined. When a pro/con style is used in a dysfunctional manner (in which issues are clouded rather than clarified), only the extremes are argued, leaving out the many positions that lie between. This seems to happen often in the popular media when controversial issues are discussed. We don't think that this has happened here.

We, like Abelard, encourage you to ask hard questions as you review debates in this book:

- How do I know a claim is true?
- Who presented it as accurate? What could be the motives of those involved? How credible are these sources?
- Are the statements of fact correct?
- Have any facts been omitted?
- Is there evidence a claim is true? How credible is this? Have any experimental studies been done? Were these studies relatively free of bias? Have results been replicated? What samples were used? How representative were these? Was random assignment used?
- Are there other plausible explanations?
- If correlations are presented, how strong are they?

Introduction xv

- What weak appeals are used (e.g., to emotion, or special interests)?
- Do authors consider both personal and environmental factors that relate to their topics of concern? (Reviews of the literature such as that by Mirowsky & Ross, 1989, make a strong argument that social factors such as poverty are primarily responsible for psychological distress, e.g., depression, alienation, hopelessness, and helplessness.)
- Do authors ignore some levels of analysis?

This book provides an opportunity for readers to hone their critical thinking attitudes, knowledge, and skills. Critical thinking can be defined as "reasonable and reflective thinking that is focused upon deciding what to believe or do" (Norris & Ennis, 1989, p. 3); it involves a commitment to using related skills to arrive at sound judgments. Examples of critical thinking "moves" suggested by Paul (1992) include the following:

- Uncover significant similarities and differences.
- Recognize contradictions, inconsistencies, and double standards.
- Refine generalizations and avoid oversimplifications.
- Create concepts, arguments, or beliefs.
- Clarify issues, conclusions, or beliefs.
- Evaluate the credibility of sources of information.
- Compare and contrast ideals with actual practice.
- Analyze or evaluate arguments, interpretations, beliefs, or theories.
- Generate or assess solutions.
- Analyze or evaluate arguments, interpretations, beliefs, or theories.
- Rethink your thinking.
- Design and carry out tests of concepts, theories and hypotheses.
- Compare perspectives, interpretations, or theories.

References

Burke, J. (1985). *The day the universe changed.* Boston: Little, Brown.
Gambrill, E., & Pruger, R. (Eds.). (1992). *Controversial issues in social work.* Boston: Allyn & Bacon.
Mirowsky, J., & Ross, C. E. (1989). *Social causes of psychological distress.* New York: Aldine de Gruyter.
Norris, S. P., & Ennis, R. H. (1989). *Evaluating critical thinking.* Pacific Grove, CA: Critical Thinking Press.
Paul, R. (1992). *Critical thinking: What every person needs to survive in a rapidly changing world* (2nd ed.). Rhonert Park, CA: Sonoma State University, Center for Critical Thinking and Moral Critique.

Annotated Bibliography: Selected Sources for Enhancing Critical Appraisal of Claims and Arguments

Caldini, R. B. (1984). *Influence: The new psychology of modern persuasion.* New York: Quill.

This book presents a readable, empirically based discussion of a variety of persuasion strategies, such as those based on liking, authority, scarcity, social proof, commitment, consistency, and reciprocity. Caldini notes that although interests in being consistent and reciprocating what we have received can work for us in many ways, others can appeal to these interests in ways that can be used against us.

Damer, T. E. (1987). *Attacking faulty reasoning* (2nd ed.). Belmont, CA: Wadsworth.

This work provides an accurate, clear presentation of informal fallacies.

Dawes, R. M. (1988). *Rational choice in an uncertain world.* New York: Harcourt Brace Jovanovich.

This is an excellent book that raises many points that should be considered in making decisions. Topics discussed include the virtues of uncertainty, basic principles of probability, representative thinking, framing consequences, sampling, significance, and effect size.

Ellul, J. (1965). *Propaganda: The formation of men's attitudes.* New York: Vintage.

This classic work on propaganda, from both sociological and psychological points of view, is fascinating reading.

Engel, S. M. (1982). *With good reason: An introduction to informal fallacies* (2nd ed.). New York: St. Martin's.

This is a readable, entertaining presentation of informal fallacies.

Gambrill, E. D. (1990). *Critical thinking in clinical practice.* San Francisco: Jossey-Bass.

This book describes how critical thinking attitudes, knowledge, and skills can be applied to clinical practice across a broad range of professions. Topics include the influence of language and persuasion strategies, formal and informal fallacies, and sources of error in making predictions and identifying causes. A chapter is devoted to enhancing the quality of case conferences, and guidelines are offered for collecting data as well as for maintaining critical thinking skills.

Gibbs, L. E. (1991). *Scientific reasoning for social workers: Bridging the gap between research and practice.* New York: Macmillan.

This book is written primarily for students learning research, but almost all the material is useful to people who have to make decisions about issues affecting children and adolescents. A chapter on unscientific reasoning describes a number of practitioner fallacies, such as appealing to tradition, newness, numbers, or popularity, and attacking a person rather than examining his or her arguments. Influence based on testimonials and manner of presentation is also described. The book includes chapters on deciding whether an intervention is responsible for changes observed, as well as a helpful format that can be used to review studies. An entire chapter is devoted to the case example fallacy.

Introduction

Gilovich, T. (1991). *How we know what isn't so: The fallibility of human reasoning in everyday life.* New York: Free Press.

This book provides a good review of influences on our thinking. Topics include the imagined agreement of others, belief in ineffective alternative practices, making too much from too little, and seeing what we want to see.

Gula, R. J. (1979). *Nonsense: How to overcome it.* New York: Stein & Day.

This entertaining volume demonstrates how thinking can go awry.

Huck, S. W., & Sandler, H. M. (1979). *Rival hypotheses: Alternative interpretations of data based conclusions.* New York: Harper.

An engaging source of practice exercises, this book lists 100 brief descriptions of studies and asks the reader to evaluate the credibility of the conclusions. Answers are provided at the back of the book.

Kahane, H. (1992). *Logic and contemporary rhetoric: The use of reason in everyday life* (6th ed.). Belmont, CA: Wadsworth.

This is an excellent classic work describing fallacies.

Nickerson, R. S. (1986). *Reflections on reasoning.* Hillsdale, NJ: Lawrence Erlbaum.

This marvelous book discusses reasoning, including material on arguments, assertions, and beliefs. Common reasoning fallacies are reviewed, such as partiality in the use of evidence, as well as stratagems such as sloganism, inappropriate dichotomizing, overgeneralization, and stereotyping.

Nisbett, R., & Ross, L. (1980). *Human inference: Strategies and shortcomings of social judgment.* Englewood Cliffs, NJ: Prentice Hall.

This classic book reviews research on social judgments. Causes and consequences of inferential errors are described, and strategies are offered for avoiding errors.

Paul, R. (1992). *Critical thinking: What every person needs to survive in a rapidly changing world* (2nd ed.). Rhonert Park, CA: Sonoma State University, Center for Critical Thinking and Moral Critique.

This volume provides a comprehensive description of critical thinking that includes guidelines for teaching it and related knowledge, skills, and attitudes. Weak sense and strong sense use of critical thinking skills are contrasted.

Phillips, D. C. (1992). *The social scientist's bestiary: A guide to fabled threats to, and defenses of, naturalistic social inquiry.* New York: Pergamon.

This book reviews false beliefs about a scientific approach to knowledge with both accuracy and style.

Thouless, R. H. (1974). *Straight and crooked thinking: Thirty eight dishonest tricks of debate.* London: Pan.

This classic work lists fallacies as well as remedies for them.

PART I

Children and Family Issues

DEBATE 1

PARENTAL COMPETENCY TESTS

➢ *Should we require all prospective parents to pass competency tests in parenting skills and values?*

EDITORS' NOTE: At first glance this may seem a rhetorical question. How could such a policy ever be implemented? Wouldn't such a policy unfairly impose norms of behavior on groups valuing different kinds of parent-child relationships? On the other hand, it is clear that many children suffer at the hands of parents who have poor parenting skills. Don't children have a right to be protected from such situations?

Roger McIntire says YES. He is Professor of Psychology at the University of Maryland, College Park, where he has taught child psychology and behavioral principles in family counseling and therapy since 1962. He has authored many books, including *Teenagers and Parents: Ten Steps for a Better Relationship*, *For Love of Children*, and *Losing Control of Your Teenager*. He has published research concerning infant vocalizations, eating problems, strategies in elementary school teaching, high school motivation, and college dropouts. He maintains that the practical principles of day-to-day success in child rearing (which he calls "adult-rearing" in *Teenagers and Parents*) are known and should be a part of every parent's education.

Robert P. Hawkins, Ph.D., argues NO. He is Professor of Psychology at West Virginia University, where he directs the Child Clinical Training Program. In 1966, he and his colleagues published (in the *Journal of Experimental Child Psychology*) the first experiment showing that a parent could successfully change her own child's maladaptive behavior in the home ("Behavior Therapy in the Home: Amelioration of Problem Parent-Child Relations With the Parent in a Therapeutic Role"). He later developed a foster-family-based treatment program that also follows the basic strategy of having treatment conducted by persons who are acting as parents, and he published a book about such programs: *Therapeutic Foster Care: Critical Issues.* Among his other books are *The School and Home Enrichment Program for Severely Handicapped Children, Practical Program Evaluation in Youth Treatment,* and *Behavioral Assessment: New Directions in Clinical Psychology.*

YES — Roger McIntire

Mother and daughter enter a supermarket and an accident occurs when daughter pulls the wrong orange from a pile and 17 oranges gain their freedom. Mother grabs daughter, shakes and slaps her. What do you do? Ignore it? Consider it a family affair—none of your business? Or do you advise the mother not to abuse her child? If she rejects your advice, do you insist or even call the police? How would you feel if I told you that the daughter is not *that mother's* daughter? Would you now be more willing to interfere? Or if the daughter had recently been adopted by the mother, would your feelings about intervention change? When do the absolute rights of motherhood begin? When do the rights of a daughter to fair and reasonable treatment begin? Where do parents' rights to treat children as they please end? Possibly the daughter has the right to a reasonable upbringing, and a parent has an obligation to be prepared to give knowledgeable care—from the very beginning.

The first consideration of the idea of licensing parents was based on the developing technology of almost-permanent contraceptives, and on the regulating by government of these new sources of birth control. The logic began with a look at adoption procedures. Adoption agencies commonly impose many restrictions on people who adopt children, but if a couple wants to have children of their own, society makes no requirements for their doing so. Regardless of how incompetent adults may be, they have the right to try parenting. The child who is an unfortunate victim of the experiment is not considered. The alcoholic father of Mark Twain's Huckleberry Finn objects to any change in this approach. When forced to send his son to school, he says, "Here's the law a-standin' ready to take a man's own son away from him . . . just as that man got that son raised at last, and ready to go to work and begun to do suthin' for him and give him a rest, the law up and goes for him. And they call that government!" We have come to accept compulsory education, yet, as selfish and abusive as Huck Finn's father was, his right to have more children would not be limited even today.

The Future of Parenthood

"Lock" was developed as a kind of semipermanent contraceptive in the early 1990s. One dose of Lock and a woman became incapable of ovulation until the antidote "Unlock" was administered. Lock required a prescription, as did Unlock. Anyone making a request had little difficulty obtaining either. Gradually, however, a subtle but significant distinction became apparent. Other contraceptives merely allowed a woman to protect herself against pregnancy at her own discretion. Once Lock was administered, however, *the prescription for Unlock required an active decision to allow the possibility of pregnancy.*

By 1998, the two drugs were being prescribed simultaneously, leaving the Unlock decision in the hands of the potential mother. Of course, problems arose. Parents protected their daughters by immunizing them with Lock and the daughters later asked for Unlock. Women misplaced the Unlock and had to ask for more. Faced with the threat of a black market, the state set up a network of special dispensaries for the contraceptive. When the first dispensaries opened in the year 2000, they dispensed Lock rather freely, because they could always regulate the use of Unlock. But it soon became apparent that special local committees would be necessary to screen applicants for Unlock. "After all," the dispensary officials asked, "How would you like to be responsible for this person or that becoming a parent?"

PROTECT OUR CHILDREN

That same year brought the school riots. A growing complex of needs could not be met by the educational system. Needs for special education, social services for needy children, and job training for teens were being more loudly demanded with each report of teen crime, child abuse by young parents, and statistics of inadequately prepared adults. Taxpayers asked increasingly about the source of all these growing societal burdens. Beyond the symptoms, they found one primary cause—low-quality parenting. That led to trouble.

Until then, people had assumed that schools existed primarily for basic education. But the advent of early job responsibilities and single-parent family responsibilities suggested the notion that the schools ought to teach what the parents seemed unable to do—other essential abilities such as social skills, self-control, time management, and study skills. The growing ranks of working parents and single parents demanded that the schools do more. The combination of the swelling population of children and the expanding demand for more practical preparation was more than the educational system wanted to accommodate. This led many of the parents to protest; some even took to the streets.

In Richmond, Virginia, parents in one school neighborhood protested over the reluctance of the board of education to take on more responsibilities. One of the demonstrators picked up a traffic sign near the school that cautioned drivers to "Protect Our Children" and found herself leading the march toward city hall. Within a week, that sign became the national slogan for the protesters, as well as for the Lock movement. It came to represent not only the demand that our children be prepared (protected) with the skills necessary for success in the ever more complex society, but also that the children should be protected from unplanned pregnancies that would add to the burden of that training.

So the distribution of Lock took on the characteristics of an immunization program under threat of an epidemic! With immunization completed, the state could control the quality of parent preparation by setting standards for the distribution of Unlock. But this did not solve the problem of deciding who should be selected to parent. As might be expected, the parent-licensing program came under attack from those who complained about the loss of their freedom to create and raise children according to their own choices and beliefs. In answer to such critics, the protect-our-children (Lock) faction argued, "It's absurd to require driver's education and a license to drive a car, but to allow anybody to raise our most precious possessions, or to add to the burdens of these possessions without demonstrating an ability to parent."

"But the creation of life is in the hands of God," said the freedom-and-right-to-parent faction (referred to by their opposition as the "far-right people").

"Nonsense," said the Lock people. "Control over life creation was acquired with the first contraceptive. The question is whether we use it with intelligence or not."

"But that question is for each potential parent to answer as an individual," said the far-right people.

The Lock people answered, "Those parents ask the selfish question of whether they want a child or not. We want to know if the child will be adequately cared for by parents and our culture."

The far-right responded, "God gave us our bodies and all their functions. We have the right to use those functions. Unlock should be there for the asking. Why should the government have a say in whether or not I have a child?"

"Because the last century has shown that the government will be saddled with most of the burden of raising your child," answered the Lock people. "Government must provide education and child support programs, medical and welfare services. The schools, the medical programs, the youth programs, and crime prevention and protection programs—they will be burdened with your child. That's why the government should have a say. The extent of the government's burden depends on your ability to raise your child. If you foul it up, society and government will suffer. That's why they should screen potential parents."

From the right again: "The decision of my spouse and myself is sacred. It's none of their damned business!"

But the Locks argued, "If you raised your child in the wilderness and the child's shortcomings burdened no one but yourselves, it would be none of their damned business. But if your child is to live with us, be educated by us, suffered by us, add to the crowd of us, we should have a say."

Those in opposition to parent licensing usually do not mention child abuse, neglect, or any other suffering produced by parents with insufficient time, information, or love for child rearing. In place of these issues they express concern for the *adult's right* to birth another human, under any circumstance, with or without any useful information or skills. The opposition emphasizes the right of *having* children, but neglects the responsibility of *raising* them. Many families have only one adult to be both breadwinner and parent, and extended family support is often unavailable. For centuries the family unit has been society's instrument for raising children; now the freedom to have a child is abused by those who ignore the responsibility to create a secure family to raise that child. How shall we be sure that the child-rearing responsibility remains intact?

Many principles concerning diet, health, and hygiene are crucial to adequate parenting and are already a part of the usual public education program. But knowledge of principles of child development, learning, communication, and behavioral control are not common subjects, and none of them is emphasized or required in current educational programs. Intense attention to these subjects at the high school level would prepare prospective fathers and mothers for parenthood and give them motivation to acquire the skills for a parenting license.

The license requirement is essential for the cognitive momentum necessary for parents to learn and to apply what they learn. Driver's education is not enough without the requirement of a driver's license, nor is training in medicine, law, or scuba diving complete without testing and certification. Parenting requires skills, patience, self-control, and knowledge to an extent at least equal to these other fields.

The benefit to the happiness of both our children and their parents would be revolutionary even without any extreme measures to enforce the licensing law. Doctors and lawyers are not closely "policed," and yet standards are well maintained out of the human inclination to meet the standards set by society. Even drivers' performance relies on the notion that most people will use safe and beneficial practices without observation and consequences from a spying government. Of course, there will always be examples of poor behavior. But occasional exceptions to the success of a law do not constitute grounds for rejecting it.

The requirements for a parenting license would involve a demonstration of knowledge of facts, principles, theories, and controversies about child rearing. Parents would carry out parenting as they see fit within the present limitations set by the laws dealing with child abuse, neglect, and the requirement of education. No parental rights to raise children by cultural standards, creeds, or religions would be violated. The notion doesn't go as far as the driver's license law, which tests for competence *and* checks to see that one uses that competence *and* provides legal consequences if one falls short. And, as with the driving laws, the parent licensing law would not eradicate poor parenting, but it would improve the confidence and comfort of parents. Laws and standards "on the books" do provide an incentive for thoughtful and beneficial behavior, even in areas where enforcement is nonexistent or never intended. The parent license would require only that one know what there is to know before taking on the responsibility of raising another human being. The law would emphasize the positive goals of child rearing beyond avoiding abuse and neglect. It would be a stated and required standard that would benefit our culture, our children, and our contentment and happiness with family life.

NO   **ROBERT P. HAWKINS**

Reservations About Government's Own Competence

Over the past few decades the American public has become increasingly educated about the waste, ineffectuality, misuse of funds, and other problems that abound in government-conducted or government-funded programs. Events such as the release of radioactive material into the air at the Twelve Mile Island atomic power plant make us aware that the Atomic Energy Commission is not as competent at protecting our safety as we assumed. The huge stockpiles of radioactive material that continue building, with no satisfactory and safe place to store them, further erode our confidence in the AEC. On another front, it is worth noting that we are running out of places to dump our solid waste, yet we are producing more and more each year. Further, the world population keeps growing at a rate that far outstrips our rate of solving the problems that such population creates, yet governments seem almost oblivious to the issue. This does not inspire great confidence in governments.

Yet it is proposed that government regulate who shall parent children. Parenting is probably the most profoundly important "job" performed in any society, for it determines the very nature of the society's future culture (Hawkins, 1972, 1974). Are we ready to let the government decide who may hold that job? Even if we are, there are several other issues to address. I will present some of them below.

Whose "Rights" Will Be Respected?

The issue of "licensing" people to be parents is similar in some ways to current conflicts in our society regarding whether a woman has a right to abort a fetus and, if so, under what conditions. Just as many thinking people argue that a woman has a right to choose whether to give birth or to abort, it can be argued that a person, or couple, has a right to bear and rear children. At the same time, just as some people believe that a fetus has a right to live, it can be argued that a child has a right to be reared in a responsible, caring home, not in an abusive or neglectful home. The issue is not simple, and some kind of compromise position will probably be necessary in both cases; but let us not yet leap to regulate who may parent a child.

Issues of Enforcement

If we license people to parent children, we must control women's ability to get pregnant. If we do not control pregnancy, we will be forced either to require abortions—a particularly unappealing action—or to take newborn children away from unsuitable parents and provide foster homes for them. We already know that the foster parent system is generally an unhealthy one (e.g., Sherman, Neuman, & Shyne, 1973)—after all, it is largely government run. Even if we could get enough foster parents, it would be tragic to condemn babies to live in such a system.

We Lack the Necessary Knowledge and Tools

A valid test. If we are to predict the competence of a person's performance at parenting, so that we can prevent the incompetent from taking on the task, we need to know what it is about individuals that is highly predictive of how well they would perform as parents. When we license people to drive automobiles, we wisely test not only their verbal skills (knowledge) about the law, we also place them in cars and require that they perform certain driving tasks. The same should apply to tests of parenting skills, but at present we have neither such tests nor sufficient knowledge on which to base them.

Knowledge of what constitutes competent parenting. The first requirement for developing a test predictive of competent parenting would be to define what competent parenting is. Would it be defined in terms of certain ways the parent behaves—such as dressing the child "appropriately," spending a certain amount of time with the child daily, or belittling the child—or in terms of the actual outcomes evidenced in the child's adjustment, such as the child's cooperation with peers, aggressive behavior, or even committing crimes? If we take the former approach, defining competence in terms of the form of parent behavior, we need to recognize that we are far from agreeing on what behaviors are important to competent parenting. For example, Gordon (1970) recommends a communications approach and decries the use of behavior-contingent consequences, whereas Becker (1971) and others adopt a science-based approach that *emphasizes* such consequences. The many other experts take still other approaches, few of them based on science and none of them adequately *evaluated* through research demonstrating their long-term effects on children. Thus it is unclear what we would look for in deciding who is parenting competently, and this prevents us from finding measurable predictors of such performance to use in a test.

A More Modest Approach Than Licensing to Parent

At present, through the absence of restrictions on parenting, it is being treated in the law as though it were an automatic right. However, it is a right that can at least be *withdrawn*. Parents who repeatedly and severely neglect or abuse their children do occasionally have their parental rights withdrawn. A modest form of further control over who does parenting—one that might be morally acceptable and sociologically beneficial—would be to expand this withdrawal approach by also taking away the right of such demonstrably incompetent parents to *bear further* children. Obviously, this would pose technical problems, because it would require that birth control measures be implemented by the government or its agents, but this modest expansion of our present approach to the issue of competent parenting seems much more palatable than an all-encompassing one based on inadequate evidence.

If our society wished to go one step beyond the withdrawal of parenting rights based on *demonstrated* incompetence, we could add *denial* of parenting rights based on *predicted* incompetence. This would require only that we be able to predict who will be unusually incompetent at parenting, a somewhat easier task than predicting general, positive competence. There is some research on what predicts the level of incompetence known as parental neglect and abuse (e.g., Wolfe, 1987), and further research could provide an adequate basis for such negative predictions. But that still leaves the question of what one does about the person predicted to be grossly incompetent as a parent.

Licensure for Parenting Requires That We Provide Training

It would be irresponsible for a society to prevent some people from becoming parents without providing some way for them to remedy whatever deficits they may have. As I have proposed before, providing such education and training in high school—and even in junior high school—seems the best approach; then everyone would get at least a modicum of training (Hawkins, 1972, 1974). But we must also provide more individualized remedial training for those who fail to pass the competency (or incompetency) test. Further, we would need an appeals process for anyone denied permission to raise children, if we are to protect everyone's rights adequately.

Summary

Before we jeopardize individual rights by preventing some people from taking the role of parent, we need to know much more about what constitutes competent parenting and what predicts it, so that we have a strong scientific basis for deciding who may parent. An alternative would be merely to prevent those who have demonstrated their incompetence as parents from bearing further children. And an expansion of that approach would be to use various kinds of measures to predict incompetence, so that those most likely to be incompetent could be prevented from bearing even one child.

However, any control over the right to parent creates the societal responsibility to provide the training necessary for individuals to acquire competence. This training should be provided to everyone in our society, through the schools. In addition, remedial training should be available to anyone who fails to meet the minimal qualifications of being an adequate parent.

References

Becker, W. C. (1971). *Parents are teachers: A child management program.* Champaign, IL: Research Press.

Gordon, T. (1970). *Parent-effectiveness training: The tested way to raise responsible children.* New York: Peter H. Wyden.

Hawkins, R. P. (1972). It's time we taught the young how to be good parents (and don't you wish we'd started a long time ago?). *Psychology Today, 11,* 28-40.

Hawkins, R. P. (1974). Universal parenthood-training: A proposal for preventive mental health. In R. Ulrich, T. Stachnik, & J. Mabry (Eds.), *Control of human behavior: Vol. 3. Behavior modification in education* (pp. 187-192). Glenview, IL: Scott, Foresman.

Sherman, E. A., Neuman, R., & Shyne, A. W. (1973). *Children adrift in foster care.* New York: Child Welfare League of America.

Wolfe, D. A. (1987). Child abuse. In M. Hersen & V. B. Van Hasselt (Eds.), *Behavior therapy with children and adolescents* (pp. 385-415). New York: John Wiley.

ROBERT P. HAWKINS RESPONDS

Dr. McIntire makes several persuasive points. For example, he points out that we protect children who are available for adoption by placing many requirements on those who wish to raise such a child, so that only those who are well suited to the task will be given that responsibility and privilege; yet no requirements are placed on those who wish to have a child by conception. He points out that—consistent with our society's usual emphasis on short-term consequences—we are more likely to identify an *adult's right* to bear children than we are to identify the *child's right* to humane and reasonably educative and supportive rearing. And he points out that parenting is *at least* as demanding a task as driving a car or scuba diving, yet we require evidence of competence for these and not for becoming a parent.

If I understand his proposed solution, he is suggesting only a very modest licensing requirement: that a prospective parent know certain facts, theories, and controversies regarding child rearing before being allowed to bear children. The word *know,* as McIntire uses it, seems to indicate only verbal knowledge. If so, his proposal is very modest and would not require the applicant to demonstrate any skill at parenting tasks, such as identifying nutritious foods to buy and serve, monitoring the safety of a playing toddler, or correcting a child who is misbehaving. The probable benefits of such a modest program so easily outweigh the probable costs and risks that I cannot oppose it. In fact, I believe that some such program *should* be developed, tried experimentally, carefully evaluated, and, after revision and further evaluation, implemented nationwide.

Several important details would need to be worked out that are left unmentioned by McIntire. He does not indicate how the required knowledge is to be acquired. I would suggest that the public schools teach it, provided that teachers do not follow the foolish practice of passing youngsters as a "social promotion" but rather require a certain level of demonstrated competence. I would further suggest that this competence be judged partly on the basis of demonstrated *skills* with actual children.

He does not indicate who would evaluate whether an applicant has or does not have adequate knowledge of child rearing. A school-based program would place this judgment in the hands of a teacher. The teacher's work should be governed by a curriculum that is adapted by each state from the experimentally tested one already mentioned and then disseminated by the state. A school-based program would also deal with the issue of what a person is to do who fails to demonstrate adequate knowledge, so that he or she would still be able to acquire it and be evaluated again; it would just be a matter of retaking the required course or a special remedial one.

It appears that the time is right for us to begin to evaluate curricula for teaching parenting skills and knowledge, and then to move cautiously toward licensing.

ROGER McINTIRE RESPONDS

Reservations About Government's Own Competence

General dissatisfaction with government is not relevant to the discussion of parent licensing. By that logic our programs of licenses for drivers, doctors, and pilots of 747s would be eliminated. The more modest approach of withdrawing the right to have a child from those who neglect and abuse children is a constructive step that the courts have sometimes taken, but it protects a pitiful few.

To assert that the government has not performed well in regulating atomic power plant safety, atomic waste management, and population growth should not lead to the conclusion that these problems, and parenting, should go unregulated. On the other side, one could list successful regulation by government of air traffic, building codes, clean water supplies, and competency requirements for doctors, police, and bus drivers.

Whose "Rights" Will Be Respected?

What is lacking from the opposition is a concern for the children, a concern that goes beyond the preoccupation of adults for adult benefits and power. Our imperfect system for licensing drivers, doctors, and pilots still allows accidents and abuse, but the limits on freedom have worked to protect us all. We owe at least that to children in need of responsible parenting.

Issues of Enforcement

Enforcement through the control of pregnancy is not possible now, but many effective regulations are not fully enforceable. Our justice system is inefficient and sometimes inconsistent in its response even to multiple offenders. We find that frustrating and continue our debates on how improvements should be made. For the most part, however, laws are obeyed, because most citizens feel the citizen's obligation. Just the existence of a law has a positive effect on behavior. Of course, child rearing will remain imperfect, and there will still be cases of child abuse, just as traffic accidents remain too frequent in spite of licensing laws, but the quality of life on the roads is better with the laws than it would be without. Enforcement of a parent licensing law by required education would be a constructive step.

We Do Have the Necessary Knowledge and Tools

The position that we should not start a parent licensing program based on competence because we don't have all the answers will lead to ever-continuous delays. The proposal itself will provide a healthy stimulus for discussion, development, and dissemination of knowledge about the positive practices that would improve parenting. Instead of only a preoccupation with what rights and choices can be exercised with or without responsibility, issues concerning punishment, diet, health, education, entertainment, rules and limits concerning abused substances, money, sex, free time, and educational and career choices would all become a part of the debate. What a benefit to the children when we focus on these subjects! What a benefit to the parents! What a benefit to our culture!

DEBATE 2

PARENT ACCESS AFTER ADOPTION

➢ *Should parents who give up their children for adoption continue to have access to them?*

EDITORS' NOTE: Dilemmas that involve children and their families often concern the rights and obligations of different players in a complex story. Certainly this is the case with the question raised here. Do biological parents who do not want records opened have a right to have their wishes respected? Or do adoptees' "rights to know" supersede those of their biological parents to have their privacy protected? And what about adoptive parents? What are their rights and interests? In addition to questions of rights, there are questions about what is best psychologically for involved participants. Are adoptees harmed or helped by searching for their biological parents? All of these questions arise in discussion of this debate's topic.

Marianne Berry, Ph.D., ACSW, says YES. She is Assistant Professor at The University of Texas at Arlington School of Social Work, where she is conducting a prospective study of adoptions. She is the author of numerous articles on family preservation, adoption, and child welfare services, and is coauthor of *Adoption and Disruption: Rates, Risks, and Responses*. She is a recipient of the Frank R. Breul Memorial Prize from the University of Chicago for outstanding scholarship in child welfare.

Mary Beth Seader, M.S.W., and **William L. Pierce**, Ph.D., argue NO. Seader is the Vice President for Policy and Practice at the National Council for Adoption. She is coauthor of *The Adoption Option: A Training Manual for Pregnancy Counselors*, contributor to the *Adoption Factbook*, and the author of numerous articles on adoption and pregnancy counseling. The National Council for Adoption is an information and advocacy group for sound, ethical practices in adoption. Pierce is the President of the National Council for Adoption. He is coauthor of the *Encyclopedia of Adoption,* editor of the *Adoption Factbook,* and author of numerous articles on adoption and child welfare.

YES MARIANNE BERRY

Adoption practice in the United States is rapidly changing, and has undergone a dramatic evolution in the past 30 years. Postponed childbearing among two-career couples, changes in the labor force participation of women, birth control and abortion practices, societal acceptance of single motherhood, and an increased push to establish permanent homes for foster children have all contributed to a decreasing availability of infants for adoption and an increased number of adoptable older children with histories of maltreatment. These changes in the adoption population have been accompanied by concomitant shifts in adoption practice; one of the most controversial of these is the establishment of open adoption as standard practice among many adoption agencies and attorneys.

Open adoption refers to the sharing of information and/or contacts between the adoptive and biological parents of an adopted child, before and/or after the placement of the child, and perhaps continuing for the life of the child. Open adoption is in direct opposition to the traditional confidential adoption practices of the recent past, under which birth parents could not maintain any contact with the child or the adoptive family after placement. In fact, until very recently, adopted children had no way of finding their biological parents in adulthood. Adoption professionals are now consolidating in their support of adoptees' access to records when they reach adulthood; most agree that adult adoptees have the right to obtain details of their genealogical and biological pasts if they so desire, and if the biological parents have made known their availability for contact.

This push for open records and adoptees' rights to information has been joined by a call for increased openness from the beginning of the placement, allowing birth parents to have continuing access to their children from the time the children are placed for adoption and throughout the children's lives. The call for continuing access is based on two distinct developments in adoption practice. First, many professionals have expressed a concern about adoptees' heightened confusion around identity in adolescence arising from the secrecy attached to information about the past. The second development contributing to increased usage of openness is related to the decreasing availability of adoptable infants, bolstering the involvement of the birth mother in adoption decision making and practice.

Access Is Antithetical to Secrecy

Adoptees are reported to be overrepresented in mental health utilization in adolescence, for emotional disturbance and identity problems. Some adoption professionals posit that it is the secrecy associated with deidentified birth certificates and sealed adoption records that contributes to adoptees' curiosity and confusion about their pasts. Information about one's origins is the right of all individuals, and continued confidentiality in adoption will contribute to further identity confusion in adolescence for adoptees.

If biological parents do have access to their children from the beginning of the placement, those children will also have access, through those birth parents, to the answers to many questions they may have about their identities or their biological roots as those questions arise, rather than in retrospect once they reach adulthood. If biological parents are known and available, they may not be idealized or villainized by the child, but seen as real people who are a part of the child's past and present.

For older children who know and remember their birth parents, contact may be especially apt. The relationship between older adopted children and their adoptive parents has been compared to that of stepfamilies (Borgman, 1982), given that the adopted child is not an infant to be socialized, but a child with a history in another family and the resulting ideas and beliefs about family life that history has spawned. For children of all ages, if adoptive parents avoid dealing with a child's history, they are denying that child a part of his or her identity. Open adoptions that acknowledge the older child's history and pre-adoptive genealogy should therefore support a more complete identity development.

Most research concerning the effects of such access consists of cross-sectional studies of small samples of adoptive parents (some also include birth parents), and findings reflect little knowledge about the actual impact of contact on children's behavior or adjustment. In one of the largest studies to date, a study of 1,396 adoptions in California, it was found that children in open adoptions had significantly better behavior scores (as rated by their adoptive parents) than children in adoptions with no access to birth parents, and the adoptive parents of children who were in contact with birth parents had more positive impressions of those birth parents (Berry, 1991). However, because this is a cross-sectional survey, it is unknown whether adoptive parents in open adoptions rated their children's behavior more positively because of those positive impressions of the birth parents, whether parents were in open adoptions precisely because of those positive impressions, or whether open adoption is truly related to more positive behavior in children. Given the recency of this practice, it may be too early to tell. This was the first wave of a longitudinal study of adoptive families, and continuing data collection will be able to shed light on how children in open adoptions adjust, relative to those in confidential adoptions.

Regarding what evidence there is concerning family adjustment and openness, several studies have found that adoptive parents in open adoptions often chose this option because they felt it was in the best interests of the child (Belbas, 1986; McRoy, Grotevant, & White, 1988). Those adoptive parents in more extensive contact with birth parents tend to show more understanding of them (Meezan & Shireman, 1985), and many studies have found open adoptions to be characterized by positive relationships between adoptive and birth parents (Belbas, 1986; McRoy et al., 1988; Meezan & Shireman, 1985). Adoptive parents' understanding of, and positive relationship with, birth parents should contribute to increased empathy toward the birth parents of the adopted child and to reduced denial of the child's biological heritage.

The child's interpretation of any contact or relationship in an open adoption is at the center of the debate over the benefits of continued access, and it is precisely this interpretation that is yet to be illuminated by research. McRoy and Grotevant's (1991) qualitative findings show varied interpretations among adopted children: Some embrace contact and some are frightened or confused by it. These researchers do not identify an age-appropriate time for contact or other correlates of adaptation. Although openness and information sharing may prevent the genealogical bewilderment and pain of searching in adulthood, research findings to date have not found a temporal relationship between openness and subsequent adjustment.

Access Increases the Role of Birth Parents

As the number of infants in adoption has decreased over the past three decades, the influence and control of birth parents in the adoption process has increased dramatically. Independent adoptions (through adoption attorneys or centers) have also flourished in the recent past, and these types of adoptions often give birth mothers increased control over the adoption process. As adoptable infants have become scarcer, attorneys and agencies have strengthened the role of the birth mother in the adoption process, allowing the birth mother to participate in the selection of the adoptive parents and becoming more responsive to requests that she be allowed continuing access to the adopted child in various forms. This participation may help relieve the birth mother of some guilt and uncertainty about relinquishing the child. It may also convince some birth mothers to relinquish who may not otherwise choose to do so, in the hopes that relinquishment will not be a total separation from the child (Barth, 1987).

McRoy and Grotevant (1988) found that adoptive parents in open adoptions were generally satisfied with the amount of contact they practiced, but biological mothers generally wanted more, regardless of how much contact they practiced. Adoptive parents in direct contact with birth mothers expressed some concern about the maturity of biological mothers and the amount of time and energy that contact with them demanded, but felt that openness was in the best interests of the children. Biological mothers often treated the adoptive families as extended family or as a source of social support.

Barth and Berry's (1988) study of older child adoptions and the more recent study of 1,396 adoptions (Berry, 1991) found that adoptive parents' comfort with contact is related to their perceptions of control over the contacts. Parents who were exceptionally stressed by contact or found it destructive to family integrity were those who felt little control over those contacts (because openness was imposed by agency policy or birth mother request).

Continued Access Must Exist in a System of Continuing Support

Because of the importance of honesty in family relationships and the need to enlist birth mothers in making positive and responsible plans for their children, continued access between birth parents and their adopted children should be available and supported. It is the social and legal responsibility of adoption agencies and attorneys, however, to balance the rights and responsibilities among the three parties in the adoption triangle—the birth parents, the adoptive parents, and the adopted child—and to support each of these parties around the decision-making process and once a decision has been made. Each of these parties has interests and rights, with the adopted child's interests and rights least likely to be heard.

The adoption attorney or social worker has the societal mandate to protect the interests of vulnerable parties in working with more powerful parties. With birth parents' rights and interests most likely to be heard, given the supply-and-demand characteristics of the current adoption market, it is the adoption worker's responsibility to support the best interests of the child. Any policy around adoption practice should consider the short- and long-term impacts such a practice will have on the adopted child. Given that empirical evidence as to the long-term effects of this practice is scarce, adoption practitioners' work is made more difficult.

Professionals generally agree that the child is least confused about loyalties to either set of parents when the open relationship between the adoptive and biological parents is clear and positive. Adoption attorneys and social workers must work toward helping birth and adoptive parents identify their beliefs and expectations about contact, and help to work out an agreeable plan for contact that respects the adoptive parents' rights as parents. Although adoption professionals have always stressed that the choice of any open adoption should be made in the course of extensive counseling and decision making with trained professionals, the extent to which this occurs in independent adoptions is unknown and is a potential source of disagreement and conflict. Some independent agents state that they help to guide the relationship between biological and adoptive parents at the beginning of the adoption, then step out of the way as both sets of parents start to form their own relationship. As social workers in child welfare agencies, however, adoption counselors should consider the child's interests the paramount concern, and this relinquishment of control to the birth parents over such a new practice is disturbing.

It is important to emphasize to birth parents who are interested in continued access the importance of a lifelong commitment to that plan, however limited or extensive that plan is. Birth parents are typically adolescents who may not understand or comprehend the long-term consequences or implications of such choices. If contact is planned and regular at first, but then the contacts drop off or unexpectedly stop (e.g., when the birth parent gets married or otherwise begins a new life), this second separation can be a source of confusion for the child.

In this changing era of adoption practices, on the basis of the two arguments of marketplace demand and rejection of secrecy, those birth parents who so desire openness will and should continue to have access to their children, throughout the children's lives. That access brings with it, however, new challenges for every member of the "adoption rectangle" (Sachdev, 1989): the birth parents, the adoptive parents, the adopted child, and the adoption agency. Birth parents must recognize the lifelong commitment they are making to the adopted child, adoptive parents must acknowledge the role of birth parents as extended family members (but not primary parents), the child must be supported in working out the unique relationships of these various family members in his or her environment, and the adoption agency must provide lifelong supportive postadoption services for all parties as they forge these new relationships.

References

Barth, R. P. (1987). Adolescent mothers' beliefs about open adoption. *Social Casework, 68,* 323-331.

Barth, R. P., & Berry, M. (1988). *Adoption and disruption: Rates, risks, and responses.* Hawthorne, NY: Aldine de Gruyter.

Belbas, N. F. (1986). *Staying in touch: Empathy in open adoptions.* Unpublished manuscript, Smith College School for Social Work.

Berry, M. (1991). *Adoptive parents' perceptions of and comfort with open adoption.* Manuscript submitted for publication.

Borgman, R. (1982). The consequences of open and closed adoption for older children. *Child Welfare, 61,* 217-226.

McRoy, R. G., & Grotevant, H. D. (1988). Open adoptions: Practice and policy issues. *Journal of Social Work and Human Sexuality, 6,* 119-132.

McRoy, R. G., & Grotevant, H. D. (1991, September 19). *American experience and research on openness.* Paper presented at the International Conference on Adoption, Edinburgh, Scotland.

McRoy, R. G., Grotevant, H. D., & White, K. L. (1988). *Openness in adoption: New practices, new issues.* New York: Praeger.

Meezan, W., & Shireman, J. F. (1985). *Care and commitment: Foster parent adoption decisions.* Albany: State University of New York Press.

Sachdev, P. (1989). *Unlocking the adoption files.* Lexington, MA: Lexington.

NO   MARY BETH SEADER and WILLIAM L. PIERCE

The way the question is phrased—"Should parents who give up their children for adoption continue to have access to them?"—reminds one of how pollsters can get very different responses from the same group of people just by asking the same question in different ways. The question evokes an immediate emotional response. The phrases "give up" and "have access" make it sound as though a parent has made a self-centered decision that she does not want the responsibilities of being a parent, but wants to continue the benefits of the relationship. In that respect, denying access would be seen as a punishment for the "crime" of "giving up" the child. This is not what the discussion about "open" adoption or "openness" in adoption is about today.

The question about whether there should be continued contact between women and men who have planned adoption and adopted persons must be addressed in terms of the possible risks and benefits of the contact for all parties, but particularly the child. The catalyst for the practice of continued contact in adoption came from reports by women who had placed children for adoption; those women said that they felt unresolved grief over adoptions that had occurred many years before.

Since the 1970s, when the idea first began to emerge, the movement for open adoption has taken on a life of its own for a variety of reasons. As practitioners who had observed some birth parents (mostly women) who had placed children for adoption and who unquestionably had unresolved grief began to write and speak on the problems of this clinical population, they began to attract others who reported problems of women who had placed, until some in the field of adoption universalized the experience of these women to all women who placed children for adoption. Open adoption was proposed as the solution, but open adoption did not "fix" the problems of unresolved grief, as evidenced by the words of Reuben Pannor and Annette Baran (1990), who now say that "relinquishment of children to a new set of parents, as a final, irrevocable act, severing all rights of the birth parents, must be discontinued. Open adoption, which we helped pioneer, is not a solution to the problems inherent in adoption. Without legal sanction, open adoption is an unenforceable agreement at the whim of the adoptive parent. Instead a form of guardianship adoption would be in the best interest of all concerned." What Pannor and Baran and others have proposed is that adoption be restructured, so that it looks more like foster care.

It is our contention that proponents of open adoption have misdiagnosed the problem; therefore, their solution not only does not address the problem, but in many cases exacerbates the problem. First, proponents of open adoption conclude that it is the separation that causes the problem. It is a fact that loss causes pain. However, it is not a fact that individuals cannot recover from loss. Life is a series of losses, and if individuals could not recover from them, this would be a planet of basket cases. It is a fact that some individuals have more trouble than others in resolving losses, for a variety of reasons, including previous life experiences, individual capacity (which may be affected by stage of development and other factors), and social supports. It is also a reality that a "problem pregnancy" itself is a crisis that precipitates losses, regardless of the decision made about how to manage the pregnancy. The role of the counselor is not to deny or obliterate the loss, but to support the client through the loss to a healthy resolution. This does not mean that the individual will forget about the loss, or that there will not be some regrets and moments of pain. Reaching a healthy resolution means that the individual can go on to lead a peaceful, happy, productive life.

Our personal experiences as counselors and a review of the literature indicate that women who have placed children for adoption who continue to experience pain from the experience have become "stuck" in the grieving process. Often what emerges is an inability to forgive themselves for getting into the situation to begin with and for not being prepared to parent. There is also often an inability to forgive the father of the baby, family, friends, and society for not providing more support, and the adoption worker and agency as representative of the source of the pain.

In her book *Saying Goodbye to a Baby,* Patricia Roles (1989), advocate of open adoption, describes the common grief reaction of "searching behavior" (which may range from scanning crowds for babies to all-out attempts to make contact with the adopted child) as generally part of the "anger phase" of mourning. The anger, which is often very intense, prevents the woman who placed her child from forgiving, which is necessary for a peaceful resolution. Unless the woman can let go of the anger, she cannot move forward to the final stage of acceptance and peace.

So what can continued access to their children do to help women who are going through this grieving process? Common sense and an understanding of grieving theory suggest, not much. The searching behavior is an attempt to undo the loss. Continued contact, or open adoption, is also an attempt to undo the loss. The reality of adoption is that the person who places the child ceases to be the parent, and continued contact can be very confusing to the person who placed, the child, and the child's family. Continued contact inhibits the grieving process because it makes it difficult to define the loss and therefore have closure.

Carole Anderson (1990), president of Concerned United Birthparents (CUB), an advocacy group for people who have placed children for adoption and who have had negative experiences, agrees with Pannor and Baran that open adoption has not resolved the problem. She writes, "The way most open adoptions are handled, with birthparents participating in their own destruction and suffering from more ambiguous losses, it may be even harder for open adoption birthparents to acknowledge and face their losses. . . . these birthparents seem to remain in a frozen, childlike state for very long periods" (p. 10).

A study at the University of Texas at Arlington on the postadoptive grief experience of women who had placed children for adoption found that

> indications were strong that biological mothers who know more about the later life of the child they relinquished have a harder time making an adjustment than do mothers whose tie to the child is broken off completely by means of death. Relinquishing mothers who know only that their children still live but have no details about their lives appear to experience an intermediate degree of grief. (Blanton & Deschner, 1990, p. 534)

There is mounting evidence that open adoption has not addressed the needs of the people who place, and there are increasing complaints that adoptive parents are not fulfilling agreements for contact they made prior to the adoption finalization, indicating that open adoption arrangements have not been satisfactory for adoptive families. There are efforts in some states to pass legislation requiring adoptive parents to comply with prefinalization agreements for contact. One could argue that this interferes with the adoptive parents' rights and responsibilities as the legal and moral parents to the child. This is precisely what Pannor and Baran refer to when they say that open adoption does not go far enough in maintaining the rights of people who place, because in adoption, the adoptive parents are more than guardians, they are the full parents, for all intents and purposes, of the child. Adoption was created out of the recognition that children need to feel secure about who their parents are and what their role is. If adoption professionals are candid, they will make sure that all people who place understand this completely before they consent to adoption.

So it would appear that open adoption does not reach its intended goal of relieving any pain resulting from a "problem pregnancy" and adoption for the person who places. And if it creates problems for the adoptive family because it interferes with the parents' role as parents to the child, what effect does it have on the child? Kathleen Silber and Patricia Martinez Dorner, in their book *Children of Open Adoption* (1989), report:

> During this honeymoon period [after the placement of the child], it is important for the adoptive parents to have some "space." That is, they need time (without interference by the birthmother) to bond with the baby and establish their own intimate relationship as a family. If there is too frequent contact with the birthmother during these first few weeks, the couple can over-identify with her and her pain, thereby continuing to view the baby as "her baby." (p. 32)

Silber and Dorner wrote *Children of Open Adoption* to show the "positive" effects of open adoption on children who have been involved. Because open adoption is a fairly new concept as currently practiced, the study was limited to children under the age of 9 or 10. The authors report that the children respond positively to and show genuine affection for the parents who placed them for adoption. Given the nature of children, one would expect that children would respond positively to caring adults. However, Silber and Dorner seem to take great leaps when they discuss children's understanding and acceptance of adoption and their birth parents: "As Alberta Taubert indicates, her three-year-old daughter, Jordan, is able to appropriately use the term birthmother and to realize that she grew in Christy's womb and, in fact, got her curly hair from Christy. Of course, Jordan only has an elementary understanding of adoption" (p. 50). A child of 3 calling a woman "birth mother" does not indicate that she understands the relationship. Certainly, the authors do not expect the readers to believe that a 3-year-old has an understanding of genetics and the transmission of "curly" genes.

Silber and Dorner say that in their work with children of open adoption they found that

> the realization and experience of loss is demonstrated by adopted children at earlier ages than previously believed. The different manifestations of grief are evidenced by the children—we see denial, sadness, and anger. Jennifer's story reflects how denial came into play for this child. At age $4\frac{1}{2}$ Jennifer began to emphatically say that she had not grown in Gloria's womb. Over time, Jennifer's mom had explained her adoption story in simple terms, including that Jennifer had grown in Gloria's womb. (p. 55)

This "theory" of grief is contrary to the findings of David Brodzinsky, Ph.D., who has examined extensively how adopted children come to understand their adopted status. His findings are consistent with learning theory. Brodzinsky (n.d.) states that "sometime around 8 to 10 years of age, children begin to understand what relinquishment means. In middle childhood, reflection begins on the adoption process itself. This is a normal part of coping with adoption." Brodzinsky does not oppose early telling, but does caution parents to recognize that children do not understand the world in the same way adults do, and that any attempt at explaining must take this fact into account.

When one considers the example used by Silber and Dorner, one questions the accuracy of their interpretation of the child's response. Because it is unlikely that the child understands what adoption means and she has clearly denied the existence of her "birth mother," it is more likely that she is responding not to feelings of loss, but to confusion at her mother's insistence that she is not her mother. *Children of Open Adoption* is full of stories like Jennifer's, and one has to wonder what this constant reminder of differences will do to these children in the long run. What will happen when the children are old enough truly to understand adoption? Will they understand what their place is between two mothers?

Marianne Berry (1991), in an extensive literature review on open adoption, concludes:

> Children, as children, are at greatest risk in open adoptions. Although openness and information sharing may prevent genealogical bewilderment and pain of outreach in adolescence, research findings so far have not found that openness leads to greater adjustment or attachment. Children do not understand the relationship in open adoption, and direct contact with a biological parent can weaken the bond between adoptive parents and child. (p. 648)

She states further:

> Without more information on the extent of open adoption practices and their long-term effects on all members of the adoption triad, practitioners must proceed with caution in prescribing openness, particularly when it includes direct contact between biological parents and children. When such openness is part of the adoptive triangle, adoption workers must be prepared to remain an integral part of the adoption triangle, providing postplacement support of all parties during the adoptee's growing up. (p. 649)

If the practice of open adoption does not improve the situation for the adopted person, the person who places the child, or the adoptive family, and in fact may increase the risks for each, it appears unwise to continue its practice. Studies of participants in adoption have shown that for the vast majority, traditional adoption has worked very well. For those who are continuing to have problems, it is first necessary to assess what is causing the problems and then to prescribe appropriate interventions to address and resolve those problems.

References

Anderson, C. (1990, September). Response to "A time for sweeping change." *CUB Communicator*, pp. 9-11.

Berry, M. (1991). The effects of open adoption on biological and adoptive parents and the children: The arguments and the evidence. *Child Welfare, 70,* 637-651.

Blanton, T. L., & Deschner, J. (1990). Biological mothers' grief: The postadoptive experience in open versus confidential adoption. *Child Welfare, 69,* 525-535.

Brodzinsky, D. M. (n.d.). "Adaptive grieving" natural for the child. *Morris County Record* (New Jersey).

Pannor, R., & Baran, A. (1990, Summer). It's time for a sweeping change. *American Adoption Congress Newsletter,* p. 5.

Roles, P. (1989). *Saying goodbye to a baby.* Washington, DC: Child Welfare League of America.

Silber, K., & Dorner, P. M. (1989). *Children of open adoption.* San Antonio, TX: Corona.

MARY BETH SEADER and WILLIAM L. PIERCE RESPOND

Marianne Berry notes several times in her argument that it is believed that continued contact with the birth parent will decrease "genealogical bewilderment" of adopted adolescents and, therefore, relieve any need to search. However, there is no proof that such genealogical bewilderment exists among adopted persons. The term was first coined in 1952 and subsequently argued by H. J. Sants in a British journal in 1965. Sants builds his case on the story of *The Ugly Duckling* by Hans Christian Andersen and Sophocles' play *Oedipus Rex*. Sants suggests that Andersen wrote the story to reflect his own genealogical bewilderment, yet it should be noted that Andersen was reared by his biological mother and his biological father until his father died when Andersen was 12 (Sants, 1965). Freud's misunderstanding of the story of Oedipus has been widely discussed in the literature. Yet even with this flimsy "proof," the concept of genealogical bewilderment has been accepted uncritically by many in the field.

If one looks at the searching activity of adoptees in the United States, the United Kingdom, and Australia, one finds that consistently the proportion of adopted persons who are interested in searching is between 2% and 4%. To suggest that adopted adolescents have "identity crises" is to report the obvious about the life stage of adolescence, when the developmental task is identity formation. The suggestion that adopted adolescents receive more mental health services than do their nonadopted peers does not adequately address all of the dynamics involved in the decision to seek mental health services. For instance, women are more likely to receive counseling than are men—are we to assume that women have more problems coping in life or are we to assume that women are more open to counseling services? It is likely, particularly when one considers that adopted adults are not overrepresented in mental health services, that adopted teens are seen more often because their parents are more likely to seek services for adolescent developmental issues than are the parents of their nonadopted counterparts. Perhaps a major reason for this use of service is the message that adoptive parents have been given for the past 25 years, that their children will suffer from genealogical bewilderment. Thus at the first sign of an adoptive child's asking "Who am I?" that child is shuffled off to a therapist.

After providing this "We're hoping 'open adoption' will help kids although there is no evidence that it will" argument, Dr. Berry gets into the real reason for open adoption—to make it more appealing to pregnant women to provide babies for hopeful, infertile couples. Increasingly, agencies are turning toward open adoption to keep their doors open. Open adoption is very appealing to an adolescent or a woman who is in the middle of a painful crisis pregnancy. It has a ring of relieving the stresses of parenting without giving up the benefits of relationship. The reality, as has been argued, is somewhat different.

It is unfortunate that some in the field have forgotten their mission, which is to assist women in crisis pregnancies to make plans that are in their best interests and the best interests of their children. For many, if not most, adoption is the solution in everyone's best interest. However, the decision must be reached only after honest discussion of the reality of adoption—the transfer of *all* rights, responsibilities, and relationships from the biological parents to the adoptive parents. Client self-determination is one of the primary ethical principles of social work, and it cannot be achieved unless clients are fully informed about the consequences of decisions they are about to make. There is no room in ethical social work practice for manipulation of information to make it more appealing to clients so they will choose the option that the counselor believes is optimal. This is particularly reprehensible when the motivation for influencing the choice of the option is based on the desire to satisfy the needs of another client, the prospective adoptive parents.

Many in the adoption field like to talk about adoption as a lifelong process. For most adopted persons, birth parents, and adoptive families, it could be argued that adoption is an event. Adoption is a means of joining a family, just as birth and marriage are. Family is a lifelong process. Living is a lifelong process. Open adoption is a means of assuring that adoption becomes a lifelong process and, as Dr. Berry argues, a process that needs professional intervention. As Dr. Berry states, many birth parents come to see the adoptive family as part of their therapeutic milieu, a role that is wholly inappropriate. Not only is the adoptive family not qualified for this role, but it keeps the birth parent always in the role of patient. Should parents who give up their children for adoption continue to have access to those children? If our job were to ensure that social workers have continuing employment opportunities, than the answer would be yes. If our job is to ensure that parents facing a crisis pregnancy, children, and their adoptive families receive the best treatment and are encouraged to move on with their lives, the answer is clearly no.

Reference

Sants, H. J. (1965, Summer). Genealogical bewilderment in children with substitute parents. *Child Adoption, 47.*

MARIANNE BERRY RESPONDS

I agree that a consideration of open adoption must weigh the risks and benefits for all parties. Unfortunately, much of the debate about risks and benefits in open adoption is not empirically based, but grounded in counselors' personal experiences and a collection of case studies and convenience samples of birth parents or adopted parents. Extrapolating a firm policy on the practice of open adoption from such sources is problematic. Openness, like many other decisions in parenthood, should be a choice guided and supported by fact and reason.

Seader and Pierce make an important point when they note the "emotional response" to the question of continued access. Family decisions often are emotional decisions. Every person knows, or has seen stories in the popular press, about children and families with either positive or negative experiences with open adoption. These emotional stories have no place, however, in the formation of family policy.

Small studies of a handful of adoptive or birth families using purely qualitative measures and narrative accounts of their experiences, such as those relied upon by Seader and Pierce (and, I might add, their opponents in the open adoption debate), add some helpful information to the discussion, but are also insufficient. In order to make informed policy and practice decisions about openness, practitioners need accurate and complete information concerning the long-term positive and negative effects of open and confidential adoption practices. Such information can best be provided by longitudinal research, some of which is currently under way in a variety of locales across the United States.

While waiting for more complete information on the impact of openness, practitioners can help birth and adoptive parents to sort out the potential consequences of openness for themselves based on larger, albeit short-term, studies of openness, which have found high levels of comfort with openness among birth and adoptive parents and few short-term ill effects for children or families (Berry, 1991; McRoy & Grotevant, 1991). These studies have also identified statistically significant relationships between preplacement information and discussions concerning openness and adoptive parents' subsequent comfort with openness.

Open adoption should be a choice for birth and adoptive parents. Adoption agencies and facilitators must support parents in making this difficult and emotional choice by providing solid and accurate information based on empirical findings of rigorous research. These findings indicate that for most families openness is a satisfactory and comfortable practice, but one in which families often would like ongoing agency support and information. Adoption social workers and facilitators can contribute best to the open adoption debate by remaining informed about the empirical evidence as it becomes available and passing this evidence along to families as they weigh the risks and benefits for themselves.

References

Berry, M. (1991). The practice of open adoption: Findings from a study of 1396 adoptive families. *Children and Youth Services Review, 13*, 379-396.

McRoy, R. G., & Grotevant, H. D. (1991, September 19). *American experience and research on openness*. Paper presented at the International Conference on Adoption, Edinburgh, Scotland.

DEBATE 3

CHILD CUSTODY AND SEXUAL ORIENTATION

➤ *Should sexual orientation be a consideration in custody proceedings?*

EDITORS' NOTE: Child custody law has undergone a revolution in the past 20 years, forcing a reexamination of all the factors that contribute to the "best interests" of the child. The establishment of no-fault divorce eliminated the need for alleging adultery as one of the most common grounds for divorce, and in most states the transformation of custody law that followed in the wake of no-fault divorce excluded specific reference to moral fitness as a factor in custody decisions. Homosexual activity on the part of one of the parents, which in previous eras would undoubtedly have been a deciding factor against that parent, is increasingly tolerated. A few states still view homosexuality as evidence of parental unfitness per se, but most require proof that homosexual activity (or extramarital heterosexual activity) is having an adverse effect upon the child. The influential Uniform Marriage and Divorce Act, Section 402, states: "The court shall not consider conduct of a present or proposed custodian that does not affect his relationship to the child." Still, changes in law do not necessarily force changes in judicial attitudes. With sexual mores, as with the maternal presumption, judges frequently find other reasons within their powers of discretion that allow them to reach the same decisions they would have reached under the old laws. Judges reflect the conflict regarding this issue that exists in U.S. society as a whole. The essence of this conflict is expressed in the following debate.

J. Craig Peery says YES. He is Professor of Family Sciences at Brigham Young University.

Michael S. Wald argues NO. He is a Professor of Law, Stanford University, and is currently serving as Deputy General Counsel, U.S. Department of Health and Human Services. He has written numerous articles and books on children's issues, including "State Intervention on Behalf of 'Neglected' Children: A Search for Realistic Standards" (*Stanford Law Review,* vol. 27, 1975).

YES   J. CRAIG PEERY

When courts perceive a conflict between parental rights and the best interests of the child, state law and common-law tradition require them to resolve the conflict in favor of the child's interests. (Susoeff, 1985, p. 864)

○ ○ ○

I do not like the title the editors have chosen for this chapter. The title I would prefer is, "Why parental homosexuality should be taken into consideration in child custody proceedings." Some of the polemics and strife over homosexuality, currently being conducted on several fronts smack of Orwellian "new speak." Terms are redefined (Gay!), old words (and concepts) are expunged from acceptable usage, some combinations of words become politically incorrect, and their use may cost professors their jobs or students their matriculation. All this can be a thinly veiled attempt at mind control, and only serves to obfuscate, rather than clarify the debate. "Homosexual" and "homosexuality" are perfectly good words; they have clear meanings. Parental homosexuality should be taken into consideration by the courts in determining custody. Why not just say it, and then the discussion can begin.

○ ○ ○

Child Policy Perspective

The child's "best interests" are the primary consideration for determining whether a parent should receive custody. Findings from social science research can help to inform these decisions, but cannot supply definitive answers on a case-by-case basis. In determining what is best for children, the presumption should favor factors that most closely accommodate community standards and values, legal requirements, personal and religious values of the parents, healthy parental personality and social characteristics, a home as free of negative stress as possible, the developmental state of the child, and a presumption that providing a normal, or average expectable, environment is preferable to an environment that is potentially pathogenic. When the conflict over custody is between two biological parents, everything else being equal, the parent who gets custody should be the one who can demonstrate parental superiority in meeting these standards.

The "best interests of the child" make perfect sense as the criterion of judgment. Even those who, like Susoeff, quoted above, advocate a change in state statues so that parental homosexuality is *not* considered in the making of custody determinations acknowledge that the child's best interests must be the governing consideration. Children are vulnerable and relatively powerless when thrust into the arena of parental strife. The state intervenes on the child's behalf in order to ensure that the child experiences the outcome most likely to benefit his or her development. Broad diversity in moral perspectives notwithstanding, something in our bones tells us that morality requires promoting optimal development in our children. Child policy questions need to be framed by this context: *What is most likely to promote optimal development for the child?* Policy recommendations, and custody decisions, can then be evaluated in terms of the potential risks.

Discussing conditions and probabilities of risk is much more scientifically acceptable than proving harm. Such a perspective shifts the discussion from whether *damage can be proved* to whether *less than optimal development is likely.* Negative outcomes or risk to children should not be tolerated if they are avoidable. Too often courts make custody decisions based on a requirement to *prove harm.* From a developmental and statistical perspective such an approach is in error. In the absence of an appropriate control group it is virtually impossible to prove harm on a case-by-case basis. Too frequently, homosexual advocates assume a priori that the role of science in this debate is to prove harm as a result of actual homosexual child rearing. Those who question the propriety of child custody by a homosexual parent are neither morally nor intellectually obligated to *prove* that homosexual parenting will *cause harm.* Rather, it is incumbent on the homosexual parent to prove that he or she provides *superior* conditions for child rearing.

Although seeking optimal situations for children may seem to be a disarmingly simple standard, the child's best interests can easily get lost in the ideological shuffle. Much of the rancor in custody hearings, and much of the debate about homosexual custody, frequently focuses on *adult* considerations quite outside the world of the child. Because children are robust and are frequently able to endure a wide variety of environmental insults, too often we tend to assume that if they are merely *surviving* then all must be well. If we determine what we know morally, socially, and scientifically about raising children in optimal circumstances, custody options can then be compared to those circumstances, and probable risk to the child can be estimated. When an optimal developmental environment is not possible, as is the case in divorce, the path of moral responsibility leads not toward mere survival, but toward providing conditions that are as close to optimal as feasible. Any potential condition of risk to the child is an *essential* component of the custody equation. As I will discuss briefly below, the moral, legal, social, and developmental problems inherent in parental homosexuality point to conditions of considerable risk. Therefore, everything else being equal, the heterosexual parent should be given preference in custody determinations. Consequently, the extreme proposal that a parent's sexual orientation should never be considered in determining child custody is completely untenable.

Research on Outcomes of Homosexual Parenting

Though the substantial body of research on normative child development can act as a guide, and the abundant research on child-rearing conditions that cause problems in development can also be enlightening, there is not now, nor is there likely to be in the future, a sufficiently definitive body of research literature to resolve most of the knotty questions involved with policy development relating to homosexual custody. In part owing to major inadequacies, research on homosexual parenting is virtually never published in the leading developmental journals. The existing body of research on outcomes of homosexual parenting is seriously, usually fatally, flawed because of one or more shortcomings, including unsuitable philosophical approaches; logical inconsistencies; inappropriate theoretical models; limitations on sample size, sample selection, control groups, data collection, and analysis; and lack of longitudinal perspective. One example: Researchers frequently compare lesbian mothers with heterosexual single mothers, but courts are never asked to decide between lesbian mothers and straight single mothers in awarding custody. The decision is between lesbian mothers and heterosexual fathers, who usually have a very high probability of remarrying and establishing households headed by two heterosexual adults. Yet virtually no research exists comparing children experiencing these two options.

A scientifically adequate body of literature on homosexual parenting will never develop, and cannot develop, from a "proving harm" perspective, partly because research adopting this posture violates the American Psychological Association's and the Society for Research in Child Development's codes of ethics for research with human subjects in general and children in particular. Both codes require researchers to inform subjects of potential risks and prohibit using children as guinea pigs in paradigms that subject them to serious risk. Because of my value preferences and my interpretation of the body of literature on normal child development, I, for one, could not ethically conduct research on children actively being raised by homosexuals without informing the children and parents of the potential risks involved in such an arrangement—as I perceive them—thereby possibly alienating the parents, probably troubling the children, and certainly biasing the potential data. A proposal for research that does not inform parents and children of the potential risks of homosexual parenting, and the hypotheses directed at examining those risks in the research design, would not pass muster when scrutinized by an internal review board at any major university. Problems of this sort are ubiquitous in homosexual parenting research; if, for example, a researcher suspected a child was being sexually abused, under the laws of many states he or she would be obligated to violate the confidentiality of the research and report the suspected abuse to the authorities, thus ultimately eliminating from the study those subjects who might best be able to "demonstrate harm."

The only research on homosexual parenting that avoids this ethical dilemma would consist of studies that collect data on children only after the homosexual parenting has been terminated. This approach places severe limits on sample selection. Further, studies that examine cross-sectional post hoc data only will never be methodologically adequate to answer the developmental questions that must be asked. Yet it is immoral and unethical to conduct the developmental research (collecting data over time while the homosexual parenting is ongoing) without informing the subject of potential risk, and thereby undoubtedly biasing the results—a classic scientific double bind.

Thus developmental research on homosexual parenting will always be limited to researchers and paradigms that do not recognize risks in homosexual parenting. Such researchers, at worst, would be advocates for homosexual parenting, considering parents' rights supreme over children's best interests; at best, their analyses would be subject to bias. Evidence of considerable pro-homosexual bias, sometimes amounting to researchers' having an ax to grind, already exists. By way of illustration, I cannot for the life of me see how Kleber, Howell, and Tibbits-Kleber (1986) can conclude that children of lesbian mothers show no enhanced "social/emotional maladjustment" (p. 86) when they cite researchers reporting children who have experienced being evicted from rental housing because of morals complaints, children of lesbian mothers displaying differences in sex role development, over half the children in one study rated as severely or moderately disturbed, children denying or repressing anger about their mothers' living arrangements (with homosexual lovers), deferring hostility toward their mothers' lovers and resenting the lovers' attempts at parenting, fearing telling friends about their home situations, and expressing concerns that they might become homosexual.

Value Preferences

Of course, discussions of optimal development are subject to value preferences and to value judgments. In the several decades during which George Gallup has been asking Americans in national polls what they value, the most frequent answer has always been a happy family life. Americans value happy families above health, wealth, or personal freedom. Nine out of ten mental health professionals believe being faithful to one's marriage partner and being committed to family needs and child rearing are important for a positive, mentally healthy lifestyle (Jensen & Bergin, 1987). From the perspective of optimal development for children, then, factors that contribute to a happy family life reflect our primary values, and factors that detract from a happy family run counter to what we most prize in our hearts. As a baseline for a happy family, the notion of identifying an average expectable environment for child rearing is helpful. Two normally devoted, natural parents (a father and a mother) should be part of this environment. There is a large volume of research pointing to the benefits of such a two-parent arrangement for both parent and child. There is another, probably even larger, volume of research documenting the adverse effects on the child when one or both of the parents is missing because of divorce, death, desertion, or whatever. So children facing parental divorce and subsequent custody proceedings are already at risk. In terms of American values, a primary question is, Which custody arrangement will most likely provide a happy home environment for the child? The absolutely crucial developmental question is, Which custody arrangement is most likely to help the child grow up to establish a happy family life of his or her own?

No state recognizes homosexual marriage, and state laws, whether or not they are actively enforced, declaring homosexual activity illegal have been found to be constitutional. The "right of privacy" extends only to circumstances involving the family, marriage, and procreation. Homosexual conduct, "long rejected by Western culture as deviant," is neither "implicit in the concept of ordered liberty" nor "deeply rooted in this Nation's history and tradition," and consequently is not deserving of constitutional protection (see Hafen, 1991, pp. 8-9). All things being equal, then, courts should give preference to custody by the heterosexual parent, who has the potential, at least, to establish a legally recognized marriage and family. Custody preference for the heterosexual parent is further emphasized in a state where homosexual behavior is illegal, and where custody by the homosexual parent would force the child to be raised surrounded by circumstances that the community has declared are in violation of law.

Beyond legal concerns, value judgments about homosexuality and child rearing cannot be avoided. It would be futile to ignore these value preferences and attempt to devise a "scientific and purely objective" set of standards for homosexual child-rearing policy. Given that only heterosexuality produces life, and that children are therefore connected only with heterosexuality, it seems reasonable that there should be a presumption in favor of it. A homosexual lifestyle is inherently sterile, and the presence of a child in such a life is a conundrum. Children are alien to homosexuality. From a strictly logical perspective, any human society in which homosexuality was normative would become extinct in one generation. From an evolutionary perspective, homosexuality is a deviation that is self-limiting. Religiously and morally, the Judeo-Christian tradition, which is the source of values for most of our civil and criminal laws, has historically seen homosexuality as a moral and social perversion deserving moral and/or physical punishment (death by stoning, according to the Law of Moses). Homosexuals in our society are continually confronted with the pain and alienation that going against these normative values implies. Their home life is of necessity more socially stressful than that of heterosexuals, and therefore riskier as a milieu for child rearing.

Risk Related to Homosexual Parenting

At a minimum, a firmly committed homosexual is making a physiological and social statement that eschews the bearing and raising of children. A committed homosexual who wants to raise children faces a de facto psychological conflict, sometimes referred to as the double deviation, that can be a major source of stress and is very likely to be psychopathogenic. A bisexual individual who does not live in a heterosexual marriage and who desires to raise children (perhaps this could be called the triple deviation) is even more likely to live a life that is psychopathogenic for children. Particularly for men, to be both homosexual and a parent is to be the victim of a divided identity. "These individuals can be described as marginal beings who are challenged by having ties to the cultural worlds of both nongays and gays" (Bigner & Bozett, 1989, p. 157). Or, more poignantly, in the words of one homosexual father with custody of his three children, "There is nothing gay about a homosexual's life. To live with a homosexual father is both unsafe and unhealthy" (Bigner & Bozett, 1989, p. 156).

Homosexuals experience social stigmata related to employment, housing, and homosexual social activities; they have other personal problems related to "coming out," moving between the straight and homosexual communities, and difficulties associated with homosexual relationships and homosexual identities. Parenting is difficult enough, single parenting even more challenging. Being a single homosexual parent is likely to multiply the sources of stress and resultant risks even further. One may well question whether homosexual lifestyles themselves may draw time and energy away from child-rearing duties and activities, thus making the homosexual parent less able by definition. Certainly a home environment filled with these stressors is not an optimal, and is likely a hostile, place for children.

Homosexual parents may subject children to conditions of health risk that are life threatening. The vast majority of individuals with AIDS in America are homosexuals, drug abusers, or homosexual drug abusers. Children living with homosexual parents, especially fathers, are at much greater risk of contracting AIDS (and consequently dying) just because of proximity to the virus.

Specifically, developmental psychology suggests numerous ways in which homosexual parenting is less than optimal. Two homosexual adults living together and exposing vulnerable children to a homosexual lifestyle and to homosexual role models, particularly when those role models are beloved and/or powerful in the child's environment and capable of shaping the child's behavior (as parents are) by manipulating rewards and punishments, will likely contribute to confusion in the child about family functioning, gender-appropriate behavior, sexual behavior, and, potentially, sexual orientation. They cannot provide the child with appropriate role models or training for behavior between husband and wife, relationships between father and mother, normal relationships between parents and children, or, and perhaps this is the most crucial problem, normal heterosexual relationships. Again, there is voluminous literature dealing with the development of *each* of these aspects of family relationships, and documenting the effects of malfunction on children.

A persuasive body of research testing these hypotheses does not exist and, as I have noted, is not likely to develop. However, there is abundant research evidence that children tend to grow up to be similar to their parents. Children from large families are more likely to have larger families. Children's educational attainment, career choices, and so on are similar to those of their parents. Children who experience their parents' divorce are more likely to become divorced. Abused children become abusers. If a child does not become homosexual when living with a homosexual parent (which is not the likely outcome), he or she is still thrown into conflict because identification with the parent on the fundamental issue of sexual orientation cannot occur. The child has to reject this primary part of the parent's life, once again creating a major potential source of conflict and psychological stress for the child that can only be exacerbated by living with the parent. Beyond the more passive influences, there is always the greatly increased likelihood of a parent or sex partner actively seeking to involve the child in homosexual practices or other forms of sexual abuse. Because physical attractiveness and youth are among the male homosexual ideals, children living with homosexual fathers may be particularly vulnerable to abuse.

The clear direction of this literature suggests that a child who fails to have healthy role models and positive life experiences during critical developmental stages, and who does not have a constructive background in these family relationships, will be at substantial risk in establishing a healthy, heterosexual marriage and family. *In none of this research literature is there ever even a suggestion that a child raised by a homosexual parent will experience the optimal environment for his or her own personality development or development of an understanding of these family relationships, or for implementing them in later life.*

Summary

Examining the narrowly limited (philosophically, ethically, logically, theoretically, and methodologically) research on outcomes of homosexual parenting provides a grossly inadequate base from which to make final determinations about child custody. The principal weight of religious and legal tradition and of social science research in family sociology and in personality/social development in children points to substantial, specific conditions of risk to children raised by homosexual parents. Although everything else is never equal, based on considerations related to parental homosexuality alone, custody preference should be given to the heterosexual parent. Custody proceedings, undertaken with the child's best interests paramount, and endeavoring to limit risk factors, must be informed about parental homosexuality and attending lifestyles and practices. The extreme assertion that parental homosexuality should never be considered in custody determinations is absurd.

References

Bigner, J. L., & Bozett, F. W. (1989). Parenting by gay fathers. *Marriage and Family Review, 14,* 155-175.

Hafen, B. (1991). Symposium on family law: Introduction. *Brigham Young University Law Review, 17*(1), 1-42.

Jensen, J. P., & Bergin A. E. (1988). Mental health values of professional therapists: A national interdisciplinary survey. *Professional Psychology, 19,* 290-297.

Kleber, D. J., Howell, R., & Tibbits-Kleber, A. L. (1986). The impact of parental homosexuality in child custody cases: A review of the literature. *Bulletin of the American Academy of Psychiatry and the Law, 14,* 81-87.

Susoeff, S. (1985). Assessing children's best interests when a parent is gay or lesbian: Toward a rational custody standard. *UCLA Law Review, 32,* 852-903.

NO   MICHAEL S. WALD

In this comment, I argue that evidence of a parent's sexual orientation should be inadmissible in legal proceedings between two parents regarding custody or visitation. I will show that excluding any reference to sexual orientation best promotes the interests of children and the integrity and fairness of the process.

Before defending this proposition, I want to comment on two assumptions embedded in the question. First, although the question is stated in neutral terms, I suspect many readers assume that my task is to argue that a parent's homosexuality[1] should not be considered as a *negative* factor. Because heterosexuality is viewed as "normal" and homosexuality "abnormal" (even immoral), many people believe that homosexual parents must prove that their sexual orientation should not be held against them.

Second, the question implies that the term *sexual orientation* has a clear meaning. However, this issue is not so simple (see Halley, 1989). Are we concerned with whether a parent has engaged in specific sexual acts? The proclaimed public sexual identity of the parent? The sex of a partner with whom the parent is living?

I view homosexuality as less common, not as less "normal," than heterosexuality. I do not think that homosexual parents should bear a special burden because of their sexual orientation; in fact, there is evidence that might justify disfavoring heterosexuals. Nonetheless, I will focus solely on the issue of whether open homosexual relations by a parent should be considered as a negative factor, because this is the issue relevant to most policy makers.

In order to evaluate this question, it first is necessary to understand the legal standards by which custody disputes are decided. Most states instruct courts to award physical custody to whichever parent will better promote the child's "best interests." Under this test, a court is supposed to evaluate the probable impact on the child of any factors that might influence the child's future development. Thus if living with a homosexual parent might, in and of itself, affect a child's development, a court must estimate the probable effects on the child's development of living with the homosexual parent. It also must consider each parent's other characteristics, behaviors, and relationship with the child that might affect the child. After weighing all these factors, the court must then estimate which placement is more likely to further the child's best interests.

Some states have modified the best interest test by adopting presumptions regarding the custody arrangement that is best for children. For example, several states presume that it is in a child's interest to continue living with the parent who has been the child's "primary caretaker." In these states, a heterosexual parent wishing to gain custody from a homosexual primary caretaker must prove that placement with the homosexual parent would result in harms that clearly exceed the harms from disrupting the child's relationship with the primary caretaker.[2]

Regardless of which test is applicable, it also is necessary to understand what type of information is acceptable as evidence in legal proceedings in order to decide whether sexual orientation should be considered. Courts may consider only information relevant to the legal question at issue; a fact is relevant only if there is a reasonable basis for believing that it sheds light on the ultimate legal issue. Thus, in custody disputes, a particular parental trait or behavior would be relevant only if it is likely to affect the child's future well-being.

Moreover, a court cannot simply speculate that any particular parental characteristic or behavior might be related to some aspect of a child's development; there must be a reasonable basis for this belief. For example, a court could not consider a parent's political affiliation, as there is no basis for assuming that a parent's political affiliation is related to children's well-being. Similarly, parental sexual orientation should not be admissible absent credible evidence that it is related to children's future well-being.

To decide whether a parent's sexual orientation might affect a child's future "best interests," it is necessary to know what aspects of a child's development are encompassed in the term *best interests*. For example, is it in a child's best interests to grow up being kind, competitive, tolerant, scholarly, aggressive? These, of course, are just some possible elements. There are no legislative definitions of the term *best interests*. Many scholars have noted the problems in developing a definition (Chambers, 1984; Mnookin, 1975). Specifying the end goals of child development requires making value judgments that no legislature has ever been willing to do.

Because there is little societal agreement as to the relative value of a wide range of possible outcomes, most commentators believe that courts should consider only those aspects of development that are unambiguously of value to a child. At present, there appears to be consensus on a few things. First, we want to avoid, to the extent possible, manifestly harmful outcomes, such as poor physical health, poor school performance, delinquency, and serious mental health problems. Second, it is in a child's interest to feel loved and wanted, and to have a sense of self-worth. Finally, it is desirable that children develop the capacities to love and to be self-sufficient.

With regard to these factors, the irrelevance of parental sexual orientation is clear. There is no evidence that growing up with a homosexual parent increases the probability that a child will do poorly in school, commit delinquent acts, or experience serious emotional problems. Nor is there any evidence that children living with homosexual parents have lower self-esteem or capacity to love others. In fact, some evidence indicates the opposite. For example, one researcher found that children of lesbian parents perceived themselves as more lovable than did children from heterosexual families; so did their teachers (Steckel, 1987). Another study found a higher sense of well-being among adult children of homosexual parents (Gottman, 1990). Finally, there is no evidence that homosexual parents provide less adequate physical care, love, affection, stability, discipline, or guidance than do heterosexual parents. As I will discuss below, all social science research has limitations. I would not use the results of these studies to disfavor heterosexuals. However, they offer no support for the claim that parental homosexuality is relevant.

Even people who contend that sexual orientation is relevant rarely assert that homosexual parents are less caring or less able to provide for their children's physical or intellectual needs, or that the children of homosexuals feel less loved or wanted. Rather, they make one or more of the following claims: (a) that living with a homosexual parent may have a negative impact on the child's gender identity or sexual development; (b) that living with a parent who is different from the majority of other parents may harm children, because children do not want their parents to be different; (c) that living with a homosexual parent increases the likelihood that the child will be sexually abused; or (d) that living with a homosexual parent may harm a child because the child may suffer from "social stigma."

There are three responses to these claims. First, I question whether two of these factors should be included in the definition of best interests. I believe that society should be indifferent with respect to an adult's sexual orientation. (I should note that there is no evidence that a parent's sexual orientation influences a child's ultimate sexual identity.) The only rational argument for preferring heterosexuality would be the claim that it is better not to be a member of a group that suffers from societal discrimination. However, public policy should be designed to combat discrimination, not to give it credence.

I also reject the notion that it is in a child's best interests to live in the most "normal" environment, if normal means typical. Any such standard would directly contradict our society's commitment to cultural, intellectual, political, and religious diversity. Children may be embarrassed about their parents for many reasons, for example, because their parents are disabled, overweight, or speak a different language. Fortunately, our society believes that it is best for children to learn to respect differences, not to see them as negatives.

Second, even if we assume that all of these concerns are legitimate, it still must be shown that there is a relationship between a parent's sexual orientation and any of these outcomes. With the possible exception of social stigma, there is no basis for assuming such a relationship.

Just recently, Charlotte Patterson (1992), a professor of psychology at the University of Virginia, reviewed the findings from a large and diverse group of studies that have examined the possible impacts of living with a homosexual parent on a child's sexual identity, gender identity, sexual orientation, emotional well-being, and social relationships. Her conclusion is unequivocal:

> There is no evidence to suggest that psychosocial development among children of gay and lesbian parents is compromised in any respect relative to that among offspring of heterosexual parents. Not a single study has found children of gay or lesbian parents to be disadvantaged in any significant respect relative to children of heterosexual parents in otherwise comparable situations. Indeed, the evidence to date suggests that home environments provided by gay and lesbian parents are as likely as those provided by heterosexual parents to support and enable the children's psychosocial growth. (p. 1040)

Professor Patterson also found no evidence that children living with homosexual parents more often become homosexual, or are at greater risk of sexual abuse, than other children. Her conclusions on all these issues match those of other scholarly reviews (Falk, 1989; Polikoff, 1990).

Proponents of considering sexual orientation sometimes dismiss this research as inadequate, biased, or irrelevant. As with almost all research relevant to child custody, many of the studies contain methodological or other problems. In particular, it is very difficult to do studies using random samples.

It must be remembered, however, that in order to consider evidence of sexual orientation a court must conclude that there is a valid reason to believe that a child will somehow be advantaged by living with a parent *solely* because the parent is heterosexual or disadvantaged *solely* because the parent is homosexual. To reach such a conclusion a court must either look to research on the issue, to psychological theories, or it must decide that the impact of a parent's sexual orientation is so clear that no proof is needed. Given that all of the empirical research refutes the claim that sexual orientation matters, research cannot serve as the source of a court's decision to consider sexual orientation. Moreover, the presence of a consistent body of evidence finding *no* advantage based on heterosexuality and *no* harms associated with homosexuality belies any assertion that the court can reasonably rely upon either theory or "common knowledge," as judges sometimes do. Allowing judges to draw inferences about sexual orientation is equivalent to allowing them to conclude that children do better living with Catholic rather than Protestant parents. In custody, as in other legal proceedings, it is simply unacceptable for judges to assume as true something for which there is not an iota of evidence.

What about the possibility that a child living with a homosexual parent may be stigmatized by his or her peers or by some adults? As Professor Patterson notes, the research on this issue is limited. Lewis (1980) reports that some children of lesbians are proud of their mothers "for standing up for what [they] believe." I believe that, regrettably, some children may be harmed by the behavior of some community members.

Still, I would exclude evidence of parental sexual orientation. First, there is reason to fear that allowing judges to consider the possibility of stigma is likely to harm more children than it would benefit. Remember that under the best interest test the impact of any such stigma on the child's development must be weighed against any factors favoring the homosexual parent, such as continuity of caretaking or greater parent-child attachment. Yet any fair reading of judicial opinions makes it clear that once a parent's homosexuality is introduced, many judges are unable to focus on anything else. Judges have ruled against homosexual parents despite undisputed expert testimony that the children were suffering no harm and were strongly attached to the homosexual parents. Because of the widespread prejudice against homosexuality, some judges will greatly exaggerate both the likelihood and the probable impact of stigma. Given the vagueness of the best interests test and the substantial discretion judges have in weighing all the factors, judges should be barred from considering any factor that is highly subject to misuse based on their personal biases, absent powerful, systematic evidence that the factor clearly is related to children's well-being. To do otherwise is to invite bad results for children.

Moreover, in any given case, both the possibility of stigma and its likely impact usually are highly speculative. The probability that a child will be harmed by stigmatization is no greater than the possibility that a child will be harmed by living with a heterosexual parent, as heterosexual parents are more likely to remarry and many children do not get along with their heterosexual stepparents. Similarly, it might be claimed that homosexual fathers should be favored over heterosexual mothers because the mother may marry someone who may molest the child, as stepfathers are a high-risk group for abusing stepdaughters. A child's best interest is not likely to be furthered by the consideration of any of these speculative claims.

Finally, promoting children's well-being is not the only interest at stake in custody disputes. There is at least one other principle that is of equal or greater importance. Courts should not legitimate societal prejudices that are based on a person's race, religion, or sexual orientation. This principle was recognized by the U.S. Supreme Court in the case of *Palmore v. Sidoti* (1984). In that case, a trial court in rural Georgia transferred custody from a white mother, who had been the child's longtime custodian, to the father following the mother's remarriage to a black man. The judge based his decision on the need to protect the child from the social stigma that would presumably accompany an interracial marriage in this rural area. The Supreme Court reversed, holding that a court cannot ratify such local prejudices, even if this requires ignoring one aspect of the child's best interests.

One can see the importance of this principle by contemplating another situation. Suppose two parents are divorcing; one parent is Christian, the other Jewish. Suppose also that the couple lives in an area where there are few Jews (being Jewish in America is "abnormal," in the sense that Jews constitute only 3% of the population, a smaller proportion than homosexuals) and where many people in the community believe Jews are immoral (they might justify this belief with biblical references to Jews as Christ killers, just as those who are prejudiced toward homosexuals often resort to the Bible for justification). Should we allow a judge to award custody to the Christian parent because the child might feel stigmatized or different or because living with Christian parents is more "normal"? I believe the answer is clearly no.

Some people will claim that cases involving race or religion are different, because the Constitution forbids state discrimination on the basis of race or religion, but not on the basis of sexual orientation. But the wrongness of racial or religious prejudice does not turn on the fact that such discrimination is forbidden by the Constitution. We should not allow courts to base decisions on community prejudices as a matter of policy, whether or not the Constitution requires this outcome. Despite the pain some children may experience, it is in children's and society's best interest that children learn that such prejudices are wrong and should be opposed, not given state sanction.

This leads to my last point, which, perhaps, in terms of importance, should be my first. To a very great extent, promoting a child's "best interests," as that term is generally defined in disputes between heterosexual couples, is not really what is at issue in many cases involving homosexual parents. These cases are not really about whether the children's academic, emotional, physical, or social development will be hindered if they live with a homosexual parent. These cases are not about minimizing stress. Either overtly or covertly, many judges, and other people, think that homosexuality is relevant because they believe homosexual behavior is immoral and therefore disqualifying, or that society should favor a heterosexual family over a homosexual one. Inherent in this position is the assumption that it is appropriate for a court (or legislature) to use a custody determination as a vehicle for declaring societal disapproval of homosexuality.

I cannot, in this short comment, hope to convince people who hold these views that their biases against homosexuals are morally wrong. Although the truth of this proposition is totally obvious to me, I recognize that prejudices based on race, religion, cultural differences, and sexual orientation are endemic in virtually all societies. Many people seem willing to condemn other human beings just for who they are, regardless of the fact that a person's race, religion, or sexual orientation does not harm anyone else. Perhaps most sadly, people often use their own so-called religious or moral beliefs as justification for denigrating other human beings.

I must, however, remind those who would base custody decisions on such beliefs that in doing so they are jeopardizing the well-being of those very children they allegedly want to protect. Allowing sexual orientation to be considered in custody proceedings inevitably will deflect attention from those factors that really might influence a child's well-being—a focus on maintaining attachments and continuity, on identifying the parent who has been best meeting the child's major needs, and on determining which parent will most likely encourage the child to maintain her or his love, respect, and attachment toward the other parent (regardless of the other parent's sexual orientation). Therefore, people who are truly concerned with meeting the needs of children, and not with pursuing some adult agenda, will reject any consideration of a parent's sexual orientation.

Notes

1. I use the term *homosexuality* to include bisexuality.
2. The burden upon a parent who wants to deny or limit visitation by the other parent is even greater yet. Most states grant all noncustodial parents the right to visitation, unless such visitation would be seriously detrimental to the child. Even restricting visitation requires a showing of a likelihood of harm.

References

Chambers, D. (1984). Rethinking the substantive rules for custody disputes in divorce. *Michigan Law Review, 83,* 477-569.
Falk, P. (1989). Lesbian mothers: Psychosocial assumptions in family law. *American Psychologist, 44,* 941-947.
Gottman, J. S. (1990). Children of gay and lesbian parents. In F. W. Bozett & M. B. Sussman (Eds.), *Homosexuality and family relations* (pp. 177-196). New York: Harrington Park.
Halley, J. (1989). The politics of the closet: Towards equal protection for gay, lesbian, and bisexual identity. *UCLA Law Review, 36,* 915-976.
Lewis, K. G. (1980). Children of lesbians: Their point of view. *Social Work, 25,* 198-203.

Mnookin, R. (1975). Child-custody adjudication: Judicial functions in the face of indeterminacy. *Law and Contemporary Problems, 39,* 226-293.

Patterson, C. (1992). Children of lesbian and gay parents. *Child Development, 63,* 1025-1042.

Polikoff, N. (1990). This child does have two mothers: Redefining parenthood to meet the needs of children in lesbian-mother and other nontraditional families. *Georgetown Law Journal, 78,* 459-575.

Steckel, A. (1987). Psychosocial development of children of lesbian mothers. In F. W. Bozett (Ed.), *Gay and lesbian parents* (pp. 75-85). New York: Praeger.

MICHAEL S. WALD RESPONDS

Professor Peery's article dramatically illustrates the problem with allowing custody decision makers to consider a parent's sexual orientation. Professor Peery is a social scientist, yet his arguments focus on his belief that homosexuality is immoral. Driven by this belief, he ignores, dismisses, or distorts the evidence regarding the actual impacts on children of living with homosexual parents. If academics behave this way, should we expect much more from judges?

Professor Peery begins by dismissing as biased all of the research showing that children raised by homosexual parents develop normally. He asserts that "objective" researchers could not conduct research given the potential risks of homosexual parenting. In this way, he tries to avoid the force of the evidence discussed by Professor Patterson (1992) in her article published in *Child Development,* the most prestigious peer-reviewed journal in the field.

Peery's claim is clearly wrong. No serious scholar believes that objective research cannot be done to *determine* whether certain factors place children at risk. Scholars conducting such research always begin with hypotheses regarding risk. If Peery's reasoning were accepted, no research examining such issues as joint custody, father custody, or interracial adoptions could be conducted, because people posit possible risks from each of these forms of custody.

It is Professor Peery's biases, not methodological issues, that should concern us. Instead of empirical support for his positions, he offers innuendo and misinformation. For example, he speculates that "homosexual lifestyles themselves may draw time and energy away from child-rearing duties and activities." What does he mean by "homosexual lifestyles"? Is he implying that lesbian mothers, or gay fathers, are sexually "promiscuous," a commonly held bias? There is no basis for this belief; if anything, evidence regarding sexual behavior following divorce raises concerns about the lifestyles of heterosexual parents. The same is true of Peery's totally unsupported claims that children living with homosexual parents are at greater risk of contracting AIDS or being sexually abused. In fact, children living with lesbian mothers may have the lowest risk of being exposed to AIDS or of being sexually abused.

Professor Peery's biases also cause him to ignore evidence inconsistent with his claims. He asserts that heterosexual parents should be preferred because they are more likely to remarry and provide a "normal" home. Yet he does not mention that many children do badly in stepfamilies or that the high divorce rate in second marriages may also put many children at risk.

Instead of proof for his claims, Peery provides misinformation. One example is his attribution of the quote "To live with a homosexual father is both unsafe and unhealthy" to a "homosexual father of three." In fact, these are the words of the nonhomosexual pastor of the Lovingway Pentecostal Church in Denver, and these words were disputed by the homosexual father in question. Unfortunately, such carelessness pervades Peery's piece.

The only real risk Professor Peery identifies is that some parents and children will be disadvantaged because of societal discrimination. We must reject the notion that it is proper to persecute people and then say that they will be bad parents because they are subject to persecution. The answer is not to remove children from good parents but to remove prejudice from custody determinations. By ending legal discrimination against homosexuals, legislatures will contribute to children's optimal development.

Reference

Patterson, C. (1992). Children of lesbian and gay parents. *Child Development, 63,* 1025-1042.

J. CRAIG PEERY RESPONDS

Professor Wald's argument contains the errors of logic and analysis typical of pro-homosexual authors who embrace the premise that their "most important" task is not protecting the child's best interests, but rather convincing people that "biases against homosexuals are morally wrong." The majority of Americans believe homosexual behavior is morally wrong. There is overwhelming evidence that, in our society, homosexuality leads to divorce, psychological hardship, personal-social trauma, and, particularly for men, increasingly to death. Common sense proscribes the immorality of dragging children through such a caustic wake.

My initial argument addresses, however briefly, most of Professor Wald's arguments. However, Wald's sweeping assertion that "no evidence" exists that demonstrates difficulties with homosexual parenting is a particularly egregious distortion of reality and deserves comment. Problems regularly reported in research involving children of homosexual parents include but are not limited to numerous social stigmata, confusion about the parent's homosexual orientation, anger at the parent and the homosexual partner(s), confusion in the child's sexual orientation, greater incidence of homosexuality, a broad range of psychological problems, and need for psychological treatment. When methodologically inadequate and developmentally naive studies using cross-sectional analyses of tiny groups of children yield no "statistical" difference, review articles with a pro-homosexual bias trumpet "no difference exists," which chorus can become alchemically transmuted during discussion of legal issues into "no evidence" for problems. Lawyers may not understand the technical research issues, but for social scientists to gloss over evidence or countenance exaggeration and misinterpretation is clearly not in children's best interests, and amounts to intellectual dishonesty.

DEBATE 4

GRANDPARENT ACCESS

➤ *Should grandparents have the right of access to their grandchildren in intact families and in the event of divorce or adoption?*

EDITORS' NOTE: Following no-fault divorce, the near epidemic of divorces, frequently followed by remarriage and sometimes second (and sometimes more) divorces, created a huge class of nonparents, such as stepparents and grandparents, who had intimate ties with children, yet their access to these children could be summarily cut off. Except in extreme circumstances, the best interests of the child framework did not allow for a custody award to a nonbiological parent. Grandparents, as blood relatives with presumably close affectional ties, did receive special consideration for visitation following divorce, if not for custody, under the new laws. Common law had not recognized grandparents' rights in this regard. In revising their custody codes, however, most legislatures gave a sympathetic nod toward visitation rights for grandparents if they were deemed in the child's best interests. The U.S. House of Representatives, in an unusual intrusion into family law, also called on the states to be generous to grandparents (U.S. Congress, Resolution 45, April 19, 1983). This issue, however, remains controversial. There are those who believe that the unwanted intrusion of grandparents into an intact family or a family following divorce will produce conflict, which is not in the best interests of the child. As with many of these issues, the rights of the parties involved must be balanced against one another. This delicate task is undertaken by our two opponents.

Ethel J. Dunn says YES. She is the Executive Director of Grandparents United for Children's Rights. She has testified before Congress and speaks widely in her efforts to further the grandparents' rights movement. She has two grandchildren, ages 5 and 7.

Ross A. Thompson argues NO. He is a Professor of Psychology and Associate Director of the Center on Children, Families, and the Law at the University of Nebraska. He is editor of *Socioemotional Development* (volume 36 of the Nebraska Symposium on Motivation), and teaches on Children and the Law at the University of Nebraska College of Law.

YES — ETHEL J. DUNN

The idea that grandparents ever should be denied access to their grandchildren is totally repugnant to me. It is counter to the body of strong evidence signifying the importance of the contribution of grandparents to family strength and preservation. The only conceivable instance in which contact should legitimately be withheld is in the unusual event of a conviction for grandchild abuse. Supervised visitation might be appropriate at times, or telephone or written contact might be the agreed-upon method in others. But, whether through visits supervised or unsupervised, long-term or five-minute telephone conversations, children should never be deprived of their grandparents' unqualified love or the sense of total completeness that a grandparent's presence represents.

What surprises me is that the assumption might ever be addressed to the contrary. An abundance of powerful information suggests that the relationship between a child and his or her grandparents is second only in emotional intensity to that between child and parents, and that severance of or intrusion upon that natural bond can have long-term unhealthy effects.

A look at some recent statistics illustrates only too clearly that families, and particularly children, are in deep trouble today. According to recent figures published by the Children's Defense Fund (1991), the number of children younger than 6 who will have mothers in the labor force in 1995 will be 14.6 million; those children will need costly day care or family child care in order to get by. Illicit drug use is on the rise, but alcohol use is legal, more widespread and, therefore, more of a threat to our children's health. Violent crime and family poverty have exploded in the past quarter century, and teen suicide is now the second leading cause of death among young white males. A total of 2.4 million children were reported abused or neglected in 1989; that figure represents a 147% increase since 1979. According to the U.S. Public Health Service, 12% of all children younger than 18 suffered mental disorders in 1989 (Committee of the Institute of Medicine, 1989); the health care statistics for children and the current number of homeless children in our country are abominable.

We know that strong relationships with parents and grandparents increase children's abilities to weather the emotional turmoil and uncertainties that they face daily. Yet today's children spend less time with their parents and grandparents (or any adults) than did children in previous generations. What kind of commentary is it on our society that, while there are children in the

United States who are suffering from such emotional and physical stresses as just related and who could benefit from a grandparent's love, there are also those who would advocate legislating grandparents out of existence?

In another era, the question of whether or not grandparents should have access to their grandchildren would never be considered. Historically, grandparents and grandchildren united with other family members to provide the cement that kept families and, in turn, society generally stable. The family unit thrived and provided its own stability and economic comfort, each generation serving as an enhancement of its own to the succeeding one.

The past few decades have seen a change in the structure, perceived social needs, and economic stability of the family. Terms have been derived that define the place of each individual within the family unit, and an aura of isolationism has evolved to envelope the individual members and sustain their conceived prerogatives. We see the Fourteenth Amendment invoked to protect family members from one another, or the First Amendment used in an opposite fashion, to assure familial attachment. We have developed an entire dictionary of terms that seemingly defy definition, and we rely on amorphous verbiage to satisfy our needs and achievements. And while we adults are busily engaged in semantic tower building, our children are suffering from abuse, neglect, inadequate educational opportunity, parental stress, and myriad other socioeconomic needs that did not burden the lives of children a generation ago. The one factor that has remained constant, however, is the willingness and ability of most grandparents and great-grandparents to help, enrich, and strengthen their grandchildren's lives.

In the normal flow of life, a child is born endowed with one set of parents, two sets of grandparents, and perhaps some great-grandparents. If a conflict occurs between the adult generations, and conflict is normal in all human relationships, it is probably soon settled amicably and life goes on. Unfortunately, in some instances anger and resentment are allowed to smolder. Ultimately some of the warring adults may conclude that conflict resolution is useless and, furthermore, undesirable. A final split occurs between the adult generations. But some parents are not content to stop there. They have an ace up their sleeves and they are now, they see, in a position to use it. They tell the grandparents that they may not have access to their beloved grandchildren now or at any time in the future. And they persist, sometimes for years on end. Time might serve to cause the adults to recognize their own dysfunction, to understand their own needs to exert power or control. But no amount of time might be able to heal the child who sadly and suddenly becomes the innocent victim in an adult war.

We call the above "parental rights." Unfortunately, our culture is so determined to protect parental rights that we disregard those who made them parents in the first place—the children. It is certainly an anachronism to speak of the rights of children in our society. They have none! The child who is denied his grandparental affiliation can be living in an intact, though dysfunctional, home and suffering intense abuse; we give little credence to that fact. A child might have limited or no access to a loving parent because of a messy divorce and might be utilizing her grandparents as confidants; we give little cognizance to that fact. The child might even have been adopted by a stepparent and still be trying to adjust to new relationships. Rather than perceiving that a child's old relationship with grandparents can be important for his or her stability, our child-care professionals and lawmakers often authorize—nay, mandate—the instant removal of that stabilizing force from the child's life. What a sad state of affairs it is that a natural, loving relationship can be obliterated by a stroke of the pen.

There is no doubt that children need and love their parents. But the unequivocal fact remains that the intense natural bonds that children share with and the emotional strength they derive from their grandparents are equally essential to children's overall well-being. The inevitable conclusion, however, is that adult behavior (or misbehavior) can cause the divorce of children from their grandparents. And, as stated before, parental needs are currently deemed to supersede those of children, individually or as a group.

Every state now authorizes grandparent visitation under certain circumstances, most frequently when the marriage of a grandchild's parents is dissolved or when the child's parents die. Only a few states offer statutes that are general. No two states share a common statute, but many use a common standard in their expression of intent, the "best interests of the child," a familiar though highly amorphous phrase. Only three states have attempted to define and characterize that term clearly (American Bar Association, 1991).

It is precisely that lack of definition, along with legislative apathy, that is causing children and their grandparents so much consternation. I maintain that the doctrine of the "best interests of the child" is a farce and is intended to function only as a legislative dodge. It is a euphemism that really means "in the best interests of the parent." Rather than preserving family strength, it serves to aid in the disintegration of overall family unity. It obviously was not in Joshua DeShaney's "best interests" to be returned time after time to his abusive father and to be beaten so severely that, today, he is confined to an institution for the profoundly retarded (*DeShaney v. Winnebago County Department of Social Services,* 1979). It was certainly not in Dennis Jurgen's "best interests" to be cruelly abused by his adoptive mother and, mercifully, killed before his fourth birthday (Siegel, 1990). The list is long and the crimes are heinous.

How long will it take our society to revolt against the treatment of our children as chattels or pawns by the very people who have been legislatively authorized to provide for their comfort and security? When will grandparents be given the legislative tools to enable them to serve in the ways that are natural and right—those of protector, mentor, educator, confidant, mediator, and ego builder to their beloved grandchildren, in whose eyes they will always represent wisdom and strength, boundless love and continuous wonder? A grandparent, in the eyes of a child, represents more than merely another member of the family who provides goods and services on a regular basis; a grandparent represents love and a sense of wholeness that a child can get in no other way. Grandparents must never be denied access to their grandchildren and, conversely, children must always have access to their grandparents, along with the unconditional love that the relationship engenders.

We should start by revoking the "grandparent visitation statutes" of each of the 50 states, thereby disposing of the diversity and confusion that is currently common in grandparent-parent disputes. We should then enact a uniform grandparent presumption statute. The presumption should be that willing grandparents will have loving and continuous relationships with their grandchildren. It should be presumed that all children and society in general will benefit from the affiliation and that the natural bonding of one generation with the other is beneficial to the preservation of the family. Further, it should be presumed that the interrelationship between the polar generations provides an educative service to each and offers the continuing trust and security that is essential to the establishment and continuation of a healthy society. If anyone should wish to dispute the grandparent presumption law, he or she should do so in court and should be forced to show cause.

That willing grandparents have calmly and with little hesitation undertaken the combined roles of social worker, stress buffer, and surrogate parent can be attested to by the vast number of grandparents within the past decade who have been called upon to assume the parenting role again. U.S. Census data from 1990 show that more than 3 million grandparents in our country are now raising or helping to raise their grandchildren. They have stepped in because of their own children's inability or unwillingness to assume their responsibilities. The trend in census data from 1980 to 1990 shows that the number of grandparents living with grandchildren is increasing; it is not unreasonable to expect this rise to continue well into the twenty-first century. The number of grandparents who have opened their homes to their own divorced or unwed children and grandchildren has reached monumental proportions. Many grandparents tell of having to refinance their homes or sell some of their holdings in order to assist their suddenly reexpanded families.

The role of grandparenting has historically been to serve as family "backbone"—a strong link in the family generative chain. Hagestad (1985) suggests that, in some cases, "effects of grandparents can be felt simply from their presence, not their actions" (p. 44). In a study by Kornhaber and Woodward (1985), 300 children clearly depicted through pictures and verbal statements what their grandparents meant to them, leaving no doubt in anyone's mind that grandparents are the necessary glue for family—and society's—preservation.

In conclusion, I reiterate: Grandparents must not be denied access to their grandchildren. Instead, their aid should be encouraged as we attempt to preserve our most important natural resource, our children.

References

Children's Defense Fund. (1991). *The state of America's children.* Washington, DC: Author.

Hagestad, G. O. (1985). Grandparents: Diversity and socialization. In V. L. Bengtson & J. R. Robertson (Eds.), *Grandparenthood* (pp. 31-48). Beverly Hills, CA: Sage.

Kornhaber, A., & Woodward, K. L. (1985). *Grandparents/grandchildren: The vital connection.* New Brunswick, NJ: Transaction.

Siegel, B. (1990). *A death in White Bear Lake.* New York: Bantam.

DeShaney v. Winnebago County Department of Social Services, 489 U.S. 189 (1979).

NO   ROSS A. THOMPSON

From the anguished testimony of older adults at legislative hearings, articles in the popular media, and survey results, it is clear that many grandparents are distressed by their limited contact with their grandchildren. Their anguish is not in question here, nor is the desirability of fostering intergenerational relationships that benefit children. What deserves careful consideration, however, is the use of legal policy to enforce grandparent visitation over parental objections. Legal remedies are not well suited to creating and maintaining supportive relationships for children, and often they exact emotional costs from the children they are intended to protect. We cannot helpfully legalize the ties that bind if those ties are not supported within the child's family. Other solutions must be sought.

There are many ways, of course, that advocates for grandparents could seek to enhance grandparents' access to grandchildren. They could foster public education efforts that underscore the benefits children receive from their relationships with grandparents. They could encourage grandparents to ally with parents, most of whom welcome the emotional support, respite care of offspring, and other assistance that grandparents can provide, and who often regard grandparents as important resources for their offspring. They could foster the development of community programs that enable children, parents, and grandparents to share common interests, or business initiatives that promote multigenerational relationships. They could support the creation of counseling and mediation services that would be available to families in conflict over grandparent access to grandchildren. But enlisting legal reform in the effort to assist grandparents requires that advocates address several important questions about the consequences of grandparent visitation laws for children, and for the family in general.

Winners and Losers in Family Law

First, who derives the benefits of grandparent visitation laws? In contrast to counseling and mediation approaches that can benefit each participant, the legal system is an adversarial system of dispute resolution that inevitably identifies some as "winners" and others as "losers." This is a problem in family law because the winners and losers are often members of the same family. Advocates of grandparent visitation laws provide a mixed message about who benefits from their policies. They claim that grandparents and grandchildren are *both* winners. It is certainly true, of course, that grandparents benefit from legally enforced visitation with grandchildren over parents' objections. Grandparents acquire guaranteed access to grandchildren that does not depend on their assuming financial, material, relational, or any other responsibilities. They are not even required to visit grandchildren regularly. This is one reason that groups representing older adults have long argued for grandparent visitation laws.

Are children also "winners" from these laws? Advocates argue that they are, because courts must determine that visitation is in a child's "best interests" before visitation privileges are awarded to grandparents. But is it worthwhile considering the costs to children of family conflict brought to the courtroom (Derdeyn, 1985)? The adjudication of grandparent visitation disputes occurs because the child's parents and grandparents cannot agree about visitation with grandchildren (if they could agree, they would have no reason to go to court). Grandparent visitation is thus decided in a context of intergenerational conflict, in which the child's parents and grandparents are courtroom adversaries and children are at the nexus of their dispute. This is highly stressful to children, and because grandparent visitation disputes often occur shortly after a parent has died, or when parents have separated or divorced, or as an accompaniment to adoption proceedings, the child's capacity to cope is limited by the other stresses the child already faces.

There is nothing in the judicial process to ensure that intergenerational hostility does not persist after visitation rights have been awarded to grandparents, especially when parents lose an expensive and bitter court battle. Consequently, children are likely to become enmeshed in continuing family conflict in which parents and grandparents vie for the child's loyalty, arouse the child's guilt, and denigrate one another. This is not solely the fault of grandparents, but it is a natural outcome of the adversarial legal procedures by which grandparent visitation disputes are decided. Whatever benefits visitation provides grandchildren, therefore, must outweigh the emotional costs that intergenerational conflict brought to the courtroom entails for them.

It is important to identify clearly the benefits and costs of grandparent visitation disputes—and who assumes them—because in these situations the interests of grandparents and the interests of grandchildren are seldom the same. Whereas grandparents seek unrestricted access to grandchildren, grandchildren also need a supportive family environment, emotional stability, and predictable life demands. Legally enforced grandparent visitation can seldom satisfy the needs of grandparents as well as grandchildren given the family conflict that visitation usually entails. Moreover, legal guarantees of grandparent visitation take precedence over the children's own desires if they do not want to meet with grandparents. Consequently, it is wise to conclude that grandparent visitation laws primarily serve the interests of older adults, whose concerted advocacy efforts have resulted in the legal benefits they currently enjoy. The benefits of these laws to children are much less certain.

Appraising the Child's "Best Interests"

Of course, if courts can sensitively weigh these emotional benefits and costs to children, we have less reason for concern about children's welfare. Thus a second question that advocates of these policies must address is, How well do courts appraise a child's "best interests" concerning grandparent visitation? Consider all the diverse factors involved in such an appraisal: the child's age and developmental needs, the nature of the relationship and amount of prior contact between the child and grandparents, the amount of conflict between grandparents and the child's parents, the child's preferences, the importance of siblings, and many other factors. Judges' legal training poorly prepares them to make such sensitive assessments, and legal language defining children's "best interests" provides judges with little guidance. Moreover, there are few clinical tools and scant research to date evaluating the quality of grandchild-grandparent relationships, so the advice of mental health experts is likely to be speculative (although potentially helpful). Most people, in fact, would be very hesitant to estimate a child's best interests in these situations, because doing so involves complex considerations and difficult interpretations of children's needs.

What do judges do in such situations? In an effort to answer this question, my students and I surveyed a large number of court decisions concerning grandparent visitation to determine the bases for the courts' decisions (Thompson, Scalora, Castrianno, & Limber, 1992). What we learned surprised us. In *none* of the cases were the child's preferences mentioned in the court's determination of the child's best interests. Rarely were psychological evaluations made of either the child or the grandparents. In a surprisingly large proportion of cases, however, judges seemed to assume that grandparent visitation *was* in the child's best interests unless there was contrary evidence. Such an assumption may not only be misleading (and inapplicable to many families), it may also reflect a bias in favor of grandparents that causes judges to endorse grandparent visitation even when it does not benefit children. In interpreting children's needs, in other words, judges may be guided less by the needs and circumstances of the particular family members before them and more by their intuitive beliefs about the family and the needs of grandparents. We concluded that there is reason for concern about the court's capacity to make a valid appraisal of a child's best interests in grandparent visitation.

This is not necessarily the fault of judges. It is inherent in the difficult judgment they are expected to make. Indeed, these concerns are similar to those voiced by scholars who have examined judicial decisions when parents divorce: Judges often have difficulty appraising a child's best interests in awarding custody. But these considerations undermine the hope that by awarding grandparent visitation, based on a judicial determination that this is in a child's best interests, we are guaranteeing that children will benefit. This is frequently likely to be untrue.

The Importance of the Grandparent-Grandchild Relationship

Despite these concerns, however, advocates of grandparent visitation rights argue that the relationship between children and their grandparents is special and worthy of legal protection. At its best, they point out, grandparents assume unique roles in the lives of grandchildren as family historians, indulgent and nonjudgmental playmates, mentors, and sources of unconditional advice and support. There is a long-standing tradition of legal protection for visitation between children and their divorced parents, they note, even though it may involve conflict between family members. In a similar manner, the relationship between grandparents and grandchildren merits legal protection, even though children may experience some difficulty. Thus a third question we must consider is, How important are grandparents to grandchildren?

There is no doubt that, at their best, the relationships between grandparents and grandchildren are mutually supportive, loving, and affirming. But grandparenting has also changed in recent decades, as older adults have become healthier, wealthier, and more mobile than previous generations, and grandparenting has become more individualized as older adults balance grandparenting roles with the other pleasures of later life. When my students and I recently reviewed research about grandparenting, we learned that the grandparent-grandchild relationship is a *contingent* relationship (Thompson et al., 1992). In other words, its benefits to grandchildren are not inherent in kinship, but are dependent on several other factors (Cherlin & Furstenberg, 1986).

The geographic proximity between grandparents and grandchildren is one influence on the relationship, because grandparents who live within a single day's drive are afforded many opportunities to develop meaningful relationships with grandchildren. The grandparent's interest in developing this relationship is another influence; in one survey by Kornhaber and Woodward (1985), the large majority (75%) of grandparents reported only intermittent or irregular contact with grandchildren, even though most lived within daily driving distance. Another national survey reported that only 15% of grandchildren included a grandparent in their definition of the family, and only 2% indicated that they would turn to a grandparent for help with a personal problem (Cherlin & Furstenberg, 1986). Other influences include the age, employment, marital, and health status of grandparents, the ages of grandchildren, as well as their ethnic and racial group identity. In short, the contemporary grandparenting role is much more variable than traditional portrayals of grandparenting suggest, and its meaning to children is contingent on many features of their life circumstances.

Above all of these influences, however, is the relationship between grandparents and their *own* offspring—namely, the child's parents. Because they are at the center of the multigenerational family, parents mediate between grandparents and grandchildren and help to define their relationship. When the relationship between grandparents and parents is harmonious, for example, parents can support grandparents' efforts to mentor, love, and indulge grandchildren. Children also gain indirectly from the emotional and material assistance grandparents can offer their parents. When the relationship between grandparents and parents is conflictual, however, many of these benefits of grandparenting to children are prevented from developing or are undermined by intrafamilial hostility. In a sense, therefore, grandparenting is a contingent relationship because it is affected by the legacy of an *earlier* parent-child relationship: How well grandparents and their own offspring get along shapes the quality of the grandparent-grandchild relationship.

Thus the meaning of grandparenting to grandchildren cannot be evaluated outside the context of multigenerational family relationships. In this light, it is hard to see how these benefits can be ensured through litigation that makes parents and grandparents adversaries in a courtroom. Legally enforced visitation rights might preserve contact with grandchildren that grandparents enjoy, but their benefits to children are much less certain when visitation results from a court fight between family members. In effect, the legal system cannot preserve extended family relationships—and, most important, their benefits to children—when those relationships are impaired by family conflict.

New Directions

In sum, the law cannot easily regulate family relationships. Families are delicate social institutions, affected by a multiplicity of factors within and outside the network of relationships they share. The law, on the other hand, is a very blunt instrument, designed to change human behavior through coercion and punishment. At times, the legal system is compelled to regulate family functioning, such as when divorcing parents cannot agree on the custody of children and ask the courts to decide. In these cases, judges make uncertain and, at times, controversial decisions because their tools of legal analysis are not well suited to the conduct of sensitive evaluations of intimate relationships. For this reason, family law reformers are cautious in extending legal regulations to other areas of family life.

Grandparents are important to children, but they are not parents. The legal traditions that safeguard visitation between children and divorced parents are based on the well-founded assumption that a child's emotional well-being depends, in part, on maintaining contact with both parents after divorce. We can make no such assumption about grandparents because grandparents do not typically assume parental roles in children's lives (indeed, one of the pleasures of grandparenting is *not* having to assume parental responsibilities!). Moreover, in the context of family conflict, visitation entails emotional costs for children. When parents divorce, these costs undermine some of the benefits children derive from visiting with a parent, and even joint custody does not benefit children when parents remain hostile toward each other. With grandparents, the emotional costs of visitation may undermine most of its benefits to children because the grandparent-grandchild relationship is so fundamentally shaped by multigenerational family relationships.

Grandparent visitation statutes are currently part of the family law of all 50 U.S. states. In most cases, legislators were concerned about rising divorce rates, the growth of single parenting, and high rates of teenage pregnancy. They concluded that enlisting members of the extended family to provide support and assistance to grandchildren would have few risks and many potential benefits for children raised in potentially troubling conditions. This is one reason legally enforced grandparent visitation can occur in most states only if the child's family has been disrupted in some significant way (such as through divorce or separation or the death of a parent). In these circumstances, legislators reasoned, children have the most to gain through legally mandated visitation with grandparents.

More recently, however, groups representing older adults have renewed the fight to extend legalized grandparent visitation to *all* families, regardless of whether they are experiencing difficulty. If they are successful, any child may be compelled to visit with grandparents through a court order, even if parents object. If the benefits of grandparent visitation for children who might need intergenerational support in troubled conditions are uncertain, the wisdom of extending visitation rights to untroubled families is even more doubtful.

There remain many good reasons for enlisting intergenerational support on behalf of children. If advocates are truly concerned with benefiting *children,* however, it may be time to question whether the law should be used to protect all the significant relationships that a child shares with adults. Grandparents can better secure access to their grandchildren through mediation and counseling, public education efforts, and the kinds of intrafamilial bargaining and conciliation that have always characterized family life. When these efforts are unsuccessful, however, grandparents should reconsider whether legalizing the ties that bind ultimately benefits their grandchildren.

References

Cherlin, A. J., & Furstenberg, F. F., Jr. (1986). *The new American grandparent: A place in the family, a life apart.* New York: Basic Books.

Derdeyn, A. P. (1985). Grandparent visitation rights: Rendering family dissension more pronounced? *American Journal of Orthopsychiatry, 55,* 277-287.

Kornhaber, A., & Woodward, K. L. (1985). *Grandparents/grandchildren: The vital connection.* New Brunswick, NJ: Transaction.

Thompson, R. A., Scalora, M. J., Castrianno, L., & Limber, S. P. (1992). Grandparent visitation rights: Emergent psychological and psycholegal issues. In D. K. Kagehiro & W. S. Laufer (Eds.), *Handbook of psychology and law* (pp. 292-317). New York: Springer-Verlag.

ROSS A. THOMPSON RESPONDS

It is instructive to note the many points of agreement between my colleague Ethel Dunn and me on the issue of grandparent visitation rights. We are mutually concerned with the conditions of children and families today, and with the extent to which families are no longer reliable, "safe havens" for children who increasingly need such havens to cope with the escalating demands of their schools, neighborhoods, and communities. We agree that many grandparents and great-grandparents are willing to help enrich and strengthen the lives of their grandchildren through the relationships they share. And we both acknowledge that strong relationships between parents and grandparents enhance a child's life experience and emotional well-being.

But none of these issues is the focus of this debate. This debate concerns legal *rights* for grandparents. Rights and relationships are not the same things. Relationships are naturally occurring, often spontaneous human commitments that enrich life, partly because they are freely chosen and maintained by mutual consent. Rights are legalized commitments that are disputed in formal settings and enforced through coercion by recognized authorities. It is partly because rights and relationships are very different that the legal system—which is primarily concerned with rights—is not a good arena for enhancing and guaranteeing human relationships. Relationships cannot be coerced, whether they concern a child who does not want to visit a noncustodial father or a spouse trying to restore a dying marriage with a partner who wishes to divorce. The debate, therefore, is not over whether relationships with grandparents are good for grandchildren. In most cases, they are. Rather, the debate is over whether or not children benefit by having their relationships with grandparents guaranteed through legal procedures when they cannot be otherwise maintained within the family.

I have argued that children stand to lose more than benefit when their grandparents and parents are adversaries in a courtroom. If intergenerational conflict has escalated to a point that these adults cannot amiably agree on access to grandchildren, then it is hard to see how enmeshing the child in the nexus of their dispute through legally mandated visitation will benefit the child. The sad fact is, however, that many families are at just such an impasse. Grandparent visitation rights provide one way out for grandparents by enabling them to enlist the legal system to guarantee access to grandchildren. The far more difficult course—but the one adopted for generations—is that adults must work out their conflict without recourse to the courtroom. I think this traditional remedy remains the best one for children, even though grandparents may, on occasion, feel unduly deprived of contact with grandchildren until remedies to their intergenerational conflict are mutually negotiated. Grandparents will be denied contact with their grandchildren only if they cannot, or will not, help to make peace within the family.

Thus nobody is considering "legislating grandparents out of existence." Grandparents will always have significant and meaningful relationships with grandchildren that are guaranteed in the manner that they have traditionally been ensured: through supportive intergenerational relationships from which the child benefits. At the same time, however, it is potentially dangerous for children for society to extend current grandparent visitation rights to encompass a broad presumption that grandparents will have loving and continuous relationships with their grandchildren. Not all grandparents (or parents) are so loving. Not all grandparents (or parents) can keep their intergenerational conflict sufficiently minimized to resist embroiling grandchildren in their disputes. Not all grandparents (or parents) are so motivated by the needs of children to use legal coercion only when it benefits children. Parents, however, must exercise their rights in the context of significant responsibilities to children—responsibilities that parents can be sanctioned for neglecting. Only advocates for grandparents seek rights without responsibilities to children. Providing such sweeping legal guarantees for grandparents risks sacrificing children to the interests and needs of an older generation and identifies grandparent visitation rights as legislation that is truly in grandparents'—but not necessarily children's—best interests.

ETHEL J. DUNN RESPONDS

People bring to the grandparent visitation debate, as to any controversial issue, their own preconceived notions and learned prejudices. Thus it appears with Ross Thompson's contribution to the current discussion. Although he has referenced worthy authors and works, he has ably managed to misconstrue statements, provide half-truths, and, in some instances, artfully rearrange my own arguments to appear as support for his position. Although I would like to offer a rebuttal for each significant error, of both commission and omission, space does not allow me to do so. Instead, I would ask readers to examine carefully the original referenced material of both authors and make their own judgments. It is particularly vital for them to read the Cherlin and Furstenberg (1986) and Kornhaber and Woodward (1985) references in their entirety for important clues. I will, however, offer a few comments that I feel are imperative.

Just as there is heterogeneity in our culture among parents, so this is the case among grandparents. Therefore, I suggest that we cannot afford to stereotype and overgeneralize in our discussion of grandparent roles and how they are played out. My opponent calls the grandparent-grandchild relationship a contingent one. Certainly it is and inherently so. Often, however, what makes the conditional nature of the relationship so tenuous are the whims, emotions, and stability or instability of those in the controlling generation—the parents. He says that grandparents want rights but no responsibilities. I suggest that (a) he acquaint himself with the literature regarding the millions of grandparents who have assumed the responsibilities of caring for their grandchildren when the parents have been either unable or unwilling to do so and (b) he give credence to the fact that grandparents walk a fine line (see Cherlin & Furstenberg, 1986) between playing their prescribed roles as intergenerational mediators, mentors, "family watchdogs" (Troll, 1983), and family negotiators and being viewed as tenacious, meddlesome, and interfering creatures.

Although it would be wonderful if we could live in a world where love, peace, and harmony transcend everything, we must accept the fact that the world we live in is harsh and difficult. It might pay here to confront a bit of reality. No culture can do without laws and a legal system that at least attempts to provide freedom from chaos. My opponent negates the desirability of legal intervention in adult intergenerational disputes over visitation and has suggested mediation/counseling as an alternative solution. It is a sound suggestion, and it was adopted by the American Bar Association as an official policy several years ago. Private mediation agencies that have been surveyed indicate that, although the concept is an excellent one, it works only when implemented by mandating regulation, as provided in state family codes. Unless mediation is mandated by the court, it is usually refused, generally by the parent of the child. This seems to be the case even when the grandparent offers to absorb the expenses necessary for private mediation. Thus we must fall back on our legal system and, regretfully, lawyers.

Census figures from 1990 indicate that 60% of all marriages end in divorce, increasing the number of single-parent households at a rapid rate and often throwing women and children into poverty. According to the ABA's National Center for State Courts (1991, p. 122), New York State alone showed a 157% increase in child abuse and neglect cases filed in family court from 1984 to 1990. Michigan saw a 316% increase in cases filed during this same period. The National Committee for Prevention of Child Abuse reported a total of 2.4 million children abused or neglected in 1989. A 1988 nationwide survey of 36 hospitals conducted by the National Association of Perinatal Addiction, Research and Education estimated that 11% of newborns (375,000 infants) had been exposed perinatally to illegal drugs, including alcohol (Gittler & McPherson, 1990).

The list can go on indefinitely. It is well known that the first thing abusers do is isolate themselves and their families from loved ones. Grandparents and other loving relatives are usually the first to go, because not only are they the first to recognize the symptoms of illness, they usually attempt to alleviate the situation. Does my opponent think that it is in the "best interests" of children for them to be separated from loving relationships at such a time? We can no longer hide our heads in the sand. We must begin to recognize that parental rights should not be sacrosanct and that external intervention into the dysfunctional family is sometimes a necessity.

In conclusion, I reiterate that easy access must be maintained between the polar generations at all costs, because grandparents' involvement in children's lives is essential to children's emotional health and often their physical well-being.

References

American Bar Association, Section on Family Law. (1991). Grandparent visitation rights. *Family Law Quarterly, 25,* 26-81.
Cherlin, A. J., & Furstenberg, F. F., Jr. (1986). *The new American grandparent: A place in the family, a life apart.* New York: Basic Books.

Committee of the Institute of Medicine. (1989). *Research on children and adolescents with mental, behavioral and developmental disorders.* Washington, DC: National Academy Press.

Gittler, J., & McPherson, M. (1990, July-August). Perinatal substance abuse. *Children Today,* pp. 3-7.

Kornhaber, A., & Woodward, K. L. (1985). *Grandparents/grandchildren: The vital connection.* New Brunswick, NJ: Transaction.

National Center for State Courts. (1991). *Who are vulnerable children? The state of America's children.* Washington, DC: Children's Defense Fund.

Troll, L. E. (1983). Grandparents: The family watchdogs. In T. H. Brubaker (Ed.), *Family relationships in later life.* Beverly Hills, CA: Sage.

DEBATE 5

CHILDREN DIVORCING THEIR PARENTS

➢ *Should children and parents be allowed to divorce one another?*

EDITORS' NOTE: There are two separate issues embedded in this question. The first explores under what conditions an adolescent may seek emancipation from his or her parents. Are there any limits on this action if the parents are willing? Generally, state emancipation statutes address the following issues: (a) the minimum age for emancipation, (b) the proper court for jurisdiction, (c) the specific standards by which the court may judge the petition (which often include the financial viability of the adolescent), and (d) the purpose of the emancipation. What if the parents do not give their consent? Are there circumstances under which the minor should be able to achieve emancipation without the parents' consent? The second issue is the flip side of the question. Under what circumstances can parents relieve themselves of the obligation to support and supervise their child? Consider the issue of the incorrigible child who creates debts and is generally out of control, and yet has broken no law that would bring him or her under the jurisdiction of the juvenile justice system. Our two authors consider both sides of this complex issue.

Dana F. Castle says YES. She is Professor of Law at the University of Akron School of Law. She is the author of "Early Emancipation Statutes: Should They Protect Parents as Well as Children?" which appeared in *Family Law Quarterly* (Fall, 1986) and from which her current argument is drawn.

Carol Sanger argues NO. She is Professor of Law at the University of Santa Clara. She is coauthor of "Minor Changes: Emancipating Children in Modern Times," which appeared in the *University of Michigan Journal of Law Reform* (1992).

YES   DANA F. CASTLE

The parent-child relationship has received considerable attention during the twentieth century. The parental right to custody and control has been established as a fundamental right. Obligations owed to the child have been recognized and strengthened by statutes and case decisions that impose criminal and civil liability, including terminating parental rights, for failure to provide support and for abuse or neglect. In addition to these developments that reinforce the established legal framework, the child's position within that framework has been the subject of extensive critical reappraisal. The consideration has focused almost entirely on the issue of children's rights, with proponents advocating greater autonomy for children to direct their own lives.

As in earlier times, most families today experience minimal disruption or survive more serious conflict during the child's adolescence and emerge with relationships intact. But today's parent is required to assure control and conformity to acceptable norms in a more difficult environment. Forces converging to reduce the family's impact on adolescent development and values have weakened parental ability to direct behavior effectively. Despite this weakened position, when failure does occur the parent not only suffers from the disruptive effect the child's uncontrolled conduct has on the family unit, but frequently, as the legal power broker and authority figure, receives the blame and possibly a penalty as well.

The extreme measure of compelling a minor, unemancipated child to leave his or her home may terminate the parent-child relationship in fact and lessen daily family conflict; it can also create a quagmire of legal uncertainty. Is the parent who would have provided for the child within the family home were it not for untenable behavior liable for additional expenses generated by the child's living elsewhere? Is the parent civilly liable to third parties or subject to criminal sanctions for failure to control the child when the ability to control, to the extent that it remains, is voluntarily and unilaterally terminated by the parent? A number of jurisdictions have enacted emancipation statutes that provide children with the mechanism to terminate the parent-child relationship prematurely and obtain the protection of legal status certainty. Should similar protection be extended to parents also?

At common law a parent was not liable for a child's acts unless the parent was involved in the wrongdoing or was negligent in failing to prevent the child's wrongful conduct. Today, most jurisdictions have "contributing to delinquency" statutes and all states have "financial responsibility" statutes that impose vicarious criminal or civil liability on parents irrespective of fault, except to the extent that the child's misconduct infers the fault of failure to control. Parental liability statutes infuse the right of custody and control with a duty to exercise control to prevent the child from engaging in prohibited behavior. But guidelines for what will satisfy parental control requirements are vague.

In *Alber v. Nolle* (1982), under a statute that imposed liability on the basis of the parent-child relationship, a father was held accountable for the acts of his 17-year-old daughter, who was a habitual runaway who had not lived at home for two years. Even though the parent had engaged in numerous attempts to assert control, including counseling, submission of the child to juvenile authorities, and subsequent placement in a detention home, the court found parental liability. As the *Alber v. Nolle* decision illustrates, liability can be imposed on a parent despite demonstrated, although unsuccessful, attempts to control a child who engages in misconduct.

Where the purpose of the statute is to compel parental assistance, a "knowledge of the need for control" prerequisite generally does not apply. The fact that the parent is without knowledge of the wrongful conduct may not constitute a defense. Moreover, even if knowledge of wrongdoing is required, a child's propensity for wrongful conduct may be the basis for imputing constructive knowledge. In instances where a child's conduct has been repeatedly disruptive and unacceptable to his or her parent, establishing knowledge or reason to know should not be too difficult for the party attempting to prove parental failure to control. Also, one court held that a parent need not be physically present at the time of the child's misconduct (*Seaman v. Hockman*, 1953). This position obliges a parent to undertake preventive steps based on forewarnings. Liability for failure to control premised on passive parental conduct may not be litigated frequently, but the potential nevertheless exists.

Judicial emancipation is frequently described as a right of the parent, but this characterization does not allow for unilateral termination of the relationship and obligations otherwise owed. Intent and conduct on the part of the child, such as leaving home and being self-supporting, are critical factors. The so-called parental right to effect an emancipation might be described more accurately as the right of negation; by refusing to consent, the parent can prevent a finding of judicial emancipation.

One of the primary arguments made to support early emancipation is that children are growing up faster today, maturing at an earlier age, and thus are more capable of handling their own affairs. The recognition of early maturity suggests allowing children increased autonomy, as proponents of the children's rights movement advocate. But other factors operate against emancipation, because it terminates not only parental control but also accompanying obligations of support and maintenance. Children may be maturing at an earlier age, but they are experiencing postponed entry into the workforce and hence are delayed in achieving economic self-sufficiency. Most reach majority age and emancipation by operation of law while still engaged in the education or training necessary for today's complex employment opportunities. This situation generally involves some degree of continued dependence within the family unit. These children are not aided by early termination of parental obligations, which emancipation pursuant to the post-1970 statutes generally entails. The post-1970 emancipation statutes may indicate changes in the perception of family relations besides an ability on the part of children to function independently at an earlier age.

"The delicate parental . . . duty requires of a child submission to reasonable restraint and demands habits of propriety, obedience, and conformity to domestic discipline" (*Stant v. Lamberson,* 1937, p. 117, quoting *Ramsey v. Ramsey,* 1889, p. 70). Successful fulfillment of parental responsibility subsumes not only that the parent will perform her or his legal and moral duties but also that the child's behavior will conform with familial and societal standards. Yet when a child fails to conform, parents frequently are charged with sharing in and perhaps being the root cause of the deviant behavior. The characterization of a disobedient child as "stubborn and rebellious" and accountable for his or her wrongful action has been widely replaced by the philosophy that "there are no delinquent children, there are only delinquent parents." But legal and social changes in the family structure challenge the efficacy of placing the blame only on the parent, as at one time it was placed solely on the child.

Legal developments of the twentieth century have eroded the framework for family autonomy, including the right of the parent to control his or her child, which existed through the nineteenth century. Compulsory education is only one of a number of developments that have narrowed the function of the family and diminished the control that parents exercise over their children.

The family has undergone even more drastic alterations as a social unit. The occurrence of a "social morphological revolution" has transformed a community-based society into a mass society and has caused profound alteration in people's attitudes, values, behavior, interpersonal relations, forms of social control, and social organizations (Hauser, 1969, p. 27). The character of the family has not been immune to the effects of this revolution; the extended family has become the nuclear family. Its role as a production, consumption, religious, educational, socialization, affectional, and protective unit has been diminished. The family has transformed from a monogamous unit into "a form of chronological polygyny and polyandry" (Hauser, 1969, p. 30). It has become less a primary group as family members are subject to greater influence from peers and other outside forces because of the segmented rather than holistic nature of contacts with one another.

As a part of, and in addition to, the altered family structure, children today experience an extended rite of passage prior to adulthood, a greatly protracted period of "useless adolescence" (Kohler, 1979, p. 147). Studies indicate that few opportunities are available to children other than the "passive restrictive" role of the student, which prolongs financial dependency (Kohler, 1979, p. 147).

Despite characterization of emancipation as a parental right, the parental participation that is recognized is usually limited to acquiescence in or negation of a child's attempted emancipation. Parental abandonment or action to terminate responsibility has been characterized as intolerable and is distinguished from a forfeiture by the child who voluntarily leaves home. Arguably, a child's extreme misconduct and refusal to abide by rules is a constructive abandonment by her or him and should have the same effect as a forfeiture, but it is unlikely that this line of defense would be sufficient to overcome the repugnance with which parental abandonment is viewed.

The idea that a person is able to divorce his or her child and benefit from terminating the relationship contradicts established perceptions of the parental role. When normal adolescent conflicts are resolvable by traditional means, the drastic measure of expulsion sanctioned by a parent-initiated emancipation adjudication is indefensible. However, the need to protect children who are justified in leaving home by means of an emancipation process not requiring parental consent has been recognized. The need to protect parents should also be recognized when their only remaining recourse in dealing with unacceptable behavior is to terminate the parent-child relationship prematurely.

The relations of family members have been regulated for centuries and should not be lightly disturbed. But the family unit has undergone considerable change of structure and function that brings into question the future of the family in its present state. The period between childhood to adulthood known as adolescence has always been a difficult time. It has become even more difficult in family units caught in a state of change and deprived of once-accepted, familiar support without effective substitutes.

Legal advocates have focused concern primarily on the rights of children. The rights of parents, as those rights relate not to protection *of* the parent-child relationship but *from* it, have been ignored. Our legal system must recognize that there are parents for whom traditional methods of exercising control are inadequate in modern society. Parents are also people with rights who may themselves be the victims of discord created by a child's extreme antisocial behavior. Parents deserve the protection that early emancipation statutes could give them, just as these statutes provide for children in need. A court procedure with specified criteria would provide the necessary control against "parental cop-out," that is, against parents' seeking to alter the obligations normally owed to children. Early emancipation initiated by parents should be granted as a last resort only, but it is an option that deserves to be considered.

References

Alber v. Nolle, 98 N.M. 100, 645 P.2d 456 (1982).
Hauser. (1969). Social science predicts and projects. In *The future of the family* (pp. 32-62). New York: Simon and Schuster
Kohler. (1979). Child advocacy: Youth's right to participate. In P. Vardin & I. Brody (Eds.), *Children's rights: Contemporary perspective*. New York: Teacher's College Press.
Ramsey v. Ramsey, 121 Ind. 215, 23 N.E. 69 (1889).
Seaman v. Hockman, 2 Pa. D. & C.2d 663 (1953).
Stant v. Lamberson, 103 Ind. App. 411, 8 N.E.2d 115 (1937).

NO   CAROL SANGER

The idea of parent-child divorce received considerable attention in 1992 as the nation followed the case of an 11-year-old Florida boy who, the newspapers assured us, "divorced" his mother so that he could be adopted by his foster parents. Although the case raises interesting questions about what constitutes parental abandonment and the age at which a child's custody preferences should be respected, it was really less a novel divorce action than a traditional case involving termination of parental rights.

That is not to say, however, that parents and children do not sometimes "divorce" one another, if by divorce we mean some type of lasting separation. Thus the question here is not so much whether parents and children *should* divorce one another as how they manage to do so already, even in the absence of a formal intergenerational divorce procedure. In this essay I report on the use of a range of mechanisms used by parents to separate from, if not divorce, their children, particularly their teenage children. My primary focus will be on the attractions and the inappropriateness of one particular divorce substitute growing in popularity: statutory emancipation, the process by which minors assume the legal status of adults before they reach the age of majority.

My starting point for thinking about both emancipation and parent-child divorce is a realistic one: Parents and teenagers sometimes cannot live together. In this culture, the "irreconcilable differences" required for divorce between spouses are simply not limited to married adults. For most families the tensions and conflict that arise during the teen years are just a phase. Adolescence is endured, the child accomplishes some degree of individuation, and the transition to adulthood advances. But in other families the period is more like a siege than a phase. Conflict may last longer and be more intense. If family members are unwilling or unable to resolve the tensions, an intractability may set in that makes daily life close to unbearable for the parent, the (often present) stepparent, and the child.

In such cases domestic tranquility seems attainable only when the child is not at home. In recent years parents have used various approaches to bring about their children's absence. Depending on family history, temperament, and resources, frustrated parents have removed frustrated teenagers in a number of ways: by declaring them incorrigible or "beyond control" and relinquishing custody to the state, by sending them to private schools or camps, by institutionalizing them, by pushing them out, and by cutting them loose, as is sometimes recommended in the Tough Love programs.

Emancipation appears to be the latest in this series of available mechanisms for getting teenagers who are in conflict with their parents out of the family home. It was enacted in California and other states in the late 1970s as a means of removing the legal impediments of minority from self-sufficient minors already living on their own, independently from their parents. Unemancipated minors cannot sign contracts, rent apartments, or work overtime; emancipated minors can. It is simply easier to function in the real world as a legal adult.

But the adult status of emancipated minors also has implications for their legal relationships with their parents. Unemancipated minors must be supported financially by their parents; emancipated minors are on their own. It is *this* aspect of emancipation that has made it attractive to the parents of troublesome teenagers, as revealed by a recent study of emancipated minors from the San Francisco Bay Area (Sanger & Willemsen, 1992). The data from this study suggest that only in some cases did emancipation work as it was supposed to—by providing independent teenagers with legal authority appropriate to their life situations. In many other cases, however, emancipation was used by parents to end their own responsibility for more typical teenagers who lacked the experience, resources, or desire to live independently. Parents frequently had initiated the idea of emancipation, presenting the option to their teenagers, and had then facilitated the process by paying the fees, getting the papers, and driving to court. In short, in the counties studied, emancipation had become a way for parents to promote their children into legal adulthood ahead of schedule.

How is it that a statute intended to empower mature minors is sometimes used to dislodge them from their positions, however unsatisfactory, within home and family? Although many factors contribute to emancipation's susceptibility to the uses described, I focus here on two central ones: the substantive and procedural benefits of the process, especially to families in conflict, and a tradition within the American legal system of uncritical judicial assumptions about parent-child relationships.

First, the benefits of emancipation. If emancipation is considered as a form of "out-of-home placement," its advantages become quickly apparent. First, emancipation ends parental responsibility for any further financial support. The parent is relieved of the obligation to provide day-to-day support as well as the fear of vicarious liability for the child's conduct, particularly parental concerns about driving. Second, in most cases the emancipated minor is gone for good. Unlike runaways, who tend to come back, or institutionalized teenagers, who are often "cured" and sent home when their parents' insurance coverage is exhausted, emancipation is intended to be permanent.

A third benefit is that the emancipation process is unintrusive and relatively nonstigmatizing. No lawyers, social workers, or other professionals need be involved. Emancipated minors are neither crazy nor delinquent; they are mature. Finally, the emancipation process is cheap and quick. In the 90 petitions studied by Sanger and Willemsen (1992), emancipations were usually granted within a week from filing the petition. The involvement of the court is minimal. When parents signed their children's petitions, as they did in all of the cases studied, no hearing was required. Indeed, despite the statutory requirement that the judge determine that emancipation is not contrary to the minor's best interests, the few hearings that were held lasted no more than 5 or 10 minutes, and most exchanges between judge and minor were perfunctory.

This judicial response—basically rubber-stamping what seems to be parental permission for the emancipation—is not unusual in matters concerning parents and their children. The law steadfastly presumes that parents act in the best interests of their children. In many cases that is probably true. For example, in custody cases arising out of divorce, courts regularly rubber-stamp whatever agreements the parents have reached regarding their children's custody. (In other circumstances, such as parents' institutionalizing their teenage children, any assumed unity of parental-child interests is far less clear.) The premise behind judicial deference to parental decisions in the custody area is the reasonable assumption that parents take the welfare of their children seriously in deciding what a child's postdivorce circumstances are going to be. Similarly, then, a judge faced with an emancipation petition that has been signed by parents may well assume that all is agreeable, as it appears on the face of the petition.

The study data show, however, that the emancipation petitions do not always accurately portray the status or the desires of many of the minors. In addition, the petitions do not at all reveal the motivations or extent of participation by the minors' parents. This is because the familial conflict that often underlies an emancipation petition is masked by certain assumptions about what emancipation is meant to do. The process originally was intended to ratify or legitimate an existing set of circumstances—a minor living in financial and physical independence from his or her parents. Neither the legislature nor the judges who implement the emancipation process foresaw that parents would persuade their children to give up the benefits of minority by filing for emancipation.

The degree of parental persuasion needed is often not very great. Recall that often parents and their adolescent children are angry and frustrated with one another. Both may want to live apart from the other. But the problem with using emancipation to bring the separation is that the consequences of emancipation for minors are often quite severe. In the California study, minors' postemancipation lives were often marked by unstable living arrangements and precariousness of income and social support. Similarly, studies of minors in runaway shelters in Michigan revealed that many of them had not run away but had instead been emancipated by parents under a Michigan process (since revoked) that permitted parents alone to request their children's emancipation. Such troubling consequences should come as little surprise. There is no reason to suppose that minors who are financially dependent on their parents will overnight gain actual independence or functioning ability simply by a change in their legal status.

Emancipated minors face other problems as well. Three-fourths of the minors in the study reported here had dropped out of school, a powerful negative determinant of future well-being. In addition to their bleak economic prospects, many of the minors interviewed spoke wistfully about their old, unemancipated, lives and were frequently disillusioned by the consequences of their new status. Emancipation had sounded a lot better before it became a reality. Many had not understood that being on their own was serious business. Others were annoyed that benefits they had expected by virtue of the emancipation did not materialize. For example, emancipated minors who commit crimes are still under juvenile court jurisdiction, and emancipated minors without sufficient income still need cosigners to qualify for car loans—two disappointments mentioned frequently.

The contrast between emancipated and unemancipated life becomes clearer if we again compare emancipation to divorce. In both procedures the parties agree to dissolve their legal relationship because they find that living together in sufficient harmony is no longer possible. But emancipation differs from divorce in several important ways. First, although divorce ends the legal relationship between the spouses, it does not necessarily end the obligations between them. Aspects of dependence during the marriage often justify continued financial support between the former spouses. With emancipation, on the other hand, the minor's "postdivorce" independent status becomes completely controlling, and no account is taken of the previous dependent relationship.

A second difference concerns the procedure itself. Because the state values the marital relationship, steps are taken within the divorce process itself to promote the continuation of marriage. For example, in California the divorce petition offers the parties the opportunity for counseling services, and there is a six-month cooling-off period before the divorce can become final. In contrast, emancipation requires no waiting period and offers no counseling. It is perhaps closest to a summary divorce, where the court grants a divorce on the basis of the pleadings alone. But even parties to a summary divorce must be offered information explaining to them in nontechnical language the "requirements, nature, and effect" of a divorce. No such notice is required with emancipation, even though the change in the minor's legal status is at least as profound as in a divorce. Thus parties to a true divorce are both more informed and more protected than the teenage child of emancipating parents.

So what should parents and teenagers who are at their wits' end do? Although emancipation is sometimes misused, it nonetheless seems to serve a function that otherwise goes unfilled: facilitating separations between parents and teenage children who can no longer live together. Thus abolishment of emancipation is an unsatisfactory solution. Not all emancipated minors, even all badly emancipated ones, are unhappy or unhinged on their own. We cannot know if emancipated minors who leave home for the partial or primary benefit of their parents are less well off on their own than they would have been had they remained at home.

We can, however, try to remedy the ways in which emancipation unnecessarily and unacceptably compromises the interests of many minors. I present three recommendations here. The first is simply that minors who file for emancipation should be better informed about what emancipation means, legally and socially. This can be accomplished through brochures and manuals such as the ones provided by Legal Services for Children in San Francisco. That organization's pamphlet titled "Choices: When You Can't Live at Home" describes four legal options in addition to emancipation that are available to teenagers: guardianship, voluntary foster home, ward of the court, and emergency shelters. The pamphlet explains what each is, how one goes about getting it, and the likelihood of getting it, and offers telephone numbers to call for information.

Second, courts granting emancipation should be more alert to its possible manipulation by parents. The object of emancipation reform is not to keep the minor in a bad home situation but rather to make sure that the minor can actually manage on his or her own. The California statute requires that the minor already be living independently, though in practice judges rarely require any proof that this is the case. Thus my second recommendation is simply that judges verify that the facts on the petition are true and not rely on the parental signature as a proxy for an independent best interests determination. This can be done with such proof as rent receipts, checking account records, or statements from employers.

Third, perhaps emancipation should be made *more* rather than *less* available. States other than California authorize emancipation prospectively; that is, children do not have to prove that they are already living independently, but rather that they have thought through what it means to live independently and can show the court where they will live and work upon emancipation.

Emancipation is not much of a solution for minors who are mad at their parents. Similarly, it is not a proper solution for parents who can no longer tolerate their children. In a society where we permit adolescents to decide very little for themselves, emancipation is an anomaly. To the extent that it can safely promote the interests of both parents and teenagers, it is an anomaly we should keep. But we should be on guard for instances where emancipation does not protect the interests of children, even the older and more troublesome ones.

Reference

Sanger, C., & Willemsen, E. (1992). Minor changes: Emancipating children in modern times. *University of Michigan Journal of Law Reform, 25,* 239ff.

CAROL SANGER RESPONDS

I have little argument with Professor Castle's position that when a teenage child is completely beyond parental authority, and the parents have done everything they can to control their teenager's behavior, and the jurisdiction holds the parents liable for damage caused by the teen, and procedures are in place to ensure that emancipation is used only as a last resort, then the law ought to provide some mechanism for parents to protect themselves from the consequences of their child's acts. But these many qualifications pull us away from what I think is a larger problem than potential tort liability for a minor's bad acts, and that is the absence of legal or social services to remedy the predicament of parents and children who can no longer live together.

The emancipation study discussed above points up the complicated interplay between law and family conflict: Families may creatively employ legal procedures enacted for one purpose, such as emancipation, when the system leaves them without other available solutions (Sanger & Willemsen, 1992). The problem with the creative use of emancipation, however, is that it puts minors, even the older ones toward whom the culture feels little sympathy, at risk. Teenagers emancipated for the convenience or concern of their parents and stepparents are often without the skills and maturity necessary for independent adult life. They are therefore at risk for immediate homelessness, for sustained poverty, and for the emotional consequences of what in its present state comes very close to a form of sanctioned abandonment.

Reference

Sanger, C., & Willemsen, E. (1992). Minor changes: Emancipating children in modern times. *University of Michigan Journal of Law Reform, 25,* 239ff.

DANA F. CASTLE RESPONDS

Professor Sanger's response to whether parents and children should be allowed to divorce raises valid concerns about the use of emancipation procedures. However, these concerns relate more to shortcomings in the process than to the concept itself. Indeed, Professor Sanger notes that "to the extent that it can safely promote the interests of both parents and teenagers, it is an anomaly we should keep."

Initially, it needs to be emphasized that an emancipation that is not sought for the primary reason for which the process was first recognized—that is, to allow minors in exceptional circumstances greater autonomy in financial matters—should be only a solution of last resort, to be used when more conventional methods, such as counseling parent and child, have failed to remedy serious problems. I agree with Professor Sanger's recommendation that emancipation be made more available rather than less; I also believe it is important that the process become somewhat different from what most emancipation statutes prescribe and considerably more stringent than something analogous to a summary divorce. To this end, I offer the following suggestions in addition to Professor Sanger's.

First, allow the action to be brought by parents as well as children, with the parents' best interests recognized as a separate "ground" for emancipation (as Connecticut does). This should eliminate instances of parental manipulation and influencing by providing for an honest approach. Some parents, for social and psychological reasons, may still attempt to cloak the process as one initiated by the child, but a diligent judiciary would, it is hoped, recognize where that is the case.

Second, require the appointment of a guardian *ad litem* to represent the interests of the child in all emancipation proceedings. The guardian *ad litem* could encourage further dialogue between the parties where merited or facilitate the legal process where emancipation appears to be truly in the best interests of both parent and child. Where it is not, the matter would proceed in an adversarial posture.

Third, where the emancipation is sought in the best interests of the parents, the burden of proof for establishing that other methods of dealing with the problem have been tried and failed should be placed upon and required of the parents.

Finally, as divorce recognizes that some obligations may continue after legal severance of the marital relationship, legislation could provide for continued support provisions, as warranted, when emancipation is being decreed for other than recognition of the child's independent financial status.

Emancipation of minors can serve important societal needs. The existence of problems in its present legislative form and judicial implementation should direct us to seek solutions, not to reject totally or even accept reluctantly the concept itself.

PART II

Health and Medical Issues

DEBATE 6

SOCIAL COSTS OF AN AT-RISK FETUS

➤ *Should prospective parents be asked to consider the costs to society of giving birth to an offspring when prenatal testing has diagnosed a fetal defect that will produce severe physical and/or mental disabilities?*

EDITORS' NOTE: We contacted a number of genetic counselors and public health academics to write the yes argument for this question, but all declined the invitation. One person said that he would argue that testing should not be permitted unless the woman is willing to consider seriously the termination of the pregnancy if the results show that she will have a seriously disabled child. Otherwise, he noted, why pay for the test—why conduct a test if it is not going to make any difference one way or the other to a decision? Some people declined to argue the yes position because they favored the no position. Others believed that yes was a reasonable position if the steps it would require could be carried out in a sensitive manner, but declined to take on the task of making the argument because taking such a position goes against mainstream thinking in genetic counseling. Are they correct in being concerned about how others will react to their taking an unpopular position? They are. Studies have shown that even when people are told that a position on a topic is randomly assigned, they associate the person making the argument with the position argued. However, suppression of unpopular opinions on controversial topics does not forward thinking in a field. So the second editor of this volume has prepared the yes statement. She is not a genetic counselor and has never been confronted with the likelihood of bearing a severely disabled child. As always, there are advantages as well as disadvantages to being an outsider. Advantages include not being subject to biases, assumptions, and stereotypes in an area that may get in the way of improving the quality of service. Disadvantages include overlooking real issues that limit options. In the spirit of this book, the main goal is to consider thoughtfully the advantages and disadvantages of a position.

Eileen Gambrill, Ph.D., presents the YES position. She is Professor of Social Welfare at the University of California at Berkeley. She has been interested in the field of child welfare for many years and has published books, articles, and chapters in this area (including *Supervision: A Decision Making Approach,* with T. J. Stein). She is also interested in the area of clinical decision making, as reflected in her recent book, *Critical Thinking in Clinical Practice.*

Rita Beck Black, Ph.D., argues NO. She is Associate Professor at the Columbia University School of Social Work, New York, and Assistant Project Director of the Maternal and Child Health Training Project. She is the author of numerous articles and book chapters on the psychosocial impact of prenatal testing, reproductive difficulties, and disabilities. She is coauthor, with Sylvia Schild, of *Social Work and Genetics: A Guide for Practice.*

YES — EILEEN GAMBRILL

Professionals often help clients to reach decisions. These decisions can be difficult ones, as in this example. It is hard to imagine a more difficult experience than being confronted with the likelihood of bearing a severely disabled infant. I was told by one genetic counselor that 75% of couples with a high probability of bearing such a child decide not to conceive to avoid facing the decision of whether or not to abort a fetus. What are some of the issues here? One is degree of risk. The question to be addressed has been worded in such a manner as to indicate high risk.

The Fragility of Clients Is Overestimated

One of the assumptions underlying the position that prospective parents should not be asked to consider the costs to society of bearing a child with severe physical and mental disabilities seems to be that this would be too much for the parents—that they are already burdened enough with the difficulty of their situation and this would add to their burden. Some individuals with whom I spoke seemed to believe that asking prospective parents to take society's costs into consideration would be cruel. Such assumptions may be untrue. In fact, the opposite may be true. Are people really so fragile? I have always been impressed by the resilience of human beings. It seems that if we hold high expectations of ourselves, we tend to approximate these. If we are treated as children and information is withheld from us we have less chance to make well-reasoned decisions and to take pride in doing so.

Counselor Skills Are Underestimated

Another assumption seems to be that asking prospective parents to consider the costs to society of bearing a severely disabled child cannot be done in a sensitive manner. I do not think this is true. Shouldn't professional training provide the attitudes, knowledge, and skills needed for counselors to be able to introduce difficult topics with care and consideration for clients? Isn't this one goal of training programs in genetic counseling?

Self-Determination Is Compromised

Genetic counselors have an obligation to help prospective parents to consider the pros and cons of different alternatives (having or not having the child) rather than assuming that they are too emotionally disadvantaged to do so. Asking couples to consider the costs to society may help them to make a decision that they are leaning toward but feel guilty about. Aborting a fetus is not an attractive idea to anyone. Could it be that pressure is on prospective parents *not* to abort, and that asking them to consider the costs to society would help them to balance the pros and cons in a manner that more accurately reflects their wishes? Failure to mention societal costs may tilt the decision-making process in a direction that is not the one desired but the one that the prospective parents may be pressured into.

The societal costs of bearing a disabled infant could be presented as one of the many possible consequences that prospective parents may wish to consider. Isn't this what genetic counseling is about—helping prospective parents arrive at informed decisions, decisions they will be happy with, not only in the short term, but in the long term as well? Isn't it the counselor's responsibility to help prospective parents to consider consequences they may overlook in their emotional distress, and perhaps regret overlooking later? It is precisely when emotions run high that counselors should help clients think through decisions that carry weighty consequences. It is precisely then that counselors should help prospective parents to consider multiple goals and alternatives and to evaluate related evidence. Their doing so does not require or imply a cold, detached manner.

Professionals often think for clients. For example, doctors may think for patients—deciding what patients should (or "want to") know and what they should not (or "don't want to") know. Who is to say that they are correct? Are they correct because they have a degree? Are genetic counselors correct in not asking prospective parents to consider the costs to society of bearing a severely disabled child because they are credentialed and/or have a degree? Does a license or degree provide sound guidelines for knowing what another person should or should not know in reaching a decision? I am not so sure that it does. Shouldn't we give clients the right to decide? Shouldn't we respect them enough to help them to think through their decision?

Opportunities to Encourage Altruism Are Lost

What is becoming of the world when we cannot even suggest that someone consider the costs to others of personal decisions? Many writers have described the individualistic nature of our society and the lack of concern for others (e.g., Bellah, Madsen, Sullivan, Swidler, & Tipton, 1985; Slater, 1976). In a world of shrinking resources, consideration of others' needs is all the more imperative. Don't professionals have an obligation to take whatever steps they can to encourage altruism in the world? Aren't we patronizing clients and underestimating their concern for humankind by assuming that they are too fragile to think about other people who may be deprived of needed medical services because hundreds of thousands of dollars have been spent on one child? Genetic counselors, like all of us, are influenced by the vividness of events. They see parents struggling to decide what to do. Their anguish and sorrow is clear. The consequences of personal decisions to unknown others in the future are not seen. We don't see the child years from now who may be refused a needed operation because there is no money left in the depleted health care system. Future costs may be enormous if a genetic defect is passed on to future generations and results in the birth of still more children with severe disabilities.

Is the assumption of a lack of money down the line to provide needed health care to all an incorrect one? I don't think so. The gap between health needs and available resources is becoming more, not less, acute, as illustrated by increasing calls for some kind of national health coverage and the suggestion that quality of life be considered in making decisions about expensive medical care. Concerns about limited funds have led to the development of a measure of the value of treatments in terms of quality as well as length of life: quality-adjusted life years (QALYs).

> Health-care experts say that the era when doctors offer most insured patients the most expensive, aggressive treatments is fast coming to an end. Rationing is looming they say. And, bowing to the inevitable, economists are seizing upon a scale that many say is the best available to rank treatments.
> ... Although no one thinks QALY's are the perfect measurement, economists and ethicists say it, or something very much like it, will almost certainly be used to rank treatments in the United States in the near future. (Kolata, 1992, p. B5)

I suspect that as the gap between available resources and health needs increases, it will become more common (perhaps even required) for genetic counselors to ask clients to consider the costs of personal decisions to others. Aren't personal decisions of this kind really social decisions as well in their consequences to others?

The Myth of Nondirectiveness

Counselors with whom I spoke said that a nondirective approach is favored in genetic counseling, and that is why they would not ask clients to consider the costs to society of decisions made. What is a nondirective approach? One definition would be allowing clients to make their own decisions without leading them in one direction or another. Can counselors be nondirective? Research suggests that they cannot. Counselor behavior within the interview influences the client's behavior, even in very nondirective helping approaches (see, for example, Truax, 1966). If we know anything about the helping process, we know that it is a social influence process in which one "cannot not communicate," as the saying goes. Intentions on the part of counselors to be neutral may not be successful. Transitory moods and attributional biases influence clinical decision making (see, for example, Gambrill, 1990; Turk & Salovey, 1988). The more nondirective a counselor is, the more controlling he or she may be in the play of unrecognized subtle influences (Jurjevich, 1974). A raising of the eyebrow, a turning of the head, a repositioning of the body at a certain time—any or all may be interpreted as the counselor's indication of favoring or not favoring a certain course of action.

Those who say that the nondirective nature of genetic counseling prohibits asking prospective parents to consider the costs to society err in both practical and ethical ways. Following the rule to "be nondirective" is not only impossible, it overlooks the need to consider values and goals prospective parents may have or may wish to consider if they think about it. Counselors cannot be purely nondirective, and in their efforts to do so they may overlook subtle sources of influence and get in the way of helping prospective parents make well-thought-out decisions.

Summary

Like it or not, prospective parents who find out about fetal defects during pregnancy are confronted with a difficult decision. Neither outcome may be one that is preferred. This decision is a moral one. It involves life either way it turns out. What is the best way to make a decision—when emotions run high and no option is liked? Should we be led by our emotions? Or should we try to think the decision through as best we can under the circumstances? Making a difficult decision, whether under emotional distress or not, requires a search for possibilities, evidence, and goals. As Baron (1985) notes, "Aside from optimal search, good thinking involves being fair to all possibilities—including those not currently strong" (p. 107). Of course, emotions may influence the decision-making process. It is for this very reason that certain rules of thumb are valuable (e.g., consider other possibilities, examine the soundness of evidence).

Rationality in decision making does not imply cold calculation with an absence of emotion, based on a single value. It involves consideration of multiple goals and consequences involved in a decision (Baron, 1985). The search for goals is a key aspect of decision making. Premature closure on a selected subset (or one) may result in a decision that is later regretted (p. 238). In not helping prospective parents to discover and to consider multiple goals in this difficult decision, counselors are not doing their job, and, in the bargain, are being paternalistic.

References

Baron, J. (1985). *Rationality and intelligence.* New York: Cambridge University Press.
Bellah, R. N., Madsen, R., Sullivan, W. M., Swidler, A., & Tipton, S. M. (1985). *Habits of the heart: Individualism and commitment in American life.* New York: Harper & Row.
Gambrill, E. D. (1990). *Critical thinking in clinical practice.* San Francisco: Jossey-Bass.
Jurjevich, R. M. (1974). *The hoax of Freudism: A study of brainwashing the American professionals and laymen.* Philadelphia: Dorrance.
Kolata, G. (1992, November 24). Ethicists struggle with judgments of the "value" of life. *New York Times,* pp. B5, B8.
Slater, P. (1976). *The pursuit of loneliness: American culture at the breaking point.* Boston: Beacon.
Truax, C. (1966). Reinforcement and nonreinforcement in Rogerian psychology. *Journal of Abnormal Psychology, 71,* 1-9.
Turk, D. C., & Salovey, P. (Eds.). (1988). *Reasoning, inference, and judgment in clinical psychology.* New York: Free Press.

NO   RITA BECK BLACK

The so-called costs to society of people with serious disabilities include the actual expenses incurred in providing for their medical and sometimes residential care as well as the loss in productivity of family members whose energies are diverted to the care of those offspring.[1] Prenatal diagnostic testing now makes possible the diagnosis of a large number of disorders that lead to serious physical and mental disabilities after birth. Many prospective parents undergo specialized testing during pregnancy because they know that, because of family history or age, they have an increased risk of carrying a fetus with a serious disorder. Other pregnant couples learn of a defect when routine prenatal tests uncover a problem. Whatever the route to discovery, the prospective parents face the decision of whether or not to continue the pregnancy. Although they are free to make this choice, the existence of prenatal testing suggests at least implicit societal support for reduction of the costs of seriously impaired newborns through the termination of affected pregnancies. However, the prospective parents themselves should not be asked to consider the costs to society as they go about arriving at their own, very personal, decision about whether to bear a child with a serious disability.

The personal and fundamentally private nature of this decision rests on the genetic and social nature of the parent-child relationship. Genetically, the fetus starts as a composite; it is part of each of the parents. For the mother, the relationship takes on added complexity because the fetus starts out as part of the mother's body and only gradually becomes separate. The personal meanings attached to this developing genetic and social relationship are unique within each family and differ for each parent. Pregnancy represents one of life's developmental crises, a critical turning point from which neither mother nor father can return to a childless state. Likewise, one's biological family offers a central arena for the development of one's sense of self and intergenerational connectedness. Adoptees' frequent searches for their genetic parents attest to the power of biological connections. Society long has recognized the unique power of family relationships through prohibitions against professionals' serving members of their own families. Family remains one of the few, if only, places in society where people develop and feel valued for being who they are, not what they are "worth" or what they "cost." Asking prospective parents to consider the costs to society of their unborn fetus is asking them to violate the basic premise of family relationships.

A positive response to the question under debate represents an extension of "economic thinking" or "economic ideology" (Whitbeck, 1991), which views each person as a potential resource. We all are familiar with the evaluation of resources using cost-benefit analyses. Under this ideology people become commodities; we speak of the commodification of life. The dangers of the commodification of life perhaps are easiest to recognize when we consider the consequences of slavery (i.e., one group of people used as a resource/commodity by another group of people) or the oppression of women (the traditional patriarchal ideology that viewed women as having few rights or little value apart from their bodies). We begin a course down the slippery slope of eugenics when we ask a couple to view their fetus as a commodity that carries either benefits or costs to society. One can only wonder if the next step would be asking parents of particularly bright or athletically capable children to consider the "benefits" to society of bearing more offspring.

Yet, having said all of this about parental privacy and individual worth, one is still left with the reality that in the United States today our society perceives the person with a disability to be expensive and is not willing to spend sufficient resources for needed services. Just as prospective parents should have full information about potential financial and social supports available to help them care for a disabled child, they also should be informed about the practical costs for themselves and other family members. In effect, given the woeful insufficiency of medical and social resources for people with disabilities, prospective parents are asked to "cost out" what bringing an affected pregnancy to term would mean to them and any other existing children. However, for couples to consider limitations in current services when making their decision about whether to continue an affected pregnancy is not the same as suggesting that they have a responsibility to reduce the demand for such services by ending their pregnancy.

Whether something costs too much or too little is a question of value. From the perspective of the rights of people with disabilities, serious disabilities are not costing enough, or at least society is not spending enough. In the face of often enormous financial costs and limited services, one can even wonder whether it is appropriate to say that most prospective parents truly have free choice in deciding whether to bear a child with serious disabilities. Given that women generally assume a disproportional share of the caretaking responsibilities for children (whether sick or well), women's ability to choose freely is even more compromised. Asking a couple whose fetus has severe abnormalities to consider the costs to society of their bearing the child is tantamount to blaming the victim. It is asking them to settle a societal question of resource allocation by making their fetus into a resource that is entered into the economic equation. The couple are in effect hit twice: once by a society that will not provide an adequate service base to help them if they continue the pregnancy and once by a society that asks them, the victims, to assume responsibility for solving the problem.

Note

1. I regret that space limitations prevent discussion of the many ways that people with severe disabilities are valued and positive members of families and society. Indeed, one should question the appropriateness of using the term *defect* when speaking of any person. Cars have defects; people have varying abilities.

Reference

Whitbeck, C. (1991). Ethical issues raised by the new medical technologies. In J. Rodin & A. Collis (Eds.), *Women and new reproductive technologies: Medical, psychosocial, legal, and ethical dilemmas* (pp. 49-64). Hillsdale, NJ: Lawrence Erlbaum.

RITA BECK BLACK RESPONDS

Dr. Gambrill's response to this question assumes that it addresses how a genetic counselor or social worker should behave in a clinical encounter with prospective parents who have recently received disturbing results after prenatal testing. By moving directly to questions of clinical decision making—for example, whether parents would be too overwhelmed by the prospect of considering societal costs—Dr. Gambrill implicitly accepts the validity of the question. In contrast, I have argued against the premises on which the question is based. If prospective parents are asked to consider the societal costs of a child with a serious disability, they are asked to violate the privacy of the parent-child relationship and consider their offspring as commodities. Questions about the couple's own emotional or intellectual "ability" to handle this difficult decision thus become irrelevant. Moreover, the suggestion that it is altruistic to terminate the pregnancy in order to save society some money may be seen as an especially cruel instance of blaming the victim. Our hypothetical prospective parents surely cannot be said to be responsible for the lack of adequate health policy and preventive health services that have led to our current crisis in medical costs. How then can we say they are less altruistic for deciding to take on the strenuous emotional and financial challenges that often accompany the parenting of a child with special needs?

Assuming that termination of the pregnancy is more altruistic also implies that the person born with a defect is by definition a negative drain on societal resources. Yes, financial costs for supporting that life probably will be greater than for the "average" person. But is money our only measure? People with severe physical and mental disabilities may grow into loving relationships with family and significant others. Such relationships may enhance the lives of all concerned.

The issues raised by the question debated here are not clinical questions of client fragility or counselor directiveness. Rather, they are larger questions of the extent to which our society chooses to value the birth and rearing of all its children, regardless of their physical and mental capabilities. The negative social and moral costs to society of asking prospective parents to consider the "societal price tags" of their children are much greater than any monetary costs.

EILEEN GAMBRILL RESPONDS

In her statement, Rita Beck Black focuses on costs and concerns related to the child and his or her immediate family. She argues that the "so-called costs to society" include the expense of providing for medical and residential care as well as loss of productivity of family members. The potential costs are much wider. They include lack of funds for helping other children/adults in other families. Money spent on caring for one seriously disabled child is money that cannot be spent on helping other children. It is not money per se that is the issue, but the good that the spent money could do for others. In a world of scarce and shrinking resources, personal decisions are social and political decisions, and they may result in the deprivation of services to others. I would argue that my thinking is humanitarian thinking, not economic thinking (as Dr. Black suggests). It is asking clients to consider the potential costs of a personal decision to other children and families.

Rather than a "commodification" of life (to use Black's term), this position reflects an altruistic concern for others. I do not see what this perspective has to do with slavery. Slavery involves the ultimate use of force—one person owning another. Asking citizens to consider the costs to society (i.e., to other people) of personal decisions involves no force. Thinking about what others may need and how personal decisions may influence this seems to me quite different from owning another person and forcing him or her to do one's bidding. Never did I imply that prospective parents should make consideration of the costs to society the sole factor in their decision; I argued merely that it should be one of many factors considered. Is asking prospective parents to consider the costs to society of bearing a child with severe physical and mental disabilities asking them to solve the problem of scarce resources, as Black alleges? No, it is not. It is asking them to play their part, as we all should, in making the most just use of scarce resources.

Even if we may be genetically programmed to focus on the parent-child relationship (as Black suggests), must we remain stuck at this level? Can we not learn to be concerned about others as well as ourselves? Black argues that "one's biological family offers a central area for the development of one's sense of self and intergenerational connectedness." (Given the fact that the family is the single greatest site of violence, is this even true?) Isn't there too much focus on the self? What about caring for and connectedness to other human beings in the family of humanity? Isn't it just this kind of self- and family-focused thinking and acting that has gotten the world in the trouble it is in, with each individual, family, or nation attending to its own special interests, with little or no concern for anyone else's? It is not at all obvious that considering others violates the basic premise of family relationships. A basic premise valued in some families *is* to consider others.

Missing from Black's argument is the possibility that some prospective parents may *want* to consider the costs to others and to society. They may be more altruistically oriented than the genetic counselors so eager to think for couples by shielding them from some of the effects of personal decisions. Also missing is recognition of the counselor's responsibility to help people think through their decisions, not to think for them by withholding information about certain consequences.

Societies consist of people: real children and families that struggle with limited resources, real children and families that may suffer because of personal decisions. Yes, it is hard to think about other, unknown families when making agonizing personal decisions. They are not as vivid as one's own needs and wants, one's own family, one's own fetus. But they are there. We can encourage a self-centered focus, or we can take small steps to encourage caring and concern for others, and we can do so in a way that offers clients what many came for: to get help with a decision and to make one that is sound for them. With enough small steps, we may build a more humanitarian world for all, not just for some.

DEBATE 7

PREVENTING TEENAGE PREGNANCY

➤ *Should public policy be directed toward preventing teenage pregnancy?*

EDITORS' NOTE: In the past three decades the numbers of babies born to unwed teenage mothers has risen sharply overall, with the greatest rise occurring among some racial minorities. The reasons for this sharp rise are many; they include our long history of racism and demotion of the traditional family model, but also changes in law and policy that have moved toward removing the stigma of illegitimacy and providing at least minimal economic support for the unwed mother and her child. This support reverses previous public policy that severely discouraged unwed motherhood and made it difficult for a young unwed mother to keep her baby. Critics of our current supportive policy claim that the circumstance of unwed teenage motherhood is not in the best interests of either the young mother or the child, and that it is an unfair economic burden on the rest of society. Advocates of support claim that the timing of teenage motherhood is not necessarily a disadvantage for mother and child, and that those who attempt to thwart these births may do so for the wrong reasons, including racism. Moreover, they argue, reproductive freedom is increasingly looked upon as a woman's individual right in America. Our authors carefully analyze this controversial issue with scientific dispassion, providing clearheaded arguments in what is often a hotheaded debate.

Jane Mauldon says YES. She is an Assistant Professor in the Graduate School of Public Policy, University of California at Berkeley. Her research and teaching interests include social welfare policies in the United States, particularly AFDC and Medicaid, and aspects of the health of children and young adults in the United States.

Kristin Luker argues NO. She is Professor of Sociology and of Law at the University of California, Berkeley. Her research interests include teen pregnancy and other aspects of reproductive law and social policy. Her many publications in these areas include "Dubious Conceptions: The Controversy Over Teen Pregnancy," copyright 1991, New Prospect, Inc., excerpts of which are reprinted here by permission from the Spring 1991 issue of *The American Prospect*.

YES JANE MAULDON

Adolescent pregnancy was first defined as a social problem in the early 1970s. Since then, hundreds of programs have tackled the so-called epidemic of teen pregnancy, with approaches ranging from "Just say no" to the provision of free contraceptives and abortions. Now some researchers are claiming that the emphasis on preventing teen pregnancy is naive and misguided and that early childbearing is not necessarily harmful for mothers or their offspring. I reject this view and argue instead that government and the private sector should expand efforts to prevent teen pregnancy and childbearing. Ignoring or minimizing these problems does a disservice to both teens and society.

The high rate of pregnancy among U.S. teens will come as a surprise to many readers. More than 40% of American women become pregnant by age 20, and 20% become mothers. Although the large majority of them are aged 18 or 19, the United States has more very young mothers (under 16 years old) than any other developed country. Few choose motherhood at this age; more than 80% of pregnancies among both black and white teens are described as unwanted, or as "too early" (even if wanted at some time). (All the preceding data are from Hayes, 1987.)

Teenagers rarely use contraception when they first have sex, and typically they delay almost a year before seeking prescription contraceptive services. About 15% of sexually active teens report never using contraception, and many more use it only intermittently. Consequently, more than a million teenagers become pregnant each year, most of them unintentionally (Hayes, 1987).

About 40% of these young women abort, close to half carry their pregnancies to term, and the rest, about 13%, miscarry (Hayes, 1987). Abortion is not a trivial procedure; for many women, it is physically painful and (at least in the short term) emotionally distressing. The very fact that nearly half a million teenagers annually undergo abortions ought to make teen pregnancy prevention a major public policy concern. Young women abort because they believe that the alternative—early childbearing—would be far worse for them or the child. They want to delay parenthood until they are ready, and all the evidence suggests that they are right to do so.

Some teens do not abort even though they would like to. They may lack money for abortions, live too far from providers, or admit their pregnancies too late. Others never contemplate abortion because they are opposed to it on principle or because it frightens them. None of these young women had planned to have children as teens, and, with better access to contraception and abortion, some would have managed not to. As it is, they find themselves mothers by mistake. All too often, their lives provide compelling evidence in support of policies to help teens avoid pregnancy.

It is true that some teens welcome pregnancy, even if they did not actively intend it. Researchers have offered plausible theories, although little hard evidence, to explain this reaction. They suggest that girls who anticipate few satisfying work, educational, or other opportunities in the near future may view motherhood as a potential source of gratification (Abrahamse, Morrison, & Waite, 1985; cited in Hayes, 1987). It is likely that emotional factors are important for some teens; for example, they may believe that having a child will bind the child's father to them, or that pregnancy will enhance their standing in the eyes of peers or family and provide an entrée into adulthood. Some teens seek in motherhood an intense, intimate relationship with another person (Furstenberg, 1991). For these young women, childbearing offers appealing immediate rewards in a life in which other options may look bleak.

Because reproductive choices are profoundly personal and the motivation for pregnancy complex, there will always be teens who become pregnant and decide to become mothers. Rather than trying to prevent all teen pregnancies, public policies should be directed at the following three goals: first, to *eliminate unwanted pregnancies* (many of which are now aborted); second, to *change the range of options available to low-income teens* so that more are motivated to avoid pregnancy and early parenthood; and third, to *encourage those who want children to postpone pregnancy* at least until they graduate from high school.

These goals overlap, but each is targeted at an aspect of teen pregnancy that involves substantial human suffering, major public and private expense, or both. Teenage abortion places a financial, physical, and psychological burden on the young women having the abortions and a fiscal burden on those states that pay for abortions under Medicaid. The solution is not to make abortion less available (research summarized in Hayes, 1987, indicates that the likely consequences would be more unwanted teen births and a higher number of risky abortions); rather, we must reduce unwanted pregnancies.

Premature childbearing, especially among teens under 18, imposes heavy burdens on young mothers, their families, their children, and, often, society in general. The educational and economic contrasts between women who start childbearing at age 17 or before and women who start at or after age 21 are stark: high school dropout rates and poverty rates are far higher for the younger than for the older mothers. Admittedly, early motherhood is not the only and may not even be the chief reason for these gaps—differences in academic aspirations, abilities, and opportunities exist even before the girls reach puberty. Nevertheless, motherhood is a profoundly important event that completely changes the options facing young mothers, and may prevent or greatly delay their training or education past high school. By age 25, more than half of very young mothers still lack high school diplomas, whereas a majority of older childbearers have gone to college. Even one- or two-year delays in childbearing, from early or mid-teens to age 18 or 19, are associated with significant gains to women's well-being later in life (though here again, we do not know how much of the gap is caused by delaying motherhood and how much is the result of other inherent differences between the mothers).

The lifetime of poverty or near poverty that many teen mothers face results partly from their low levels of education, but also from their unmarried status. Fewer than half of teen mothers are married before their first births, and these early unions—or those begun after the first child's birth—are even less stable than the average marriage in the United States today. The typical teen mother spends most of her child-rearing years unmarried, and, bluntly, mothers and children who do not have access to husbands' income are usually poor. The timing is also important: During her late teens and early 20s, the years when other young women are acquiring work experience or education, the teen mother is caring for her young children. When she does enter the paid labor force, her lack of education and limited work experience put her at a significant disadvantage (Hayes, 1987).

Finally, the children of teenagers are in turn disadvantaged. Teen mothers often do not receive adequate prenatal care, and they may be less ready than older mothers to alter their diets and other behavior to ensure healthy pregnancies. Consequently, problems such as low birth weight, prematurity, and other complications of pregnancy are quite common. In addition, research consistently shows that children of less educated mothers score lower on academic achievement tests. Poverty exacerbates these children's problems in a host of ways. One long-run effect is that the daughter of a teen mother has a higher risk of having children early herself. Thus the cycle of poor health, low education, and poverty repeats itself across generations.

As noted above, for the many teen mothers who grow up poor early pregnancy may not be the only, or even the major, cause of their lifelong poverty. In fact, some young women become mothers precisely *because* they intend to drop out of high school, do not expect to find good jobs, and want some satisfying activity to fill their lives. But the fact that, from the perspective of some disadvantaged teens, it "makes sense" to have a baby when young is an indictment of the inequities in our society, not evidence that early childbearing is benign. Certainly many women who had their first children when they were teenagers believe, in retrospect, that early childbearing did significantly alter their educational, employment, and marriage options. Even if they eventually caught up educationally and economically with their peers who delayed having children, the difficulties they faced in doing so were considerable. Such women are usually adamant in saying that they do not want their own daughters following the same path. A teen mother's own mother and other relatives often take on much of the additional work and the financial responsibility of the new baby. In households already facing multiple stresses the arrival of an infant can be a huge burden. Former teen mothers may discourage their daughters from having babies because they know all too well how it affects the whole family, especially the new baby's grandmother (Furstenberg, 1991).

Given that rates of teen pregnancy and childbearing in the United States are unacceptably high, it is natural to wonder what policies, if any, could lower them. Here, the experiences of Western Europe and Canada offer hope. Although European teens are probably about as sexually active as American teens, teen pregnancy and childbearing are far less common in Europe than in the United States. Not coincidentally, the relevant public policies in these countries are crucially different. Three strategies are common: giving teens very easy access to contraception and abortion, educating teens about sex and contraception (rather than urging them to "just say no"), and offering education, training, and employment programs that broaden the opportunities available to disadvantaged teens (Jones et al., 1985).

Teenagers are most inclined to use family planning services that are free or very low cost, have a high degree of community acceptance, and are convenient. Simply increasing the availability and visibility of contraceptive services will make some teens aware that they need to use them. Confidentiality is also crucial in appealing to teens. Many teens who use clinics for family planning services say that their parents do not know of their visits and admit they would not use the services if health workers had to notify parents before dispensing contraceptives. Yet only 29 states and the District of Columbia have laws authorizing physicians to provide family planning services to minors without their parents' consent (Hayes, 1987).

The policy implications of the preceding analysis are obvious: Expand funding to family planning clinics, encourage them to extend their hours and strengthen their ties to their local schools and community organizations, and eliminate parental notification requirements for contraceptive and abortion services. Unfortunately, during the 1980s most public policies moved away from, not toward, these strategies. Between 1980 and 1990, total government expenditures for family planning, adjusted for inflation, declined by one-third. Many states passed laws requiring parental notification or permission before a minor could have an abortion. Meanwhile, teen birthrates rose between 1986 and 1989, after declining for more than two decades. The sharpest increases have been among the youngest teens; between 1986 and 1989 the birthrate increased by 19% among teens aged 15-17 (McKeegan, 1993).

Making contraception widely available will help some teens—those who feel relatively comfortable about their sexual behavior, are aware of the risk of pregnancy, and are determined to avoid it. But other approaches are needed to reach the many sexually active teens who, although they do not want to become pregnant, do not believe they need to protect themselves. They may think that they are not fertile, or believe that, magically, "pregnancy just won't happen to me."

Changing such widely held views and teaching teens to make informed decisions about sex are the ostensible goals of sex education programs in the United States. Unfortunately, there is no evidence that America's very restricted version of sex education has reduced teenage childbearing or pregnancy rates. In contrast, Swedish sex education teachers, for example, invite candid student discussion about sexuality and present quite young students with specific information about contraception. Sweden also has a system of special clinics where young people receive contraceptive services and counseling free, and abortion is widely available. Sweden's teen pregnancy rate is less than one-half the U.S. rate, and the teen birthrate is correspondingly low also (Jones et al., 1985).

An alternative strategy is to use radio, television, and other mass media to influence and educate teens. Again, the European experience is instructive. In several countries contraceptives are advertised on television, and public service announcements and billboards recommend condom use. In contrast, although sex pervades television and radio commercials and popular shows in the United States, the link is rarely made to unintended consequences such as pregnancy or sexually transmitted disease. Permitting condom and spermicide makers to advertise on television, or running public service announcements similar to the memorable antismoking advertisements aired in California in 1991, could make teens and adults more aware of the risks of unprotected sex.

Providing contraceptives and creating effective media messages to help teens avoid unwanted pregnancy will cost public dollars. Broadening the opportunities available to disadvantaged teens so that they want to avoid early childbearing will be even more expensive. However, the full costs of premature pregnancy and unwanted childbearing to young women, their children, and society are very great. The costs of a complicated birth, poor health, and low economic productivity are quantifiable. Other costs are not as easily measured. How should we value the benefit to a young woman and society of an abortion averted through the use of contraception—or the full cost, to society and individuals, of an education interrupted by premature motherhood?

Even if we evaluate programs only in terms of savings to taxpayers, preventing teen pregnancy still looks like a good investment. The savings are hard to measure because we cannot know exactly how much teen mothers' use of such programs as Aid to Families with Dependent Children (AFDC, or welfare), food stamps, or Medicaid is caused solely by their early childbearing. Given their disadvantaged circumstances, many of them would probably turn to these programs no matter when they had their first child. However, if their early motherhood *causes* them to, for example, drop out of high school, the additional public costs are certainly large. One study has estimated that delaying a young woman's first birth from age 16 until age 18 saves $7,182 in public funds. Thus if a program costs $700 per participant, it need delay only 1 pregnancy in 10 to break even in terms of public funds (Burt & Levy; cited in Hayes, 1987).

Every year in the United States, hundreds of thousands of young women become pregnant inadvertently, and many of them give birth. These unintended pregnancies and births are the indirect results of the decisions of public policy makers and others who shape the American social, economic, and cultural landscape. American teens live in a society where access to contraception and abortion is, for many, restricted; where the popular media glamorize sexual intimacy while ignoring its consequences; and where disadvantaged teens are offered only the most limited educational and economic opportunities. These realities need to be changed. When they are, and only then, we will see adolescent pregnancy, abortion, and childbearing become less common.

References

Abrahamse, A. F., Morrison, P. A., & Waite, L. J. (1985). *How family characteristics deter early unwed parenthood*. Paper presented at the annual meeting of the Population Association of America, Boston.

Furstenberg, F. F., Jr. (1991). As the pendulum swings: Teenage childbearing and social concern. *Family Relations, 40,* 127-138.

Hayes, C. (Ed.). (1987). *Risking the future: Adolescent sexuality, pregnancy, and childbearing* (Vol. 1). Washington, DC: National Academy Press.

Jones, E. F., Forrest, J. D., Goldman, N., Henshaw, S. K., Lincoln, R., Rosoff, J. I., Westoff, C. F., & Wulf, D. (1985). Teenage pregnancy in developed countries: Determinants and policy implications. *Family Planning Perspectives, 17*(2), 53-62.

McKeegan, M. (1993). *Abortion politics: Mutiny in the ranks of the Right.* New York: Free Press.

NO   KRISTIN LUKER

The conventional wisdom has it that an epidemic of teen pregnancy is today ruining the lives of young women and their children and perpetuating poverty in America. In polite circles, people speak regretfully of "babies having babies." Other Americans are more blunt. "I don't mind paying to help people in need," one angry radio talk-show host told Michael Katz (1989), a historian of poverty, "but I don't want my tax dollars to pay for the sexual pleasure of adolescents who won't use birth control."

By framing the issue in these terms, Americans have imagined that the persistence of poverty and other social problems can be traced to youngsters who are too impulsive or too ignorant to postpone sexual activity, to use contraception, to seek abortions, or, failing all that, especially if they are white, to give their babies up for adoption to "better" parents. Defining the problem this way, many Americans, including those in a position to influence public policy, have come to believe that one attractive avenue to reducing poverty and other social ills is to reduce teen birthrates. Their remedy is to persuade teenagers to postpone childbearing, either by convincing them of the virtues of chastity (a strategy conservatives prefer) or by making abortion, sex education, and contraception more freely available (the strategy liberals prefer).

Reducing teen pregnancy would almost certainly be a good thing. After all, the rate of teen childbearing in the United States is more similar to the birthrate among the rates prevailing in the poor countries of the world than to birthrates in the modern industrial nations we think of as our peers. However, neither the problem of teen pregnancy nor the remedies for it are as simple as most people think. In particular, the link between poverty and teen pregnancy is a complicated one. We do know that teen mothers are poorer than women who wait past their twentieth birthday to have a child, but, stereotypes to the contrary, it is not clear whether early motherhood causes poverty or the reverse (Hofferth & Hayes, 1987). Worse yet, even if teen pregnancy does have some independent force in making teen parents poorer than they would otherwise be, it remains to be seen whether any policies in effect or under discussion can do much to reduce teen birthrates.

These uncertainties raise questions about our political culture as well as our public choices. How did Americans become convinced that teen pregnancy is a major cause of poverty and that reducing one would reduce the other? The answer is a tale of good intentions, rising cultural anxieties about teen sex and family breakdown, and the uses—and misuses—of social science.

How Teen Pregnancy Became an Issue

Prior to the mid-1970s, few people talked about "teen pregnancy." Pregnancy was defined as a social problem primarily when a woman was unmarried; no one thought anything amiss when an 18- or 19-year-old got married and had children. And concern about pregnancies among unmarried women certainly did not stop when the women turned 20.

But in 1975, when Congress held the first of many hearings on the issue of adolescent fertility, expert witnesses began to speak of an "epidemic" of a "million pregnant teenagers" a year. The new concept of "teen pregnancy" had a remarkable impact. By the mid-1980s, Congress had created a new federal office on adolescent pregnancy and parenting; 23 states had set up task forces; the media had published more than 200 articles, including cover stories in both *Time* and *Newsweek*; American philanthropy had made teen pregnancy into a high-priority funding item; and a 1985 poll by Louis Harris and Associates showed that 80% of Americans thought teen pregnancy was a "serious problem" facing the nation, a concern shared across racial, geographic, and economic boundaries.

Certainly, they had reasons to worry. Numerous studies have documented an association between births to teenagers and a host of bad medical and social outcomes (for an overview of these studies, see Hofferth & Hayes, 1987). Compared with women who have babies later in life, teen mothers are in poorer health, have more medically treacherous pregnancies, have more stillbirths and newborn deaths, and have more low birth weight and otherwise medically compromised babies.

Later in life, women who had babies as teenagers are also worse off than other women. By their late twenties, women who gave birth as teenagers are less likely to have finished high school and thus not to have received any subsequent higher education. They are more likely to have routine, unsatisfying, and dead-end jobs; to be on welfare; and to be single parents either because they were never married or their marriages ended in divorce (see Hofferth & Hayes, 1987). In short, they often lead what writer Mike Rose (1989) has called "lives on the boundary."

Yet an interesting thing has happened over the past 20 years. A description of the lives of teenage mothers and their children was transmuted into a causal sequence, and the often-blighted lives of young mothers were assumed to flow from their early childbearing. Indeed, this is what the data would show if the women who give birth as teenagers were the same in every other way as women who give birth later. But they are not.

Two kinds of background factors influence which teens are likely to become pregnant and give birth outside of marriage. The first is inherited disadvantage. Young women from families that are poor, or rural, or from a disadvantaged minority, or headed by a single parent are more likely to be teen mothers than are their counterparts from more privileged backgrounds. Yet young mothers are not just disadvantaged; they are also discouraged. Studies suggest that a young woman who has other troubles—who is not doing well in school, has lower "measured ability," and lacks high aspirations for herself—is also at risk of becoming a teenage mother.

Race plays an independent part in the route to teen motherhood. Within each racial group, according to Abrahamse, Morrison, and Waite (1988), teen birthrates are highest for those who have the greatest economic disadvantage and lowest academic ability. The effects of disadvantage vary, however, depending on the group. Waite et al. found that among young, high-ability, affluent black women from homes with two parents, only about 1 in 100 becomes a single, teenaged mother. For comparable whites, the risk is 1 in 1,000. By contrast, a poor black teenager from a female-headed household who scores low on standardized tests has an astonishing 1 in 4 chance of becoming an unwed mother in her teens. Her white counterpart has 1 chance in 12. Unwed motherhood thus reflects the intersecting influences of race, class, and gender; race and class each has a distinct impact on the life histories of young women.

Given that many, if not most, teenage unwed mothers are already both disadvantaged and discouraged before they get pregnant, the poor outcomes of their pregnancies as well as their later difficulties in life are not surprising. It is difficult to sort out the effects of a teen birth apart from the personal and social factors that predispose young women to both teen motherhood and less education. Few would argue that having a baby as a teenager enhances educational opportunities, but the exact effect of teen birth is a matter of debate.

Raising children as a single mother presents economic problems for women of all ages, but the problem is especially severe for teenagers with limited education and job experience. Partly for that reason, teenagers became a focus of public concern about the impact of illegitimacy and single parenthood on welfare costs. Richard Wertheimer and Kristin Moore (n.d.) estimate that if by some miracle we could cut the teen birthrate in half, welfare costs would be reduced by 20%. Many of these young women would still need welfare for children born to them when they were no longer teens.

Other research suggests that most young mothers spend a transitional period on welfare while finishing school and entering the job market. Other data also suggest that teen mothers may both enter and leave the welfare ranks earlier than poor women who postpone childbearing. Thus teen births by themselves may have more of an effect on the timing of welfare in the chain of life events than on the extent of welfare dependency. In a study of 300 teen mothers and their children originally interviewed in the mid-1960s,

Furstenberg, Brooks-Gunn, and Morgan (1987) found 17 years later that two-thirds of those followed up had received no welfare in the previous five years, although some 70% of them had received public assistance at some point after the births of their children. A quarter had achieved middle-class incomes despite their poverty at the time their children were born.

None of this is to deny that teen mothers have a higher probability of being on welfare in the first place than women who begin their families at a later age, or that teen mothers may be disproportionally represented among those who find themselves chronically dependent on welfare. Given the disproportional number of teen mothers who come from socially disadvantaged origins (and who are less motivated and perhaps less able students), it would be surprising if they were not overrepresented among those needing public assistance, whenever they have their children. Only if we are prepared to argue that these kinds of women should never have children—which is the implicit alternative at the heart of much public debate—could we be confident that they would never enter the AFDC rolls.

Rethinking Teen Pregnancy

The original formulation of the teen pregnancy crisis seductively glossed over some of these hard realities. Teen motherhood is largely the province of those youngsters who are already disadvantaged by their position in our society. The major institutions of American life—families, schools, job markets, the medical system—are not working for them. But by framing the issue as teenage pregnancy, Americans could turn this reality around and ascribe the persistence of poverty and other social ills to the failure of individual teenagers to control their sexual impulses.

Framing the problem as teen pregnancy, curiously enough, also made it appear universal. Everyone is a teenager once. In fact, the rhetoric has sometimes claimed that the risk of teen pregnancy is universal, respecting no boundaries of class or race. But clearly, although teenage pregnancies do occur in virtually all walks of life, they do not occur with equal frequency. The concept of "teen pregnancy" has the advantage, therefore, of appearing neutral and universal when in fact it is directed at people disadvantaged by class, race, and gender.

If focusing on teen pregnancy casts the problem as deceptively universal, it also casts the solution as deceptively simple. Teens just have to wait. In fact, the tacit subtext of at least some of the debate on teen pregnancy is not that young women should wait until they are past their teens, but until they are "ready." Yet in the terms that many Americans have in mind, large numbers of these youngsters will never be "ready." They have already dropped out of school and will face a marginal future in the labor market whether or not they have babies. And, as William J. Wilson (1987) has noted, many young black women in inner-city communities will not have the option of marrying because of the dearth of eligible men their age as a result of high rates of unemployment, underemployment, imprisonment, and early death.

Not long ago, Arlene Geronimous (1987), an assistant professor of public health at the University of Michigan, caused a stir when she argued that teens, especially black teens, had little to gain (and perhaps something to lose) in postponing pregnancy. The longer teenagers wait, she noted, the more they risk ill health and infertility, and the less likely their mothers are to be alive and able to help them rear their children. Some observers quickly took Geronimous to mean that teen mothers are "rational," affirmatively choosing their pregnancies.

Yet, as Geronimous herself has emphasized, what sort of choices do these young women have? Although teen mothers typically report knowing about contraception (which they often say they have used) and knowing about abortion, they tell researchers that their pregnancies were unplanned. In the 1988 National Survey of Family Growth, for example, a little more than 70% of pregnancies among teens were reported as unplanned; the teenagers described the bulk of these pregnancies as wanted, but just arriving sooner than they had planned (Williams & Pratt, 1989).

Researchers typically layer their own views onto these data. Those who see teens as victims point to the data indicating most teen pregnancies are unplanned. Those who see teens as acting rationally look at their decisions not to use contraceptives or seek abortions. According to Frank Furstenberg (1990), however, the very indecisiveness of these young people is the critical finding. Youngsters often drift into pregnancy, and then into parenthood, not because they affirmatively choose pregnancy as a first choice among many options, but rather because they see so few satisfying alternatives. As Laurie Zabin, a Johns Hopkins researcher on teen pregnancy, puts it, "As long as people don't have a vision of the future which having a baby at a very early age will jeopardize, they won't go to all the lengths necessary to prevent pregnancy."

Many people talk about teen pregnancy as if there were an implicit social contract in America. They seem to suggest that if poor women would just postpone having babies until they are past their teens, they could have better lives for themselves and their children. But for teenagers already at the margins of American life, this is a contract that American society may be hard put to honor. What if, in fact, they are acting reasonably? What can public policy do about teen pregnancy if many teenagers drift into childbearing as the only vaguely promising option in a life where options are already constrained by gender, poverty, race, and failure?

The trouble is that there is little reason to think any of the "quick fixes" currently being proposed will resolve the fundamental issues involved. Liberals, for example, argue that the answer is more access to contraception, more readily available abortion, and more sex education. Some combination of these strategies probably has had some effect on teen births, particularly in keeping the teen pregnancy rate from soaring as the number of sexually active teens has increased. But the inner logic of this approach is that teens and adults have the same goal: keeping teens from pregnancies they do not want. Some teens, however, do want their pregnancies, and others drift into pregnancy and parenthood without ever actively deciding what they want. Consequently, increased access to contraceptives, sex education, and abortion services are unlikely to have a big impact in reducing their pregnancies.

Conservatives, on the other hand, often long for what they imagine was the traditional nuclear family, where people had children only in marriage, married only when they could prudently afford children, and then continued to provide support for their children if the marriage ended. Although no one fully understands the complex of social, economic, and cultural factors that brought us to the present situation, it is probably safe to predict that we shall not turn the clock back to that vision, which in any event is highly colored by nostalgia.

This is not to say that there is nothing public policy can do. Increased job opportunities for both young men and young women, meaningful job training programs (that do not slot young women into traditional low-paying "women's jobs"), and child support programs (see Skocpol, 1990) would all serve either to make marriage more feasible for those who wish to marry or to support children whose parents are not married. But older ages at first marriage, high rates of sex outside of marriage, a significant portion of all births out of wedlock, and problems with absent fathers tend to be common patterns in Western industrialized nations.

In their attempts to undo these patterns, many conservatives propose punitive policies to sanction unmarried parents, especially unmarried mothers, by changing the "incentive structure" young people face. The welfare reform bill of 1988, for example, made it more difficult for teens to set up their own households, at least in part because legislators were worried about the effects of welfare on the willingness to have a child out of wedlock. Other writers have called for such draconian solutions as forcible removal and placement in foster care for the children of unwed teen parents, or for the reduction of welfare benefits for women who have more than one child out of wedlock. Leave aside, for the moment, that these policies would single out only the most vulnerable in this population, the more troublesome issue is that the burdens of such policies would often fall most heavily on the children. Americans, as legal historian Michael Grossberg (1985) has shown, have traditionally and justifiably been leery of policies that regulate adult behavior at children's expense.

The things that public policy could do for these young people are unfortunately neither easy to implement nor inexpensive. However, if teens become parents because they lack options, public policy toward teen pregnancy and teenage childbearing will have to focus on enlarging the array of perceived options these young people face. And these must be changes in their real alternatives. Programs that seek to teach teens "future planning" while doing nothing about the futures they can expect are probably doomed to failure.

We live in a society that continues to idealize marriage and family as expected lifetime roles for women, even as it adds on the expectation that women will also work and be self-supporting. Planning for the trade-offs entailed in a lifetime of paid employment in the labor market and raising a family taxes the skills of our most advantaged young women. We should not be surprised that women who face discrimination by race and class in addition to that of gender are often even less adept at coping with these large and contradictory demands.

Those who worry about teenagers should probably worry about three different dangers as Americans debate policies on teen pregnancy. First, we should worry that things will continue as they have and that public policy will continue to see teens as unwitting victims, albeit victims who themselves cause a whole host of social ills. The working assumption here will be that teens genuinely do not want the children they are having, and that the task of public policy is to meet the needs of both society and the women involved by helping them not to have babies. What is good for society, therefore, is good for the individual woman. This vision, for all the reasons already considered, distorts current reality and, as such, is unlikely to lower the teen birthrate significantly, though it may be effective in keeping the rate from further increasing. To the extent that it is ineffective, it sets the stage for another risk.

The second risk is that the ineffectiveness of programs in lowering teen pregnancy dramatically may inadvertently give legitimacy to those who want more punitive control over teenagers, particularly minority and poor teens. If incentives and persuasion do not lead teenagers to conduct their sexual and reproductive lives in ways that adults would prefer, more coercive remedies may be advocated. The youth of teen mothers may make intrusive social control seem more acceptable than it would for older women.

Finally, the most subtle danger is that the new work on teen pregnancy will be used to argue that because teen pregnancy is not the linchpin that holds together myriad other social ills, it is not a problem at all. Concern about teen pregnancy has at least directed attention and resources to young, poor, and minority women; it has awakened many Americans to the diminished life chances among that population. If measures aimed at reducing teen pregnancy are not the quick fix for much of what ails American society, there is a powerful temptation to forget these young women altogether and allow them to slip back to their traditional invisible place in American public debate.

Teen pregnancy is less about young women and their sex lives than it is about restricted horizons and the boundaries of hope. It is about race and class and how those realities limit opportunities for young people. Most centrally, however, it is typically about being young, female, poor, and nonwhite and about how having a child seems to be one of the few avenues of satisfaction, fulfillment, and self-esteem. It would be a tragedy to stop worrying about these young women—and their partners—because their behavior is the measure rather than the cause of their blighted hopes.

References

Abrahamse, A. F., Morrison, P. A., & Waite, L. (1988). *Beyond stereotypes: Who becomes a single teenaged mother?* Santa Monica, CA: RAND Corporation.

Furstenberg, F. F., Jr. (1990, November). *As the pendulum swings: Teenage childbearing and social concern.* Paper presented at the annual meeting of the National Council on Family Relations, Seattle, WA.

Furstenberg, F. F., Jr., Brooks-Gunn, J., & Morgan, S. P. (1987). *Adolescent mothers in later life.* Chicago: University of Chicago Press.

Geronimous, A. (1987). On teenage childbearing in the United States. *Population and Development Review, 13,* 245-279.

Grossberg, M. (1985). *Governing the hearth: Law and family in 19th century America.* Chapel Hill: University of North Carolina Press.

Louis Harris & Associates. (1985). *Sex education, family planning and abortion* (a poll for the Planned Parenthood Federation of America, Reference No. 85pf8).

Hofferth, S. L., & Hayes, C. L. (Eds.). (1987). *Risking the future: Adolescent sexuality, pregnancy, and childbearing* (Vol. 2). Washington, DC: National Academy Press.

Katz, M. (1989). *The undeserving poor: From the War on Poverty to the war on welfare.* New York: Pantheon.

Rose, M. (1989). *Lives on the boundary: A moving account of the struggles and achievements of America's educational underclass.* New York: Free Press.

Skocpol, T. (1990, Summer). Sustainable social policy: Fighting poverty without poverty programs. *American Prospect.*

Wertheimer, R., & Moore, K. (n.d.). *Teenage childbearing: Public sector costs.* Washington, DC: Urban Institute.

Williams, L. B., & Pratt, W. B. (1989). *Wanted and unwanted childbearing in the United States, 1973-1988: Data from the 1988 National Survey of Family Growth.* Hyattsville, MD: U.S. Department of Health and Human Services, National Center for Health Statistics.

Wilson, W. J. (1987). *The truly disadvantaged: The inner city, the underclass, and public policy.* Chicago: University of Chicago Press.

KRISTIN LUKER RESPONDS

The truth of the matter is that Professor Mauldon and I agree more than we disagree. We are both worried about the lives of young women whose options are constrained by the fact of being born female, and who are, in a disproportionate number of cases, poor and minorities. I suspect that if either of us felt that teenage motherhood was a free choice among "goods," as the economists say, rather than a constrained choice among "bads," both of us would be substantially reassured. Yet all of the available evidence suggests that even to speak of a "choice" among teenage mothers is probably a mistake.

I have insisted in my work that young mothers cannot simply be seen as losers, victims of their own incompetence and stupidity. But as Mauldon makes clear, even competent and skillful young women (and men, who are typically left out of discussions of teenage pregnancy) have problems negotiating the maze of programs and decisions that are needed to prevent pregnancy.

Professor Mauldon calls for three overlapping public policy changes: to reduce unwanted pregnancies, to change the range of options available to low-income teens so that motherhood does not seem the most attractive of a limited range of options, and to encourage women who want children to postpone the birth of the first child at least until after high school graduation.

I agree enthusiastically with the first two of these suggestions. No one can seriously argue against programs that prevent unwanted pregnancies, and we would be foolish to limit further the options of young people whose lives are already limited. However, I find Professor Mauldon's third policy suggestion, namely, to encourage young women to postpone pregnancy until after high school graduation, to rest more on presumptions about young people than on hard data.

In the late nineteenth century, firm boundaries were drawn for the first time between children and adults, and a new category of "adolescence" was carved out between the two. New notions of age-appropriate behavior meant that adolescence were deemed "not ready" for sexuality, childbirth, or work. This was a departure in American attitudes. For much of the nineteenth century, for example, the "age of consent"—the age at which a young woman was deemed capable of consenting to sexual intercourse—was between 7 and 10 in most states. The age at which young people could get married without parental permission was typically 14 for girls and 16 for boys. And even early child labor laws protected only rather young children, usually below the ages of 10 or 11.

As our attitudes have changed, we have come to assume that there is something wrong about having a child during the high school years. As sociologists would say, a pregnant high schooler (or junior high schooler) is a role anomaly, as we have historically come to think that one is either a parent or a schoolchild, but not both. Yet the truth of the matter is that there is no good time to have a child in American society, which is notoriously skimpy in its provision of day-care services that would allow women to combine motherhood with work in the paid labor force.

More affluent women have chosen to deal with this dilemma by postponing childbearing until after they have become fully established in the paid labor force and can pay for appropriate child care. But we know that less affluent women are more likely to use kin-based child care when they work. Thus Arline Geronimous (1987) has argued that there are real incentives for less affluent women to have children *before* full-time entry into paid work: There is more of a likelihood that the young mother's own mother will be alive and well, and, in a competitive situation, young mothers have more of a claim on kin-based child care than do others.

Are there concrete costs to having a child during (or before) high school? The data are far from clear. There are some data to suggest that very young women (under 15) do have extra physical burdens associated with young motherhood itself (whether there are social and economic burdens as well awaits further research). With respect to high schoolers, however, the data are even less clear. Because young mothers are typically poorer and less motivated than either those who do not become pregnant or those who end their pregnancies by abortion, there is likely to be a powerful selection effect operating. The exact magnitude of the costs of high school motherhood is still being examined. What *is* clear, however, is that easy assumptions about high school motherhood—for instance, that such motherhood dooms a young woman to a more limited life than she otherwise would have—are not supported by the data.

A fresh look at teenage parenthood calls for new research strategies and findings. Already alluded to is the question, now being examined by scholars, of the exact costs of having a child while in high school. Other areas for research include an attempt to get a better feel for what young women (and men) perceive as their realistic futures, and how they imagine work and parenthood (and occasionally marriage) fits into their dreams for the future.

In short, the work of debunking the conventional wisdom on teenage pregnancy has begun. What lies before us is the hard, multilevel work of creating lives for teenage parents and their children so that teenage pregnancy is not a central part of—although not necessarily a central cause of—poverty across generations.

Reference

Geronimous, A. (1987). On teenage childbearing in the United States. *Population and Development Review, 13,* 245-279.

JANE MAULDON RESPONDS

Professor Luker notes that I have "two out of three right": Government ought to help teens prevent unwanted pregnancies and should also expand the economic and educational options available to low-income teens. We differ, however, on one point: I remain convinced that postponing childbearing until after high school graduation is advisable, and that public policies should encourage young women to do so. The issue between us is not whether we should enable young people to prevent unintended births completely, but whether to spend public dollars on efforts to discourage births that are "semi-intended."

Let us start with the question of why a young woman becomes a mother, assuming that it is not simply because of an accidental pregnancy with no chance of an abortion. Teenagers are on the verge of adulthood, and long to break away from parental authority. In the past, young men often escaped through military service, and young women typically used marriage, leading to motherhood. For disadvantaged black teen girls today, marriage is not often an available route into adulthood, but motherhood and welfare receipt are. As unmarried mothers, they are entitled to very modest AFDC checks, food stamps, and perhaps subsidized housing; they also acquire a new, adult, status. That for so many young women motherhood should still be the most obvious route to emancipation and adulthood, even now when women are acquiring education and entering the labor force in unprecedented numbers, is very disturbing.

The adult "freedom" offered by early motherhood is short-lived if it ultimately leads to long-term dependence on welfare or a succession of low-paid, low-status jobs. Teenagers who become mothers are taking an important step toward "specializing" in child rearing at the expense of economic self-sufficiency while other young people are acquiring an important credential—a high school diploma—and holding their first jobs. Because child rearing interferes with the acquisition of skills and experiences valued in the marketplace, teen mothers are greatly disadvantaged in a society in which, for example, high school graduation is required for higher education, vocational training, and most jobs.

Early motherhood has psychological as well as economic and educational consequences, for it tends to socialize young women into caretaker roles. Motherhood requires women to subordinate their own needs to their children's. Teen mothers enter this training ground young, at an age when most would be better off cultivating a healthy self-centeredness that would allow them to explore different life choices and take seriously their own needs.

Although delaying childbearing until after the teen years (or at least until after high school graduation) obviously does not prevent poverty, it might significantly broaden the opportunities a woman encounters later on. Looking back, she might say, "I'm glad I finished school" or "I was lucky to have had that job." Certainly, many women who began their families as teens wish in retrospect they had waited. In comparison with other developed countries, the United States employs social, health, and economic policies that neglect or are downright hostile to mothers and children. Women whose chief work and greatest skills are in child rearing increasingly find themselves, along with their children, consigned to the lowest rungs of U.S. society. Teen mothers enter adulthood heading in that direction.

DEBATE 8

PARENTAL CONSENT FOR ABORTION

➢ *Should parental consent to or notification of an adolescent's abortion be required by law?*

EDITORS' NOTE: Challenges to state parental consent or notification requirements in cases of adolescent abortion are probably the most closely watched legal issue today. Prochoice and prolife forces both believe that U.S. Supreme Court decisions regarding these challenges indicate the future of abortion rights. Outside of this critical legal arena, however, this issue triggers fundamental social questions regarding the control that parents should have over the reproductive rights of their adolescent children. Under what circumstances should an adolescent girl be allowed to make her own choices regarding pregnancy-related issues? Does this decision making include contraception and the decision to have a child as well as abortion? Even if we grant the adolescent the right to make a choice, should the parents be notified, or should the girl preserve the right to confidentiality? Yet another issue is whether both parents should be involved. In a society where so many adolescents live with only one parent, is it appropriate to require the consent or notification of both? So far the U.S. Supreme Court has struck a compromise. In states requiring parental consent, the girl can ask a judge to declare her a mature minor or to decide for some other reason that her decision is correct. This judicial bypass is also available in states that require two-parent notification. Our two sets of authors take positions at both sides of the Supreme Court's compromise. One believes that adolescents deserve more autonomy; the other argues for stronger parental involvement.

Everett L. Worthington, Jr., Ph.D., **David B. Larson**, M.D., M.S.P.H., **John S. Lyons**, Ph.D., **Malvin W. Brubaker**, J.D., **Cheryl A. Colecchi**, M.S., **James T. Berry**, M.S., and **David Morrow**, M.A., M.S., say YES. Worthington, Colecchi, Berry, and Morrow are associated with Virginia Commonwealth University. Larson is on leave from Duke University Medical Center and is working at the National Institute for Health Care Research in Arlington, Virginia. Lyons is at Northwestern University Medical School, and Malvin W. Brubaker, attorney at law, operates a private practice in Richmond, Virginia. Their argument in this debate appeared previously as "Mandatory Parental Involvement Prior to Adolescent Abortion" in the *Journal of Adolescent Health* (vol. 12, no. 2, 1991) and is reprinted by permission of the authors.

Margaret C. Crosby, J.D., and **Abigail English**, J.D., argue NO. Crosby is with the ACLU Foundation of Northern California. English is on the staff of the National Center for Youth Law, San Francisco. Their argument in this debate appeared previously as "Mandatory Parental Involvement/Judicial Bypass Laws: Do They Promote Adolescents' Health? in the *Journal of Adolescent Health* (vol. 12, no. 2, 1991), copyright 1991 by the Society for Adolescent Medicine, and is reprinted by permission of Elsevier Science Publishing Company, Inc.

YES — EVERETT L. WORTHINGTON, Jr., et al.

Since 1973, more than half of the U.S. states have enacted legislation calling for some form of mandatory parental involvement prior to a minor's securing an abortion (*Roe v. Wade,* 1973). Such laws generally require parental consent or notification before a minor's pregnancy is aborted. The permissible scope of these laws has been defined in decisions handed down by the Supreme Court (*Bellotti v. Baird,* 1979; *H.L. v. Matheson,* 1981; *Planned Parenthood of Kansas City v. Ashcroft,* 1983; *Zbaraz v. Hartigan,* 1976). Even without legislative mandate, more than 50% of pregnant adolescents already involve their parents in decision making about abortion (Lewis, 1987; Rosen, 1980).

Proponents and opponents of mandatory parental involvement tend to emphasize the communal responsibility of the family or the individual liberty of the adolescent. Clearly, it is quite difficult to reconcile the individual liberty of the adolescent with the responsibilities of the parent within the family unit. In most similar circumstances, laws have tended to favor the responsibilities of the parent over the civil liberties of the adolescent (Gardner, Scherer, & Tester, 1989). For instance, it is illegal to sell alcohol to a minor, but parents are free to buy alcohol and serve it to their adolescents should they choose to do so. Similar logic holds for an adolescent's viewing of an R-rated movie or smoking a cigarette. In the event of potential psychological or physical harm to the adolescent, the civil liberties of minors have often been restricted with the parental mandate to allow such liberties at their discretion. In states requiring parental notification, this same logic holds. In states where parental notification is not required, it becomes the adolescent's responsibility to choose whether to abort and whether to consult her parent(s).

It is this inherent conflict between an adolescent's right to an abortion and the parents' responsibility for the health and welfare of their adolescent that characterizes the controversy regarding legally mandated parent involvement in abortion. Opponents of legislative mandate argue that requiring parental involvement may in fact damage the adolescent and restrict her liberty to decide about her pregnancy. Proponents, on the other hand, argue that allowing abortions without parental notification undercuts the parents' responsibility for the well-being of their daughter and may damage both the girl and the (usually already imperiled) family.

Given the stark philosophical difference between the individual rights and communal responsibility positions within the legislative and judicial process for resolving these issues, it is not surprising to see a variation in laws across states. There is, however, a clear consensus among major medical and mental health professional organizations against parental notification. These organizations have consistently taken the position that parental notification may cause harm to the pregnant teenage girl considering abortion.

These clinical professional organizations are in need of research assessing the clinical impact of a legislative mandate. Research is needed to assess whether an adolescent who would have aborted without consulting her parents would be helped, harmed, or unaffected by a requirement of parental involvement. Little of this research has been undertaken, thus other relevant literature must be considered. To begin addressing this important issue, we will consider relevant decision-making research. In particular, we will review the scientific evidence regarding the impact of parental involvement in pregnancy-related decision making on the well-being of a pregnant minor.

Parental Reactions to Pregnancy

A major hypothesis regarding the negative impact of legislative mandate for parental notification is that anticipated parental anger or possible rejection will decrease the likelihood that an adolescent will come forward about her pregnancy until it is too late to abort safely. Several studies suggest that when adolescents become pregnant, they often feel guilty, ashamed, anxious, and fearful of telling their parents because of anticipated parental anger (Adler, 1981; Bolton, 1980; Musick, Handler, & Waddill, 1984; Osofsky & Osofsky, 1978; Swigar, Breslin, Pouzzner, Quinlan, & Blum, 1976). Research shows that these expectations are partially justified. When parents are informed about a daughter's pregnancy the expected anger usually takes place, but, on adjusting to the news, most parents are supportive (Bowerman, Irish, & Pope, 1966; Figley, 1983; Friedman, 1966; McCubbin & Patterson, 1983; Smith, 1975; Swigar et al., 1976). From two-thirds to four-fifths of parents have been reported to be supportive (Baptiste, 1986; Bolton, 1980; Bowerman et al., 1966; Litton-Fox, 1980; Olson, 1980; Rue, 1985), even in research conducted prior to *Roe v. Wade* (1973), when attitudes concerning illegitimate birth were more judgmental than today. Generally speaking, evidence suggests that parents react much less negatively than adolescents anticipate (Clary, 1982; Furstenberg, 1976; Maracek, 1987).

Adolescent Decision Making

Opponents of parental involvement in adolescent decision making suggest that including parental input will not improve the quality of decision making, and that, in fact, there are no differences in decision-making abilities between adolescents and adults (Interdivisional Committee on Adolescent Abortion, 1987). The American Psychological Association's brief in *Thornburgh v. American College of Obstetricians and Gynecologists* (1986) concluded that "there is no empirical basis for concluding that minors fourteen and older are less capable of making informed decisions than adults" (p. 27). Consistent with the position of others (e.g., Gardner et al., 1989) and based on the research reviewed, we believe this conclusion is inappropriate.

Contrary to the American Psychological Association's brief, we believe there is substantial literature suggesting not only that adolescents differ from adults, but that younger and older adolescents differ in how they make decisions. First, younger adolescents consult different people for advice more frequently than do older adolescents and adults (Ashton, 1979; Clary, 1982; Lewis, 1980; Torres, Forrest, & Eisman, 1980). The relative influence of parents and peers on decisions appears to change with age as well as the type of decision under consideration (Larsen, 1972).

Second, adolescents and adults differ in their abilities to view situations from the perspective of their significant others. For example, 52 two-parent families with adolescents between the ages of 13 and 16 responded to a moral decision-making questionnaire viewed from three different perspectives. Each subject completed the questionnaire once for him- or herself and then two more times, estimating how specific other family members would respond. Adults were able to view decisions more accurately from the perspectives of other family members than were adolescents (Whitbeck & Mullis, 1987).

Third, adolescents at age 15 years consider different factors in their pregnancy decisions from those considered by adults (Hatcher, 1976). They also differ from adults in estimating their potential for childbearing (Leibowitz, Eisen, & Chow, 1984; Lewis, 1980; Musick et al., 1984).

Fourth, in decision making, adolescents are less likely than adults to consider the importance of future solutions and goals (Rowe, 1984; Verstraeten, 1982). Adolescents differ from adults in their consideration of future consequences in hypothetical dilemmas. For example, Lewis (1981) found that adolescents' abilities to consider the consequences of having cosmetic surgery increased with age. Eisen, Zellman, Leibowitz, et al. (1983) conclude that many adolescents do not have sufficient ability to foresee future consequences or to reason abstractly concerning many decisions about sexuality. Finally, adolescents are more likely to delay or procrastinate about a decision than are adults (Bracken & Kasl, 1975; Russo, 1986).

Further discussion of the relationship between theories of cognitive development and adolescent pregnancy decision making can be found in a study by Gardner et al. (1989). These authors point to the reliance on Piaget's theory of developmental stages for support of the conclusion that adolescents and adults are developmentally similar in their decision-making abilities. However, they point out that recent work in theories of cognitive development does not support a uniform adolescent-adult stage model, but rather suggests that cognitive abilities develop at different rates and thus occur at different stages.

It is difficult to assess the implications of these findings for an adolescent's ability to make a competent decision without some definition of what *competence* might mean. Janis and Mann (1977) propose a theory of decision making that emphasizes assessing competence based on the process rather than the decision made. According to this model, "effective" decision making (a) seeks multiple perspectives; (b) understands these perspectives; (c) considers the potential costs and benefits of multiple, reasonable alternatives; (d) identifies future solutions and goals; (e) considers the consequences of potential outcomes; and (f) does not result in long delays or procrastination in acting on a decision, nor is decision making prematurely foreclosed through hasty, impulsive acts.

Thus, applying the six criteria of Janis and Mann to the above differences between adolescents and adults, older adolescents and adults would be expected to engage in effective decision making more frequently than would younger adolescents. Thus a parent should in general be a more competent decision maker than that parent's younger adolescent. Consequently, involving the parent with the adolescent in decision making may contribute to improvement of the quality of decision making.

Co-opting the Minor's Right to Decide

An additional concern expressed about the parental mandate is that once the parent is notified, he or she will either not include the adolescent in deciding the fate of her pregnancy or elicit sufficient guilt to pressure a decision in accordance with the parent's wishes. Thus the parent might, in essence, make (or induce) an "ineffective" decision. This form of parental decision making can cause guilt, postdecision regret, and psychological problems. Regardless of whether the decision was to abort (Adler & Dolcini, 1986; Bracken, Hachamovitch, & Grossman, 1974) or to bear the child, this form of ineffective parental decision making has been reported to occur in a small minority of instances.

However, parental notification may have little or no impact on this type of parental pressure. For example, perceived parental pressure has been reported to occur even when the girl does not consult her parents (Lewis, 1980). This finding is particularly troubling given research that suggests that teenage girls see their parents as less accepting than they really are (Furstenberg, 1976). Even counselors, who usually make a conscious effort to avoid influencing the final decision of the adolescent, may still be perceived by the teenager as exerting pressure toward a particular decision (Maracek, 1987). Thus it may be a mistake to base conclusions about how parents will react to notification on the perceptions of the teenage girl. Likewise, it may be a mistake to assume that parental ignorance about a pregnancy will have either no impact or less impact than will parental notification.

Social Support

One of the primary mechanisms that adults use to cope with the stress of pregnancy and childbirth is to seek social support (Levitt, Weber, & Clark, 1986). This is done first in the context of the immediate family, next by involving the extended family, and finally by reaching out to peers (Belsky & Rovine, 1984). Social support by family members appears to be even more important for pregnant adolescents than for pregnant adults, because adolescents are in general more dependent on their parents financially, physically, and emotionally than are adults (Lee, 1980).

There are no empirical data available regarding the impact of parental notification on social support. Indeed, social support from the family has been shown repeatedly to be related to less negative reactions to either abortion or childbirth (Adler, 1976; Illsley & Hall, 1976; Levitt et al., 1986; Olson, 1980; Rue, 1985; Shusterman, 1976). Children who are neither loved nor supported by their parents are the most likely to experience adjustment problems, regardless of the outcome of their pregnancies.

Given that the foundations of social support include communication and a sense of belonging, it is difficult to believe that support would be endangered by parental notification. An adolescent who is not experiencing support from her parents may not wish to consult them. However, there is no evidence that required parental notification regarding the pregnancy termination decision will make this already troubled relationship worse. Nor is there evidence that not notifying parents will support the adolescent in her differentiation from her parents.

Conclusion

In summary, although medical and mental health organizations are uniformly against parental notification statutes, there is little evidence in the limited decision-making literature reviewed to suggest that parental notification legislation does harm to a teenager or her family. If anything, such requirements might support family communication and facilitate decision making.

We believe that the natural study of adolescent decision making on pregnancy termination with and without parental notification is the necessary next step in beginning to resolve this controversy. The varying state laws on this subject provide a natural laboratory for just such research. In addition, in-depth comparison of adolescent and adult decision-making processes in real-life situations is needed to resolve the issue of the ability of adolescents to make clearly informed pregnancy decisions.

References

Adler, N. E. (1976). Sample attrition in studies of psycho-social sequelae of abortion: How great a problem? *Journal of Applied Social Psychology, 6*, 240-257.

Adler, N. E. (1981). Sex roles and unwanted pregnancy in adolescent and adult women. *Professional Psychology: Research and Practice, 12*, 56-66.

Adler, N. E., & Dolcini, P. (1986). Psychological issues in abortion for adolescents. In G. B. Melton (Ed.), *Adolescent abortion: Psychological and legal issues* (pp. 74-95). Lincoln: University of Nebraska Press.

Ashton, J. R. (1979). Patterns of discussion and decision-making among abortion patients. *Journal of Biosocial Sciences, 12*, 247-259.

Baptiste, D., Jr. (1986). Counseling the pregnant adolescent within a family context: Therapeutic issues and strategies. *Family Therapy, 13*, 163-176.

Bellotti v. Baird, 443 U.S. 622 (1979).

Belsky, J., & Rovine, M. (1984). Social network contact, family support and transition to parenthood. *Journal of Marriage and the Family, 46*, 455-462.

Bolton, F. G., Jr. (1980). *The pregnant adolescent: Problems of premature parenthood.* Beverly Hills, CA: Sage.

Bowerman, C. E., Irish, D. P., & Pope, H. (1966). *Unwed motherhood: Personal and social consequences.* Chapel Hill: University of North Carolina, Institute for Research in the Social Sciences.

Bracken, M. B., Hachamovitch, M. D., & Grossman, A. (1974). The decision to abort and psychological sequelae. *Journal of Nervous and Mental Disease, 15*, 154-162.

Bracken, M., & Kasl, S. (1975). Delay in seeking induced abortion: A review and theoretical analysis. *American Journal of Obstetrics and Gynecology, 121*, 1008-1019.

Clary, F. (1982). Minor women obtaining abortions: A study of parental notification in a metropolitan area. *American Journal of Public Health, 72*, 283-285.

Eisen, M., Zellman, G. L., Leibowitz, A., et al. (1983). Factors discriminating pregnancy resolution decisions of unmarried adolescents. *Genetic Psychology Monographs, 108*, 69-95.

Figley, C. R. (1983). Catastrophes: An overview of family reactions. In C. R. Figley & H. I. McCubbin (Eds.), *Stress and the family: Vol. 2. Coping with catastrophe* (pp. 3-20). New York: Brunner/Mazel.

Friedman, H. L. (1966). The mother-daughter relationship: Its potential in the treatment of young unwed mothers. *Social Casework, 47*, 502-506.

Furstenberg, F. F., Jr. (1976). *Unplanned parenthood: The social consequences of teenage childbearing.* New York: Free Press.

Gardner, W., Scherer, D., & Tester, M. (1989). Asserting scientific authority: Cognitive development and adolescent legal rights. *American Psychologist, 44,* 895-902.

H.L. v. Matheson, 450 U.S. 398 (1981).

Hatcher, S. (1976). Understanding adolescent pregnancy and abortion. *Primary Care, 21,* 29-47.

Illsley, R., & Hall, M. H. (1976). Psychosocial aspects of abortion: A review of issues and needed research. *Bulletin of the World Health Organization, 53,* 83-106.

Interdivisional Committee on Adolescent Abortion. (1987). Adolescent abortion: Psychological and legal issues. *American Psychologist, 42,* 73-78.

Janis, I. L., & Mann, L. (1977). *Decision making: A psychological analysis of conflict, choice, and commitment.* New York: Free Press.

Larsen, L. E. (1972). The influence of parents and peers during adolescence: The situation hypothesis revisited. *Journal of Marriage and the Family, 34,* 67-74.

Lee, G. T. (1980). Kinship in the seventies: A decade of review, research and theory. *Journal of Marriage and the Family, 42,* 923-934.

Leibowitz, A., Eisen, M., & Chow, W. (1984). *An economic model of teenage pregnancy decision making* (Paper no. 6.009). Austin: University of Texas, Texas Population Research Center.

Levitt, M. J., Weber, R. A., & Clark, M. C. (1986). Social network relationships as source of maternal support and well-being. *Developmental Psychology, 22,* 310-316.

Lewis, C. C. (1980). A comparison of minors' and adults' pregnancy decisions. *American Journal of Orthopsychiatry, 50,* 446-453.

Lewis, C. C. (1981). How adolescents approach decisions: Changes over grades seven to twelve and policy implications. *Child Development, 52,* 538-544.

Lewis, C. C. (1987). Minors' competence to consent to abortion. *American Psychologist, 42,* 84-88.

Litton-Fox, G. (1980, Spring). Teenage sexuality and the family. *Change, 9.*

Maracek, J. (1987). Counseling adolescents with problem pregnancies. *American Psychologist, 42,* 89-93.

McCubbin, H. I., & Patterson, J. M. (1983). Family transitions: Adaptation to stress. In H. I. McCubbin & C. R. Figley (Eds.), *Stress and the family: Vol. 1. Coping with normative transitions* (pp. 5-25). New York: Brunner/Mazel.

Musick, J. S., Handler, A., & Waddill, K. D. (1984). Teens and adoption: A pregnancy resolution alternative? *Children Today, 30,* 24-29.

Olson, L. (1980). Social and psychological correlates of pregnancy resolution among women: A review. *American Journal of Orthopsychiatry, 42,* 48-60.

Osofsky, J. D., & Osofsky, H. S. (1978). Teenage pregnancy: Psychological considerations. *Clinical Obstetrics and Gynecology, 21,* 1161-1173.

Planned Parenthood of Kansas City v. Ashcroft, 462 U.S. 476 (1983).

Roe v. Wade, 410 U.S. 113, 93 S.Ct. 705 (1973).

Rosen, R. H. (1980). Adolescent pregnancy decision-making: Are parents important? *Adolescence, 15,* 43-45.

Rowe, K. L. (1984, August). *Adolescent contraceptive use: The role of cognitive factors.* Paper presented at the annual meeting of the American Psychological Association, Toronto.

Rue, V. M. (1985). Abortion in relationship context. *International Review of Natural Family Planning, 9,* 95-121.

Russo, N. F. (1986). Adolescent abortion: The epidemiological context. In G. B. Melton (Ed.), *Adolescent abortion: Psychological and legal issues* (pp. 40-73). Lincoln: University of Nebraska Press.

Shusterman, L. R. (1976). The psychological factors of the abortion experience: A critical review. *Psychology of Women Quarterly, 1,* 79-106.
Smith, E. W. (1975). The role of the grandmother in adolescent pregnancy and parenting. *Journal of School Health, 24,* 278-283.
Swigar, M. E., Breslin, R., Pouzzner, M. G., Quinlan, D., & Blum, M. (1976). Interview follow-up of abortion drop-outs. *Social Psychiatry, 11,* 135-143.
Thornburgh v. American College of Obstetricians and Gynecologists, 106 S.Ct. 2169 (1986).
Torres, A., Forrest, J. D., & Eisman, S. (1980). Telling parents: Clinic policies and adolescents' use of family planning and abortion services. *Family Planning Perspectives, 12,* 284-292.
Verstraeten, D. (1982). Level of realism in adolescent future time perspective. *Human Development, 23,* 177-191.
Whitbeck, D. A., & Mullis, R. L. (1987). Parent and adolescent perspective taking. *Family Perspective, 21,* 39-47.
Zbaraz v. Hartigan, 763 F.2d 1532 (1976) (7th Cir. 1985), cert. granted, 55 U.S.L.W. 3247 (U.S. Oct. 14, 1986) (No. 85-673).

NO   MARGARET C. CROSBY and ABIGAIL ENGLISH

More than one million teenagers become pregnant each year in the United States; nearly half of these young women choose to terminate their pregnancies by abortion (Hayes, 1987; Henshaw, Kenney, Somberg, & Van Vort, 1989). More than half of U.S. states have at some time enacted a law requiring minors (under age 18) to involve their parents or to obtain court orders before they can have abortions (Donovan, 1992). As of 1991, at least nine of these laws had been enjoined by the courts and were not being enforced (Donovan, 1992). The constitutionality of these laws has been the subject of extensive litigation in state and federal courts. The factual records developed in the course of this litigation, in addition to studies conducted in some of the states in which such laws have been implemented, provide important information about the impact the laws may have on the minors they affect.

The U.S. Supreme Court has addressed the federal constitutionality of state statutes mandating parental involvement in the abortion decisions of their minor daughters (e.g., *Bellotti v. Baird,* 1979; *Hodgson v. Minnesota,* 1990). State appellate courts also have examined the constitutionality of similar laws under the privacy provisions of state constitutions (*American Academy of Pediatrics v. Van de Kamp,* 1989; *In re* T.W., 1989). At issue in these cases is the question of how far states may go in mandating parental involvement consistent with the constitutional rights of the pregnant adolescents.

In reviewing parental involvement laws, the courts have addressed such fundamental issues as the scope of minors' privacy rights, the nature of the parents' interest in a minor's abortion decision, and the government's interest in mandating parental involvement. Additional factors that are important in assessing parental involvement laws include a comparison of laws regulating abortion with those governing the delivery of other health care services to adolescents, the competence of adolescents to make health care decisions, the effects on adolescents and their families of laws mandating parental involvement, and the alternative means available to meet the stated goals of these laws.

Medical Consent Laws for Adolescents

Although the law traditionally requires parental consent for medical care provided to minor children, many exceptions to this requirement exist for adolescents. In every state one or more of the following groups of adolescents may consent to their own medical care: emancipated minors, minors living apart from their parents, mature minors, high school graduates, minors over a certain age, pregnant minors, and minors who are parents (English, 1990; Gittler, Quigley-Rick, & Saks, 1990; Morrissey, Hofmann, & Thrope, 1986). In addition, every state authorizes adolescents to consent to one or more of the following services: contraceptive services, prenatal care, childbirth and delivery services, diagnosis and treatment of sexually transmitted and/or contagious diseases, HIV-related care, treatment and counseling for substance abuse, and inpatient and outpatient mental health services (English, 1990; Gittler et al., 1990; Morrissey et al., 1986).

The laws containing these exceptions to the requirement of parental consent are sometimes referred to as "medical emancipation" statutes. They reflect a policy of encouraging minors to seek health care and a recognition that mandatory parental involvement may deter adolescents from seeking sensitive medical services. Some of these laws explicitly encourage, but do not require, parental involvement; others are silent on the issue (English, 1990; Gittler et al., 1990; Morrissey et al., 1986). The laws requiring parental involvement in decisions concerning abortion thus represent a significant departure from the medical emancipation laws that exist in every state.

Adolescents' Competence to Consent to Medical Care

The medical emancipation laws enable minors to consent to a variety of medical services for a range of conditions, sometimes in circumstances that involve decisions about complex problems or treatment involving considerable risks. One premise implicit in most of these laws is that, despite a general presumption in the law that minors lack the capacity to consent to medical care, many adolescents are competent to consent. This premise has been confirmed by empirical studies (Ambuel & Rappaport, 1992; Kaser-Boyd, Adelman, Taylor, et al., 1985, 1986; Lewis, 1980, 1981; Weithorn & Campbell, 1982). In a recent comprehensive analysis of several of these empirical studies, Gittler et al. (1990) found "considerable consistency"; they conclude:

> What can be said with some confidence is that the findings of the empirical studies reviewed, at a minimum, provide no support for the assumption that minors, especially adolescent minors fourteen years of age and older, as compared to adults, lack the capacity to make health care decisions. Hence, these studies challenge the traditional assumption of the law that adolescents are unable to make these health care decisions as well as adults. (p. 49)

Constitutional Framework for Minors' Abortion Decisions

Beginning in the 1970s, the U.S. Supreme Court has issued a series of opinions establishing a framework for reviewing the constitutionality of state laws mandating parental involvement in minors' abortion decisions. These opinions have established several basic principles. The constitutional right of privacy protects minors as well as adults (*Carey v. Population Services International*, 1977; *Eisenstadt v. Baird*, 1972; *Planned Parenthood of Central Missouri v. Danforth*, 1976). States may not grant parents the power to veto their minor daughter's decision to terminate a pregnancy (*Planned Parenthood of Central Missouri v. Danforth*, 1976).

If states require either parental consent or notification they must also establish an alternative procedure, usually referred to as "judicial bypass," to enable a minor to seek a court order authorizing the abortion without first going to her parents (*Bellotti v. Baird*, 1979). In reviewing an abortion petition, a court must allow a mature minor to make her own decision and must determine whether it is in the best interest of an immature minor to have an abortion without notifying her parents (*Bellotti v. Baird*, 1979). More than a decade ago, the Supreme Court established the basic framework (*Bellotti v. Baird*, 1979) that remains in place today (*Hodgson v. Minnesota*, 1990).

This framework emerged from an analysis of the constitutionally recognized interests of the pregnant minor, her parents, and the state. The state has a strong interest in the welfare of minors and in ensuring careful decision making in matters related to their health (*Bellotti v. Baird*, 1979; *Hodgson v. Minnesota*, 1990). Parents have an interest in guiding and controlling the upbringing of their minor children (*Meyer v. Nebraska*, 1923; *Pierce v. Society of Sisters*, 1925). However, the Constitution does not recognize any independent interest of the parents in the outcome of the abortion decision (*Doe v. Irwin*, 1980; *Hodgson v. Minnesota*, 1990). The parents' interest is protected for the purpose of furthering the child's welfare. The pregnant minor has a privacy interest that encompasses both independence in decision making and nondisclosure of intimate information (*Whalen v. Roe*, 1977). Her interest is especially weighty because of the serious burdens associated with teenage pregnancy and childbearing and because of the short time within which a decision must be made (*Bellotti v. Baird*, 1979).

According to the framework established by the Supreme Court in balancing these interests, parental consent or notification may be required, but only if pregnant minors are allowed to go to court without involving their parents and courts allow mature minors to make their own decisions. Evidence from those states where laws embodying this framework have actually been implemented suggests that they do not necessarily further the interests of the government, of the parents, or of the minors who are affected.

Consequences of Implementing Parental Involvement/Judicial Bypass Laws

Because parental involvement statutes must give adolescents the option of seeking court authorization for abortion, these laws do not in fact achieve the objective of increasing the number of teenagers who consult their parents. Rather, the laws induce a significant number of young women to bypass their parents altogether and go to court. Empirical studies have shown that more than 50% of pregnant teenagers seeking abortions consult a parent without any legal compulsion (Torres, Forrest, & Eisman, 1980). A 1984 study found that in Minnesota, which had a parental notification law with a judicial alternative in effect, the percentage of Minnesota teenagers (65%) who advised at least one parent of their abortion decisions was virtually the same as the percentage of Wisconsin teenagers who did so but were subject to no legal requirement of parental involvement (Blum, Resnick, & Stark, 1987).

Adolescents from families who will be supportive upon learning the news of a daughter's pregnancy generally do not need a law to encourage them to turn to a parent at a time of crisis. However, parental involvement laws do not increase family consultation in dysfunctional families. Teenagers who believe that their parents will not be supportive, based on extensive experience with patterns of communication in their families, are unlikely to be persuaded by a law to confide in their parents. Instead, they choose among the alternatives of court authorization, unwilling parenthood, or attempts at dangerous, extralegal methods of abortion. Those who reluctantly consult parents under legal compulsion sometimes suffer adverse consequences. Experts on adolescent care overwhelmingly oppose mandatory parental involvement legislation and have testified against such laws when they are challenged in court (*American Academy of Pediatrics v. Lungren,* 1992; *Hodgson v. Minnesota,* 1986) because all of these options present dangers to adolescents' health.

A large percentage of pregnant adolescents faced with the prospect of notifying their parents seek court authorization for their abortions. In Minnesota, Blum et al. (1987) found that 32% chose to go to court without notifying either parent. Many such adolescents are from dysfunctional homes (Donovan, 1983). The courts hearing these petitions have granted virtually every one; in Minnesota, for example, over a five-year period, 3,558 petitions were granted, 6 were withdrawn, and 9 were denied (*Hodgson v. Minnesota,* 1990). Judges grant most petitions on the basis that the minor is sufficiently mature to make an informed choice about the outcome of her pregnancy (*Hodgson v. Minnesota,* 1986). Judges have also found that it is usually in the best interest of a very young teenager seeking court authorization, who may not be sufficiently mature to make an independent choice, to terminate her unwanted pregnancy without parental notification (*Hodgson v. Minnesota,* 1986). The brief (10-minute) court hearings held on abortion petitions do not enhance the quality of adolescents' decisions because judges are neither trained nor disposed to offer counseling to pregnant teenagers. Indeed, judges view their role as a "rubber-stamp" clerical function (*American Academy of Pediatrics v. Lungren,* 1992; *Hodgson v. Minnesota,* 1986).

Although virtually all teenagers who go to court are successful, the experience is detrimental to the adolescents' health. First, the judicial process is extremely burdensome, humiliating, and stressful. Juvenile court judges, whose work exposes them to troubled youths, have testified that young women seeking authorization for abortions are unusually agitated (*Hodgson v. Minnesota,* 1986). Counselors at family planning clinics have testified that preparing teenagers for their court appearances distracts them from medical and contraceptive counseling (Wendt, 1986). Finally, the process of securing judicial authorization often delays the abortion by a week or more (American Medical Association, 1992; Donovan, 1983), which exposes adolescents to significantly increased expenses and health risks (Cates & Grimes, 1981; *Hodgson v. Minnesota,* 1986).

Some young women who cannot involve their parents but lack the resources to navigate through the court system unwillingly carry their pregnancies to term, although the number who do so for this reason is not known. These young women and girls from unhappy families are often the least prepared for motherhood. By inducing them to bear babies unwillingly, parental involvement legislation imposes significant burdens. As young parents, these minors are financially responsible for their infants' support, a responsibility that is not shared by the adolescents' own parents. Studies have documented that early childbearing is correlated with negative outcomes in economic status, marital stability, and health (Hayes, 1987). One extensive study indicates that teenagers who become pregnant and choose abortion attain higher levels of education and experience greater economic well-being than do those who bear children (Zabin, Hirsch, & Emerson, 1989). Thus a law that compels a young woman to become a mother may well influence the course of her adult life.

Mandatory parental involvement laws occasionally induce young women to turn in desperation to dangerous or self-induced abortion. Although the literature does not contain extensive accounts of such episodes, some tragedies have occurred. An example is a 17-year-old Indiana high school student who died from the complications of an abortion that was not legal and was apparently performed outside of a clinical setting. Her parents learned only after her death that she was pregnant and had felt unable to tell them or to obtain court authorization. She had apparently considered but not pursued the option of traveling out of state (Tribe, 1990), as many young women do to avoid both parental involvement and judicial proceedings (Cartoof & Klerman, 1986).

Some pregnant teenagers who tell their parents of their decisions to obtain abortions under the compulsion of law suffer adverse consequences. The news can cause enormous stress in a family with parents who are abusive, addicted to drugs or alcohol, or who suffer from severe mental disabilities. In these dysfunctional families, which unfortunately are not rare in modern American life, compelled disclosure of sexual activity, pregnancy, and a contemplated abortion may induce parents to abuse or reject their daughter (Henshaw & Kost, 1992).

The experience of young women with parental involvement laws is quite different from the theoretical objectives that such laws would appear to promote. The laws do not in fact foster family harmony or assist troubled teenagers in a time of crisis. The laws affect teenagers who do not believe that they can tell their parents potentially explosive news, and they present these young women and girls, often from troubled families, at a difficult time in their lives, with burdensome and sometimes dangerous options.

Alternatives to Mandatory Parental Involvement

In upholding parental consent and parental notification laws that contain judicial bypass options, the U.S. Supreme Court has allowed, but has not required, states to enact such laws consistent with the federal Constitution. In some states, however, legislatures may be prohibited by *state* constitutional privacy guarantees from passing laws requiring parental involvement. State constitutions protect individual rights independently of the federal Constitution. Two state courts, in Florida (*In re* T.W., 1989) and California (*American Academy of Pediatrics v. Van de Kamp,* 1989), have barred enforcement of parental consent laws to protect the state constitutional privacy rights of adolescents.

Many states have decided not to require parental involvement for adolescents seeking abortions (Donovan, 1992). Some states, such as Maine (1992) and Connecticut (1993), have simply passed legislation to ensure that pregnant teenagers receive guidance from an adult who may or may not be a relative, or adequate counseling and encouragement to confide in supportive parents from clinicians. Other states have mandated only informed consent for abortion (*Ballard v. Anderson,* 1971), as for other surgical procedures, and have left the design of counseling protocols to the discretion of trained professionals. These states have recognized that the worthy goals of promoting adolescent health and strengthening families are best fostered by laws that allow teenagers to obtain confidential access to health services and that provide teenagers from different families the support and guidance best suited to their individual needs.

Conclusion

Laws mandating parental involvement in adolescents' abortion decisions contrast with medical emancipation laws permitting competent minors to give consent for other medical care. The federal Constitution permits, but does not require, states to enact mandatory parental involvement laws if they include the option of a judicial bypass. These laws do little to further family consultation or to promote careful decision making by pregnant adolescents. Compulsory parental and judicial involvement can have adverse consequences for adolescents' health. Alternative models exist that address more directly the goal of providing adult guidance and support to ensure that careful decisions are made and adolescents' health is promoted.

References

Ambuel, B., & Rappaport, J. (1992). Developmental trends in adolescents' psychological and legal competence to consent to abortion. *Law and Human Behavior, 16,* 129-154.
American Academy of Pediatrics v. Lungren, No. 884574 (Super. Ct. San Francisco, June 8, 1992).
American Academy of Pediatrics v. Van de Kamp, 214 Cal. App. 3d 831, 263 Cal. Rptr. 46 (1989).
American Medical Association. (1992). *Induced termination of pregnancy before and after Roe v. Wade: Trends in the mortality and morbidity of women.* Chicago: Author.
Ballard v. Anderson, 4 Cal.3d 873, 95 Cal. Rptr. 1 (1971).
Bellotti v. Baird, 443 U.S. 622 (1979).
Blum, R. W., Resnick, M. D., & Stark, T. A. (1987). The impact of parental notification law on adolescent abortion decision-making. *American Journal of Public Health, 77,* 619-620.
Carey v. Population Services International, 431 U.S. 678 (1977).
Cartoof, V. G., & Klerman, L. V. (1986). Parental consent for abortion: Impact of the Massachusetts law. *American Journal of Public Health, 76,* 397-400.
Cates, W., & Grimes, D. A. (1981). Morbidity and mortality of abortion in the United States. In J. Hodgson (Ed.), *Abortion and sterilization: Medical and social aspects.* New York: Academic Press.

Connecticut. Conn. Gen. Stat. Ann. § 191-601 (West Supp. 1993).
Doe v. Irwin, 615 F.2d 1162 (6th Cir.), cert. denied 449 U.S. 829 (1980).
Donovan, P. (1983). Judging teenagers: How minors fare when they seek court authorized abortions. *Family Planning Perspectives, 15,* 259-267.
Donovan, P. (1992). *Our daughters' decisions: The conflict in state law on abortion and other issues.* New York: Alan Guttmacher Institute.
Eisenstadt v. Baird, 405 U.S. 438 (1972).
English, A. (1990). Treating adolescents: Legal and ethical considerations. *Medical Clinics of North America, 74,* 1097-1112.
Gittler, J., Quigley-Rick, M., & Saks, M. J. (1990). *Adolescent health care decision making: The law and public policy.* Washington, DC: Carnegie Council on Adolescent Development.
Hayes, C. D. (Ed.). (1987). *Risking the future: Adolescent sexuality, pregnancy, and childbearing.* Washington, DC: National Academy Press.
Henshaw, S. K., Kenney, A. M., Somberg, D., & Van Vort, J. (1989). *Teenage pregnancy in the United States: The scope of the problem and state responses.* New York: Alan Guttmacher Institute.
Henshaw, S. K., & Kost, K. (1992). Parental involvement in minors' abortion decisions. *Family Planning Perspectives, 24,* 196-213.
Hodgson v. Minnesota, 648 F. Supp. 756 (D. Minn. 1986)
Hodgson v. Minnesota, 110 S.Ct. 2926 (1990).
In re T.W., a minor, 550 So.2d 1186 (Fla. 1989).
Kaser-Boyd, N., Adelman, H. S., Taylor, L., et al. (1985). Minors' ability to identify risks and benefits of therapy. *Professional Psychology: Research and Practice, 16,* 411-417.
Kaser-Boyd, N., Adelman, H. S., Taylor, L., et al. (1986). Children's understanding of risks and benefits of psychotherapy. *Journal of Clinical Child Psychology, 15,* 165-171.
Lewis, C. C. (1980). A comparison of minors' and adults' pregnancy decisions. *American Journal of Orthopsychiatry, 50,* 446-453.
Lewis, C. C. (1981). How adolescents approach decisions: Changes over grades seven to twelve and policy implications. *Child Development, 52,* 538-544.
Maine. Me. Rev. Stat. Ann. tit. 22 § 1597-A (West 1992).
Meyer v. Nebraska, 262 U.S. 390 (1923).
Morrissey, J. M., Hofmann, A. D., & Thrope, J. C. (1986). *Consent and confidentiality in the health care of adolescents: A legal guide.* New York: Free Press.
Pierce v. Society of Sisters, 268 U.S. 510 (1925).
Planned Parenthood of Central Missouri v. Danforth, 428 U.S. 52 (1976).
Torres, A., Forrest, J. D., & Eisman, S. (1980). Telling parents: Clinic policies and adolescents' use of family planning and abortion services. *Family Planning Perspectives, 12,* 284-292.
Tribe, L. (1990). *Abortion and the clash of absolutes.* New York: W. W. Norton.
Weithorn, L. A., & Campbell, S. B. (1982). The competency of children and adolescents to make informed treatment decisions. *Child Development, 53,* 1589-1598.
Wendt, P. (1986). [Testimony]. In *Hodgson v. Minnesota,* U.S. District Court No. 3-81-538 (D. Minn. 1986).
Whalen v. Roe, 429 U.S. 589 (1977).
Zabin, L. S., Hirsch, M. B., & Emerson, M. R. (1989). When urban adolescents choose abortion: Effects on education, psychological status and subsequent pregnancy. *Family Planning Perspectives, 21,* 248-255.

MARGARET C. CROSBY AND ABIGAIL ENGLISH RESPOND

Unable to point to any evidence that mandatory parental involvement actually helps adolescents who are making abortion decisions, Worthington and his coauthors offer more indirect support of such laws. They suggest that the laws are consistent with the legal framework that customarily defines the parent-child relationship, that there is no evidence that these laws cause harm, and that further research is needed.

Overall, their argument seems to rest on a premise with a major flaw. Mandatory parental involvement laws do not, as Worthington et al. seem to assume, require parental consent or notification in all cases. Since the U.S. Supreme Court decision in *Bellotti v. Baird* in 1979, states have been required to offer minors who do not wish to involve their parents the alternative of a judicial bypass proceeding. Thus the laws result in parental involvement only when the daughters prefer that option to seeking the approval of the juvenile court. The available evidence suggests that, in fact, such laws do not increase the percentage of adolescents who involve their parents (Blum, Resnick, & Stark, 1987).

In addition to this major flawed premise, Worthington et al.'s other major points either rest on incorrect assumptions or are contradicted by the available empirical evidence. First, they suggest that notifying parents about their minor daughters' abortions gives them the same discretion to control the daughters' behavior that parents have with respect to cigarette smoking and watching R-rated movies. However, the decision whether to terminate a pregnancy or have a baby is far weightier and, therefore, not comparable to decisions about watching restricted movies or smoking cigarettes. This difference has constitutional significance, as consistently recognized by the Supreme Court beginning with the 1979 *Bellotti* decision.

Second, Worthington et al. maintain that adolescents differ from adults (and among themselves) in how they make decisions. Even if adolescents make decisions somewhat differently from adults, or younger adolescents make decisions somewhat differently from older adolescents—in terms of whom they consult or the factors they consider—this is not the same issue as whether they have the cognitive capacity to give informed consent for an abortion. All serious reviews of the literature on this issue have concluded that they do (see, e.g., Gittler et al., 1990). Moreover, the courts that have been asked to rule on petitions from minors seeking abortions without parental involvement have concluded, in the vast majority of cases, that the adolescents are sufficiently mature to make the decision on their own (*Hodgson v. Minnesota,* 1990).

Finally, Worthington et al. assert that existing research does not clearly demonstrate whether minors will be harmed or helped by mandatory parental involvement, that there is no evidence that required parental involvement will worsen a relationship in which parents are unsupportive and little evidence to suggest parental involvement legislation does harm to teenagers. Even assuming this to be true, which it is not, there is also little evidence to suggest that parental involvement statutes help minors. They do not increase the percentage of minors who involve their parents (Blum et al., 1987); rather, most of those who choose not to do so go to court, and the judges who hear their petitions have testified under oath that they feel like they perform a "rubber-stamp" function (*Hodgson v. Minnesota,* 1990).

Moreover, there *is* evidence to suggest that the statutes are likely to harm some minors. For example, the court proceedings and the logistics surrounding having to go to court are burdensome, as health care and judicial personnel involved in these proceedings have testified in numerous lawsuits (*American Academy of Pediatrics v. Lungren,* 1992; *Hodgson v. Minnesota,* 1990). These statutes also are associated with delay among minors seeking abortions and increases in the proportion of minors seeking riskier second-trimester abortions (Donovan, 1992). In addition, a recent study based on a representative national sample of adolescents receiving abortions in states without mandatory statutes found that among those adolescents whose parents found out without their daughters' telling them voluntarily, more than half suffered adverse reactions, with at least 12% suffering serious consequences such as being punished, beaten, forced to leave home, or experiencing violence in the family (Henshaw & Kost, 1992).

The body of evidence already available is sufficiently compelling that there is no justification for further experimentation with the lives of pregnant adolescents who wish to terminate their pregnancies. Those who believe they will benefit from their parents' counsel are already seeking it. Forcing the remainder to navigate a judicial proceeding (or, worse, to bear an unwanted child) does not enhance their decision making or protect their health.

References

American Academy of Pediatrics v. Lungren, Calif. Superior Court No. 884574 (permanent injunction issued June 8, 1992).
Bellotti v. Baird, 443 U.S. 622 (1979).

Blum, R. W., Resnick, M. D., & Stark, T. A. (1987). The impact of a parental notification law on adolescent abortion decision-making. *American Journal of Public Health, 77,* 619-620.

Donovan, P. (1992). *Our daughters' decisions.* Washington, DC: Alan Guttmacher Institute.

Gittler, J., Quigley-Rick, M., & Saks, M. J. (1990). *Adolescent health care decision making: The law and public policy.* Washington, DC: Carnegie Council on Adolescent Development.

Henshaw, S. K., & Kost, K. (1992). Parental involvement in minors' abortion decisions. *Family Planning Perspectives, 24,* 196-213.

Hodgson v. Minnesota, 110 S.Ct. 2926 (1990).

EVERETT L. WORTHINGTON, Jr., et al. RESPOND

Crosby and English address the question of whether parental involvement/ judicial bypass laws promote adolescents' health, implying that adolescents' health is the only concern. This is an inadequate formulation of the problem. Parents are not considered, yet, in most cases, parents will provide financial, emotional, and health support for their pregnant adolescent daughters. Within their inadequate statement of the problem, Crosby and English argue (a) that there is no benefit and (b) that there is potential harm in parental involvement legislation.

Is there benefit? Crosby and English cite weak research to claim that parental consultation by adolescents does not improve adolescent decision making. That evidence has been questioned by psychologists (see Gardner, Scherer, & Tester, 1989; Worthington et al., 1989), who have adduced additional evidence (omitted by Crosby and English) and concluded that adolescents make more mature decisions when adults are involved. (This rebuttal will not consider benefits to parents.)

Is there harm in parental involvement legislation? Crosby and English adduce an emotional case study of a 17-year-old student who resorted to a self-induced abortion and subsequently died. That is indeed tragic. There are equally tragic cases in which adolescents obtain secret abortions, only later to become guilt ridden, estranged from their parents, severely depressed, or suicidal. Crosby and English do not report such cases. In fact, arguing from an "occasional" (their word) emotional instance, as they do, and omitting counterexamples manipulates the reader's judgment.

Adolescents (and their parents) do benefit from parental involvement in decision making by pregnant teens, assuming a judicial bypass is available to protect those adolescents who really need the protection. Further, presentation of an emotional "occasional" case notwithstanding, there is no reliable evidence that *more* harm is caused by having than by not having parental involvement/judicial bypass legislation. Critics of the legislation cannot logically answer the question of which is more harmful without addressing the tragedies that occur under the absence of parental involvement/judicial bypass legislation, but Crosby and English have not considered such potential harm. Crosby and English do not make their case convincingly, but even if they had, they addressed only one aspect of a complex problem.

References

Gardner, W., Scherer, D., & Tester, M. (1989). Asserting scientific authority: Cognitive development and adolescent legal rights. *American Psychologist, 44*, 895-902.

Worthington, E. L., Jr., Larson, D. B., Brubaker, M. W., Colecchi, C., Berry, J. T., & Morrow, D. (1989). The benefits of legislation requiring parental involvement prior to adolescent abortion. *American Psychologist, 44*, 1542-1545.

DEBATE 9

MAINSTREAMING AIDS CHILDREN

➤ *Should confidentiality be maintained when children with AIDS are mainstreamed in regular classrooms and nursery schools?*

EDITORS' NOTE: The issue of confidentiality and AIDS has many facets. Under what circumstances do medical providers need to know if a patient is HIV positive? Conversely, when does a patient need to know the HIV status of his or her doctor? Employees fear that knowledge of their HIV-positive status may provoke discrimination in the workplace or perhaps termination of employment. Are lovers legally obliged to disclose to their sexual partners? And must therapists who learn the nature of an HIV-positive client's condition in therapy warn sexual partners who have not been told? When it is a child who has AIDS, the issue is more complicated. Although adults are naturally sympathetic toward sick children in general, they are also fiercely protective of their own children. Even when there is no real threat of contagion in a classroom situation, irrational fears may provoke hostile behavior toward children with AIDS. The parents' fears may also influence the behavior of their children, who may treat the child with AIDS cruelly. As the number of children who have AIDS swells, there is an increasing need to confront this issue. Our authors deal with both actual incidents and health policy initiatives. Their disagreements center perhaps more on appropriate strategy than on the shared goal of positive integration of the child with AIDS into the classroom.

Ronald Bayer says YES. He is a Professor at Columbia University School of Public Health. He is the author of *Private Acts, Social Consequences: AIDS and the Politics of Public Health* (1989) and coeditor, with David L. Kirp, of *AIDS in the Industrialized Democracies: Passions, Politics, and Policies* (1992).

David L. Kirp argues NO. He is a Professor of Public Policy and Lecturer in Law at the University of California, Berkeley. He is coauthor of *Learning by Heart: AIDS and Schoolchildren in America's Communities* (1989) and coeditor, with Ronald Bayer, of *AIDS in the Industrialized Democracies: Passions, Politics, and Policies* (1992).

YES   RONALD BAYER

The protection of confidentiality of medical information has long been recognized as crucial for two quite distinct reasons. In the first place, it serves to protect individuals from the misuse of clinical data by those who would impose upon them unreasonable burdens, those who would deprive them of the right to work and the right to participate in the full range of social activities of which they are capable. In the case of conditions that carry with them social stigma, confidentiality serves to protect individuals from the burden of shame and embarrassment. As such, respect for confidentiality is focused on the rights of the individual. But confidentiality also serves a second purpose. It has long been recognized that in the absence of strong protections against the disclosure of medical information, individuals would be reluctant to confide in their caregivers, to open their bodies to examination. Thus confidentiality has been viewed as a precondition for the effective practice of medicine. Without it, physicians could not do their work. The sick would be discouraged from seeking timely care. Not only would those with illness suffer as a result, but so would society, which is dependent on the appropriate care of those who are sick.

But even so important a principle as confidentiality has its limits. Physicians who discover that a child is being severely abused are widely held responsible for reporting such facts to the relevant public authorities. A physician who knows that a patient is about to commit a serious crime is typically held accountable for acting to notify the authorities to prevent grave injury or harm. And physicians have long been expected to report the presence of dangerous contagious diseases to public health officials so that appropriate measures can be taken to protect the common good. In each of these instances it is crucial to note that the exception to the rule of confidentiality is predicated on an overriding public interest.

Even here, however, there have been disagreements, because many fear that with the exception of truly extraordinary cases involving the immediate danger of grave harm, breaches of confidentiality will inhibit candor on the part of patients, thus depriving society of the benefits that would follow from having patients counseled by their physicians. Would we really be better off, at the end of the day, if physicians breach confidentiality in the name of protecting individuals if the social consequence is a diminution of our ability to protect society?

These background factors are crucial to, but not sufficient for, an understanding of the extent to which considerations about confidentiality have played a role in the policy response to the AIDS epidemic. Even before the discovery of HIV, the virus that causes AIDS, deep concerns had been raised about the protection of information bearing on the identity of those with or at risk for the new disease. Because the early epidemiology revealed that vulnerable populations were especially at risk—gay and bisexual men, intravenous drug users, recent immigrants from Haiti—it was clear that research on the factors that could explain the origins of the new disease could not go forward without ironclad promises of confidentiality. In subsequent years confidentiality has played a crucial role in debates about testing for HIV, counseling, and the provision of medical care. Instances of discrimination in the workplace and in the classroom, incidents of violence directed at those with or thought to be at risk for HIV infection, and stigmatization have all underscored the importance, from the perspectives of both the individual and the public health, of the protection of confidentiality.

AIDS, we know, is transmissible only through sexual intercourse, the sharing of drug injection equipment, and blood contact; pregnant women can pass HIV to their fetuses, and, under rare circumstances, HIV may be transmitted during clinical procedures. Because those with AIDS or asymptomatic HIV infection pose no threat to those with whom they come into contact, there are no public health grounds for discrimination or for revealing their medical conditions to those with whom they interact in the workplace. On grounds of civil liberties, breaching confidentiality would represent an unwarranted violation of their right to privacy. The surgeon general, the Institute of Medicine and the National Academy of Science, the federal Centers for Disease Control, and many state health department leaders, as well as the Presidential Commission on the HIV Epidemic, have all endorsed the protection of confidentiality as crucial in the struggle against AIDS.

AIDS in the Classroom

Given the nature of its communicability, there are no grounds for revealing the HIV status of teachers to school boards, school health officials, school principals, or parents. Teachers with HIV place no children at risk, and disclosing information about their medical condition, against their wishes, can serve no educational or public health end. That said, there might be great good that could be achieved if a teacher with AIDS chose to reveal his or her situation to appropriate school officials and then to schoolchildren as a way of humanizing the face of AIDS, as a way of teaching children about the nature of AIDS and its transmission, as a way of underscoring the importance of tolerance and compassion. Given that most infected teachers would be gay or bisexual men, such a revelation might also serve to make students aware of the human face of homosexuality, of the plight of gay men and women in America. But such lessons should follow only from a teacher's own decision based upon his or her consideration about how revealing important private information will affect his or her interests. No one should be forced to assume such an exemplary role. Much as we may want heroes, we cannot draft them into existence.

There might also be circumstances when a teacher with AIDS or HIV-related diseases may need to explain his or her condition to relevant school authorities, when illness or medical treatment may require absences from work. Making such information available in these circumstances can be crucial to both the teacher and school officials; it will be facilitated if it is clear that such information will not be used to harm the teacher's interests and if it is made clear that such information will be treated as privileged and confidential.

The case of schoolchildren with AIDS or HIV infection is more complicated. Early in the AIDS epidemic, in 1985, there was enormous anxiety about the risks such children could pose for their classmates. America witnessed some truly execrable displays of panic and exclusionary behavior. There were, of course, also examples of the opposite behavior, cases of schools that welcomed children with AIDS. Guided by public health officials who were able to convince parents that their children were not at risk because of the presence of those with AIDS, schools across the country rejected calls for exclusion. Nevertheless, the question remained: Who should be told about a child's disease? In most instances it was decided that special school board committees, with the advice of physicians, should consider each case. There were, in general, no grounds for telling teachers or parents about the presence of specific children with AIDS or asymptomatic HIV infection. Such secrecy was predicated on the assumption that the child's interests may require—indeed, might necessitate—cloaking the medical condition from those who might willfully or inadvertently misuse such information. Furthermore, no educational interests and no interests of other children were implicated.

Of course, it would be best if a child's parents could choose to share that information with the child's teacher. And certainly it might be best for the child not to have to bear the burden of maintaining a secret on so crucial a matter from teachers or classmates. On the other hand, there are clearly circumstances when the child's well-being would be best protected by secrecy. Nothing is gained by exposing a child to shunning and stigmatization. In the face of making decisions under painful medical and socially uncertain circumstances, wisdom dictates that those committed to the child by bonds of blood and/or love, the parents, be free to decide when and to whom to reveal the fact of AIDS or HIV infection.

There will be times when the clinical course of HIV disease in a child will impose great pressure on the parents to disclose the nature of his or her medical condition to the teacher. Repeated absences caused by bouts of illness must be explained. In some cases, neurological impairments may result in learning disabilities of which teachers must be made aware. The situation has become more complex with the availability of a range of clinical interventions that may prolong the lives and improve the well-being of those with HIV. Some children may need school nurses to administer medication during the school day. It seems inevitable that increasingly such children's interests will require that both school nurses and teachers be made aware of the children's HIV status. But here again, it is for the parents to make the ultimate choice, balancing the risks and benefits of any course for their children.

Respect for confidentiality does not require secrecy. Rather, it requires that the decision to disclose and to whom to disclose be made by those for whom the information is an intimate fact of existence. There are no good public health grounds for breaching the confidentiality of teachers or schoolchildren with HIV infection or AIDS. There are, however, very good public health grounds for working to create a social climate within which the discussion about whether to disclose such information can be made without fear of reprisal or stigma. For very few does the public persona of a Magic Johnson permit disclosure with impunity. The task is to create a context within which such invulnerability is unnecessary. We need to shape a world that does not need more AIDS heroes.

NO   DAVID L. KIRP

In 1986, one day after her daughter Melissa's fifth birthday, Joan Milne got some awful news: the perky blond girl whom everyone called Missy was infected with HIV. Tainted blood, used in a transfusion shortly after Missy's birth, was the cause of the infection. Outwardly, Missy was healthy. Indeed, the infection was discovered only when her pediatrician, fearing possible exposure to contaminated blood, ordered an HIV test. But the news was a likely death sentence.

At first, Joan Milne kept her daughter's condition a secret, with good reason—she feared that Missy would be prevented from attending school in Walnut Creek, a San Francisco suburb, or would be shunned by her classmates. Just a year earlier, parents and school officials in Kokomo, Indiana, had turned against 13-year-old Ryan White when he told the world he had AIDS. Some students had spray-painted "queer" across Ryan's locker. Townspeople had lobbed rocks through the picture window at the Whites' home. In August 1986 in Arcadia, Florida, when Louise and Clifford Ray had enrolled their three sons, all hemophiliacs with HIV, in school, the family's home was torched.

Joan Milne wanted to protect her daughter and her family from that kind of tragedy. That is why she kept her own counsel, why she made privacy her credo. In 1987, she wrote to columnist Ann Landers: "Tell [parents] I am their mother, their daughter, their sister, their friend, the mother of their child's friend. And I am suffering alone because of the ignorance about this terrible disease." The letter was printed without a signature. That same year she contacted her daughter's school, but again insisted on remaining anonymous.

Gradually, however, Mrs. Milne began revealing the secret to other family members and close friends. In 1989, she told Missy's older brother Michael. Finally, in January 1991, she told her daughter, and that same month, she informed school officials.

In Walnut Creek, as in many school districts across the country, policy in place specifies that the presence of an HIV-positive child triggers a medical review. But because AIDS is spread only by direct exposure to blood or semen and not through the kinds of contact that students usually have with one another, this review is typically just a formality. Even in extraordinary instances, when the local medical experts have proposed to keep a youngster out of school —as in one case involving a 5-year-old child, enrolled in a special education class, who did not have full control of her bowels—judges have invariably rejected the recommendation and ordered the child's enrollment. Medical review does serve the useful purpose of highlighting who would benefit from knowing about the child's condition: the classroom teacher, for instance, who could take sensible precautions if Missy scraped and bloodied her knee.

The decision whether to inform school officials was Mrs. Milne's to make, for the law does not require such notification. Legally, she also had veto power over who—if anyone—inside the school would be let in on the secret that she had chosen to reveal to the administration. Such secrecy is remarkable in an institution that keeps few things secret. The rationale is concern for the family's privacy. Privacy is your legal right, Mrs. Milne was told, you don't have to go public. More than that, it is a way of avoiding the kind of misery that Ryan White and the three Ray youngsters had to endure.

Generally, privacy is the option that families with HIV-infected children choose. Of the more than 3,000 reported AIDS cases among American children below the age of 13—and the uncounted additional thousands of cases of HIV infection—only a handful of these families have discarded the protective mask of privacy. Although the pediatric AIDS unit of the Oakland, California, Children's Hospital knows of more than 30 HIV-positive children in the county where Melissa Milne lives, hers is the only story that has been made public. All the others, as her mother says, remain "families in the shadows."

For these families, the image of that burning house in Arcadia, Florida, is too potent and menacing. Who could fault them? Where the good medical sense—and common decency—of school officials cannot be relied upon, where the choice is between keeping silent and being ostracized, there is no choice at all. What parents would willfully expose their children to the hyenas of Kokomo?

What is less obvious is that, in this context, privacy exacts an awful price. It means that a very central fact of a family's existence—that one of its members will likely die young—must remain a secret. The fear of ostracism that drives families to silence means that parents cannot share their anguish with their friends or deliver the medical facts of life to the parents of their child's playmates. Siblings cannot confide in their friends. And, perhaps worst of all, the child infected with HIV must carry that awesome truth as a private burden. Retreating into privacy thus adds to the family's pain. To avoid the possibility of being shunned, the disease becomes a secret. And secrets have a way of being understood—internalized—as shames.

In this case, Walnut Creek school officials were cautious and Mrs. Milne was worried; it was Missy's determination to tell her schoolmates that eventually carried the day. When the educators learned that Missy carried the virus that causes AIDS, and that she intended to talk about her condition, they began educating the affected community—school-site administrators, teachers, and parents—about AIDS. An AIDS awareness curriculum was introduced for elementary school children. "We're talking about the virus at school," Missy said to her mother, "so I don't have to worry."

In June 1991, just days before the end of the school year, parents of the youngsters in Missy's third-grade class had a meeting. Experts were on hand; so was Mrs. Milne. At the end of the session, a few parents remained unhappy—two reported that they would transfer their children to another class—but most were satisfied with what they had learned. There was only praise—applause—for the Milne family's courage in coming forward, for their expressed commitment not to the idea of rights, but to the ideal of the good community. Shortly afterward, when Missy told her classmates, no one sniggered. No one ran. All the children hugged Missy and some gave her a kiss.

Although such stories have not made headlines, there is nothing unique about the Milne family's odyssey. In cities and towns across the country, enlightened administrators confronted with news of a child with AIDS have made themselves into educators for the community. Parents have come to meetings on AIDS armed with hard questions, for almost every parent is fiercely protective of his or her child's well-being. In community after community, from affluent Wilmette, Illinois, to the Chicago barrio neighborhood of Pilsen, the cycle of response has been much the same: As fear is replaced by knowledge, teachers and parents come to accept that having a child with AIDS in school means taking an infinitesimally small risk—far less of a risk than teaching the lesson of intolerance through the act of exclusion. As that new knowledge sinks in, many people begin empathizing with the plight of the family and the child.

At about the same time Ryan White was being ostracized in Kokomo, the socially conservative and mainly working-class town of Swansea, Massachusetts, was taking another 13-year-old with AIDS, Mark Hoyle, to its heart. The response was the same in St. Augustine, Florida, where the Ray family fled after their house in Arcadia was burned down—and in another Arcadia, this one in Indiana, where Ryan White and his family moved after quitting Kokomo. In all those places school officials were supportive. AIDS education was intense. Fears were taken up directly and talked through. The result was the antithesis of a privatistic world. It was community support, and something more—understanding, affection, involvement; the public equivalent of love.

One final story underlines my point. I recently appeared on a Bay Area television show together with a San Francisco woman whose school-aged son is infected with HIV. The woman talked from behind a barrier that hid her face and preserved her anonymity. Privacy was vital, she said. Initially, she had gone to the principal of her son's grade school with word of his condition. She expected understanding—after all, this was San Francisco, at a time when AIDS had become a medical commonplace, and not Kokomo in the epidemic's early years—but the boy was hounded out of the school by a frightened administrator. The family moved to a new neighborhood and enrolled the boy in another school. This time, no one was told.

"What did you think of this mother's impassioned defense of privacy?" the interviewer asked me. "In her situation, I'd do exactly the same thing," I replied. "But at a personal level, it must be awfully hard to keep that secret."

Then, from behind the barrier, there came the sound of weeping. "I'd give anything, anything, to be able to take down this curtain, to be able to talk openly and to let my son live openly," the woman said between her sobs. For that sad woman—as for any parent of a child carrying the virus that causes AIDS—the right to privacy offers at best only the solace of being free from a lynching, not the public equivalent of love.

DAVID L. KIRP RESPONDS

As Ronald Bayer recognizes, confidentiality is a backstop—a hedge for the fearful—not an ideal. It embraces the procedural justice of secrecy, not the substantive justice of caring. It represents not a strategy to nurture the kind of support that the society should offer its members, but instead a way to protect individuals against abuse.

These are important concerns, particularly in a nation such as ours, which has often treated badly those with AIDS. About that point, Bayer and I do not disagree; nor would I quarrel with his assertion that, in most instances, disclosure of one's HIV status in school should be voluntary. But this is hardly a cost-free strategy. As Bayer recognizes, informed teachers and nurses are often better prepared to cope with the classroom difficulties a child with AIDS may encounter; furthermore, knowledge of a student's HIV status encourages protective measures in those rare instances (involving spilled blood, for instance) when transmission is theoretically possible.

But more divides us than the description of the policy water glass as half full or half empty. To emphasize privacy over community is to encourage a retreat into the self. To stress the perils of disclosure and the virtues of silence is to risk ceding to the abusers the power to define the moral climate. How teachers and families afflicted with AIDS respond, whether through silence or openness, is not only a matter of great personal moment; it also, and importantly, contributes to the kind of community that, past all self-delusion, we really are.

THE EDITORS RESPOND TO DAVID L. KIRP

Ronald Bayer was unavailable to prepare his own rebuttal, so, based on his initial argument, we undertake this response.

Professor Kirp effectively portrays the positive, even transformative, effects that disclosure of a child's HIV infection may have on the school community and beyond. In the best of worlds that would always be the case, and the misfortune of a child with AIDS would be mitigated by the spirit of love and cooperation that it evokes. But we all know, and Professor Kirp acknowledges, that this is not always the predictable effect. Instead, ostracism and worse can be the result of disclosure. His anecdotes, although moving, provide no empirical evidence that the trend is toward support, or even that certain regions of the country are predictably more tolerant than others. Until such evidence is available, it would be irresponsible to advise parents to share their secret. Certainly the more productive strategy is to continue educating parents and the public at large about the disease, using real people, when possible, as with Ryan White, but not suggesting that parents offer their own children for the purposes of public education.

Kirp also suggests that the secret of AIDS can become internalized as shame. Perhaps that is true for some, but privacy has its positive side as well. Our tradition of confidentiality protects the rights of individuals from unfair discrimination in the workplace and elsewhere, but it also supports a basic right in our society to maintain a private life that is not subject to public scrutiny. Families maintain this right as well. For some families, misfortune, of whatever sort, is something they prefer to deal with as a family. They may not want even well-meaning outsiders to become involved, unless absolutely necessary. They may feel the same way about good tidings. To suggest that disclosure removes shame may be closer to psychotherapy than to our American tradition of family privacy.

PART III

Child Abuse and Neglect Issues

DEBATE 10

MANDATORY ABUSE PREVENTION PROGRAMS IN SCHOOLS

➤ *Should children be required to participate in school programs to prevent molestation?*

EDITORS' NOTE: School programs designed to help children avoid being molested have become popular over the past 10 years. Do they help children? Even if they help only a few children, aren't they worth it? Or are such programs a waste of time? Is it possible that they harm rather than help children? The arguments presented here should help you decide what you think.

Jon R. Conte, Ph.D., says YES. He is Associate Professor at the School of Social Work, University of Washington, Seattle, where he teaches clinical social work and specializes in the study and treatment of childhood sexual abuse. He is the author of numerous publications on the effects of sexual abuse prevention and treatment as well as other aspects of childhood sexual abuse.

Jill Duerr Berrick, Ph.D., and **Neil Gilbert**, Ph.D., argue NO. Berrick is Director of the Berkeley Child Welfare Research Center at the Family Welfare Research Group, University of California, Berkeley. She has published articles in several journals, including the *International Journal of Child Abuse and Neglect* and *Children and Youth Services Review* and is coauthor, with Neil Gilbert, of *With the Best of Intentions: The Child Sexual Abuse Prevention Movement.* Gilbert is Milton and Gertrude Chernin Professor of Social Welfare and the Social Services at the University of California, Berkeley, and Director of the Family Welfare Research Group. He has published 13 books and more than 50 articles; among his books is *The Enabling State,* coauthored with Barbara Gilbert.

YES   **JON R. CONTE**

As a professional and as a parent, I react negatively to the notion that children should be required to participate in certain programs. Schools are asked to meet many social agendas, from teaching math and social studies to prevention of social problems such as drug abuse and sexual abuse. Establishing an agenda should, in my view, be the responsibility of parents and local communities based on an assessment of the relative educational needs and social/psychological risks for certain problems faced by children. Notwithstanding this concern about the word *required,* I will nonetheless answer in the affirmative: Yes, children may benefit from sexual abuse prevention efforts.

Nature of the Problem

Although estimates of the extent of childhood sexual abuse vary (see Peters, Wyatt, & Finkelhor, 1986), most of us would agree that it is an experience of childhood that should be avoided if at all possible. It not only can be stressful, painful, and unwanted for children while it is going on, it is clear that such experiences in childhood are associated with a wide range of social and psychological problems in childhood and throughout development.

Current efforts to identify children who are at greater risk for sexual abuse than other children have not generally yielded consistent findings that would make it possible to target prevention to those children at greatest risk (Finkelhor & Baron, 1986). For example, given that girls are more often victims of sexual abuse, should prevention programs not deal with boys as potential victims? I doubt that the parents of boys or boys themselves would favor such a strategy. Nor have research efforts to identify factors (e.g., psychological characteristics) that predict what types of adults are more likely to abuse children sexually been successful; thus it is difficult to target control measures toward those adults causing the problem of sexual abuse (Conte, 1990a, 1990b, 1990c).

It is increasingly clear what sexual abuse involves for the child. Sexual abuse consists of specific actions employed by the offender to engage a victim and maintain that victim in an abusive situation, and also includes the specific sexual behaviors and practices of the offender. The elements of sexual abuse that make up these actions include manipulation of the child (e.g., psychologically separating the child from his or her mother), coercion (e.g., using adult authority or size differential), force (e.g., holding the victim or showing a weapon), threats (e.g., "If you tell I will kill your mother" or "I will go to jail"), and virtually every kind of sexual behavior (Conte, Wolf, & Smith, 1989).

For many reasons (some only partly understood), sexual abuse inherently involves elements that directly function to keep the child from disclosing the abuse, such as offender threats or bribes, and some elements that indirectly serve the same function. Indirect functions may not be present in every case and are only beginning to be understood. For example, a child may have a sense of duplicity about ongoing abuse because he or she did not tell about the first abuse incident, or the child may have feelings of guilt generated from an irrational belief that going along with the behavior implies responsibility. Some of the effects of sexual abuse (e.g., fear, emotional or physical separation from adults who could protect the child, diminished self-esteem, unassertiveness, dissociation) also work against a child's disclosing abuse. Some children will not report because they wish to protect a parent from the pain associated with sexual abuse. Other children may be indoctrinated by offenders into not telling (e.g., by being forced to abuse other children, thereby convincing them that they too are offenders). Some children, especially young ones, appear not to know that sexual abuse is something to tell anyone about (see, e.g., Berliner & Conte, 1990).

Implications for Prevention

In all the years that I have worked with the problem of childhood sexual abuse, I have never heard anyone say that targeting small children is the best or most preferred way to approach prevention. Rather, it is our inability to identify the children at greatest risk for sexual abuse and our inability to identify sexual offenders prior to their identification by children already victimized by them that gave birth to the effort to prevent sexual abuse through work with children.

This work is based on a core set of assumptions: Many children do not know what sexual abuse is, that sexual touch need not be tolerated, that many adults (e.g., parents or professionals) want to know about sexual touching by older persons (i.e., no secrets about touching), and that it is possible to tell about sexual abuse in order to have it cease. These efforts target some but not all of the dimensions of sexual abuse that make children vulnerable. Prevention programs seek to impart to children knowledge (e.g., the difference between a safe and unsafe touch or who to tell about abuse) and skills (e.g., how to say no assertively to unwanted touch) that will be useful to them in preventing or escaping their own abuse. These assumptions underpin a large number of programs and materials designed to help children prevent or escape sexual abuse (for reviews, see Kolko, 1988).

Research on Prevention Training

An expanding research literature is available that answers questions about prevention program effectiveness. Improvements in children's knowledge about prevention concepts have been found in evaluations of several different programs using a variety of training formats (for a review, see Conte & Fogarty, 1990), although many evaluations also indicate that not all children learn all that the programs hope to teach. To date, only a few studies have assessed longer-term follow-up (see Conte & Fogarty, 1990). Although evaluations have generally found overall knowledge gains following prevention program implementation, there is evidence that some concepts are more difficult to learn than others. For example, in one study, preschoolers had difficulty explaining the abstract idea of why specific touches would create specific feelings, and could not give examples of why feelings about a touch might change (Gilbert, Daro, Duerr, Le Prohn, & Nyman, 1988).

In addition to knowledge of prevention concepts, many programs attempt to teach prevention skills (e.g., children are taught to say no, to get away from the assailant or dangerous situation, and to report the incident to a trusted adult). Assessment of skill learning is difficult for researchers, as it is virtually impossible to test children's skills in real-life situations. Some evaluations have presented children with scenarios including appropriate and inappropriate touch and asked the children what should be done in such situations. In an attempt to design a behavioral skills measure that approximates reality more closely, some researchers have created "stranger abduction situations" in which a child is approached by a confederate of the experimenter, unknown to the child, and the child's help is solicited (Fryer, Kraizer, & Miyoshi, 1987). For example, the adult confederate might approach a child sent into the hallway by the teacher with the statement, "Hi, I'm here to surprise my daughter for her birthday. Can you help me bring in the cupcakes from my car?" In a sample of 44 kindergarteners through second graders, children in the education program were more likely to refuse to help the unknown confederate than were those in a control group (Kraizer, Fryer, & Miller, 1988). However, 22% of the children in the experimental group still failed the test after the education program. Notwithstanding the methodological problems in measuring skill acquisition, most research on this aspect of prevention is quite promising, suggesting that most, but not all, children do learn most prevention skills.

There has been a great deal of well-meaning (and some not so well-meaning) concern about the negative effects of prevention. There has been a considerable amount of research on this topic, and virtually none has found serious or long-term negative effects of prevention training (for discussion, see Conte & Fogarty, 1990).

The ultimate question—Are children able to prevent, escape, or avoid their own abuse?—has not yet been systematically examined in evaluation research. Although some prevention programs have anecdotal information about successful cases of children escaping abuse, it is not clear what effort has been necessary to produce how many such successes.

Arguments Against Prevention

There are a number of arguments offered against prevention efforts. Some of these arguments (e.g., that prevention has negative side effects) are simply not consistent with the evaluation literature. Another argument is that prevention efforts shift the burden of responsibility for protecting children from adults to young children. If it were clear what adults could do to make children safe from abuse, such an argument might deserve serious attention. As it is not clear, the argument should be analyzed for the underlying political ideological sentiments that give birth to it (e.g., that women belong at home, protecting children). Another argument is that children, especially young children, have a difficult time learning prevention content. Although to some extent this is true (most studies do show that young children are more difficult to teach), this argument is a classic example of the difference perspective can make—does one view the glass as half full or half empty? Some young children have a difficult time learning to read, others have trouble learning to ride bicycles. Reading, recreation, and prevention skills are all important for children. Perhaps teaching efforts with young children deserve renewed and special efforts.

Conclusion

It is not clear that many social problems can be prevented through educational efforts (e.g., drug use). Although it is extremely important to obtain data on the extent to which prevention programs actually help children prevent, avoid, or escape sexual abuse, current research data suggest that children can learn prevention content and that there are no adverse consequences associated with prevention training. Until research efforts are more successful in identifying factors that define risk for victimization or for sexual offending, sexual abuse prevention presents a relatively cost-efficient and potentially powerful intervention that may make the battle between children and sexual offenders a bit more equal.

References

Berliner, L., & Conte, J. R. (1990). The process of victimization: The victim's perspective. *Child Abuse and Neglect, 14,* 29-40.

Conte, J. R. (1990a, June). Child molesters: Images in the shadows. *The World & I,* pp. 501-513.

Conte, J. R. (1990b). Child sexual abuse. In R. T. Ammerman & M. Hersen (Eds.), *Treatment of family violence: A source book* (pp. 50-76). New York: John Wiley.

Conte, J. R. (1990c). The incest perpetrator: An overview and introduction. In A. Horton (Ed.), *The incest perpetrator: The family member no one wants to treat* (pp. 19-28). Newbury Park, CA: Sage.

Conte, J. R., & Fogarty, L. (1990). Programs for children on child abuse. *Education & Urban Society, 22,* 270-284.

Conte, J. R., Wolf, S., & Smith, T. (1989). What sexual offenders tell us about prevention. *Child Abuse and Neglect, 13,* 293-302.

Finkelhor, D., & Baron, L. (1986). High-risk children. In D. Finkelhor & Associates (Eds.), *A sourcebook on child sexual abuse* (pp. 60-88). Beverly Hills, CA: Sage.

Fryer, G. E., Kraizer, S. K., & Miyoshi, T. (1987). Measuring actual reduction of risk to child abuse: A new approach. *Child Abuse and Neglect, 11,* 173-179.

Gilbert, N., Daro, D., Duerr, J., Le Prohn, N., Nyman, N. (1988). *Child sexual abuse prevention: Evaluation of educational materials for pre-school programs* (Department of Health and Human Services, National Center on Child Abuse and Neglect, Grant 90-CA-1163). Berkeley: University of California, School of Social Welfare, Family Welfare Research Group.

Kolko, D. J. (1988). Educational programs to promote awareness and prevention of child sexual victimization: A review and methodological critique. *Clinical Psychology Review, 8,* 195-209.

Kraizer, S. K., Fryer, G. E., & Miller, M. (1988). Programming for preventing sexual abuse and abduction: What does it mean when it works? *Child Welfare, 67,* 69-78.

Peters, S. D., Wyatt, G. D., & Finkelhor, D. (1986). Prevalence. In D. Finkelhor & Associates (Eds.), *A sourcebook on child sexual abuse* (pp. 15-59). Beverly Hills, CA: Sage.

NO   JILL DUERR BERRICK and NEIL GILBERT

In recent years the child sexual abuse prevention movement has spawned a veritable industry that produces an array of educational paraphernalia used in a variety of programs. Comic books, puppets, theater, films, role plays, and other methods have been designed to engage children and deliver the prevention message. In addition, schools and agencies in every U.S. state deliver classroom programs to alert children about child abuse. In fact, one study found that almost half of all school districts in the country *mandate* regular classroom presentations on sexual abuse for children. This approach dominates the field of primary prevention and is, in many instances, the sole form of abuse prevention.

Prevention workshops often are delivered by community-based visitors within classroom settings; some prepackaged programs are delivered by classroom teachers as well. The workshops generally last between one and two hours and are offered to children of all ages—from preschool through high school.

It is estimated that 400 to 500 curricula have been designed for sexual abuse prevention training programs (Plummer, 1988). Some of these curricula are local products whose use is limited to the communities in which they were developed; others are profit oriented and are marketed nationally to reach a vast number of children. Beyond the program providers, few people, parents of participating children included, are familiar with the precise form and content of prevention curricula. Claims for the uniqueness of programs and their delivery of material tailored to age differences are difficult for parents and policy makers to judge. Although many programs claim to be unique, research on these efforts indicates that most of the programs focus on the empowerment model; that is, they seek to empower children to develop skills to protect themselves.

The content of child sexual abuse prevention programs centers on increasing children's knowledge and expanding their capacity to respond to potential threats to their safety. The typical approach is to identify the child's private parts (parts of the body covered by bathing suits) and to explain that it is bad or dangerous for anybody, even parents, to touch these private parts except when the child is being bathed or examined by a doctor. The "bad" or "dangerous" touch should be resisted and reported to an adult. Some programs try to avoid discussion of private parts and simply tell the child that a bad touch is any touch that makes them feel bad or uncomfortable. Children are told about a number of skills to use once they have identified their abuse. They are told to say no, to run away, to tell someone, or to use self-defense skills to ward off the offender.

Typical programs are especially appealing to parents and school staff because they seem to offer a quick and simple solution—an "inoculation" in the words of program providers—to an extremely complex problem. Although songs and role plays are part of the act, the lighthearted performance masks the seriousness of the message children receive. Parents' views of the programs are also influenced by the programs' good intentions. But good intentions do not always produce positive effects. Many professionals have expressed concerns about unintended consequences for both parents and children that might result from these programs.

For parents, the unintended consequence is essentially that of cultivating a false sense of security. Told by providers that these programs will teach children how to protect themselves from sexual abuse, parents have little reason to question whether these good intentions can be realized. Why else would the schools allow these programs to be given? Few parents are aware that the research on this matter reveals a distinct lack of evidence of program effectiveness, nor are they cognizant of the fact that there is considerable disagreement among professionals concerning the value of these programs. Although research in this area indicates that children show both immediate and long-term gains in knowledge after exposure to prevention presentations, these gains in knowledge are in fact rather limited. More important, there is no evidence that children are able to translate the few concepts they may learn into effective behavior that would protect them in potentially abusive situations.

In the absence of substantive knowledge about the research findings on these programs, it is psychologically comforting for parents to think that prevention training has been well tested and really works. If the programs are effective, there should be less need to worry about the child's safety. To the extent that parents believe that these programs provide a blanket of protection for children, their concern and vigilance are likely to diminish. With parents thus lulled into a false sense of security, the overall level of family protection for young children might well decline.

With regard to children, questions have been raised as to whether the programs might increase their anxiety, make them less comfortable with family intimacy, contribute to their forming excessive fear of strangers, and interfere with the normal development of their sexuality. Regarding these concerns, several studies have documented parental observations of some degree of negative side effects in their children's behavior. The adverse behavior reported by parents cannot be attributed unequivocally to the children's participation in prevention programs, but the research findings contribute to some apprehension about the potential for negative effects. Although a few studies also report parents detecting no adverse changes, the weight of the evidence suggests a small but perceptible level of immediate negative effects.

In addition to the risk of immediate, though limited, negative side effects, there is the possibility that sexual abuse prevention training may have more harmful long-term consequences with regard to the way children come to experience sexuality and physical intimacy. Given annual messages about "bad" touches from sexual abuse prevention programs, in addition to workshops that now teach children to beware of sexually transmitted diseases, teen pregnancy, and AIDS, some question whether these negative messages will ultimately affect children's perceptions of their developing sexuality. Finkelhor and Strapko (1992), two well-respected researchers in the field, state:

> If children have already had peer sexual experiences (playing doctor, etc.) what sense do they make of it after all the discussion about good and bad touching. Are they apt to feel guilty or confused, especially since the programs are unlikely to give such sex play specific endorsement? How many of the children exposed to these programs get the idea that sexual touching is always or almost always bad or dangerous or exploitative? (p. 163)

Is the possibility of negative consequences something parents should view as an appreciable matter of concern or a negligible cost for the prevention of sexual abuse? Some program providers would dismiss the potentially negative effects as inconsequential. But most parents would probably be inclined to weigh the risks to their children against the potential benefits of participating in prevention programs. If, on the one hand, these programs have no influence on preventing sexual abuse of children, even a small possibility of negative effects would appear a matter of serious concern and thoroughly unwarranted. On the other hand, if the programs serve to inoculate children against abuse, as many providers claim, then the risks would be considered no more serious than the soreness and physical discomfort sometimes following a smallpox vaccination and equally acceptable.

The problem is that no one knows how effective this training is in preventing abuse, and it remains a matter extremely difficult to test through social experimentation. Researchers have raised serious questions about whether the central lessons of prevention training—teaching young children that their parents and relatives could sexually molest them, trying to heighten their awareness of good and bad touches, and showing them how to fight against adults—are appropriate or effective measures to prevent abuse. Thus, for example, after analyzing the curricula and reviewing the research findings on a variety of prevention programs, six psychologists, writing in *School Psychology Review,* recommended that schools should not adopt programs "based on empowering children to trust their feelings, to say no, and to be assertive" (Tharinger et al., 1988). Similar recommendations were put forth by a blue-ribbon task force on preschool curricula in California in 1989 (Preschool Curricula Task Force, 1990). Finally, whether or not these lessons are appropriate, there is much uncertainty about the extent to which young children are able to absorb the ideas and make practical use of them in real-life situations.

Professionals disagree about the benefits and express much uncertainty about the risks of sexual abuse prevention programs. Advocates and critics of prevention training weigh these risks and benefits according to their own lights. But the question of whether the potentially negative effects should be of serious concern to parents cannot be affirmed or dismissed at this stage by the existing evidence from social science. It is a matter that remains for parents to judge for themselves. Truly, if children are *required* to participate in school programs designed to teach them sexual abuse prevention techniques, parents would not be given this opportunity; such a condition would lend a degree of credibility to programs that are, as yet, experimental in nature.

Child sexual abuse prevention training cannot be likened to other required curricula in the schools such as math or reading. Several well-tested techniques have been devised to present math materials to students, all with verifiable outcomes. That is, once children are taught a few math concepts, their understanding of the material and their application of the theory can be tested easily. Although we can test the number of concepts children might learn from a prevention program, scientific methods cannot readily determine whether or not these concepts would ever be applied in a real-life setting. Further, there is widespread agreement about basic math. All would concede that one plus one equals two, but do we have community standards that tell us what defines a child's private parts? For example, is a girl's chest a private part when she is 3 years old? Or when she is 10? Finally, whereas most would agree that math is an essential skill for today's technological society, we cannot use the same logic to promote prevention training for children; there is no evidence that prevention training imparts useful skills.

Child sexual abuse is a profound social problem. In many instances, sexual abuse can be devastating to a child. Nevertheless, although the problem is great, the solution does not necessarily lie within the child's capabilities. When we increase our reliance on children to protect themselves against abuse, we decrease adult society's responsibility to protect its youngest and most vulnerable citizens. Therefore, in the absence of normative standards that define the parameters of acceptable adult-child relations and given the as yet undetermined results of sexual abuse prevention training, informed parental consent becomes paramount.

Indeed, many schools require parental consent before children are allowed to participate in prevention training programs. However, this consent is often a pro forma request on a slip of paper asking parents to check a box if they agree to have their children participate. In California, for example, most schools ask for only "passive" consent. Under this procedure, if permission forms are not returned with an explicit refusal, it is assumed that parents agree to their children's participation in the program.

In general, as they are currently written, parental consent forms for sexual abuse prevention training convey neither the experimental nature of these activities nor the potential risks of participation. By this omission, they lend an implicit legitimacy to these programs, suggesting a degree of professional consensus about the harmlessness and effectiveness of prevention training for which there is little evidence. Until further data are available that lend real credibility to the effectiveness of this approach in meeting developmental, cultural, and educational standards for children, sexual abuse prevention training should not be required of young students.

References

Finkelhor, D., & Strapko, N. (1992). Sexual abuse prevention education: A review of evaluation studies. In D. J. Willis, E. Holden, & M. Rosenberg (Eds.), *Prevention of child maltreatment: Developmental and ecological perspectives* (pp. 150-167). New York: John Wiley.

Plummer, C. (1988). Prevention education in perspective. In M. Nelson & K. Clark (Eds.), *The educator's guide to preventing child sexual abuse*. Santa Cruz, CA: ETR Network.

Preschool Curricula Task Force. (1990, January 1). *First step: A report to the Office of Child Abuse Prevention*. Unpublished manuscript, California State Office of Child Abuse Prevention.

Tharinger, D. J., Krivacska, J. J., Laye-McDonough, M., Jamison, L., Vincent, G. G., & Hedlund, A. D. (1988). Prevention of child sexual abuse: An analysis of issues, educational programs, and research findings. *School Psychology Review, 17,* 614-634.

JILL DUERR BERRICK and NEIL GILBERT RESPOND

Despite some reservations about requiring children to participate in sexual abuse prevention training programs, Professor Conte seems to support such a public mandate. His two main reasons for giving an affirmative answer to the question we were asked to address are (a) research evidence indicates that the programs are effective in teaching children how to prevent sexual abuse and (b) research evidence suggests that there are no "serious or long-term negative effects of prevention training."

On the evidence regarding the positive effects of sexual abuse prevention training, we agree with Professor Conte that some children learn some of the material presented in these programs. However, as we have indicated, these gains in knowledge are often very small. A review of 14 evaluations of sexual abuse prevention programs around the country, for example, reveals that in 6 of the studies with experimental and control groups the students' scores increased by 10% or less after training; the other studies showed gains somewhat higher than 10%, but still rather limited (Berrick & Gilbert, 1991).

The essential question, however, is whether a gain in the knowledge that these programs offer (for example, a 4-year-old child who learns the lesson that it is unsafe for her parents to touch her private parts, including her chest, except when bathing her) has anything to do with effectiveness in children's preventing sexual abuse. The answer, as Haugaard and Reppucci's (1988) review of the research reveals, is "no evidence, not even one published case example indicates that primary prevention has ever been achieved" (p. 332). Conte would seem to agree with this point when he notes that "the ultimate question—Are children able to prevent, escape, or avoid their own abuse?—has not yet been systematically examined in evaluation research." In other words, there is no reliable evidence that sexual abuse prevention training has any effect. Research on other forms of prevention training (e.g., programs to reduce adolescent pregnancy, alcohol abuse, and drug abuse) indicates that although gains in knowledge usually follow program participation, knowledge of prevention in these areas is rarely related to changes in behavior (Kirby, 1984; Moskowitz, 1989; Williams, Ward, & Gray, 1985).

Regarding unanticipated consequences, as we have indicated in our initial argument, there are a number of studies in which 5% to 35% of parents report some observations of negative effects, such as their children's loss of sleep, nightmares, and expressions of anxiety, after participation in prevention programs (Berrick & Gilbert, 1991). We interpret the evidence on this issue as suggesting a small but perceptible level of immediate negative effects. Whereas Professor Conte finds the research yielding virtually no serious negative effects, we think that the issue of whether these effects are "serious" is a matter for parents to judge. Professor Conte dismisses the possibility of negative long-term effects, but other experts believe that this is an important concern that deserves more serious consideration by researchers (Finkelhor & Strapko, 1992; Kraizer, 1986; Reppucci & Haugaard, 1989; Tharinger et al., 1988).

Another reason Professor Conte supports mandated prevention training in the schools is that, given our inability to identify children at risk or potential offenders, we don't know what else to do. We share Professor Conte's sense of frustration in the face of a grave social problem for which there is no clear or immediate solution. But we think it is neither good social policy nor good social science to mandate programs for children about which we have no evidence of effectiveness and for which serious concerns about potentially negative consequences have been expressed by a number of researchers. If these programs are given in schools, they should be voluntary and parents should be informed of their experimental nature.

References

Berrick, J. D., & Gilbert, N. (1991). *With the best of intentions: The child sexual abuse prevention movement.* New York: Guilford.

Finkelhor, D., & Strapko, N. (1992). Sexual abuse prevention education: A review of evaluation studies. In D. J. Willis, E. Holden, & M. Rosenberg (Eds.), *Prevention of child maltreatment: Developmental and ecological perspectives* (pp. 150-167). New York: John Wiley.

Haugaard, J. J., & Reppucci, N. D. (1988). *The sexual abuse of children: A comprehensive guide to current knowledge and intervention strategies.* San Francisco: Jossey-Bass.

Kirby, D. (1984). *Sexuality education: An evaluation of programs and their effectiveness.* Santa Cruz, CA: Network.

Kraizer, S. F. (1986). Rethinking prevention. *Child Abuse and Neglect, 10,* 259-261.

Moskowitz, J. (1989). The primary prevention of alcohol problems. *Journal of Studies on Alcohol, 50,* 54-88.

Reppucci, N. D., & Haugaard, J. (1989). Prevention of child sexual abuse: Myth or reality? *American Psychologist, 44,* 1266-1275.

Tharinger, D. J., Krivacska, J. J., Laye-McDonough, M., Jamison, L., Vincent, G. G., & Hedlund, A. D. (1988). Prevention of child sexual abuse: An analysis of issues, educational programs, and research findings. *School Psychology Review, 17,* 614-634.

Williams, R., Ward, D., & Gray, L. (1985). The persistence of experimentally induced cognitive changes: A neglected dimension in the assessment of drug prevention programs. *Journal of Drug Education, 15,* 33-42.

JON R. CONTE RESPONDS

In somewhat typical fashion, Berrick and Gilbert distort the intent of sexual abuse prevention, misrepresent the research evidence, and offer no meaningful alternatives to current prevention efforts. They offer a number of statements for which empirical evidence simply does not exist. These include the following: "Typical programs are . . . appealing to parents and schools . . . because they . . . offer a quick and simple solution"; "for parents, the unintended consequence is . . . a false sense of security"; "it is psychologically comforting for parents to think . . . prevention training has been well tested"; and "there is the possibility that sexual abuse prevention training. . . may have more harmful long-term consequences. . . . " My personal experience in speaking to and talking with parents about sexual abuse is that the outcomes claimed by Professors Berrick and Gilbert are not common. I find that parents develop no such sense of false security, and few see anything as a "quick and simple solution" for the dangers of childhood. But my experience means as little as their own, without data. Let them present the results of their research that support these claims. Until then, we may well conclude that they have created straw devils to knock over with their wind.

More disturbing, they suggest that "several studies have documented parental observations of some degree of negative side effects." This distorts the research and misleads the reader. In fact, there is *substantial evidence* that prevention is not associated with adverse consequences. These findings only contribute to apprehension about prevention in the minds of those ideologically opposed to prevention efforts.

Berrick and Gilbert also suggest that knowledge gains are "rather limited." The problem in prevention is not that knowledge gains are limited. Rules of data analysis define what is significant or not. A large number of studies have found gains in knowledge beyond what would be expected by chance. Our problem is that we do not know how much knowledge is associated with children's abilities to prevent or escape abuse. No one knows how much knowledge is necessary or sufficient. Certainly, Berrick and Gilbert give us no idea how much is enough or too little. Again, they make a claim that they cannot support.

They suggest that current prevention efforts reduce society's responsibility to protect children. Given the large amount of public and professional attention to child sexual abuse and the increasing levels of research, new legislation, and efforts to treat victims and offenders, I see no evidence that society feels less interested in child sexual abuse. The problem remains, and Berrick and Gilbert offer us no new ideas and no data.

It is not clear what we as adults can do to prevent abuse and protect children. Until we have better ideas, helping children to equalize what is an inherently unfair fight may be worth the effort. I know that if it is my child who is helped, it is worth everything.

DEBATE 11

INTERVENING WITH DRUG-DEPENDENT PREGNANT WOMEN

> *Should the state have the right to intervene when a pregnant woman is found to be dependent on drugs or alcohol?*

EDITORS' NOTE: Babies born with drugs, usually crack cocaine, in their systems have received a great deal of publicity and evoked a huge public response. Although most of the concerned public believes that the mothers are acting irresponsibly, there is a lively debate on what the legal response should be, and when it should be invoked. The Florida judge who jailed a drug-addicted pregnant woman forced the issue. Those who agreed with his decision claimed the mother was guilty of child neglect as well as drug possession. They would argue that the appropriate child protective measure is to restrict the mother's intake of drugs, even if that means imprisonment. Opponents of the action claim that criminal child neglect statutes apply when the child is born. Furthermore, under *Roe v. Wade,* the mother has control over the fetus until the third trimester, and even then the intervention of the state is limited to abortion issues. The argument is further confused by the fact that not all babies born with drugs in their systems are at risk of impaired development. An even more complicated issue is alcohol addiction. Although the damaging effects of fetal alcohol syndrome have been identified for many years, there has been little attempt, until recently, to control alcoholic pregnant women. The predictable effect of maternal alcoholism on the fetus is even less clear-cut than with maternal drug addiction. In addition, there are accusations that there is a class bias in favor of alcoholism, given that there are more middle-class alcoholic mothers than drug abusers. Our authors are in agreement on many aspects of this problem, but disagree about the most sensitive issue, the timing of the intervention.

John E. B. Meyers says YES. He is Professor of Law at the University of the Pacific, McGeorge School of Law. His specialty is family law, and he has published numerous articles on legal aspects of child abuse and neglect.

Douglas J. Besharov argues NO. He is a lawyer and a resident scholar at the American Enterprise Institute for Public Policy Research. He has published widely on child abuse and neglect. An earlier version of his argument here appeared as "Whose Life Is It Anyway?" in the *National Law Journal.* It is reprinted with the permission of *The National Law Journal,* copyright 1992, The New York Law Publishing Company.

YES — JOHN E. B. MEYERS

Someone is about to poison a 6-month-old baby! Does society have authority to intervene? Of course. Society has the moral as well as the legal authority to prevent adults from hurting children. Thus a police officer may physically restrain the adult, and, if help does not arrive in time, the adult may be prosecuted and sent to prison.

Now, consider a different situation. Suppose a woman is 6 months pregnant and is about to inject crack cocaine into her arm. The cocaine will circulate in the woman's blood and will pass through the placenta into the unborn child, where the cocaine may damage or kill the child. For the unborn child, cocaine is poison. Society has authority to protect the 6-month-old baby; does society have authority to protect the 6-month-old fetus? May the pregnant woman be stopped before she injects the cocaine? If the woman injects the cocaine and the child is handicapped or stillborn, should the woman be prosecuted?

These are difficult questions, and the answers are far from clear. Yet society can no longer ignore the moral and legal issues raised by maternal drug abuse during pregnancy. As many as 1 baby in 10 is born with side effects from illegal drugs taken by the mother during pregnancy. It is estimated that 300,000 infants are born annually to women who use crack cocaine during pregnancy. An additional 10,000 babies are born each year to women using opiates such as heroin. Use of drugs such as cocaine and heroin during pregnancy inflicts serious short- and long-term harm on thousands of children (Bays, 1990).

How should society respond to this tragic problem? Few would disagree that the most promising and humane response to maternal drug abuse during pregnancy is increased medical and social services for women. There is a desperate need for more drug treatment programs and prenatal medical care, particularly for poor women. Yet some women are not interested in treatment. Moreover, the incredible craving caused by crack cocaine and heroin so overpowers some users that they simply cannot stop. Because there are pregnant women who cannot or will not take advantage of voluntary services, society must ask whether the law has a role to play in preventing harm to unborn children.

Some argue that because the legal system is inherently coercive, the law cannot play a constructive role in responding to maternal drug abuse during pregnancy ("Symposium," 1990). Although the argument against such intervention has merit, opponents of legal intervention ignore the harsh reality of drug abuse and its effects on children. So long as the primary emphasis remains on increased voluntary services, the law can play a valuable subsidiary role.

The law can respond in two ways to maternal drug abuse during pregnancy: First, women whose drug abuse harms their unborn children may be prosecuted; second, rather than prosecute women *after* the harm of drug abuse occurs, the law may intervene during pregnancy to *prevent* harm.

Prosecution After the Child Is Born

A defensible argument can be made for prosecution of some women whose drug use during pregnancy harms their unborn children. The argument for prosecution begins with the well-accepted premise that society has authority to punish individuals who seriously harm others (Feinberg, 1984; Mill, 1859/1982). The criminal justice system is founded on this premise. Maternal drug use during pregnancy carries a high risk of serious harm to unborn children. Although there is some uncertainty regarding the legal status of the fetus, there is no denying that the unborn child has the *potential* to become a "person" in every sense of the word. This potential deserves the law's protection. Thus society has a strong interest in protecting unborn children from the ravages of maternal drug abuse. Moreover, opponents of prosecution cannot argue that prosecution infringes on the rights of pregnant women because there is *no* right to take illegal drugs.

Although prosecution can be defended on moral as well as legal grounds, prosecution is not a viable response to drug abuse during pregnancy. There is a very real likelihood that the threat of prosecution will frighten drug-abusing women away from the prenatal care they desperately need. Thus the social utility of prosecution is low. As I have noted elsewhere, "The ultimate irony of prosecuting maternal drug use during pregnancy could be that the state harms more children than it helps" (Myers, 1991, p. 758).

Juvenile Court Intervention Before the Child Is Born

Everyone is familiar with the highly visible criminal justice system. Fewer people are aware of the equally important juvenile court system. The primary responsibility of the juvenile court is to protect abused and neglected children. When abuse or neglect comes to the attention of police, social workers, doctors, or teachers, proceedings are commenced in juvenile court to protect the child. The juvenile court judge has authority to remove children from their homes and to order parents to obtain counseling and other assistance. Proceedings in juvenile court are less adversarial than in criminal court cases. In juvenile court, parents are not prosecuted, and the goal is not to punish, but to protect children and help parents learn more effective ways to interact with their children. Although the juvenile court system is terribly overburdened and underfunded, the juvenile court helps many families.

Although prosecution is not an effective response to maternal drug abuse during pregnancy, the juvenile court can play a constructive role. Involvement of the juvenile court is possible at two times: shortly following the birth of a drug-affected baby and prior to birth. It is clear that once a drug-affected baby is born, the juvenile court has authority to intervene if the mother is unable to care for the child. The more difficult question is whether the juvenile court should be allowed to intervene *prior to birth* in order to stop drug abuse that threatens to harm the unborn child.

If the unborn child could speak, the child would certainly favor intervention during pregnancy, *before* drugs do their dirty work. In addition to the child's unspoken desires, society has a strong interest in protecting unborn children. Thus the interests of society and those of the child dovetail. The pregnant woman has no right to take illegal drugs, particularly when such conduct may cause serious harm to the unborn child. Thus at first blush it is difficult to find a reason to deny juvenile court judges authority to intervene prior to birth. But reasons there are. Suppose a juvenile court judge orders a pregnant woman to stop abusing drugs, but the woman disobeys the judge's order? How is the judge to enforce the order? With some women, particularly addicts, the only way to stop drug abuse is to deprive the woman of her liberty —to lock her up! Thus, with some women, authorizing juvenile court intervention prior to birth is certain to infringe on the fundamental right to physical liberty. Is society justified in depriving a woman of her liberty in order to protect her unborn child? When the potential harm to the child is considered, the answer is yes. Limited juvenile court intervention during pregnancy is morally and legally defensible.

The prospect of government interference in the lives of pregnant women is frightening, and it is clear that strict limits must be placed on intervention. Moreover, the enthusiasm to protect unborn children must be tempered with caution. As Justice Brandeis of the U.S. Supreme Court warned long ago, "Experience should teach us most to be on our guard to protect liberty when the government's purposes are beneficent.... The greatest dangers to liberty lurk in insidious encroachments by men of zeal, well-meaning but without understanding" (*Olmstead v. United States,* 1928, p. 479).

Despite the fact that juvenile court intervention will impair women's civil liberties, the brutal truth is that in the time it took to read this essay, a drug-affected baby was born. Because the baby's mother used illegal drugs, the baby may be robbed of a full and meaningful life. Society does not ask too much when it insists that women refrain from drug abuse during pregnancy, and when a woman's abuse of drugs endangers her unborn child, society is justified in temporarily compromising the woman's liberty to save the child. Indeed, it is morally bankrupt to suggest that society is powerless to act. When voluntary help is refused, the juvenile court is the child's last best hope.

References

Bays, J. (1990). Substance abuse and child abuse: The impact of addiction on the child. *Pediatric Clinics of North America, 37,* 881-904.
Feinberg, J. (1984). *Harm to others.* New York: Oxford University Press.
Mill, J. S. (1982). *On liberty.* New York: Viking Penguin. (Original work published 1859)
Myers, J. E. B. (1991). A limited role for the legal system in responding to maternal substance abuse during pregnancy. *Notre Dame Journal of Law and Public Policy, 5,* 747-781.
Olmstead v. United States, 277 U.S. 438 (1928) (Brandeis, J., dissenting).
Symposium: Criminal liability for fetal endangerment. (1990). *Criminal Justice Ethics, 9,* 11-51.

NO DOUGLAS J. BESHAROV

Five years after the first crack babies appeared in inner-city hospitals, we are still arguing about whether a pregnant woman's use of drugs constitutes child abuse. Although no one wants to see endangered children go unprotected, many fear that equating prenatal exposure to illegal drugs with child abuse could be a first step toward legal recognition of the fetus as a person, thus undermining abortion rights. These concerns are misplaced.

The issue is important: Some drug-using mothers want help for their children and treatment for their addictions. But many others do not. For them, only a report of suspected child abuse will initiate a social work investigation to see whether the child can safely be sent home with the mother and whether the family needs supportive social services.

In 1991, from 30,000 to 50,000 children were born after having been exposed to illegal drugs in their mothers' wombs. Perhaps twice that number of older children live at home with drug addicts (Besharov, 1989). Prenatal drug exposure can cause serious injury and even death to the developing fetus. Pregnant women who use heroin, methadone, cocaine, or large quantities of barbiturates or alcohol—or, as is common, a combination of these drugs—are much more likely to give birth to children with severe problems. Crack, for example, constricts the blood vessels in the placenta and the fetus, thus cutting off the flow of oxygen and nutrients and creating a higher probability of miscarriages, stillbirths, and premature and low-birth-weight babies, often with various physical and neurological problems. Death rates may be twice as high for crack babies as for others (Gordon Avery, Children's Hospital, Washington, DC, personal communication, March 27, 1989; see also Whitaker, 1988).

Labeling drug use while pregnant as child abuse makes many women's rights and abortion rights advocates apprehensive, as they see it as a potential narrowing of reproductive freedoms. Their opposition—and threats of litigation—has led some jurisdictions to circumscribe sharply their efforts to protect drug babies. For example, speaking for the New York State Department of Social Services, Susan Demers (1990), deputy commissioner and general counsel, has argued that "child protective statutes were not intended to apply, nor can they constitutionally be applied, to prenatal conduct by a woman in relation to a fetus." She contends that "although there was a fetus, there was no child in existence at the time the woman committed the acts. Furthermore, such prenatal conduct falls within the woman's constitutional right to privacy and to bodily integrity."

Such arguments are strengthened by the fact that the harmful effects of prenatal drug exposure are only probabilities. Rough estimates are that only about a third of exposed babies suffer serious damage. Although medical studies have yet to develop specific measures of prediction, it appears that the existence and severity of symptoms are functions of the timing, type, dosage, and regularity of drug use, the mother's metabolism, and a host of other, little-understood factors.

One can understand the concerns about abortion rights, but they have not been borne out by experience. For example, in the past five years, at least eight states have passed laws making prenatal drug exposure subject to mandatory child abuse reporting statutes. Each of these laws is carefully drafted to apply only after the child is born.

Similarly, in states without legislation specifically aimed at prenatal drug exposure, many courts have held that a mother's use of illegal drugs while pregnant falls under existing statutory definitions of child abuse or child neglect, based on the harm or threatened harm to the developing fetus. These court decisions also have been careful to distinguish between their rulings and any restriction on abortion rights. Thus in one case, the court explained: "We are concerned here not with a woman's privacy right in electing to terminate an unwanted pregnancy, but with the protection of the child who is born when a woman has elected to carry that child to term and deliver it" (*In re* Stefanel C., 1990, p. 285). Even the few criminal prosecutions that have taken place, which many oppose on policy as well as constitutional grounds, involve live births.

For those who might say that it is only a matter of time before such rulings are twisted to undermine abortion rights, it is worth remembering that, since 1974, courts in New York City and other jurisdictions have held that "a newborn baby having withdrawal symptoms is prima facie a neglected baby" (*In re* Vanesa F., 1974, p. 340). Through all these years, no one has seriously argued that these laws and court decisions are a backdoor recognition of the fetus as a living person. In short, there is no slippery slope here.

Another concern has been that drug-using mothers—for fear of being reported—will not come into hospitals to deliver their babies. But there is no evidence that this is happening. Since 1986, about 20,000 drug-exposed newborns have been reported in New York City alone. In hospitals such as Harlem Hospital, drug testing of newborns is routine. And yet there is no evidence that more mothers are having their babies at home.

A greater possibility is that some drug-using mothers will not come in for prenatal care because they fear the legal consequences. Unfortunately, they do not come in anyway, regardless of reporting policy. In Boston, prenatal care is free for all low-income mothers, and pregnant women who use drugs are not reported by the clinics. And yet, between August 1988 and February 1989, of the 38 babies born at Boston City Hospital to mothers who had not obtained prenatal care, 37 tested positive for cocaine (Elizabeth Brown, personal communication, December 12, 1990).

Nevertheless, given the unease that so many feel about basing government action on harm (or threatened harm) to the fetus, it is important to recognize that there is a second basis for deciding that a child prenatally exposed to drugs should be considered abused or neglected—a basis totally independent of the legal status of the fetus.

The tragic nature of their condition has focused most media attention on crack babies while they are still in the hospital. But these children face even greater dangers when they leave and go home with their parents. Severe prenatal drug abuse (or alcohol abuse, for that matter) can so strikingly impair a parent's judgment and ability to cope that serious harm to the child becomes likely. Parents suffering from such severe drug habits that they are unable to care for themselves cannot care for their children. Moreover, drug use can make parents more violent toward their children. The author of a Ramsey County, Minnesota, Department of Human Services report, after reviewing 70 cases of "cocaine-attached" households in mid-1988, found that these parents are "extremely volatile with episodes of 'normal' behavior interspersed with episodes of unpredictable, dangerous and even violent behavior" (Douglas, 1989). In 1989, 70% of child abuse fatalities in which the situations were already known to New York City's child protective agency were drug related.

The home situations of heavy drug users need to be investigated even if the newborn child has suffered no damage in utero. For a newborn to evidence the symptoms of drug exposure—even to have a positive toxicology when born—means the mother was probably a regular user while pregnant. And, as a New York court held, "Repeated past behavior is a substantial predictor of future behavior" (*In re* Milland, 1989, pp. 998-999). This in turn would establish the possibility of serious harm to the baby when he or she goes home with the addicted mother. A Michigan appeals court put it succinctly: "Prenatal treatment can be considered probative of a child's [future] neglect" (*In re* Baby X, 1980, p. 739).

Waiting until the children of severe drug and alcohol abusers show signs of actual abuse or neglect would unreasonably endanger many children. In the absence of suitable arrangements, state intervention is essential and foster care may be necessary, even if such children have not yet been harmed and even if they have never been in their parents' custody.

Yet the presumption of heavy drug use during pregnancy is only that: a presumption. A parent's drug abuse does not necessarily mean that the child must be removed from parental custody. If an investigation determines that the home is safe and the mother can adequately care for her new child, then, of course, the baby should go home. In many cases, supportive services provided by the child protective agency or another public or private agency may enable the parents to care for their children.

The point is, we can help protect the children of addicts without subverting abortion rights—and we should. Rather than being diverted by an unnecessary controversy over a remote threat to reproductive freedom, we should focus on what needs to be done to protect the children of addicts—and to treat their mothers. Both desperately need our help.

References

Besharov, D. (1989, Fall). The children of crack: Who will protect them? *Public Welfare*, p. 7.
Demers, S. (1990, August 21). [Letter to Barbara Gill, American Enterprise Institute].
Douglas, C. (1989, March). Babies in trouble. *Minnesota Monthly*, p. 49.
In re Baby X, 293 N.W.2d 736, 97 Mich.App. 111 (1980); accord *in re* Troy D., 215 Cal.App.3d 889, 263 Cal. Rptr. 869 (Ct. App. 1989), basing its decision on "prognostic deprivation."
In re Milland, 146 Misc.2d 1, 548 N.Y.S.2d 995 (Fam. Ct., N.Y. Co., 1989).
In re Stefanel C., 157 A.D.2d 322, 556 N.Y.S.2d 280 (1st Dept., 1990).
In re Vanesa F., 76 Misc.2d 617; 351 N.Y.S.2d 337 (1974).
Whitaker, B. (1988, July 11). Tiniest tragedies of drugs. *Newsday*, p. 9.

DOUGLAS J. BESHAROV RESPONDS

Professor Myers has presented a straightforward and moving argument for why we should be concerned about drug use by pregnant women. As I hope is clear from my own contribution to this volume, I share his distress about the effects on children of their exposure to drugs in utero.

Professor Myers also says that he opposes criminal prosecution of pregnant addicts because, even though constitutionally allowable under *Roe v. Wade,* it would be of low "social utility." Again, I agree on both counts.

Where we disagree is in what he says next: Although there should not be criminal prosecutions, "the juvenile court should be allowed to intervene *prior to birth* in order to stop drug abuse that threatens to harm the unborn child." Giving the juvenile court such jurisdiction would be the functional equivalent of authorizing criminal prosecution, for, as Myers himself recognizes, "the only way to stop drug abuse is to deprive the woman of her liberty —to lock her up!"

No matter how great the need, incarcerating pregnant drug addicts raises serious practical and ethical concerns. First, although drug use during pregnancy unquestionably endangers the child and the mother, the plain truth is that many drug-exposed babies escape any serious harm. Some, in fact, are asymptomatic. Unfortunately, medical science has no way of predicting which drug-using pregnant women pose actual versus potential danger to their children.

Second, any plan that seeks to enforce court orders by locking up uncooperative women is not likely to work, because the possibility of incarceration would be so remote. There are not enough prison cells available now for serious criminals, and any new ones that are built will not be used for pregnant drug users. One is reminded, for example, of the outcome of a Washington, D.C., case of a pregnant women awaiting trial on theft charges. Because she had tested positive for cocaine use, the judge ordered her to remain in jail until she delivered her baby. Jail overcrowding, however, forced officials to release her weeks before she was due to give birth ("Pregnant?" 1988).

Finally, there is a real danger that, when faced with the possibility of court-ordered treatment enforced by incarceration, many more pregnant drug users will not seek prenatal care.

Therefore, I am afraid that, however attractive, using courts to impose treatment on pregnant addicts is not a realistic option. To find solutions to this terrible problem, we must look in other places.

Reference

Pregnant? Go directly to jail. (1988, November 1). *ABA Journal,* p. 20.

JOHN E. B. MYERS RESPONDS

Mr. Besharov and I agree that the state should have authority to protect drug-affected babies. However, Mr. Besharov does not go far enough. He defends legal intervention after a drug-affected baby is born, but he appears to stop short of defending intervention *before birth*. Yet intervention before birth is the *only* way to protect infants from the ravages of maternal substance abuse during pregnancy. Although legal intervention prior to birth is a frightening prospect, settling for anything less consigns thousands of children to harm that could be prevented. Parents have no right to abuse their children, *before* or *after* they enter the world.

DEBATE 12

CORPORAL PUNISHMENT BY PARENTS

➢ *Should the use of corporal punishment by parents be considered child abuse?*

EDITORS' NOTE: Corporal punishment (i.e., any hitting of children, in any form) is common in this country as well as in many others. Is it a form of abuse, or is it a necessary option for parents to use in socializing their children? Is it the reflection of cultural differences in parenting practices that should be respected? In this debate, two authors provide arguments against considering corporal punishment child abuse, one an academic and one the director of an organization called the Center for Affirmative Parenting.

Murray A. Straus, Ph.D., says YES. He is Professor of Sociology and Co-Director of the Family Research Laboratory at the University of New Hampshire. He has served as president of the National Council on Family Relations (1972-1973), the Society for the Study of Social Problems (1988-1989), and the Eastern Sociological Society (1990-1991). In 1977, he received the Ernest W. Burgess Award of the National Council of Family Relations for outstanding research on the family. He is the author of many articles and author or coauthor of 15 books, including the *Handbook of Family Measurement Techniques* (3rd ed., 1990) and *Physical Violence In American Families* (1990). He is currently writing a book on corporal punishment titled *Beating the Devil Out of Them: Corporal Punishment in American Families.*

Robert E. Larzelere, Ph.D., argues NO. He is Director of Residential Research at Boys Town, where he is doing research on treatment of childhood sex abuse victims and on parental discipline. He is the author of the methodology chapter in *The Handbook of Marriage and the Family* and has published 17 articles in a variety of social scientific journals.

John K. Rosemond also argues NO. He is a family psychologist and Director of the Center for Affirmative Parenting in Gastonia, North Carolina. He is the author of *John Rosemond's Six-Point Plan for Raising Happy, Healthy Children, Ending the Homework Hassle* and *Parent Power!*

YES　　　　　　　　　　　　　　　　　MURRAY A. STRAUS

Corporal punishment is the use of physical force with the intention of causing a child to experience pain but not injury, for purposes of correction or control of the child's behavior. The most frequent forms are spanking, slapping, grabbing or shoving a child "roughly" (i.e., with more force than is needed to move the child), and hitting with certain traditionally acceptable objects such as a hairbrush, belt, ruler, or paddle. Such acts by parents are legal and considered morally correct everywhere in the United States. In a 1986 National Opinion Research Center survey of persons age 18 and over, 84% agreed with the statement "It is sometimes necessary to give a child a good hard spanking." Between 90% and 100% of parents have actually used corporal punishment (Wauchope & Straus, 1990).

One way to answer the question of whether a certain type of parent behavior is abusive uses the criterion of whether the behavior puts the child at risk of injury (either physical or psychological) that is greater than the risk of alternative modes of child rearing. That criterion will be used in this argument.

It is well known that physical "abuse" (i.e., physical force that causes injury or has a high probability of causing injury) also tends to cause serious psychological problems and increases the probability of juvenile delinquency. It is also well recognized that when abused children grow up, they are more likely than those who were not abused to abuse children physically and to engage in crime (Elmer & Gregg, 1967; Widom, 1989; Wolfe, 1987), even though such outcomes are far from inevitable. However, one almost never hears about the research showing that ordinary and legal corporal punishment of a misbehaving child has the same consequences as physical abuse, even though not as strong. One reason these findings are not accepted is that they imply that almost all American parents are guilty of abuse, including those who write books of advice for parents and child psychology textbooks. So it is no wonder that the existence of research showing the harmful effects of spanking is one of the best-kept secrets of American child psychology.

The evidence linking corporal punishment to aggression comes from many different studies (Lefkowitz, Eron, Walder, & Huesmann, 1977; Maurer, 1974; Parke & Slaby, 1983; Straus, 1991). The evidence linking corporal punishment with other psychological problems comes from analyses of the 2,143 families in the First National Family Violence Survey (Straus, Gelles, & Steinmetz, 1980) and 6,002 families in the Second National Family Violence Survey (Straus & Gelles, 1990). Both surveys found that close to 100% of parents of toddlers and half of parents of early teenage children used corporal punishment with their children. About the same proportion reported that they themselves were hit by their parents when they were adolescents.

These high rates of hitting adolescents indicate the pervasiveness of corporal punishment in the rearing of American children. They are also important because some of the research findings are based on whether the children were hit by parents when they were adolescents. As that is the majority of American children, those findings cannot be dismissed as representing only a small group of exceptional cases. Moreover, the findings from these two surveys are based on analyses that controlled statistically for possible overlap of corporal punishment with the age and socioeconomic status of the parents, the gender of the parent and the child, whether the parents explained what they were doing, and whether there was also violence between the parents.

Corporal Punishment Increases Aggression and Delinquency

The survey that asked about whether children sometimes need "a good hard spanking" also asked if spanking would be appropriate in three situations. For a child's not cleaning up his or her room, only 9% felt that spanking was appropriate. For stealing something, the figure went up to 27%. For hitting another child, it was 41%. If the survey had asked about hitting a parent, the percentage might have reached 90%.

There is a double message in these statistics. On the one hand, the parents are saying that hitting another person is a terrible thing to do. On the other hand, they are also saying *by example* that when someone does something that is clearly wrong, it is morally correct to hit. The child learns both messages, and then has to apply both principles. When the child applies those principles it is likely to produce an *increase* in that child's hitting other children. This is because children usually hit other children precisely because they are doing something that is clearly wrong, such as taking toys or throwing water at someone they shouldn't.

Corporal punishment therefore teaches the morality of hitting. But that lesson is only one part of the "hidden curriculum" that accompanies each use of corporal punishment. Another key element of the hidden curriculum is that "those who love you are those who hit you." This is because virtually the only adults who hit infants and toddlers are those they love most—their parents. This creates the confusion of love and violence that is such a pernicious aspect of relationships between men and women. It also implicitly teaches

Corporal Punishment by Parents

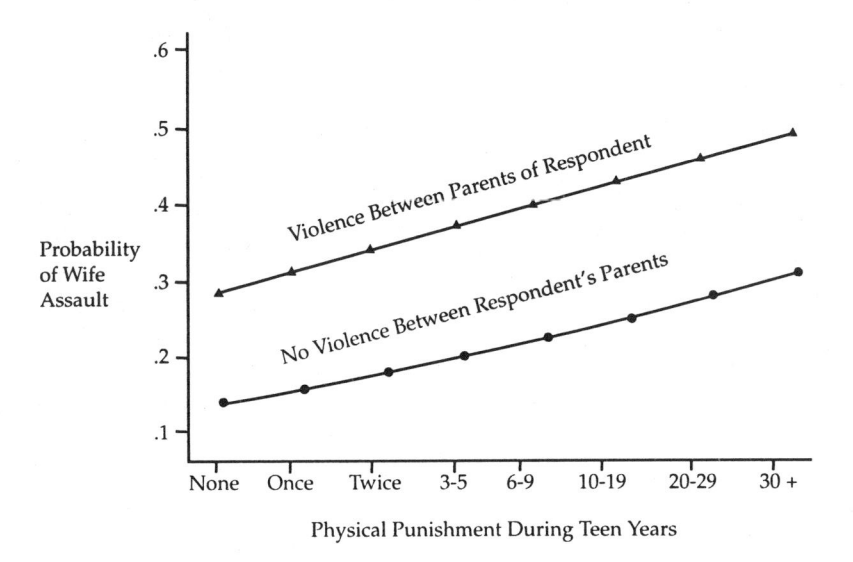

[Figure: graph with y-axis "Probability of Wife Assault" ranging from .1 to .6, and x-axis "Physical Punishment During Teen Years" with categories None, Once, Twice, 3-5, 6-9, 10-19, 20-29, 30+. Upper line labeled "Violence Between Parents of Respondent" rises from about .29 to .50. Lower line labeled "No Violence Between Respondent's Parents" rises from about .14 to .31.]

Figure 12.1. Probability of Wife Assault by Physical Punishment During Teen Years

that it is morally acceptable to hit those you love when they "do wrong." The trouble with these parts of the hidden curriculum is that they are almost a recipe for violence between spouses later in life, because, sooner or later, almost all spouses "do wrong" and "won't listen to reason," as the other spouse sees it. The results can be seen in Figure 12.1. It shows that the more corporal punishment individuals experienced as children, the greater the percentage who, only a few years later in life, hit their spouses. Figure 12.1 also shows that the increased risk of marital violence occurs among both those whose parents were violent to each other (upper line) and those whose parents were not (upper line). These findings help explain the high rate of violence between couples found in many recent studies (Gelles & Straus, 1988; Straus & Gelles, 1990).

Figure 12.2 shows that the more physical punishment individuals experienced as children, the greater the proportion who, as adults, went beyond ordinary corporal punishment and attacked their children severely enough for it to be considered child abuse. The two plot lines in Figure 12.2 show that this occurs regardless of whether there was also violence between the parents. Relationships similar to those in Figure 12.1 were also found between corporal punishment and delinquency, and between corporal punishment and assaults on people other than family members (Straus, 1991).

```
                                                    Wife Assault in Previous 12 Months
        .5
        .4
Probability
 of Child   .3
  Abuse                                 No Wife Assault
        .2
        .1
          None   Once  Twice  3-5   6-9  10-19  20-29  30 +
                    Physical Punishment During Teen Years
```

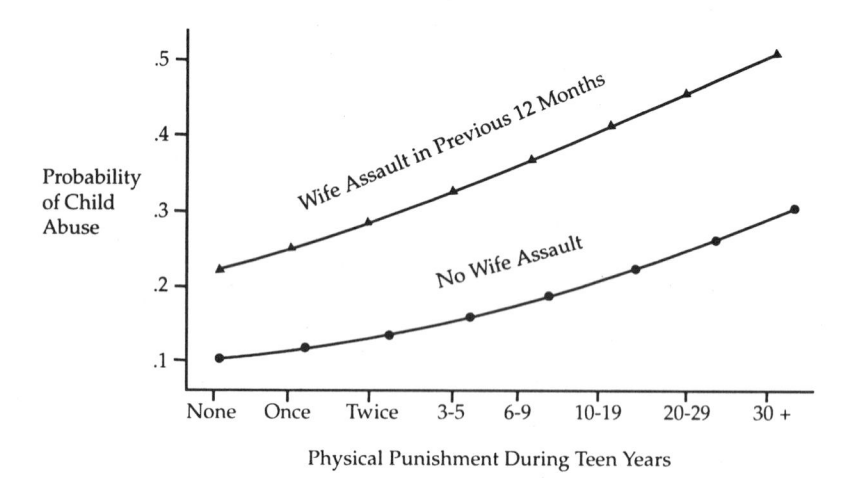

Figure 12.2. Probability of Child Abuse by Physical Punishment During Teen Years

Drinking Problems, Depression, and Suicide

In a recent study, a colleague and I analyzed physical punishment while holding constant the effects of other variables that might be the real explanation for the seeming adverse effects (Straus & Kaufman Kantor, 1992). We found that regardless of whether there was marital violence, for men as well as women, and for persons of both low and high socioeconomic status, the more corporal punishment experienced in the teen years, the higher the percentage who have a drinking problem (Figure 12.3), the higher the percentage who have depressive symptoms, and the higher the percentage who thought about killing themselves during the 12 months prior to the time they were interviewed (Figure 12.4).

Corporal Punishment Is a Risk Factor

It would be a mistake to think that the findings illustrated in Figures 12.1-12.4 show that corporal punishment inevitably leads to aggression, drinking problems, suicide, and so on. That could hardly be the case, or the human race would not have survived. Instead of a one-to-one causal relationship, corporal punishment is what epidemiologists call a "risk factor." A war is an example

Corporal Punishment by Parents

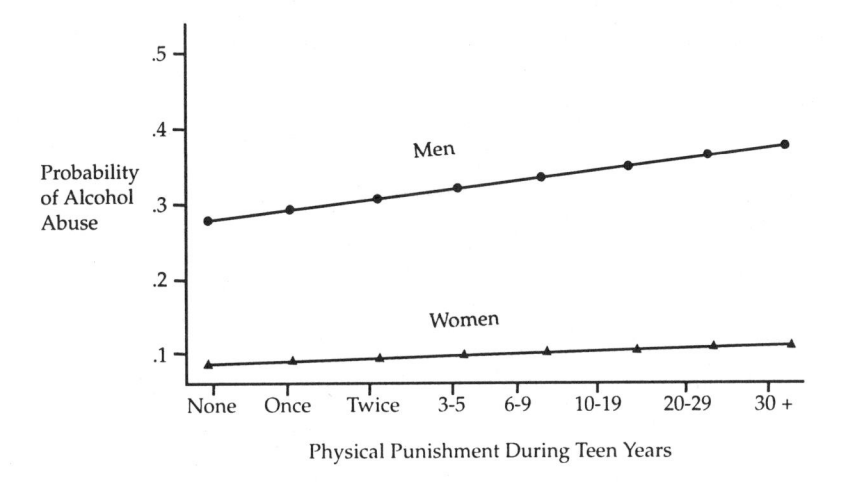

Figure 12.3. Probability of Alcohol Abuse by Physical Punishment During Teen Years

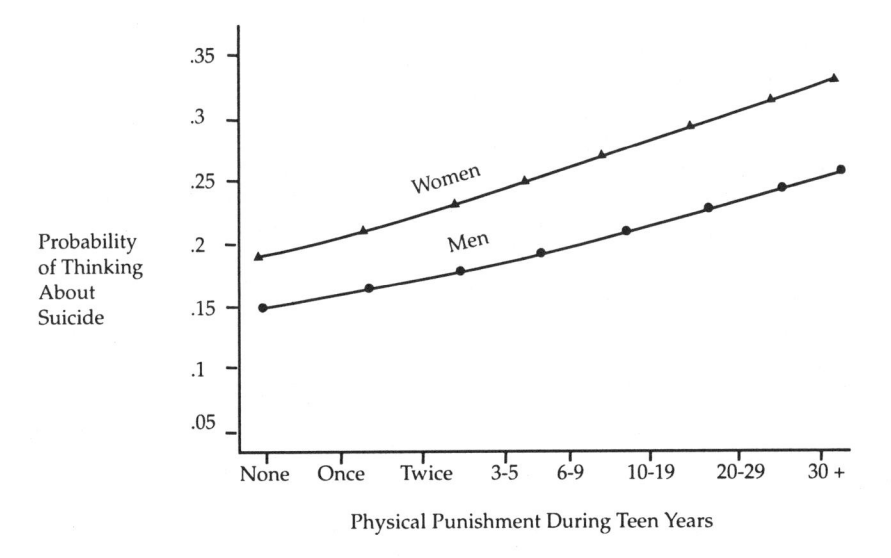

Figure 12.4. Probability of Thinking About Suicide by Physical Punishment During Teen Years

of a risk factor. It increases the risk of being killed, but even in countries that suffered millions of casualties in World War II, only a small percentage of the population were killed. Heavy smoking (a pack a day or more) is a risk factor. It increases the risk of dying of lung cancer 34 times, but despite that, two-thirds of those who smoke this much do *not* die of any smoking-related diseases (Mattson, Pollack, & Cullen, 1987). Corporal punishment is also a risk factor. Like most pack-a-day smokers, most children who are hit by parents will experience few or no long-term problems, but the proportion who do is 1.8 to 3.9 times greater, depending on the type of problem.

Spanking Is Not Necessary

By and large, parents do not like to hit children. They do so because they want to produce well-behaved children and adults. So it is ironic and tragic that using corporal punishment to deal with immediate problems *increases* the probability that the child will ultimately engage in delinquent and criminal acts, have a drinking problem, become depressed or suicidal, and so on. Moreover, research now under way shows a number of other adverse effects that, because of space limitations, cannot be discussed in this chapter, including an increased probability of drug use, alienation, and lowered occupational and economic achievement.

There is no need to expose our children to these risks for the sake of the immediate control that corporal punishment seems to provide, because the evidence is that corporal punishment is not more effective than alternative modes of dealing with misbehavior. There is an almost limitless list of alternatives, such as expressing outrage at the misbehavior, explaining, time-out, removing the child from the situation, denying privileges, and refusing to continue an activity unless the child corrects his or her behavior.

Spanking Should Be Illegal

The laws of every state permit parents to use corporal punishment, and the informal cultural norms verge on requiring it "when necessary." This cultural norm should be replaced by one that says that a child should *never* be hit. Those are the rules for employees and even prisoners. We owe our children and ourselves nothing less. That has been the law in Sweden since 1979, and several other countries have followed that lead. If a Swedish parent does use corporal punishment, he or she is not punished. Instead, the transgression is taken as evidence that the parent is having trouble managing the child and needs help, and the help is provided.

There are signs that other industrial nations are moving to outlaw corporal punishment. Many long-run benefits are likely to accrue when this happens in the United States. For parents it will mean, on average, less hassle in bringing up children; it should also result in better-behaved children. For children it will mean less risk of being physically abused and less risk of being delinquent. For the next generation of Americans it will mean less wife beating, "street crime," drug and alcohol abuse, and depression and suicide, and greater occupational and economic achievement. For American society, bringing up children without any use of corporal punishment is likely to result in less money being expended on treatment for the many social and psychological problems that the use of corporal punishment engenders; the nation will be healthier, less violent, and wealthier.

References

Elmer, E., & Gregg, G. (1967). Developmental characteristics of abused children. *Pediatrics, 69*, 596-602.

Gelles, R. J., & Straus, M. A. (1988). *Intimate violence*. New York: Simon & Schuster.

Lefkowitz, M., Eron, L., Walder, L., & Huesmann, L. (1977). *Growing up to be violent: A longitudinal study of the development of aggression*. New York: Pergamon.

Mattson, M. E., Pollack, E. S., & Cullen, J. W. (1987). What are the odds that smoking will kill you? *American Journal of Public Health, 77,* 425-431.

Maurer, A. (1974). Corporal punishment. *American Psychologist, 29,* 614-626.

Parke, R., & Slaby, R. (1983). The development of aggression. In P. Mussen (Ed.), *Handbook of child psychology* (Vol. 4, pp. 547-621). New York: John Wiley.

Straus, M. A. (1991). Discipline and deviance: Physical punishment of children and violence and other crime in adulthood. *Social Problems, 38,* 101-123.

Straus, M. A., & Gelles, R. J. (Eds.). (1990). *Physical violence in American families: Risk factors and adaptations to violence in 8,145 families*. New Brunswick, NJ: Transaction.

Straus, M. A., Gelles, R. J., & Steinmetz, S. K. (1980). *Behind closed doors: Violence in the American family*. Garden City, NY: Doubleday.

Straus, M. A., & Kaufman Kantor, G. (1992). *Corporal punishment by parents of adolescents: A risk factor in the epidemiology of depression, suicide, alcohol abuse, child abuse, and wife beating*. Durham: University of New Hampshire, Family Research Laboratory.

Wauchope, B. A., & Straus, M. A. (1990). Physical punishment and physical abuse of American children: Incidence rates by age, gender, and occupational class. In M. A. Straus & R. J. Gelles (Eds.), *Physical violence In American families: Risk factors and adaptations to violence in 8,145 families*. New Brunswick, NJ: Transaction.

Widom, C. S. (1989). The cycle of violence. *Science, 244*(4901), 160-166.

Wolfe, D. A. (1987). *Child abuse: Implications for child development and psychopathology*. Newbury Park, CA: Sage.

NO ROBERT E. LARZELERE

Some corporal punishment used by parents *is* clearly abusive, as evidenced by unacceptable rates of physical child abuse in our society (Straus & Gelles, 1986). The controversial aspect of this issue concerns whether *all* corporal punishment by parents should also be considered abusive. Because of the high rates of child abuse, several advocates are pushing an Eighteenth Amendment type of approach to its prevention. Just as that amendment failed to stop alcohol abuse, the available evidence suggests that a blanket prohibition of all parental spanking would also be counterproductive, an overly simplistic solution to the child abuse problem.

An alternative preventive approach is to clarify the distinctions between abusive and beneficial forms of corporal punishment. The available data, though sketchy, indicate that parental spanking is generally beneficial to the child at least under the following conditions:

1. Spanking is limited to a maximum of two slaps to the buttocks with an open hand.
2. The child is between ages 2 and 6.
3. Spanking is used to supplement positive parenting, not to replace it.
4. Spanking is used primarily to back up less aversive discipline responses, such as verbal correction or time-out.

Behavioral parent training programs have done an excellent job of documenting their own effectiveness for reducing children's behavior problems. These programs include a time-out discipline response to targeted misbehavior. Most behavioral programs for children from ages 2 to about 10 also prescribe a detailed spanking procedure to be used only for noncompliance with time-out. For example, Forehand and McMahon (1981) specify:

> The parent is then instructed what to do if the child decides to leave time out while it is still in force. The child should be immediately returned to the chair. The first time this ever occurs, the parent states, "If you get off the chair again, I will spank you." This warning is only presented once.... If the child gets off the chair again, the parent returns the child to the time out area. She or he then administers two (and only two) spanks on the child's bottom with an open hand. (pp. 79-80)

They go on to say, "While we are basically opposed to physical punishment, we have found a mild spanking to be the most feasible backup for the child leaving the time out chair" (p. 80). Research has shown that such a backup procedure improves the effectiveness of time-out (Bean & Roberts, 1981). Further, the only alternative backup procedure that has done as well at improving time-out compliance is the "barrier" method, which could be considered even more aversive than a mild spanking (Day & Roberts, 1983; Roberts, 1988; Roberts & Powers, 1990). It involves using a barrier (e.g., a 4-foot-high plywood sheet) to prevent a child from escaping the time-out room. Other backups, such as a holding procedure (Roberts & Powers, 1990) and response cost (McMahon & Wells, 1990), work significantly less effectively. Other behavioral parent training programs for children under 9 years of age also explicitly prescribe a mild spanking to enforce time-out compliance (e.g., Barkley, 1987; Dangel & Polster, 1984).

A second line of research has found that a combination of punishment and reasoning delays the next misbehavior recurrence in toddlers significantly longer than does punishment alone, reasoning alone, or other discipline responses (Larzelere, in press; Larzelere & Schneider, 1991). This holds true for both corporal and noncorporal punishment and for both fighting and disobedience. The combination of punishment and reasoning was found to reduce the subsequent probability of a fighting recurrence by 32% and a disobedience recurrence by 16%. The only response that was as effective as a combination of reasoning and corporal punishment was a combination of noncorporal punishment and reasoning. The latter combination was equally effective for fighting incidents and slightly but not significantly more effective for disobedience incidents (Larzelere & Schneider, 1991).

A further advantage of pairing reasoning with punishment during the toddler years is that it increases the effectiveness of reasoning alone. Sather (1992) found that reasoning alone delays the next misbehavior recurrence longer to the extent it had been recently combined with punishment. This increased effectiveness of a reasoning-alone response occurred whether the recent backup consisted of corporal or noncorporal punishment.

Together, these results suggest the following view of optimal parental discipline responses: In the toddler years, parents should first respond with the least aversive discipline they think will stop the misbehavior. If that does not elicit compliance, they should then turn to more aversive responses, such as noncorporal consequences (e.g., time-out). If the child still fails to comply with the noncorporal consequences, such noncompliance should result in a mild prescribed spanking, patterned after Forehand and McMahon's (1981) guidelines. Such a sequence will make both nonpunitive discipline responses (e.g., reasoning) and noncorporal punishment (e.g., time-out) more effective in achieving compliance later on. Consequently, parents will use such discipline responses more frequently and more effectively, and they will thus use more aversive responses less frequently as the child grows older. This developmental pattern will lead to the effectiveness of noncorporal punishment documented by parent trainers and to the subsequent tendency for parents of well-behaved preadolescents to resort more frequently to reasoning alone than do other parents (Hoffman, 1977).

This view of parental discipline responses is consistent with other lines of research. For example, Baumrind (1973) found authoritative parenting to be associated with optimal child development, both in social responsibility and in individual initiative. According to Baumrind, authoritative parenting is characterized by firm control, high nurturance, and nonrestrictiveness. Authoritative parents are as willing as authoritarian parents and more willing than permissive parents to use corporal punishment as part of their firm control. Baumrind concludes, "The evidence . . . does not indicate that negative reinforcement or corporal punishment per se were harmful or ineffective procedures, but rather that the total pattern of parental control determined the effects on the child of these procedures" (p. 36).

Many readers may be asking, But what about all the empirical evidence against spanking? The major evidence against ordinary parental spanking is that its use correlates positively with antisocial aggression in children. In a review of the relevant literature, the average correlation was a meager .16, explaining only 3% of the variability in children's antisocial aggression (Steinmetz, 1979). Further, some or all of that 3% may be accounted for by the children's effect on the parents instead of the parents' effect on the children. In four longitudinal studies, only 1 of 26 tests showed a significant association between spanking and subsequent aggression. The average correlation between spanking at the first measurement occasion and antisocial aggression at the second measurement occasion was .03 (Chamberlin, 1978; Johannesson, 1974; Lefkowitz, Huesmann, & Eron, 1978; Sears, 1961).

Other evidence against the aggression-modeling view of spanking is that the outlawing of all parental spanking in Sweden may have increased that country's child abuse rate. Gelles and Edfeldt (1986) found that, one year after spanking by parents was abolished, the Swedish rate of child beating or threatening to use or using a weapon against a child was two to four times as large as the U.S. rate. However, they report that this did not produce a significant difference on their indices of severe violence. (It probably would have been significantly higher than the 1985 U.S. rate reported in Straus & Gelles, 1986.) This high rate of child abuse is surprising, because Sweden is less violent than the United States on other measures. For example, the Swedish murder rate is less than half that of the United States. Further, the antispanking law would supposedly suppress self-reports of child abuse, even phone reports made anonymously. So there are several reasons to expect a lower child abuse rate in Sweden than in the United States, and the effect of outlawing spanking is one of the few possible explanations for why it was so high in 1980.

But what mechanism might lead to the paradoxical result that banning spanking would increase rates of child abuse? We have little empirical evidence on this issue because of the widespread assumption that decreased spanking would decrease child abuse. Baumrind (1973) does report that permissive parents, who were the most antispanking of her three parenting groups, admitted more often to "explosive attacks of rage in which they inflicted more pain or injury upon the child than they had intended. . . . Permissive parents apparently became violent because they felt that they could neither control the child's behavior nor tolerate its effect upon themselves" (p. 35). So it could be that a prohibition against all spanking eliminates the type of mild spanking that serves to maintain control before a child's misbehavior leads to an escalation into a coercive cycle of violence (Patterson, 1982). The use of mild spanking as a backup for less aversive discipline responses may subsequently make those less aversive responses more effective by themselves, thereby eliminating the need for further corporal punishment.

Given the meagerness of the data against moderate spanking, the antispanking movement is in danger of becoming merely an attempt to impose the values of one segment of society upon others. Well-educated social scientists tend to be highly verbal and thus to favor exclusively verbal solutions to interpersonal conflict of all kinds. To others, however, actions may speak louder than words, a reasonable alternative as long as those actions are not abusive. For example, one parent training program that used lower socioeconomic groups of parents as an advisory committee in its development found that those parents advocated the inclusion of additional material about spanking in the program (Dangel & Polster, 1984). Asian immigrants who have traditionally included spanking as part of parental socialization but hear that spanking may result in their children being taken away from them in the United States often end up abdicating their parental responsibility altogether (Thomas, 1992). At a minimum, some implementations of the current child abuse laws have been insensitive to cultural differences (Thomas, 1992), and these problems of cultural insensitivity may be increased if moderate forms of spanking also come to be considered abusive.

In conclusion, the available evidence suggests that some moderate spanking of children from 2 to 6 years of age is effective, particularly as a backup to less aversive discipline responses such as reasoning and time-out. We need more research if we are to be able to distinguish further between appropriate from inappropriate uses of corporal punishment. Until we do our research homework on potentially beneficial spanking, it is premature to impose a guilt trip on the vast majority of parents for ordinary spanking. However, we are in a position to suggest spanking guidelines to parents who intend to include it in their discipline repertoire. It is conceivable that such an approach may do more to reduce child abuse and other negative effects on children than would a premature call to consider all spanking abuse in order to abolish it.

References

Barkley, R. A. (1987). *Defiant children: A clinician's manual for parent training.* New York: Guilford.

Baumrind, D. (1973). The development of instrumental competence through socialization. In A. D. Pick (Ed.), *Minnesota Symposia on Child Psychology* (Vol. 7, pp. 3-46). Minneapolis: University of Minnesota Press.

Bean, A. W., & Roberts, M. W. (1981). The effect of timeout release contingencies on changes in child noncompliance. *Journal of Abnormal Child Psychology, 9,* 95-105.

Chamberlin, R. W. (1978). Relationships between child-rearing styles and child behavior over time. *American Journal of Diseases of Children, 132,* 155-160.

Dangel, R. F., & Polster, R. A. (1984). Winning! A systematic, empirical approach to parent training. In R. F. Dangel & R. A. Polster (Eds.), *Parent training* (pp. 162-201). New York: Guilford.

Day, D. E., & Roberts, M. W. (1983). An analysis of the physical punishment component of a parent training program. *Journal of Abnormal Child Psychology, 11,* 141-152.

Forehand, R. L., & McMahon, R. J. (1981). *Helping the noncompliant child.* New York: Guilford.

Gelles, R. J., & Edfeldt, A. W. (1986). Violence towards children in the United States and Sweden. *Child Abuse and Neglect, 10,* 501-510.

Hoffman, M. L. (1977). Moral internalization: Current theory and research. In L. Berkowitz (Eds.), *Nebraska Symposium on Motivation* (Vol. 25, pp. 169-217). Lincoln: University of Nebraska Press.

Johannesson, I. (1974). Aggressive behavior among school children related to maternal practices in early childhood. In J. DeWit & W. W. Hartup (Eds.), *Determinants and origins of aggressive behavior* (pp. 413-426). The Hague: Mouton.

Larzelere, R. E. (in press). Empirically justified uses of spanking: Toward a discriminating view of corporal punishment. *Journal of Psychology and Theology.*

Larzelere, R. E., & Schneider, W. N. (1991, August). *Does parental punishment reduce misbehavior in toddlers? Testing predictions from behavioral vs. survey research.* Paper presented at the annual meeting of the American Psychological Association, San Francisco.

Lefkowitz, M. M., Huesmann, L. R., & Eron, L. D. (1978). Parental punishment: A longitudinal analysis of effects. *Archives of General Psychiatry, 35,* 186-191.

McMahon, R. J., & Wells, K. C. (1990, November). *Parent training for the treatment of noncompliance in young children.* Preconvention institute at the annual meeting of the Association for Advancement of Behavior Therapy, San Francisco.

Patterson, G. R. (1982). *Coercive family process.* Eugene, OR: Castalia.

Roberts, M. W. (1988). Enforcing chair timeouts with room timeouts. *Behavior Modification, 12,* 353-370.

Roberts, M. W., & Powers, S. W. (1990). Adjusting chair timeout enforcement procedures for oppositional children. *Behavior Therapy, 21,* 257-271.

Sather, P. (1992). *Side effects of parental punishment of toddlers.* Unpublished doctoral dissertation, Biola University.

Sears, R. R. (1961). Relation of early socialization experiences to aggression in middle childhood. *Journal of Abnormal and Social Psychology, 63,* 466-492.

Steinmetz, S. K. (1979). Disciplinary techniques and their relationship to aggressiveness, dependency, and conscience. In W. R. Burr, R. Hill, F. I. Nye, & I. L. Reiss (Eds.), *Contemporary theories about the family* (Vol. 1, pp. 405-438). New York: Free Press.

Straus, M. A., & Gelles, R. J. (1986). Societal change and change in family violence from 1975 to 1985 as revealed by the national surveys. *Journal of Marriage and the Family, 48,* 465-479.

Thomas, J. (1992). An interview with Amy Okamura. *Advisor, 5*(2), 16-18.

NO JOHN K. ROSEMOND

Discussion (hah!) of this volatile topic generally begins with someone asking, Do you *believe* in spanking children? Strange—as if spanking is some sort of religious principle or experience. There are some, in fact, who would have parents believe that by spanking children on a regular basis, they are pleasing God and doing His (this is definitely a guy-God) will, but I am not one of those.

Speaking for myself, spanking has never been a religious experience. I do not believe that one spoils the child by sparing the rod, or switch, or belt, or hand. But, true confession time, I have, on occasion, spanked my children. When they were much younger, that is (they're both adults). And, in retrospect, given the same situations and outrageous behaviors, I would probably do so again. I have no regrets. But I don't *believe* in spanking.

I am not of an extremist persuasion on this issue. I issue that disclaimer realizing that by admitting I've taken an occasional hand (and only a hand, I assure you) to my children, I join, in the minds of some, the ranks of the vile. Nonetheless, I do not believe that spankings are necessary to the proper rearing of children. Nor do I believe that spankings are, in and of themselves, abusive.

So, what *do* I believe? I believe that spankings are a lousy form of discipline. In fact, I believe they do not warrant being classed as discipline at all. At best, a spanking is nothing more, nothing less, than a dramatic form of nonverbal communication. It is a means of getting the attention of a child who needs to give that attention quickly; of terminating a behavior that is rapidly escalating out of control; of putting an exclamation point in front of a message the child needs to hear.

The spontaneously delivered (as in without warning) spank to the child's rear end says, "Stop!" and "Now hear this!" Having terminated the behavior in question (a tantrum, for example), having secured the child's attention, it is necessary that the parent follow through with a consequence of one sort or another. The spank is merely the prelude to the consequence. In the final analysis, the spank is, therefore, inconsequential. The follow-through is what's important. Without proper follow-through a spanking is, at the very least, stupid.

The parent might send the child to his or her room for a time, or take away a privilege for the remainder of the day, or simply give the child a stern reprimand. For the most part, and for the purposes of our discussion, the form the consequence takes is fairly arbitrary. All-important is that the spanking not be the consequence, the end in itself. When spankings are treated as an end in and of themselves, parents misuse, overuse, and edge ever closer to abuse. No doubt about it, spankings can be administered abusively.

But, then, banishing a child to his or her room can be done abusively. It would be abusive, for instance, to lock the child's door and keep the child in confinement for days. And one can reprimand a child about his or her misbehavior abusively. It would, for example, be abusive to refer to the child as a "little shit." But sending children to their rooms and reprimanding them are not, in and of themselves, abusive. Nor are spankings. But, in the wrong hands, they can be.

At this point, the naysayer is probably inclined to say, Given that there's no way of knowing in advance who will spank abusively and who will not, let's just bypass the risk by making spanking illegal. The same argument can be made for sending children to their rooms and talking to them, thus it is absurd, rhetorical (as all the naysayer's arguments will prove to be).

The term *corporal punishment* is problematic to this, uh, discussion because a properly administered spanking is not, strictly speaking, a punishment. Nor, for that matter, is a wrongly administered spanking. According to the scientific definition, a punishment is a consequence that renders the behavior that preceded it less likely to reoccur. But people who believe they can spank certain behaviors out of existence are going to discover otherwise. Their frustration is likely to drive them to spank more often and harder. Almost inevitably, these folks wind up spanking abusively. But it is important to understand that these are not necessarily abusive people. Often, perhaps more often than not, these are people who want to do right by their children. The proper intervention here is education, not legislation.

When I am asked, by the courts or social services, to counsel parents who have spanked a child or children abusively, I rarely waste time attempting to persuade these folks to stop spanking. Instead of trying to paddle back up the stream of their upbringing, I advise them on how to spank *strategically*, as in occasionally, at carefully selected times, and only to secure the child's attention. This has not won me friends at social services (where one can generally find one of the largest concentration of emotionally charged zealots in the free world), but has definitely reduced recidivism among these clients.

It is appropriate, at this point, to define what, in my estimation, constitutes an appropriate manner of applying a spank to a child's rear end. I believe (that word again) in spanking as a first resort; in spanking in anger; in spanking only with one's hand; in spanking only the child's rear end; in administering only one, certainly no more than two, spanks at a time. I also believe that the more often one spanks, the less effective the spankings will be at terminating undesirable behaviors and securing the child's attention. In order to retain a spank's effectiveness, parents must spank only once in the proverbial blue moon.

Spank as a first resort? That's right. Spontaneously. As soon as you see that the child is losing control or as soon as the child commits whatever completely outrageous act (e.g., spitting on an adult). Whack! "Now hear this!" Send the child to his room. Done. As one builds up to a spanking with warning and threat, one builds frustration. When, under those "last resort" circumstances, the spanking finally comes, it is likely to consist of a whack, whack, whack, whack, whack, whack, whack, whack, whack. That's when spankings become abuse.

Spank in anger? That's right. If you're going to spank a child's rear end, it is rightful to make perfectly clear you disapprove of the child's behavior. You are displeased, as in angry. Not in a rage, however. You are not in a rage because you've spanked as a first resort. You are just angry, and you are able to communicate that emotion clearly.

Add the hand only, not belts, switches, spoons, or whatever. Add to the child's rear end only, not thighs, face, arms, or whatever. Add once, maybe twice. Add the message and the consequence, the follow-through, and you've got a properly administered spanking. But I don't *believe* in spanking. You can do without them, if you choose.

"So, then, let's do without them!" No, I said *you* can do without them. You choose for you. I'll choose for me. You accept responsibility for your behavior, but do me the favor of not trying to accept responsibility for mine, okay? I'll handle that myself, thank you.

You see, what really, truly bothers me about the naysayers is they think they know what's best for everyone. Beneath the veneer of social concern, they're pseudointellectual, politically correct megalomaniacs. If you don't agree with them, they want to pass laws that make you agree, or at least conform to their ideas of what constitutes appropriate behavior. They believe they are ordained, by virtue of moral superiority, to create a perfect world, and have a right to impose that vision on us all, by whatever means necessary.

They say spankings are abusive. Why? Because they are acts of violence. I say not necessarily. Spankings can be violent. On the other hand, spankings can simply be dramatic. But the naysayers' swollen egos prevent acceptance of any other point of view. There is but one proper point of view. Theirs.

They say that spankings teach children that violence is an acceptable means of responding to interpersonal conflict. This, they assert, is "proven" by the "fact" that violent and/or abusive adults, almost to the person, were abused as children. Accepting the truth in the latter, it nonetheless proves nothing about spanking. By assuming, a priori, that spankings are abusive, the argument violates one of the precepts of rational inquiry. Furthermore, the argument fails to consider the many, many, many people who were spanked as children (some, like myself, fairly often) who are not, as adults, violent or abusive. (I realize, however, that by admitting I was spanked as a child and that I spanked my children, I've "proven" their argument.)

They wave research that "clearly proves" that spanking destroys self-esteem, promotes violent behavior, and so on. The research stinks. All of it. There is not one study into the effects of spanking on children that's worth the paper it's written on. Every single one of them (I've reviewed them all, I think) is rife with design problems. This so-called research would be ridiculed in a sophomore course in experimental psychology.

In the first place, there is no research that tracks children who were spanked properly as opposed to improperly. To my knowledge, that distinction has never been made by any researcher. That reveals something important about many, if not most, of these so-called researchers. They're not doing research at all. They're trying to promote their own personal agendas. And they cloak this promotion, this shameless propaganda effort, in the guise of "science."

But as long as we're talking lousy research, I'll bring out some of my own. We'll compare lousy research with lousy research. That way, we'll stand on equal ground. My lousy research involves me and my two children. As I said, I spanked them. They're fine, thank you. They're achievement oriented, but not compulsively so. They're responsible, but do not take life seriously. They're gregarious, but not self-centered. They've never given one indication of an inclination toward violence. They're not perfect. They have their share of problems, as do we all, but not big ones. Just typical ones, the ones that come with lack of experience and maturity. Therefore, the research—my research—disproves all the other research. My research "clearly proves" there is a proper way of spanking children that is not abusive, that does not result in damage to a child's self-esteem or significant emotional damage of any other description.

When all is said and done, this argument isn't about spanking, or corporal punishment. It's about people. It's about people who want to create a perfect world. It's about politics and political correctness. It's about people who want to impose their ideology on everyone, by hook or crook. And the more frustrated they become, the more outrageous they become, the more dangerous they become. That's the problem with moral superiority, in any form. Frustrated, it inclines toward totalitarianism.

The problem with spanking is not spanking, it's people. It's a people problem that will not be solved through legislation. It will, in fact, never be completely solved, only mitigated. It can be mitigated through education. So, let's begin the education, keeping in mind that the best, most effective educators, the ones who cause people to truly want to listen, inquire, and learn, don't promote extremist points of view.

JOHN K. ROSEMOND RESPONDS

I've come to the conclusion that this debate is more about politics than it is about psychology. The hidden agenda is the desire on the part of a vocal minority within my profession and related fields to write social policy and thereby impose their vision of a perfect world upon the rest of us.

Everyone would agree that *at some point* a spanking does indeed become abuse. Likewise, a reprimand, at some point, becomes abuse. According to the logic of the antispanking argument, therefore, we should ban the use of all "negative language" when addressing children. Or, because confining a child to his or her room puts the child at greater risk for claustrophobia, parents should be prohibited, by law, from exercising this "riskier" form of discipline. If you think these are absurd parodies of the antispanking mentality, you are naive. Let me assure you that we are talking about folks who, if given an inch in the social policy realm, will want a mile.

We are to believe spanking has a "hidden curriculum" that teaches children, first, that hitting is morally acceptable and, second, "those who love you, hit you." Antispankers cannot, of course, prove any of this. The rhetoric of the argument is emotionally seductive (which is, after all, the point of rhetoric), but in the final analysis it is nothing more than undiluted psychobabble—a construction of language, not of fact.

On the matter of studies that demonstrate a correlation between spanking and the later abuse of wives, children, and self, it should be noted that these studies—*all* of them—are characterized by design problems so obvious and pervasive as to send a graduate student of experimental methods into gales of laughter. For one thing, the self-reports of people who have run afoul of authorities because of such problems can hardly be relied upon. For another, correlation is not cause. For another, as every text on experimental methods will tell you, ex post facto investigations are next to worthless. For yet another, the authors of such studies cannot be accused of objectivity. In other words, despite the impressive bibliography, this isn't science. What we have here is a shrewd attempt on the part of social policy activists within the professional community to use psychobabble and pseudoscience as the basis for law.

According to the politically correct argument, a hand laid to a child's rear end is abuse. Americans are engaged in mass denial of this "fact." Only the chosen few see through the wall of denial. As the rest of us are unwilling to admit our error, the only option is to pass laws that turn the average parent into a criminal. Not to worry, however, because offending parents won't be punished. They will be given "help." And who, pray tell, will provide this help? Why "helping professionals," of course. So the hidden agenda is not just political, but economic as well.

We are told that antispanking laws will transform us into a "healthier, less violent, and wealthier" society. In truth, such laws will only line the pockets of desperately codependent professionals whose lust for power and need to "help" people know no bounds.

ROBERT E. LARZELERE RESPONDS

Here and elsewhere, Murray Straus provides better data to support the blanket antispanking position than do other advocates for that position. The juxtaposition of his data and mine suggests some important differences between potentially abusive and beneficial uses of corporal punishment. The most relevant distinctions seem to depend upon the age of the child, the intensity of spanking, whether or not spanking is used in combination with reasoning, and whether or not spanking is used to back up less aversive discipline responses.

He also suggests an important hypothesis about the hidden curriculum of corporal punishment: Does it teach people to hit the ones they love? It will be important to get adequate data on this hypothesis and to determine whether this hidden curriculum applies to all parental uses of corporal punishment or to some types more than others.

Straus's data do show that the frequency of parental spanking of teenagers is at least a marker variable for increased risk of a wide variety of negative outcomes. The crucial question is whether such corporal punishment is a causal or noncausal marker variable. For example, being in a hospital would be a marker variable indicating an increased risk of dying. That does not imply, however, that we can reduce premature deaths by eliminating hospitals. Instead, hospitalization is a noncausal marker variable indicating that something is medically wrong, which in turn increases the risk of death. Straus has shown that frequently spanked teenagers are at increased risk for negative outcomes, but the data do not yet indicate whether spanking itself increases that risk or whether it is a noncausal marker variable. It might merely reflect the level of teenage antisocial behavior or a breakdown in the parent-child relationship. This by no means justifies parental spanking of teenagers, but simply points out that the current data do not conclusively support even a blanket prohibition of parental spanking of teenagers.

The evidence is clear that mild parental spanking is beneficial for the child under certain circumstances at least between ages 2 and 6. Straus provides a list of alternative discipline responses, but the effectiveness of the most important alternatives (explanation and time-out) has been shown to improve after being backed up with a mild spanking. This suggests that many nonspanking parents of well-behaved teenage children may have arrived at that point by shaping the effectiveness of nonspanking discipline responses with a mild-spanking backup in earlier years. Such an optimal pattern of discipline responses should not be undermined by a premature conclusion that all spanking is abusive.

MURRAY A. STRAUS RESPONDS

Response to Larzelere

Although I admire the care and scientific skill with which Robert Larzelere has investigated this critically important issue, I would like to present here some critical points on which we disagree.

Larzelere writes as though the sole issue is whether corporal punishment is effective in correcting misbehavior. But that is only one of the issues. Just as important are the harmful side effects, such as increased risk of the child using those same methods later in life to correct the misbehavior of *a spouse,* increased risk of depression and suicide, and the danger that what starts out as ordinary corporal punishment can escalate into physical abuse. The last of these is not just a theoretical possibility; research by Kadushin and Martin (1981) shows that it is typical of the majority of physical abuse cases.

Even if, for the moment, we restrict the discussion to whether spanking is effective in correcting misbehavior, the studies cited by Larzelere *and his own research* found that "a combination of *non*corporal punishment and reasoning" was as effective as corporal punishment (emphasis added). Given that the best that can be said for spanking is that it is just as effective as noncorporal punishment, why risk the possibility of harmful side effects by using corporal punishment?

The issue is not whether punishment should ever be used. Even informing a child that what he or she has done wrong has a punishment element, because that information is painful. This approach therefore combines punishment with information. I agree with Larzelere when he says that "parents should first respond with the least aversive discipline they think will stop the misbehavior." However, I disagree that spanking should ever be one of the punishments used when less aversive steps do not work.

Larzelere cites an excellent study by Baumrind, but the children of Baumrind's "authoritative" parents are socially responsible and self-directed because their parents use a combination of firm control, love, and nonrestrictiveness, not the fact that these parents also used corporal punishment occasionally. My hypothesis is that if those parents had been equally firm, loving, and nonrestrictive, but left out the corporal punishment, they would have been even more effective in producing responsible and self-directed children.

Gelles and Edfeldt's (1986) study of the Swedish law banning corporal punishment cannot be used to evaluate that law. The study was done only a year after the law was passed, and that is too short a time for it to have had much effect. Even if the study had been done 5 or 10 years after, it would not provide data on whether the law reduced corporal punishment and physical abuse, because the rates in existence before the law was passed are unknown.

I agree that nonspanking would be a disaster if parents were to take this to mean being permissive regarding children's misbehavior. Children do need firm but loving control, as in Baumrind's authoritative group. But spanking is not needed to achieve this. Some parents, if denied the opportunity to spank, will "give up" on trying to correct misbehavior, but my guess is that these parents would be very few, because most parents are deeply committed to producing responsible children. A more likely danger is that efforts to correct misbehavior will shift from physical aggression (spanking) to verbal aggression (attempts to cause psychological pain by insulting or depreciating the worth of the child). That would truly be disastrous, because psychological attacks have even more harmful effects than do physical attacks (Vissing, Straus, Gelles, & Harrop, 1991). Consequently, educational programs to end corporal punishment must give equal weight to ending verbal attacks on children. Such programs are also needed for parents who spank, because my research shows that parents who spank the most also tend to use the most verbal aggression.

Response to Rosemond

I agree with Rosemond's view that "without proper follow-through a spanking is . . . stupid." But I also disagree with him; in my opinion, what Rosemond thinks of as "follow-through" (such as sending the child to his or her room, taking away a privilege, or administering a stern reprimand) should be the *first* step, not a follow-up. In most cases, such steps alone will do the job.

A related issue concerns Rosemond's advice "to spank *strategically,* as in occasionally, at carefully selected times." The problem is that he contradicts himself by repeated advice to "spank first" (e.g., three paragraphs earlier) and advice to use "spanking as a first resort" (the following paragraph). How limited and strategic can it be if every misbehavior is *first* dealt with by "a spank to the child's rear end"? I think that Rosemond does genuinely want parents to use spanking only rarely, but his advice to do it as a first resort almost guarantees they will do it frequently, with all the adverse effects that he himself notes.

I readily admit to starting from the assumption that spanking is "abusive," just as Rosemond starts from the opposite assumption. The difference between scientists, such as Robert Larzelere and myself, and the "zealots" and "pseudointellectual, politically correct megalomaniacs" (who are well illustrated by John Rosemond!) is that scientists *test* their assumptions and are willing to let the findings of scientific tests have the last word. My research was designed to give the assumption that all spanking is abusive a chance to be either supported or disproved. Unfortunately for prospanking zealots such as John Rosemond, the research found that spanking is associated with harmful side effects. For various technical reasons, we cannot be sure this proves that spanking causes these problems, but we can be sure that the assumed harmful effects of spanking were given the opportunity to be disproved but were not.

Rosemond accuses researchers of shameless propaganda efforts in the name of science. I accuse him of just plain shameless propaganda. He uses the typical propagandist tools of the "big lie" and inflammatory language. He seems to think that the research can be dismissed by calling it "lousy" and saying that it "stinks."

Moreover, Rosemond's idea of evidence is to cite the example of his children and himself—both were spanked and both are okay. Smokers used to make a similar argument; now, however, we know that heavy smoking increases the risk of death from lung cancer and other smoking-related diseases 34 times. But because "only" a third of heavy smokers die from it, two-thirds can say, "I've smoked more than a pack a day all my life and I'm okay," just as Rosemond can say that he spanked his children and they're okay.

Response to Both

Although Larzelere would not put it that way, both he and Rosemond think the previous research "stinks." Some does, but much is excellent, including the study by Larzelere himself, which shows that corporal punishment is *not* more effective than other methods of discipline. In fact, all studies have design defects. However, when many studies are done that have different defects and they all nonetheless find that spanking is associated with harmful side effects, the weight of the evidence supports the idea that spanking is not necessary for bringing up children and should therefore be avoided.

Larzelere and Rosemond favor limited use of spanking but not frequent spanking. The research does show the most harmful side effects occur with frequent spanking. However, my research also shows that even when spanking is used only rarely, there is an increase in the probability of harmful side effects, but only a small increase.

Both Larzelere and Rosemond argue that it is wrong to impose the values of those opposed to spanking on groups and individuals who favor it. I strongly agree with this principle. However, I also strongly agree with another, conflicting, principle: that it is wrong to treat children in ways that threaten their mental and physical health. The evidence is not all in, but when it is, we will have to work out an accommodation between our commitment to individual freedom and our commitment to the well-being of children and of society. In Sweden, this is done by not having a penalty for spanking. Instead, the law assumes that when parents spank, it is because they are having trouble managing a child. The Swedes try to help such parents achieve the kind of control the parents want and that children and society need. This does not involve imposing on people's values, because even parents who approve of spanking "when necessary" prefer that it never be necessary.

References

Gelles, R. J., & Edfeldt, A. W. (1986). Violence towards children in the United States and Sweden. *Child Abuse and Neglect, 10,* 501-510.

Kadushin, A., & Martin, J. A. (1981). *Child abuse: An interactional event.* New York: Columbia University Press.

Vissing, Y. M., Straus, M. A., Gelles, R. J., & Harrop, J. W. (1991). Verbal aggression by parents and psychosocial problems of children. *Child Abuse and Neglect, 15,* 223-238.

DEBATE 13

POSITIVE METHODS

➤ *Should only positive methods be used by professionals who work with children and adolescents?*

EDITORS' NOTE: There is a spirited debate currently taking place about whether or not behavior, no matter how self-injurious or dangerous to others, can be altered by the use of positive methods alone. Some argue that this is possible. Others argue that it is neither possible nor ethical to rely solely on positive methods. The very definitions of *positive* and *aversive methods* are controversial. In the debate presented here, one team of authors argues in favor of using only positive methods, and two separate authors argue against this position. We hope that their discussion will help readers to form their own informed opinions.

Wayne Sailor, Ph.D., and **Edward G. Carr**, Ph.D., say YES. Sailor is Director of the KUAP and Professor in Special Education at the University of Kansas. He is coauthor of "Research on Community Intensive Instruction as a Model for Building Functional, Generalized Skills," which appeared in *Generalization and Maintenance: Lifestyle Changes in Applied Settings* (R. Horner, G. Dunlap, and R. Koegel, eds., 1988). Carr is Professor of Psychology at the State University of New York at Stony Brook, where he is engaged in research on developmental disabilities and severe problem behavior. He is coauthor of *In Response to Aggression* (1981).

James A. Mulick, Ph.D., argues NO. He is a pediatric psychologist specializing in early childhood and developmental disabilities at The Ohio State University, where he is Professor of Pediatrics and Psychology. He is the author of more than 100 research and scholarly publications in psychology, behavior analysis, and developmental disabilities, and coeditor of *The Handbook of Mental Retardation, Parent Professional*

Partnerships in Developmental Disability Services, Prevention of Developmental Disabilities, and the five-volume *Transitions in Mental Retardation* series.

Jay S. Birnbrauer, Ph.D., also argues NO. He is Associate Professor of Psychology at Murdoch University in Perth, Western Australia. Previously he held appointments at the University of Washington, University of North Carolina at Chapel Hill, University of Western Australia, and the Dejarnette Center for Human Development in Staunton, Virginia. In addition to research and teaching, he has been continuously involved in applying behavioral principles to program development and treatment in the area of developmental disabilities and child-family problems. Since 1989, he has codirected the Murdoch Early Intervention Program for Children with Autism. His most pertinent publications are cited in his contribution to this debate.

YES   **WAYNE SAILOR and EDWARD G. CARR**[1]

In the old days, sadly not long ago, people who had disabilities were grouped together for their own safety and protection. Needed social services could be organized in these protective environments in arrangements that were maximally convenient for service providers from a variety of helping professions. Unfortunately, institutional needs took precedence over individual needs and, because difficult-to-manage behavior was disruptive to smooth institutional functioning, it became the major target for an all-out assault.

Happily, the days of institutional prominence have faded. A citizenry possessed of significant disabilities is now to be encountered in public school classrooms, in all areas of public commerce and recreation, and in regular workplaces. Large institutions are rapidly being replaced with smaller shared-living circumstances, and services often need to be provided in public rather than secluded environments.

Imagine for a moment a third-grade classroom in a public school. Ricky, a child with significant disabilities, screams loudly and shoves Jessica, his peer tutor, who has been assisting him to the crafts table. A teacher assistant suddenly appears in the midst of the children and slams his hand, palm down, onto the table in front of Ricky and screams "No! Ricky!" in a very loud and startling manner. Ricky is then forced to do 10 push-ups in front of the classroom while his peers watch. We believe that most of you will agree that such a punishment scenario is unlikely—regardless of its probability of success in the ultimate management of Ricky's problematic behavior. The school is unlikely to tolerate any but the mildest applications of a traditional aversive technology. More complex circumstances, such as those inherent in a child's placement in a public school, call for a more complex technology, and those circumstances will entertain only a *positive* technology of behavior management. Thus professionals who are oriented toward the use of aversives are not bad guys, but simply outdated.

What, then, is the status of the new "nonaversive" technology? What is the changed mission of the practitioner, and what are the different questions posed with respect to the challenge of difficult behavior in community settings? First, it can be argued that when confronted with difficult behavior in complex circumstances, one is less inclined to focus on simply managing the problem behavior; rather, the focus is on determining what is causing, supporting, and maintaining the behavior in these circumstances. The mission of the practitioner is less likely to be to find a single-purpose solution to the behavior problem and more likely to be that of putting together a set of interventions designed to rearrange an entire microsocial system. The outcome of such interventions might well be reduction or elimination of problematic behavior, but might also include measures to assist a social unit (i.e., classroom) in becoming more tolerant of and accommodating to behavior that is outside of the bounds of middle-class, normative expectations.

A perusal of the scientific literature reveals an emerging consensus on at least the following discrete aspects of a positive behavioral technology:

1. the conduct of a systematic *functional analysis* of the problem behavior, that is, trying to discover what *purposes* the problem behavior might serve
2. a systems theory, or *multicomponent* approach to the treatment intervention, rather than a linear or single-component attack on the problem, with all of the interventions geared to the results of the functional analysis, that is, related to the purposive nature of the problem behavior
3. a *skill-development* orientation that emphasizes building behavioral repertoires that are functionally equivalent to the problem repertoires; that is, providing the person with new skills that he or she can use to achieve the same goals that could previously be achieved only through the display of problem behavior
4. *constellational* interventions that are designed to promote changes in the whole-life circumstances (i.e., "lifestyle") of the individual rather than just the modification of his or her problem behavior; that is, a focus on life enhancement, not just behavior reduction
5. an increased emphasis on *antecedents,* or events that precede behavioral problems, rather than an excessive concern for the selection of contingent consequences of the behavior
6. concern for the *ecology* of problem behavioral repertoires; scrutiny of such "setting event" factors as diet, sleeping patterns, exercise regime, noise level, and rapport with others for potential interventions
7. *social validation,* a commitment to the preservation of the civil rights and the dignity of the individual in mainstream society, a guiding principle in structuring interventions, particularly in terms of the level of treatment intrusiveness employed (Horner et al., 1990)

What about crisis management? Some argue that it will always be necessary to have aversive procedures at the ready to deal with dangerous outbursts of self-injurious or aggressive behavior, even when the general approach to behavior management is positive (e.g., Gerhardt, Holmes, Alessandri, & Goodman, 1991). In our opinion, there is sufficient reported progress even in this constricted arena to raise serious questions about the need for aversive measures.

Stimulus control procedures (e.g., altering curricula and staff assignments) now exist to manage crises (Touchette, MacDonald, & Langer, 1985).

As Carr, Robinson, and Palumbo (1990) point out, the critical issue in the 1990s is not the relative efficacy of aversive versus nonaversive behavior management. The question of interest is rather how to develop a technology of assistance that is founded on the establishment of a socially acceptable behavioral repertoire that is functionally equivalent to a problematic repertoire. Historically, under conditions of a "captive population" held in relative isolation from the society at large, we have witnessed the development of a rather extensive technology that has focused on making undesirable behavior less probable. We argue that the time has come to develop, as rapidly as possible, a positive technology that is at least as extensive as the negative one and is focused on making desirable and socially acceptable behavior more probable.

Note

1. This effort was supported in part by a federal grant to the authors as part of the National Research & Training Center on Nonaversive Behavior Management (1987), U.S. Department of Education, National Institute on Disability and Rehabilitation Research, Cooperative Agreement G0087C0234. No official endorsement should be inferred.

References

Carr, E. G., Robinson, S., & Palumbo, L. W. (1990). The wrong issue: Aversive versus nonaversive treatment. The right issue: Functional versus nonfunctional treatment. In A. C. Repp & N. N. Singh (Eds.), *Perspectives on the use of nonaversive and aversive interventions for persons with developmental disabilities* (pp. 361-379). Sycamore, IL: Sycamore.

Gerhardt, P. F., Holmes, D. L., Alessandri, M., & Goodman, M. (1991). Social policy on the use of aversive interventions: Empirical, ethical, and legal considerations. *Journal of Autism and Developmental Disorders, 21,* 265-277.

Horner, R. H., Dunlap, G., Koegel, R. L., Carr, E. G., Sailor, W., Anderson, J., Albin, R., & O'Neill, R. (1990). Toward a technology of "nonaversive" behavioral support. *Journal of the Association for Persons With Severe Handicaps, 15,* 125-132.

Touchette, P. E., MacDonald, R. F., & Langer, S. N. (1985). A scatter plot for identifying stimulus control of problem behavior. *Journal of Applied Behavior Analysis, 18,* 343-351.

NO　　　　　　　　　　　　　　　　　JAMES A. MULICK

I oppose the proposition that professionals should always use exclusively positive methods in work with children and youth. This view is based on a career spent to date mostly in pediatric psychology and clinical child psychology. My professional viewpoint derives from my working with and studying children and youth who have chronic illnesses, children with chronic physical and developmental disorders, and children with unpleasant but transient acute medical problems, as well as children from troubled families, children experiencing the direct and indirect effects of poverty, shattered homes, and unsuccessful school careers, and children who have been abused or neglected or just misunderstood. Although much involved with education and issues related to schools, I have always worked and studied childhood problems from outside the institutional structures of the schools. I have worked as much or more with parents, caregivers, and teachers as I have with the children who were nominally the focus of concern, because scientific understanding and beneficial behavioral change can be achieved only through the personal world of the child in question. In this kind of role, the professional represents a transient influence, whereas the community, its institutions, and the family are the sources of lasting influence and great practical significance for the child. I have come to understand that if beneficial change is to be achieved on behalf of a youngster, the cause of the change must derive to a great extent from the child's natural environment and be of value in the child's family and community. My values, as a person and as a professional, have had to be tempered by an appreciation of the values and goals of the people who will remain important to the child long after my conscious influence has been forgotten.

I will first discuss the conceptual basis for understanding positive methods in behavior analysis and behavioral psychotherapy. I will then discuss the role of aversive motivation in adaptive and maladaptive behavior. Finally, I will attempt to show that aversive motivation has a role in therapeutic intervention.

The Appeal of a Positive Approach

The idea that only positive methods have an appropriate place in therapy with children is an appealing one. Certainly, it feels good to most people when children are happy. Likewise, it feels good to most professionals to be recognized as a source of pleasure by children. It feels good to almost anyone to commend, to approve, to help, to be positive. It feels good to most people when children approach, smile, laugh, and try to stay nearby. Without elaboration, however, these truisms are too vague to discuss with respect to methods to be used by professionals who work with children and youth. The statements lack specificity regarding the additional information needed to judge whether or not therapeutic methods to be employed with children will produce reliable, specific, and beneficial behavioral change.

Indeed, children are best served by an environment that helps them to realize and elaborate their potentialities. *Positive reinforcement* is the behavior-analytic term that describes a contingency between an act and a consequence that leads to the enhanced likelihood that the same act, and ones somewhat like it, will be performed again under similar circumstances—an "elaborative" behavioral relation that describes the accelerative, approach-inducing selective action of certain behavior-environment transactions. Further, there is good reason to believe that the hedonic experience of people capable of demonstrating such a behavioral functional (i.e., causal) relation is one of positive value, a *feeling* of "pleasure." The ability to respond to such positive transactions is a major adaptive mechanism, one that is responsible for much of the growth of behavior that is useful for individual survival and for what is generally accepted as desirable change in the behavioral development of children.

Additional Behavioral Relations

There is another kind of behavioral relation that produces similar elaboration of acts performed by an individual. This relation, called *negative reinforcement*, refers to the accelerative selection of behavior that precedes, or produces, the cessation of events that evoke unconditioned withdrawal. This type of behavior-environment transaction is positive in terms of its effect on behavior, but not in its motivational underpinnings.

Both positive and negative elaborative mechanisms are dependent on more basic motivational systems, specifically, those expressed by appetitive-approach tendencies on the one hand and aversive-withdrawal tendencies on the other hand. The hedonic response to an event or stimulus that evokes withdrawal is negative in the sense that unpleasant feelings and emotional correlates are associated with them. Withdrawal is associated with conscious negative valuation—*aversion* in the sense of its Latin root *verto*, or "turn away." But the emotional correlates of the elaborative contingency of negative reinforcement may be less undesirable, often appropriately characterized as "relief" in everyday discourse. Healthy human infants demonstrate exquisite sensitivity to appetitive and aversive stimuli through unconditioned selective approach and withdrawal reactions at birth (Lipsitt, 1984). It is very likely that both these motivational systems and the behavioral adaptations (i.e., learning) they make possible are essential for normal development.

Punishment, too, is a very heavily laden term. It has a range of meanings that depend on the context in which it is used. There is a judicial meaning that depends on the context of formal codes of law and administrative procedures. There is a cultural context in which punishment is understood as just or unjust, moral or immoral, fair or unfair. There is an emotional context in which the term is recognized by most people as an undesirable type of experience. All these are valid contexts, because they are derived from the past experiences of the people who use the term and the people who understand the term when it is used by others. None of these contexts is precisely what is invoked by the technical use of the term *punishment* in learning theory or its application in behavior modification. Unfortunately, the negative valuation of the term *punishment* is frequently carried over by people, possibly as a result of simple classical conditioning, when it is used as a technical term for a functional behavior-environment relation (Grant & Evans, 1992).

Behavior Modification

Behavior modification is a form of psychotherapy in which the environment of an individual is restructured according to the scientific principles of learning to promote beneficial behavior change. *Punishment,* in this context, has a technical meaning in terms of a functional analysis of behavior. It refers to the planned, response-dependent use of a class of events that evoke active or passive escape and, eventually, promote avoidance of cues that predict the occurrence of such events. By *promote,* I want to suggest the behavioral sense of increased likelihood and increased frequency of behavior under similar conditions in the future. A punishment effect in this context is recognized only in terms of the behavior change it produces. In such terms, then, punishment is reserved for the escape from or avoidance of response-produced or contingent stimuli by means of decreasing performance of the act that has led to the stimuli. In everyday terms, punishment is observed when behavior that produces it stops for a while and then fails to occur as readily the next time similar consequences seem likely to result from the action. Stimuli that can be used this way are also referred to as *aversive.* The focus of interest in such a behavioral relation has traditionally been on the behavior that decreases in frequency, the punished behavior, and not the other behavior that may simultaneously increase in frequency. To be sure, when one behavior decreases in frequency, something else increases, if only to fill the temporal gap created by its absence. The focus is not on emotional distress, pain, humiliation, or other disagreeable, and quite possible, side effects of some stimuli that can function as punishment. Psychotherapy can hardly proceed effectively if people are simply subjected to disturbing experiences without some compensatory benefit. If this were to be allowed to occur, the only result would be avoidance of the therapist.

Even when understood functionally, the use of punishment in behavior modification to suppress or eliminate unwanted behavior is far from straightforward. Arranging to change behavior in the natural environment is a complex affair. The environment of any individual is heterogeneous, consisting of differentially valued components, or potentially appetitive and aversive stimuli, and many cues previously imbued with predictive significance (and acquired value) as a result of past experience. We cannot determine the meaning of an element of another person's environment except by inference from observation of the individual's behavior, indeed, except by performing a functional or causal analysis. Personal experience, to the extent that it is similar, can suggest a starting point for a functional analysis of the environment in terms of another person's behavior, but the very young or the very different (in terms of experience) may regard things so differently as to make our values and expectations irrelevant or even diametrically wrong.

One of the paradoxes of behavioral psychotherapy is that it is not requested when people behave predominantly in harmony with their own goals or in a satisfactory manner with other people. But the functional analysis of behavior assumes that the individual has acquired behavior by interacting with the environment in a lawful, understandable way. How can the lawful and adaptive interaction of an individual with the environment result in a maladaptive outcome? The answer lies in understanding that adaptive capacity differs from person to person, or even in the same person over time, and that environments can change more rapidly or radically than an individual's adaptive capacity can accommodate. The first stage of therapy always consists of assessing the adaptive capacity of an individual, including the person's general health and effectiveness within his or her daily routine, and then determining just what sort of failure of adaptation led to the request for therapy. To oversimplify greatly, but more or less accurately, maladaptation consists of behavior that is ineffective in the long run because it is too "elaborated" (or too frequent, or too forceful, or too invariant, or whatever) in some way, deficient in some way, or both—most often, both.

Problems as Motives for Change

People arrive in therapy in a variety of ways. Some seek therapy for themselves, some have it sought for them. In some cases the request for therapy comes from a true "significant other," a father or mother, a grandparent, a member of the same household with a serious stake in the behavior of other members of the household. Other people who seek therapy for others may be less directly or intimately involved with them. A teacher may refer a child for therapy because of personal concern, because of annoyance, or even as a result of professional ambition—different levels of personal involvement to be sure. Referrals for therapy may be made institutionally in an effort to save or redistribute human or material resources, even to uphold a principle or theory.

By the time the professional judgment is made regarding therapeutic measures to be employed, the legitimacy of the desire for change has already been accepted. But there may be reason to question the legitimacy of the request for behavior change. Determining the legitimacy of the request is among the early tasks of the therapist, for both ethical and practical reasons. Ethically, psychological intervention should benefit the individual or group receiving the services directly, and not solely a caregiver or institutional representative making the request. Practically, the behavior of seeking psychological services is usually functionally related to the behavior to be changed. For example, people may wish to accomplish some shared goal together, or one person's behavior may be unpleasant for others but in part caused by their mutual style of interaction.

There are two reasons a person seeks therapy to alter his or her own behavior. The first, and by far the more common, is that some of the direct effects of the individual's behavior have become undesirable. A teenager may believe that the long-term benefits of weight loss, such as increased attractiveness and greater social opportunity, would be extremely desirable, but be unable on a day-to-day basis to forgo the pleasure of excessive eating. An 11-year-old may wish to experience an important ceremonial activity at school or in a religious organization, but be afraid to do so because of a stutter or a tic, indiscriminate fear, or a problem in learning the necessary actions. In each case, the desirable outcome is prevented by some other behavior that is presumably maintained by more immediate or more powerful influences. Whether grounded in observable behavior that interferes with reaching the desired goal or a lack of behavior needed to achieve the desired outcome, the individual is experiencing an unpleasant—or aversive—circumstance that itself is undesirable.

A second major source of aversive motivation that impels a person to seek therapeutic help involves the social feedback that may typically follow some behavior. Others may ostracize or ridicule an individual because of the way that persons acts or the image he or she presents, resulting in considerable social punishment of the person's attempts to interact. If the social punishment is poorly timed, or is aimed at the person and not the undesirable behavior, no useful or relevant behavior change will be promoted. The mere approach of the unfortunate individual may be all that is punished. Much negative social feedback that is unplanned and emotionally mediated is of this nature; consequently, people feel impelled to change but experience only inconsistent or misdirected social feedback. Such people come to feel there may be something wrong with them, but remain unable to determine just what. A functional analysis in the everyday social environment often reveals these behavioral relations, helping to pinpoint the individual peculiarities that have led to the undesirable social feedback. This process, in turn, indicates the possible goals of behavior change and the environmental intervention that will serve to increase desirable feedback for the distressed individual.

Another reason people arrive in therapy is that their behavior has become intolerable to someone with the power to cause them to go there. This is the most frequent reason for parents to bring young children to therapy. Frequent nighttime awakening, bad habits, tantrums, biting or hitting others, and so forth are common clinical problems of young children. Seriously disturbed individuals sometimes fall into this category as well. Young children and people with serious disturbance may have no desire for change, but others may strongly perceive such a need on their behalf. The parent or caregiver may have a realistic perception of a problem or be motivated by his or her own needs to have the child change. In either case, the current behavior of the "patient" could be adaptive in the sense that it leads to desirable outcomes for him or her, at least in some sense. Effective intervention, depending on the results of a functional analysis of the source of the mismatch between the people, may emphasize change by either the nominal patient or the person(s) making the request for therapy.

Normative Adaptation

The very young seem especially likely to acquire behavior that parents will do anything to stop. In fact, the young of many species exhibit the same ability, that of evoking caregiving by emitting behavior aversive to the parents. The ability has obvious survival value when the young are born helpless and dependent on parental caregiving. For example, the distress cries of newborns seem to be particularly salient stimuli for adults of many species (Pryce, 1992). They are easily elicited by discomfort, such as a decrease in body temperature or hunger. As development proceeds, in many species, they are evoked by the absence of the parent. They tend to cease immediately when parental contact or suckling is initiated. They cease not as a result of punishment at such times, but because the newborn is engaged in some hedonically positive alternate activity (e.g., feeding and often emitting nondistress vocalizations). Suckling provides nourishment, stimulates the release of endogenous opioid peptides called endorphins in the newborn that act as natural analgesics similar to morphine, and decreases general activity leading to drowsiness (Blass, 1990).

It is no accident that newborn distress cries usually are perceived as aversive (evoking escape efforts designed to terminate them) by parents. This aversive behavioral relation is supplemented by appetitive mechanisms that keep parents close to their offspring, such as the pleasurable feedback afforded mothers during nursing via the reduction of pressure in the breast from the buildup of milk, or tactile interactions such as mutual touching and grooming. Suckling, in turn, stimulates the release of the maternal hormones prolactin and oxytocin, which then, respectively, increase milk production and its release from the breast (Larson & Smith, 1974). Without such behavioral mechanisms that help to maintain parental proximity, of course, adults would just leave offspring to their own devices when their behavior becomes noxious. These mutual bonding mechanisms, as they are sometimes called, clearly depend upon both appetitive and aversive behavioral transactions.

The astute reader will have noticed something about the behavioral relations just described. They represent mutually reinforcing relations. The behavior of the one serves to increase the behavior of the other, and vice versa. The newborn's distress calls are followed by desirable consequences, positive reinforcement, such as restoring bodily warmth or becoming quietly satiated with nourishing mother's milk. If developmentally capable of such learning, the newborn will be more likely to do the same things the next time it gets cold or hungry. In turn, the parent has succeeded in acting to turn off the aversive distress calls, reducing the newborn to a state of satisfied near unconsciousness. This behavioral relation is negative reinforcement. The parent can be expected to try doing some of the same things the next time distress calls begin, drawing the newborn close, sharing the warmth of her body, and feeding the newborn.

The normative importance of sensitivity to noxious stimulation, and the aversively motivated learning it makes possible in development (and in parenting), is not to be minimized. Weaning usually occurs partly through a process of reciprocal aversive conditioning (Pryce, 1992); so that, for example, the newborn's sharp teeth and increasing strength and weight decrease the net hedonic valuation of the experience for the mother, while her increasingly vigorous attempts to free herself from such stimulation by force decrease the offspring's tendency to approach her preferentially for nourishment. Motor development and coordination are facilitated in part by the push and pull, respectively, of avoidance of uncomfortable falls or too intense stretching and the relentless pursuit of appetitive goals. Quite clearly, absence of sensitivity to pain and other forms of negative feedback poses a danger to children who might otherwise pursue potentially injurious methods without inhibition to achieve some attractive goal.

Aversive Intervention Strategies

When accelerative learning processes have led to a maladaptive excess of some behavior, a clear therapeutic goal is to decrease the behavior to lower levels of performance. The young need to learn what not to do, as well as what to do. There are a number of ways to accomplish this outcome, at least theoretically. Reinforcement could be restricted, allowed only for some alternate adaptive behavior, arranged exclusively for lower-intensity or more adaptive forms of the same behavior, or just withheld completely following the maladaptive behavior. These all would urge the maladaptive behavioral excess in the desired direction. It should be noted, however, that nonreinforcement of behavior is experienced as a negative event (Leitenberg, 1965) in that an individual would work to avoid it.

Sometimes feasible positive interventions are not practical. The therapist may be unable to alter aspects of a child's environment or to persuade all people involved with the child to change their styles of interaction. Some reinforcement contingencies responsible for maladaptive behavior may not even be controllable in principle, such as the direct effects of successful theft on the robber or the taste for sexual violence on the perpetrator. In such cases a therapist may still hope to remove the opportunity for performing the maladaptive behavior. This can be done by reorganizing the young person's daily routine in a way that would provide little or no occasion for the maladaptive behavior to occur (Touchette, MacDonald, & Langer, 1985). If the effort is successful, and if the young person can learn new and equally rewarding behavioral alternatives in the meantime, then it can be hoped that gradual reintroduction of the old routines will not lead to a resumption of the behavior. Therapists rarely have such potent influence over even a very young child's complex daily routine and all the people involved in it that such a feat can be engineered and maintained. Most often, in practice, reintroduction of the opportunity for the maladaptive behavior results in relapse. Finally, sometimes the behavior is very dangerous or intolerably disruptive to the child's essential social support system.

Under critical circumstances, maladaptive behavior must be stabilized at a low level quickly as a practical necessity, or further attempts to engineer positive aspects of the total environment will never have a chance. Some circumstances call for the use of direct decelerative consequences, the functional behavioral relation called punishment. Other circumstances, such as the unalterable availability of strongly attractive incentives for the maladaptive behavior, might need to be offset by even stronger concurrent disincentives. To this extent, the proposition that only positive means should be employed by professionals who work with children and youth is clearly inappropriate. Aversive motivation has a place in therapy, albeit no doubt a small one, just as it has a role in normal development. Its use, directly by therapists or by caregivers with professional instruction and supervision, calls for systematic assessment of the functional behavioral relations shared by the participants in the social network of the child, the long-term goals and values of these participants, and the expected risks, costs, and benefits of various feasible intervention alternatives (Meinhold & Mulick, 1990, in press). The decision to employ aversive motivation in comprehensive therapeutic interventions (those with multiple aversive and nonaversive components) will sometimes need to be made.

References

Blass, E. M. (1990). Suckling: Determinants, changes, mechanisms, and lasting impressions. *Developmental Psychology, 26*, 520-533.

Grant, L., & Evans, A. N. (1992). Acceptance of labels for response-reduction procedures and the users of those procedures. *Psychological Record, 42*, 355-368.

Larson, B. L., & Smith, V. R. (Eds.). (1974). *Lactation: Vol. 3. Nutrition and biochemistry of milk maintenance.* New York: Academic Press.

Leitenberg, H. (1965). Is time-out from positive reinforcement an aversive event? A review of the experimental evidence. *Psychological Bulletin, 64*, 428-441.

Lipsitt, L. P. (1984). Mental retardation: A view from the infant learning laboratory. In J. A. Mulick & B. L. Mallory (Eds.), *Transitions in mental retardation: Vol. 1. Advocacy, technology, and science.* Norwood, NJ: Ablex.

Meinhold, P. M., & Mulick, J. A. (1990). Risks, choices, and behavioral treatment. *Behavioral Residential Treatment, 5*(1), 29-44.

Meinhold, P. M., & Mulick, J. A. (in press). Social policy and science in the treatment of severe behavior disorders: Defining and securing a healthy relationship. *Clinical Psychology Review.*

Pryce, C. R. (1992). A comparative systems model of regulation of maternal motivation in mammals. *Animal Behavior, 43*, 417-441.

Touchette, P. E., MacDonald, R. F., & Langer, S. N. (1985). A scatter plot for identifying stimulus control of problem behavior. *Journal of Applied Behavior Analysis, 18*, 343-351.

NO   JAY S. BIRNBRAUER

The methods that should be used by professionals who work with children and adolescents are those that have the greatest chances of success in the short and long term for both clients and their communities. (By *communities,* I mean the persons directly affected by the program and client behavior, such as family, neighbors, teachers, and other carers. Discussion of negative methods as deterrents is a paper in itself. In a nutshell, I think we will get society's problems right if we learn to get relations between individuals and their communities right.) As scientists, we should place no conditions or exclusions on methods unless they are supported by reliable findings. We should instead be supporting the research necessary and utilizing functional methods, as Carr, Robinson, and Palumbo (1990) have argued very effectively. Although I agree with them that this question is the wrong one to ask, the issue is most commonly stated in terms of positive versus negative methods or aversive versus nonaversive methods. So I shall stay at that level.

Defining *positive* and *negative* methods is very much part of the problem. Definitions vary and usually are based on form or appearance, even though arguments based on form of behavior are futile. A few examples will suffice to secure agreement. For example, I don't think anyone is suggesting that professionals should use only such words as *yes* and *good* when working with a child or youth, the old saying "If you can't say anything nice, don't say anything at all" notwithstanding. As a second example, it is acceptable to consider giving a youth pocket money for washing the family car, but not for sexual favors. Both involve the same behavior, payment, which is generally regarded as a positive method. But, of course, professionals are prohibited by consensus from "committing" the latter, whereas they may "program" the former with impunity.

Both positive and negative methods are subject to abuse. Indeed, one might argue that positive methods are more dangerous because they are less noticeable and their potential for harm less often recognized. I have heard, for example, that juries are more likely to side with a defendant who repudiates his or her confession if it was extracted by coercion than if was obtained through acts of kindness, offers of cigarettes, and promises of leniency. Safeguards against abuses are found in training competent professionals and providing working environments that reinforce and maintain ethical and effective practice as defined in the short statement of ethical practice prepared by the American Association for Advancement of Behavior Therapy (1977). This statement does not discriminate between positive and negative methods. The arguments for and against positive methods do not hinge on potential for abuse.

Moreover, abuses are not diminished by rules that are based on false premises and stated ambiguously. Such rules engender hairsplitting, apparently much litigation, which fortunately has not reached Australia, and ingenious euphemisms (as an exercise, generate a list of names for what we used to call isolation rooms and solitary confinement). Azrin and Holz (1966) define punishment as *any* response-contingent procedure, that is, any procedure that follows some behavior that reduces the probability of that behavior. There are three criteria: It follows behavior, is contingent on behavior, and reduces the rate of behavior in the future. That definition includes both positive and negative methods of behavioral reduction and was once generally accepted as the technical definition. The idea of punishment, however, has not been in favor among learning psychologists and many segments of the population for many years.

At the same time, we are quite likely to employ punishment in our interactions with others every day, and since 1966, numerous studies dealing with reduction of problem behaviors have accumulated in the applied research literature, with procedures waxing and waning in acceptability. Overcorrection provides an instructive example. Although it certainly met the technical definition of punishment, overcorrection was touted as not an aversive method by some investigators and for a period of time gained acceptability, probably on the basis of those claims plus the inclusion of positive practice and restitution in the package. The latter, in particular, is apt to win much support among the general public. As Foxx and Bechtel (1982) express it, because the area had become so "muddled," they were compelled to devote considerable space in their paper to clarifying the rationale and procedures.

Some texts have separated positive punishment and negative punishment, possibly to suggest that the former is better than the latter. The former is response-contingent removal of positive reinforcers—response cost, time-out from positive reinforcement, temporary loss of a privilege, and the like. Negative punishment includes applying some pain-inducing procedure—spanking, electric shock, and so on. Using the word *wrong* may also be painful, but it is part of "feedback" that is generally acceptable. Most recently, Sulzer-Azaroff and Mayer (1991) have reserved the term *punishment* for the application of aversive stimuli; they place punishment at the bottom of their list of behavior-reducing methods (pp. 397-398), on the grounds of its generally being the most intrusive and restrictive method, but recognize that this depends upon context and other variables. Interestingly, Sulzer-Azaroff and Mayer find a reprimand with only the boss present to be more acceptable than a reprimand in front of coworkers, and they classify the two differently, the latter being an example of punishment, the former not. I am not sure which is more negative and can imagine circumstances in which reprimanding in front of peers would be positive—no doubt so can you and Sulzer-Azaroff and Mayer. I cite this example because their table separates procedures in ways that have a number of commendable features.

Any rules about the use of *yes* and *no* and all positive and negative treatments will need to contain reference to prior history, circumstances, behavior, and contingencies. Perhaps that is the only point that all research supports, and that the method alone is not sufficient basis for exclusion. I have to admit to two exceptions of which I approve. Throughout Australia, no capital punishment under any circumstances is still the law. A social consensus has been achieved for the time being and is enforceable by its very clarity. The second exception is the banning of corporal punishment (caning) in schools. That, incidentally, is only recent in Western Australia and may yet be the law in all the Australian states.

It follows that research to date does *not* support positive methods as more effective and safe for all concerned. For example, Vollmer and Iwata (1992) conclude from their review that differential reinforcement procedures have met with only moderate success. On the other hand, research does not support the opposite conclusion, that negative methods are more effective, either. Consequently, very persuasive arguments based on evidence can be employed by both sides (Repp & Singh, 1990; Sidman, 1989) and people will choose on the basis of their experience and competencies. The critical determinants of views on this issue are the experiences that we, professionals and other decisions makers, have had.

It can be seen also that positive methods alone are effective only in rare circumstances naturally and often practically impossible to establish and maintain by professionals. Parents of infants often come as close as anyone. It usually is not recognized that the prerequisites of success with positive methods alone are themselves negative. What we think we know now about operant behavior and contingencies of reinforcement was discovered with subjects who were deprived of food or water and confined in exquisitely designed spaces, and who received one-to-one instruction. The challenge for applied investigators has been to design spaces, training programs, and contingencies that are functionally equivalent and as successful in achieving objectives.

We have tried to design better study, work, and living environments for clients of all sorts, but at some point negative features are required. Otherwise, we have to depend upon volunteers in the first instance and accept truanting and opting out subsequently. Schools operating under permissive philosophies claim they are successful with only positive methods, but they are voluntary and may sacrifice achieving some number of educational objectives. I know of no evidence on that, however.

Given that most of us work under circumstances that do not permit our redesigning spaces, we will often fail if we insist on designing only positive programs. Many parents and other allies will reply, "It won't work"; "I can't do that"; "I tried that"—and you know they're right. The reason I like working with preschool children is that their spaces are so much more limited, the control of antecedents and reinforcers is potentially so much easier, and if the parents need help it can be obtained through volunteer assistants. Even here I cannot escape negatives, however, especially when it comes time for the child to enter regular school programs.

But I cannot close the case against positive methods at this point either, because everything just said also applies to negative methods. There are no circumstances in which punishment or negative methods alone have been shown to be more effective when measured against achieving objectives and quality of life for youth and community. The complexities of using negative methods correctly are just as great as those using positive methods; in earlier work I reported on a painful and disappointing experience to help others avoid the same pitfalls (Birnbrauer, 1968).

One exception that might occur to some of you is the case of applying very severe punishment analogous to a traumatic event. There, however, we run the risk of the individual's avoiding the situation entirely and thus not learning alternative means of achieving legitimate ends; that is, that method fails because it does not consider the client's benefit. Very severe punishment, however, is supportable if the behavior has no legitimate ends, as in some forms of self-injurious behavior, sexual behavior, and assaultive behavior. The foregoing is one instance in which I argue for the use of negative methods on the grounds of effectiveness. That is, when behavior produces automatic reinforcement that cannot be gained acceptably by other means, I don't know any option now except to introduce aversive consequences to compete with the inherent positive ones. The overriding purpose is simply to stop the behavior.

Other situations for inclusion of negative methods (along with provisions for success through alternative behavior) are those in which it is necessary to capitalize upon the instantaneous stopping of behavior that negative methods often yield. Nonreinforcement and differential reinforcement procedures allow behavior to occur, and sometimes that is unsafe. As I have pointed out elsewhere, we need to pay equal attention to the safety and well-being of carers, peers, siblings, and so on in designing educational and treatment programs (Birnbrauer, 1990). The safety of others is not *more* important, as advocates of punishment would have it, but it is *as* important. To secure their cooperation, we need to train carers in specific ways of preventing harm to themselves and others. Because instantaneous effects of punishment are often positive (e.g., the tantrum stops), disallowing anything but positive techniques does not conform with the experiences of our potential collaborators. Most will have enjoyed the temporary relief that negative methods often gain. Second, they may not have read or be persuaded by the research that worries us—that effects of negative methods are temporary, do not generalize to other persons and situations, and diminish the child's self-esteem, induce learned helplessness and generalized apprehension or apathy, or increase aggressiveness and teach the child to use negative methods when it is his or her turn to be parent or carer ("That may be true of other people, but punishment hasn't harmed me. I'm okay"). Third, all of the negative effects just listed can result from nonreinforcement and withholding positive reinforcement until appropriate behavior occurs. Nonreinforcement also elicits anger and aggressive behavior, feelings of helplessness, and so on. Whether the methods are classed as positive or negative, the outcome depends more (dare I say *entirely*?) on the aspects of the program that induce successful alternative behavior. For these reasons, in many instances, a program that includes well-controlled negative methods is more likely to be tried and successful.

I am suggesting that we apply the same principles in working with collaborators as we apply with clients directly. That is, we start from the level of skills they demonstrate and prompt and shape new repertoires from there. In other words, we change the experience of carers and thereby increase their willingness to try new things and share our respect for the powerful roles positive methods, careful analysis, and monitoring play.

In summary, my position is that positive methods are powerful and necessary, but *only* positive methods are rarely applicable. As a rule, programs will require carefully selected and applied negative methods. Abuses occur with either. Effects may be good or bad with any method, because methods are indifferent to the desirability or offensiveness of behavior. The long-term effects associated with punishment are also found when alternatives to punishment are tested. The key to avoiding unwanted emotional effects is found in the provisions within programs to increase client competencies and thereby their rates of success.

References

Association for the Advancement of Behavior Therapy. (1977). Ethical issues for human services. *Behavior Therapy, 8,* 763-764.

Azrin, N. H., & Holz, W. C. (1966). Punishment. In W. K. Honig (Ed.), *Operant behavior: Areas of research and application* (pp. 380-447). New York: Appleton-Century-Crofts.

Birnbrauer, J. S. (1968). Generalization of punishment effects: A case study. *Journal of Applied Behavior Analysis, 1,* 201-211.

Birnbrauer, J. S. (1990). Responsibility and quality of life. In A. C. Repp & N. N. Singh (Eds.), *Perspectives on the use of nonaversive and aversive interventions for persons with developmental disabilities* (pp. 231-236). Sycamore, IL: Sycamore.

Carr, E. G., Robinson, S., & Palumbo, L. W. (1990). The wrong issue: Aversive versus nonaversive treatment. The right issue: Functional versus nonfunctional treatment. In A. C. Repp & N. N. Singh (Eds.), *Perspectives on the use of nonaversive and aversive interventions for persons with developmental disabilities* (pp. 361-379). Sycamore, IL: Sycamore.

Foxx, R. M., & Bechtel, D. R. (1982). Overcorrection. In M. Herson, R. M. Eisler, & P. M. Miller (Eds.), *Progress in behavior modification, 13* (pp. 227-288). San Diego: Academic.

Repp, A. C., & Singh, N. N. (Eds.). (1990). *Perspectives on the use of nonaversive and aversive interventions for persons with developmental disabilities.* Sycamore, IL: Sycamore.

Sidman, M. (1989). *Coercion and its fallout.* Boston: Authors Cooperative.

Sulzer-Azaroff, B., & Mayer, G. R. (1991). *Behavior analysis for lasting change.* New York: Holt, Rinehart & Winston.

Vollmer, T. R., & Iwata, B. (1992). Differential reinforcement as treatment for behavior disorders: Procedural and functional variations. *Research in Developmental Disabilities, 13,* 393-417.

JAY S. BIRNBRAUER RESPONDS

Sailor and Carr have addressed this issue from the perspective of working with persons with developmental disabilities, whereas I have taken a much broader view. They were correct in doing so in that this controversy rages principally among the advocates, parents, and professionals involved with those client groups. I chose not to because the notion that *only* positive methods should be used affects other groups as well.

Similarly, often disagreements arise only about the use of particular kinds of aversive procedures—electric shock, smacking, and the like. But again, because others have generalized to everything *they* consider aversive, we need to be specific about the procedures in question. Otherwise, we may have rules imposed that make it difficult to use positive methods correctly. As I have pointed out, positive methods always involve some elements of deprivation, unpleasantness, negative emotions, disappointment, and pain for someone.

Judging from their example of Ricky, Sailor and Carr are more inclusive. They appear also to advocate judging an intervention on appearance and acceptability even though it is not consistent with a functional analytic stance. Ironically, contingent exercise, the method in their example of Ricky, was developed as an alternative that often would be acceptable and useful. After all, teachers, coaches, and parents have been using repetitive work and exercise for eons. Before judging any particular case, we should ask: How did Ricky's team arrive at that plan? What was the total plan for Ricky? How is it being monitored?

Sailor and Carr argue that aversives should be used under no circumstances, whereas I say we should not close the door on the possibility that some circumstances require aversive consequences—that using them would be the most ethical path to follow. Lovaas (1987), for example, on the basis of 25 years of controlled investigations unmatched in the field of infantile autism, concludes, "Contingent aversives were isolated as one significant variable. It is therefore unlikely that treatment effects could be replicated without this component" (p. 8). I have been conducting an early intervention program for children with autism and have chosen not to use physical aversives. I worry that I may thereby have reduced their chances of leading significantly richer lives. The children, for their part, have not made informed choices to live out their lives with autism.

I fail to see anything new in Sailor and Carr's "new behavioral technology" and anything more (or less) complex about present circumstances. Nor do I work in systems that will entertain only a positive technology of behavior management. I wish I did. Indeed, in my experience, people do not welcome rearrangements of their microsocial systems. Initially at least, they blame the client and are much more likely to advocate and accept quick and easy solutions, and it is a matter of whose behavior is most influenced by the other. That is, will the behavior analyst succeed in changing the system or will he or she succumb or flee from it? Historically the latter has often been the result, and there is no evidence that the rules governing human behavior have changed.

I can distinguish only five points of consensus on a "positive behavioral technology":

1. Conduct a functional analysis before intervening.
2. Intervene holistically.
3. Build alternative repertoires that enable persons to achieve their goals.
4. Emphasize antecedents.
5. Respect each person's rights.

Although each is important, only the last is pertinent to a discussion about aversives and nonaversives and can be adequately addressed by a system of safeguards for selecting and monitoring programs. The other four are essentially the definition of behavior analysis, which has always been misnamed. The fundamental axiom is that behavior is controlled by its environment. Therefore, for behavior change to occur, behavior's relationship to environmental variables requires analysis and the environment needs to be redesigned accordingly. The vast majority of people, professional and nonprofessional, psychologists and nonpsychologists, dispute that axiom.

Finally, Sailor and Carr's analysis is incomplete. First, evidence suggests that some self-injurious and aggressive behavior is not "purposive"; that is, the function of the behavior is self-stimulatory or elicited ("respondent") behavior. In those cases, we may not be able to achieve control of critical stimuli. Second, behavior that was functional at one time, such as neurotic and compulsive behavior, continues at excessively high rates and is extremely resistant to change. It is difficult to offer alternatives that achieve the same goals as do highly effective escape and avoidance behavior. The treatment of choice currently is exposure with prevention of escape. That treatment is likely to be unpleasant for a while. Third, as I mentioned, some behavior has no safe, social purpose. Teaching people acceptable means of achieving an unacceptable goal is simply not an alternative. We know little about how to decrease the value of reinforcers. What I think we know entails the use of aversive consequences.

In the final analysis, we probably agree that the big challenge is teaching and maintaining correct use of behavioral technology. Finally, in the heat of this debate we should not lose sight of the fact that most research has been about the application of positive methods. Historically, it was common among behavior analysts to regard the use of punishment as an admission of defeat. I believe that view still is the prevalent one.

Reference

Lovaas, O. I. (1987). Behavioral treatment and normal educational and intellectual functioning in young autistic children. *Journal of Consulting and Clinical Psychology, 55,* 3-9.

JAMES A. MULICK RESPONDS

I tried to convey in my initial statement that appetitive and aversive motivation are involved in the genesis of all behavior, normal and abnormal, and can be discerned in the everyday give and take of behavioral transactions between people. The functional analysis of behavior is not a new approach to behavior analysis and psychology; rather, it is a fundamental approach to behavior and psychology that traces its roots to many late nineteenth- and early twentieth-century thinkers. These include Darwin's views on environmental trait selection in evolution (see Boakes, 1984), Angell's (1907) emphasis on the adjustment of the organism to the environment, James's (1893) philosophical dedication to practical empiricism, Thorndike's (1933, 1935) law of effect, and, later, Skinner's (1938, 1948) selection of behavior by its consequences. Functionalism has no special relation to nonaversive therapeutic intervention, except as a naive application of Thorndike's (1935) observation that the strengthening effect of reward was asymmetrical, more direct, and more effective than the weakening effect of punishment, a conclusion subsequently overturned by much research (Azrin & Holz, 1966) and our justifiable pedagogical bias in favor of teaching new skills over mere suppression of bad habits. Clearly, an intervention used with a child, if it is to be effective and work as planned, must be based on a functional approach to the problem behavior or skill deficit *and* the treatment. This is, as I have said, the hallmark of the modern scientific school of applied learning theory referred to as behavior analysis. However, an oversimplified view of strict early twentieth-century functionalism has to be augmented by more modern views of individual biological limits on behavior modifiability and a more complex and extended view of functional analysis in a broad social context.

The other major point I tried to convey in my initial statement is that aversive motivation, whether or not we choose to recognize it (or to use it) in a therapeutic rearrangement of behavioral contingencies, is inherent already in the request for intervention. All that is necessary to realize this is to extend the boundaries of functional analysis beyond the immediate context. Someone is seeking relief whenever a request for intervention is made. The aversive behavioral relation is already a factor before *our* intervention begins. This means the intervention really begins with the behavioral contingencies that produce the request.

A related issue pertains to the functional relations that caused the behavior problem. A mother's unselective positive reinforcement of her toddler's actions, even those that hurt her, that disrupt family meals and nighttime sleeping patterns, that decrease her opportunities for spousal intimacy, can be changed by redirecting her reinforcement only to that toddler behavior that fits better with competing family and social needs. The *intervention* is nonaversive, but the motivational condition established in the child is partly aversive. Just as cues associated with deprivation or failure become negative signals and hence are avoided, the toddler "turns away" from nonreinforced behavior and toward positive outcomes. Without *differential* reinforcement, nonreinforced behavior would not be abandoned, but rather would likely gain in strength during reinforcement of new "functionally equivalent" members of its wider response class. Putting on blinders to the interplay of appetitive and aversive motivation will only serve to decrease effective problem solving.

Let's pursue an expanded perspective, then, despite my hesitation in principle to grapple with someone else's straw man, by looking at Sailor and Carr's imaginary behavioral example in the classroom. The little boy in their example is given a consequence that just might decelerate the preceding misbehavior (as would many feasible consequences, but let's stick with their exercise idea). The authors grant this point, but deem it too disagreeable for imagined onlookers. Sadly, that probably is true. A little boy, we'll call him Mark, chooses to display behavior that disrupts the classroom. Disruptive behavior takes many forms. In my experience, many children like Mark hit, bite, kick, and spit too when peers thwart their desires. I have three or four such little Marks and Sallys referred to me every year. The complex repertoire of obnoxious behavior seems to covary as a hierarchy of choices, or a branching series of alternative actions, and forms a response class.

How did Mark get that way? Children like Mark learn progressively elaborated coercive strategies more or less appetitively; their behavior is shaped, mostly via positive reinforcement, in a variety of culturally deprived and permissive earlier environments. For example, children of mothers or fathers whose lifestyle includes unlawful behavior and who value being inconspicuous often learn to keep their children quiet via placation, and so are themselves being negatively reinforced for positively reinforcing obnoxious behavior. Children of unhappy or mentally ill parents, children of parents who are enmeshed in conflict, children of parents who are distracted by pressing fears and concerns, all these children readily acquire elaborated repertoires of behavior that accomplish the basic goal of the helpless child; namely, to get and maintain parental attention long enough to meet their needs in a world they are too young and too small to act upon directly. Such children learn to behave more forcefully to get through to their distracted caregivers. In addition, forceful behavior, even outright aggression, sometimes leads to direct reinforcement from attaining a specific goal, social conflict resolution, or material gain. When these children get to school, they arrive with well-practiced repertoires of aggressive behavior that are different from those of many of their classmates.

Now, at least some of the time, Mark may not only scream and push, but may also bite his peer tutor. A human bite, leaving two neat, curved rows of indentations, a corona of ugly blue and red discoloration from broken capillaries under the skin, and lingering pain, is likely to ruin the peer tutor's mother's day. This mother will subsequently express her distress by calling the principal, threatening to sue, asking for the teacher to be fired, and requesting that Mark be expelled or her daughter moved to a safer class "immediately." The peer tutor's father will have been audible to the principal on the telephone, barking encouragement for the mother's demands in the form of more direct promises of retribution to "that kid's parents and the damned principal." Now, instead of being able to assure the distressed parent that the school indeed has a well-understood method to help youngsters like Mark learn to withhold biting others in the future, we must agree with Professors Sailor and Carr that a few push-ups or deep knee bends *would* be deemed too drastic an intervention. Professor Sailor is, after all, a well-respected and successful teacher-trainer who ought to know better than us what his graduates have been taught to believe when they were recently in college. The principal, as one long familiar with responding under negative reinforcement contingencies, will feel compelled to take some action, but lacking a regiment of social caseworkers and publicists who can effect spin control on the public relations impact of this incident, is in a bind. The principal cannot assure the parent that her daughter will be free from danger at some future date, because an effective decelerative strategy involving aversive motivation cannot be used in the school. The principal has no resources to transfer income to Mark's parents and no power to instill middle-class values in them, much less effect an ecological sea change in Mark's community. Instead of exercise as a consequence for performing any member of a small class of disruptive or aggressive acts, on perhaps a dozen or so future occasions (because when punishment works it is not used very long or very often), *exile* is the only administrative option. Mark probably would be expelled, or shunted into a "special" segregated program (where, incidentally, the curriculum would move at a much slower pace because the teachers need to concentrate on the concatenated behavior management ordeal of dealing with an entire room full of children with habits like Mark's). Now Mark faces educational deprivation as well as the unfortunate home experiences that have led to his disruptive behavior. In the future, of course, Mark will be able to have the best possible individual care from young professionals like the ones Professor Carr trains in his graduate program in clinical psychology. He will need them, too, because when his aggressive behavior continues to elaborate along more mature lines, when biting is replaced by its *functional equivalent* of using knives or guns to win material or social gain and peer admiration (all of which are positive reinforcers that no professional will be able to control because they will derive from a peer group socialized along similar lines), he will find it more difficult than ever at school to make teachers and peer tutors like him. He will probably get poor grades. He will have remarkably poor self-esteem as a result of all the aversion his behavior engenders. He will, to say the least, most likely find it hard to take school seriously or even to attend school.

Would the partly aversive treatment have allowed Mark to receive the benefits of regular education and middle-class peers? We will never know, but there is reason to believe so. The moral victory will go to Professors Sailor and Carr. The material gain may go to their students. The expectation of failure will be their indirect legacy to little Mark.

References

Angell, J. R. (1907). The province of functional psychology. *Psychological Review, 14*, 61-91.

Azrin, N. H., & Holz, W. C. (1966). Punishment. In W. K. Honig (Ed.), *Operant behavior: Areas of research and application* (pp. 380-447). New York: Appleton-Century-Crofts.

Boakes, R. (1984). *From Darwin to behaviorism: Psychology and the minds of animals*. New York: Cambridge University Press.

James, W. (1893). *Psychology*. New York: Holt.

Thorndike, E. L. (1933). A proof of the law of effect. *Science, 77*, 173-175.

Thorndike, E. L. (1935). *The psychology of wants, interests and attitudes*. New York: Appleton-Century-Crofts.

Skinner, B. F. (1938). *The behavior of organisms: An experimental analysis*. New York: Appleton-Century-Crofts.

Skinner, B. F. (1948). Superstition in the pigeon. *Journal of Experimental Psychology, 38*, 168-172.

WAYNE SAILOR and EDWARD G. CARR RESPOND

Response to Mulick

Interestingly, there are many points of convergence between Mulick's approach and ours. All of us acknowledge the importance of context (ecology) in understanding and treating problem behavior. All of us see a major role for functional analysis in planning treatment. Finally, all of us agree on the necessity of multicomponent interventions for dealing with serious problem behavior.

As is true in any scholarly debate, there are areas of disagreement as well. The core disagreements are definitional in nature. First, Mulick seems to equate positive approaches with a hedonic (pleasure) principle. Positive approaches help children to feel good, smile, and laugh. Although it is true that these outcomes might occur, they do not define the nature of positive approaches. As the term has emerged in the scientific literature, positive approaches are interventions that are designed to make socially desirable responses more probable, thereby undermining the necessity for an individual to continue to perform severe problem behavior (Carr, Robinson, Taylor, & Carlson, 1990). In other words, the focus is on skill development and restructuring living environments rather than on pleasure per se.

Second, Mulick defines punishment in very broad terms. His definition is technically correct, however, the debate in the field, for most people, has focused on the use of extreme forms of punishment, such as contingent electric shock and forced inhalation of fumes from ammonia pellets. There is still a role for such naturally occurring punishers as reprimands, brief time-out (e.g., being sent to one's room), or response cost (e.g., losing one's allowance for a week because of misbehavior). However, there is nothing natural about electric shock in the management of children's behavior, nor can one make much of an argument for using it with most of the child populations mentioned by Mulick (e.g., children with acute medical problems or children evidencing delinquency or school failure). Even in populations that have traditionally received extreme forms of punishment (e.g., people with developmental disabilities) there is a strong trend away from the use of highly intrusive procedures, as Mulick himself notes when he cites the classic study by Touchette, MacDonald, and Langer (1985) on managing severe problem behavior through environmental reorganization.

Third, Mulick stresses the maladaptive nature of problem behavior. This point of view invites parents, teachers, and other treatment agents to focus on the punishment issue. After all, if a behavior is maladaptive, why not get rid of it as soon as possible? If punishment can do the job, then so be it. Our view is that problem behavior is adaptive, not maladaptive. The reason that it lasts so long and is so resistant to change is that it is very often an effective means, sometimes the only means, for an individual to control other people and get what he or she wants from them. This point of view invites parents, teachers, and other treatment agents to discover why the individual misbehaves in the first place and then teach the individual alternative (socially appropriate) ways of achieving goals, thereby making problem behavior unnecessary. When we alter our view of problem behavior and recognize its adaptive qualities, we can better see the merits of an approach that emphasizes education over behavior reduction—in other words, a positive approach.

Response to Birnbrauer

We agree with most of what Birnbrauer says on the issue of positive versus negative methods. Positive methods can indeed be misused. For example, employing a differential reinforcement procedure in which a boy diagnosed as retarded is given juice every 10 seconds that he does not engage in head banging may not have the slightest effect if the reason the child is head banging is related to his having to go to the bathroom. The example, however, is not an indictment of positive methods as such, but rather of the lack of expertise of the treatment providers who failed to analyze the reasons for the misbehavior correctly in the first place. Unfortunately, inadequate analysis commonly occurs in the area of behavior management. Also, paradoxically, as Birnbrauer notes, positive methods can indeed be aversive. For example, withholding reinforcers (e.g., candy, toys) from a child contingent on a child's aggression is technically, and probably hedonically as well, aversive. However, as we note above in our response to Mulick, we do not reject all procedures that may have aversive effects. Withholding reinforcers, providing reprimands, and sending a child to his or her room for misbehavior are normative disciplinary practices in our culture. No doubt, positive procedures alone may often be ineffective unless accompanied, at least occasionally, by some of the negative procedures just listed. However, the real debate in the field is not about the use of reprimands but rather about punishers such as electric shock, forced inhalation of ammonia fumes, and being sprayed in the face with ice water. These are not normative procedures in our culture, therefore, how can one justify their use?

Birnbrauer suggests that very severe punishment may be justified when individuals engage, for example, in self-injury that is under internal control and, by implication, not susceptible to environmental influence. However, what if the reason an individual is engaging in head banging is related to a middle ear infection, severe gastrointestinal problems, or allergies (Bailey & Pyles, 1989; DeLissovoy, 1963; Gardner, 1985; Gunsett, Mulick, Fernald, & Martin, 1989)? Should we proceed with electric shock treatment? We believe that Birnbrauer would not do so and neither would we. The point is that ascribing the control of self-injury to internal factors is often no more than an admission of ignorance rather than a reasoned, analytic approach. Further, temporary control of self-injury through the use of electric shock often has the effect of discouraging further inquiry into why the person is self-injurious. After all, if the person begins to misbehave again, there is always the shock option. That is bad clinical practice and very bad science.

What then of the practical question of what to do at the moment that severe problem behavior is occurring? Surely we cannot wait for scientists to discover the truth when we have a crisis happening right in front of our eyes. Surely the instantaneous relief provided by strong aversives is the only solution that is workable. No, it is not. As has been argued elsewhere, the real question is, Why has the situation been allowed to develop into a crisis in the first place (Carr, Robinson, & Palumbo, 1990)? That is, have steps really been taken to educate the individual, to teach him or her the skills that undermine the necessity for self-injury? Has a rich, stimulating social and physical environment been created that provides the individual many discriminative stimuli for nonproblem behavior? Or has the person been put in a barren institution, with nothing to do, and with few people around for social support? Our point is that good treatment is preventive and positive in nature; bad treatment is neither and, instead, focuses on responding to crises that are the result of inadequate educational and social opportunities.

Still, even with the best of planning, there will be times when crises occur and something must be done right away. However, why assume that the response to a crisis must be aversive, that is, must involve the use of electric shock or the like? As Touchette, MacDonald, and Langer (1985) show, it is possible to deal with even very severe problem behavior by rearranging the person's environment. Their strategy resolved dangerous crises without the use of extreme aversive procedures.

Birnbrauer makes a very good point when he notes that the safety of caregivers must also be considered in the design of treatments. Thus caregivers will certainly favor procedures that minimize danger to themselves. They will favor a procedure that quickly stops aggression over one that acts more slowly. Implicitly, the suggestion is that negative procedures work faster and reduce danger to caregivers. However, a case can be made against this argument. Negative procedures may themselves require a long time to work (Guess, Helmstetter, Turnbull, & Knowlton, 1987). Even when these procedures produce quick effects, it is a mistake to believe that danger to the caregiver is minimized. For example, the overcorrection procedure mentioned by Birnbrauer often results in clients' fighting back (Foxx & Bechtel, 1983), thereby posing a danger to the caregiver. People with developmental disabilities are not passive; they often use their problem behavior to influence others (Carr, Taylor, & Robinson, 1991). Thus, clinically, it is common to see recipients of electric shock or forced inhalation of ammonia fumes fighting back against the individuals attempting to administer such treatments.

In sum, there is no quick fix with negative procedures. Indeed, the main issue, one that Birnbrauer and we both agree on, is that education is the real long-term solution to severe problem behavior. Ultimately, education is about positive procedures.

References

Bailey, J. S., & Pyles, D. A. M. (1989). Behavioral diagnostics. In E. Cipani (Ed.), *The treatment of severe behavior disorders* (pp. 85-107). *Monographs of the American Association on Mental Retardation, 12.*

Carr, E. G., Robinson, S., & Palumbo, L. W. (1990). The wrong issue: Aversive versus nonaversive treatment. The right issue: Functional versus nonfunctional treatment. In A. C. Repp & N. N. Singh (Eds.), *Perspectives on the use of nonaversive and aversive interventions for persons with developmental disabilities* (pp. 361-379). Sycamore, IL: Sycamore.

Carr, E. G., Robinson, S., Taylor, J. C., & Carlson, J. I. (1990). Positive approaches to the treatment of severe behavior problems in persons with developmental disabilities: A review and analysis of reinforcement and stimulus-based procedures. *Monograph of the Association for Persons With Severe Handicaps, 4.*

Carr, E. G., Taylor, J. C., & Robinson, S. (1991). The effects of severe behavior problems in children on the teaching behavior of adults. *Journal of Applied Behavior Analysis, 24,* 523-535.

DeLissovoy, V. (1963). Head banging in early childhood: A suggested cause. *Journal of Genetic Psychology, 102,* 109-114.

Foxx, R. M., & Bechtel, D. R. (1983). Overcorrection: A review and analysis. In S. Axelrod & J. Apsche (Eds.), *Punishment: Its effects on human behavior* (pp. 133-220). New York: Academic Press.

Gardner, J. M. (1985). Using microcomputers to help staff reduce violent behavior. *Computers in Human Services, 1,* 53-61.

Guess, D., Helmstetter, E., Turnbull, H. R., III, & Knowlton, S. (1987). Use of aversive procedures with persons who are disabled: An historical review and critical analysis. *Monographs of the Association for Persons With Severe Handicaps, 2*(1).

Gunsett, R. P., Mulick, J. A., Fernald, W. B., & Martin, J. L. (1989). Brief report: Indications for medical screening prior to behavioral programming for severely and profoundly mentally retarded clients. *Journal of Autism and Developmental Disorders, 19,* 167-172.

Touchette, P. E., MacDonald, R. F., & Langer, S. N. (1985). A scatter plot for identifying stimulus control of problem behavior. *Journal of Applied Behavior Analysis, 18,* 343-351.

PART IV

Children's Legal Issues

DEBATE 14

DISCRIMINATION IN JUVENILE JUSTICE

➢ *Does the juvenile justice system discriminate against racial minorities?*

EDITORS' NOTE: The rates of arrest and detention of juveniles involved in violent and drug-related crimes have escalated over the past several years. In addition, an ever-greater percentage of the juveniles detained and incarcerated are African American males. These facts have set off a heated controversy regarding the fairness of the juvenile justice system toward racial minorities. In a related incident, the televised recording of the Rodney King beating forced the public to face the issue of racially motivated police brutality in dealing with adult offenders. It is sometimes difficult for scholars to maintain a dispassionate and fair posture in dealing with such emotionally and politically charged issues as racism and juvenile offenders. In this debate, Professor Gibbs argues the pro side with skill, good evidence, and well-reasoned logic. We could not find anyone to do the same for the con side. For whatever reasons, the juvenile justice experts we contacted both in and outside of academia declined. In the belief that all controversial issues have at least two sides, we have written the con argument ourselves. It may not be the best such argument, but in it we attempt to set the debate in a wider arena, addressing possible causes, and therefore solutions, for juvenile crime outside the juvenile justice system.

Jewelle Taylor Gibbs says YES. She is the Zellerbach Family Fund Professor of Social Welfare at the University of California, Berkeley, and the editor of *Young, Black and Male in America: An Endangered Species* (1988).

Mary Ann Mason and **Eileen Gambrill** argue NO. Mason is an Associate Professor of Social Welfare at the University of California, Berkeley, and coeditor of this volume. Gambrill is a Professor of Social Welfare at the University of California, Berkeley, and coeditor of this volume.

YES JEWELLE TAYLOR GIBBS

In 1990, the Sentencing Project in Washington, D.C., issued a startling report that claimed that 23% of young black males, or nearly 1 in 4, in the 20-29 age group were involved in the criminal justice system, in jail, on probation, or on parole (Mauer, 1990). This compares with 1 in 16 white males and 1 in 10 Latino males in similar stages of involvement. Black males now account for nearly half of the state prison population; that is, prisons are among the few American institutions that provide equal access to blacks. In 1985, when black males accounted for about 15% of youth under the jurisdiction of the juvenile court, they represented more than 40% of all incarcerated male juveniles. Black male juveniles had the highest rate of incarceration of any race-sex group, and they were disproportionally placed in public rather than private correctional facilities (Krisberg, Schwartz, Fishman, Eiskovitz, & Guttman, 1986).

These statistics dramatize the increasing trend toward incarcerating young black males, 14-30 of age, who are convicted of crimes ranging from petty theft to homicide. The crucial issue in evaluating the figures is whether black males are receiving equal treatment and equal justice in the American juvenile and criminal justice system, from the initial point of arrest to the final disposition of a case.

Black males are imprisoned in the United States at a rate four times greater than that of black males in South Africa (3,109 versus 729 per 100,000). In 1990, the District of Columbia Department of Corrections reported that more than 12,500 people (9 out of 10 inmates) in jail in Lorton and in various other state and federal institutions were black or Latino (Bryant, 1990).

In spite of their equal numbers in the state prisons, black inmates are less likely to be enrolled in programs of rehabilitation, education, or drug treatment than are white inmates. Thus prison serves primarily as an instrument of social control rather than as an avenue of rehabilitation for these young men. The liberal philosophy of rehabilitation and reform of the 1960s has been displaced by the conservative philosophy of retrenchment and revenge of the 1970s and 1980s. In the absence of enlightened prison policies and lack of attention to the underlying causes of crime, the national recidivism rate for adult offenders is 63%; the rate is 70% for juvenile offenders (Bryant, 1990).

Contrasting Perspectives on Racial Disparities in the System

Why is it that a young black male who steals $100 may go to prison for several years, whereas a white savings and loan executive who embezzles millions of dollars from unsuspecting citizens may pay a fine and be given a sentence of "community service"? There are two major competing hypotheses about the observed racial disparities in the criminal justice system, particularly to explain the disproportional number of black males in prison (blacks are 12% of the general population but constitute nearly half of the state prison population): (a) *differential involvement,* that is, that blacks commit more crimes and more serious offenses (in proportion to their population) than do whites; and (b) *differential processing,* that is, that differential rates of incarceration reflect selective law enforcement at every stage of the juvenile and criminal justice systems, from the police, to the prosecutors, to the juries and judges.

Dozens of studies have been conducted to produce supporting evidence for both of these theories. Because this volume's format precludes an exhaustive review or critique of these studies, I will summarize several of the more recent studies, which are more sophisticated conceptually and methodologically than the earlier studies. Studies published in the 1980s employed the technique of multivariate analysis to sort out and control for the numerous variables that influence the dispositions of felony cases, including prior offense record, severity of offense, age and sex of victim, use of a weapon, and other relevant factors that could account for variations in sentencing.

Several studies in California and New York, and two studies that analyzed national patterns of the impact of race in the criminal justice system, arrived at some surprising findings. First, nearly all of these studies found that *blacks and Latinos are more likely to be arrested than whites,* but are also more likely to have their cases dismissed before trial or at preliminary hearings (Dehais, 1987; Petersilia, 1983; Smith & Visher, 1981; Zatz, 1981). There are several hypotheses advanced to explain this apparent anomaly: that there are more unjustified arrests among blacks, that many blacks are arrested without valid warrants, and that evidence and witnesses against black suspects may not be strong enough to sustain convictions against them. Hepburn (1978) concludes that "powerless persons are more likely to be arrested on less sufficient evidence" (p. 54) in his study of all felony arrests in a large midwestern city in 1974; Petersilia (1983) comes to the same conclusion in her study of California offenders.

Second, in many jurisdictions minority defendants (blacks and Latinos) are *less likely to be convicted than whites,* which should result in a lower ratio of black to white prisoners in the jails and prisons, yet this is not the case. This finding suggests that the major racial disparities in the criminal justice system appear to be two polar ends of the system, first at the point of arrest, and last at the point of sentencing and disposition of cases, in which a much higher proportion of *those blacks who are convicted of a crime,* compared with convicted whites, *are more likely to be sentenced to prison* and less likely to be placed on probation or fined. In a review of 23 studies of sentencing in *noncapital* cases, Dehais (1987) found that there was partial or full support for racial discrimination in sentencing outcomes, even when prior offense record was factored in or controlled.

Studies of sentencing for felonies in the mid-1970s in Michigan (Zalman, Ostrom, Guilliams, & Peaslee, 1979) and Alaska (Rubenstein, Clarke, & White, 1980) found that there was a significantly higher probability of imprisonment of nonwhites for index crimes. In Michigan, blacks received longer sentences than whites for four felony offenses (sex, drugs, burglary and larceny), and in Alaska, Indians and blacks received much longer sentences of all for drug-related crimes (*by 467%*).

Results from studies of sentencing decisions in Los Angeles County (Petersilia, 1983) and New York State (Frederick & Zimmerman, 1983) also demonstrated that blacks and Latinos were more likely than whites to be incarcerated rather than paroled in cases where they were all eligible for parole, but Charles (1987) concludes that there is significantly less racial bias in sentencing in New York City than in the suburbs or upstate areas of New York. A study of drug offenders in Miami found that black drug offenders were sentenced more severely than whites, despite their committing less serious offenses and having fewer charges filed against them (Unnever, 1982).

There are two other decision points in the dispositions of criminal cases at which black and white defendants are treated differently. In a review of bail as an important factor in preventing or delaying incarceration of defendants in criminal cases, research has shown that whites are more likely than blacks to be released on bail, even when prior offense records are taken into account. Similarly, white defendants are more likely than blacks to be involved in plea bargaining before or during trials, frequently resulting in reduced charges, probation, fines, or shorter sentences.

Summary

A fair assessment of these studies is that "there is convincing evidence of racial disparity at the sentencing stage, which contributes to the disproportionate incarcerations of minorities in several states" (Dehais, 1987). It is also important to note the findings of the 1982 Report by the National Center for State

Courts, which analyzed data from multiple jurisdictions in the United States and concluded that "the impact of race in criminal sentencing varies with the locus of the study"; for example, the researchers found no evidence of racial disparity in the Denver, Colorado, District Court, but did find that blacks had an 11.8% higher probability of incarceration than whites in the common pleas court of Philadelphia.

The most significant and severest disparities occur at the level of death penalty sentencing. *Black defendants are more likely to receive the death penalty than are white defendants in capital cases,* but the significant factor is the *race of the victim*; that is, blacks who commit capital crimes against whites (murder, kidnap, rape) are more likely to receive the death penalty than are blacks who kill blacks, whites who kill whites, or any other racial combination of offender and victim (U.S. General Accounting Office, 1990).

Implications for Public Policy

The disproportional involvement of young black males in the criminal justice system reflects on their relationship to the broader society, which has narrowly limited their opportunities and their life options through implicitly condoning poverty and discrimination, and reinforcing their sense of alienation, anger, and hopelessness. Their experience in the criminal justice system is simply a further reflection of their own victimization and powerlessness, as well as an indictment of the democratic tenets of a just society. We have to look at three levels of public policy to address the increasing trend of funneling young black males into the criminal justice system and the increasing cost of keeping them incarcerated: federal government policies, federal and state programs, and local community programs. For example, at the federal and state levels, there is a need to reform the current welfare system to increase self-sufficiency of the recipients through education, job training, and child-care subsidies, so that young blacks will grow up in homes where they have *working parents* as role models and where they will see incentives for education and employment in the legitimate sector of the economy. Our educational system needs major reforms, with particular attention to be paid to early childhood education programs such as Head Start, curriculum reform to meet the needs of a changing school population, incentives for teachers to work in inner-city schools, innovative dropout prevention programs, and *enriched* rather than remedial programs for inner-city schoolchildren. Job training and job placement programs for disadvantaged youth should be increased and strengthened. Finally, the juvenile justice and criminal justice systems are in need of extensive reform to assure equal treatment and equal justice to all defendants.

References

Bryant, M. (1990, June 24). Crime and punishment. *Washington Post*, p. 1.

Charles, B. (1987). *Crime and the black community: An assessment of the impact of selected criminal justice issues in New York State*. Albany: Governor's Advisory Committee for Black Affairs.

Dehais, R. J. (1987). *Racial discrimination in the criminal justice system: An assessment of the empirical evidence*. Albany: State University of New York, New York African American Institute.

Frederick, B. C., & Zimmerman, S. E. (1983). *Discrimination and the decision to incarcerate*. Albany: New York State Division of Criminal Justice Services, Office of Program Development and Research.

Hepburn, J. R. (1978). Race and the decision to arrest: An analysis of warrants issued. *Journal of Research on Crime and Delinquency, 15*, 54ff.

Krisberg, B., Schwartz, I., Fishman, G., Eiskovitz, Z., & Guttman, E. (1986). *The incarceration of minority youth*. Minneapolis: University of Minnesota, Humphrey Institute of Public Affairs.

Mauer, M. (1990). *Young black men and the criminal justice system: A growing national problem*. Washington, DC: Sentencing Project.

Petersilia, J. (1983). *Racial disparities in the criminal justice system*. Washington, DC: U.S. Department of Justice, National Institute of Corrections.

Rubenstein, M. L., Clarke, S. H., & White, T. J. (1980). *Alaska bans plea bargaining*. Washington, DC: U.S. Department of Justice, National Institute of Justice.

Smith, D. A., & Visher, C. A. (1981). Street-level justice: Situational determinants of police arrest decisions. *Social Problems, 29*, 167-177.

U.S. General Accounting Office. (1990). *Death penalty sentencing: Report to Senate and House Committee on the Judiciary*. Washington, DC: Government Printing Office.

Unnever, J. D. (1982). Direct and organizational discrimination in the sentencing of drug offenders. *Social Problems, 30*, 212-225.

Zalman, M., Ostrom, C. W., Jr., Guilliams, P., & Peaslee, G. (1979). *Sentencing in Michigan: A report of the Michigan Felony Sentencing Project*. Lansing: Michigan Felony Sentencing Project.

Zatz, M. S. (1984). Race, ethnicity, and determinate sentencing: A new dimension to an old control. *Criminology, 22*, 147-171.

NO   MARY ANN MASON and EILEEN GAMBRILL

In a major report recently published by the National Council on Crime and Delinquency (NCCD), the principal finding is that African Americans are significantly overrepresented at every stage of juvenile justice processing in California (Austin, Dimas, & Steinhart, 1992). The report identifies institutional racism as the number-one cause of this disproportion: "African-Americans are expected to act violently; when this stereotype is held by law enforcement officers and other juvenile justice officials, it leads to selective over-arrest and over-incarceration of Black youth" (p. 35).

The report, however, reveals two other striking facts that contradict the primacy of this explanation. The first is the statistical finding that "African-American youth have violent felony and drug arrest rates that are three times the same rates for Latino youth and ten times the identical rate for Anglo-American youth. This correlates with high indices of African-American representation at post-arrest processing points" (p. 27). The other fact is that the number of youth from the major minority groups incarcerated in California increased by about 50% between 1985 and 1989. This is the same time frame in which mandatory sentencing for drug offenses led to a population explosion in California's court and prison system.

Isn't this a case of shooting the messenger? Even granting there is some institutional racism in California's juvenile justice system, it alone cannot explain the huge disparity in arrest and detention for violent crimes and drug offenses between African American males (females have a much lower rate of arrest and detention) and Anglo-American males. In fact, the racism explanation is weakened further by the fact that Latino youth, who constitute the largest racial minority population in California (43.4% Latino versus 8.67% African American), are not overrepresented at any stage of juvenile justice processing. Moreover, Asian Americans, who make up 10.29% of the population, are significantly *underrepresented* at all stages.

The real issue is that young African American males are committing crimes of violence and drug abuse at a frightening and escalating rate. A racist juvenile justice system is not creating that fact, nor will sensitivity training and affirmative action in the juvenile justice system abolish that fact. Far more to the point are problems of institutional poverty, and of families headed by unwed teenage mothers in the African American community. These problems are much more difficult and costly to solve than a housecleaning of the juvenile justice system. Although most observers, and the National Council on Crime and Delinquency report as well, allude to these problems as a cause of African American juvenile crime, they give them only a passing nod, either because they are too big to tackle or because they are in somebody else's jurisdiction. In doing so, they seriously distort the nature of the problem and its solutions.

Another issue, not addressed at all by the NCCD report, is the fact that many of these crimes are committed by mentally ill youth who are then incarcerated because there is no other facility available in which to treat them. An official of the California Youth Authority estimates that 26% of youths in custody are severely emotionally disturbed. Other studies of the California adolescent population suggest that acutely ill African American youth are far more likely to be held in detention centers than in psychiatric hospitals. One study indicates that 80% of all adolescent patients in psychiatric hospitals are white, although only 52% of youths in California are white. Most of these adolescents are in private hospitals, where all minority groups are seriously underrepresented. The controlling factor identified for this disparity is not racism per se, but the presence or absence of private health insurance (Mason & Gibbs, 1992; Schwartz, 1989). The availability of health care reflects the income level of the family. Families with full employment are more likely to have access to private health insurance. In California, white families have significantly higher incomes than either African American or Hispanic families. Providing equal access to mental health care for adolescents might go further than changing the personnel of the juvenile justice system in eliminating racial disparities in arrest and detention—but it is far more costly and attached to the larger behemoth of our failing health services and delivery system.

The NCCD report is perhaps closer to the mark of institutional racism when it compares the disposition of juveniles with the same offenses in secure detention in juvenile hall and in secure commitment to training school. African American youths are significantly more likely to be detained in both these facilities than are Anglo-American youths. Is this a clear instance of institutional racism, as the report suggests? Perhaps—but consider other explanations. The report establishes that African Americans are greatly overrepresented at this juncture in the process, particularly with relation to drugs and violent crime. In considering a disposition, a judge must consider the alternatives. Sending a youth back to a neighborhood where violent juvenile crime has become a way of life for too many is not necessarily the best approach. The underlying philosophy of a separate court for juveniles is that the disposition can be tailored to the needs of the adolescent. Anglo-American youth may have more family or community resources available to them, or they may have access to mental health services through their parents' health insurance. The NCCD report itself recommends the establishment of alternative, nonsecure placements and programs, such as nonsecure residential placements, currently lacking in the system. In the absence of such alternative placements, secure detention, rather than a return to the community that promoted juvenile crime, may be the only appropriate solution.

Racism has become an emotionally charged and all-embracing term in American rhetoric, and it often helps to obscure and even exonerate more compelling societal failures. The predominance of young African American males at every step of the juvenile justice process cannot be attributed principally to racism in that system. That is too easy, and it is not correct. The more difficult and more accurate policy approach is to identify and tackle potential problems even before these young people are born. What is the family environment for these children? What are the educational and medical opportunities, including mental health services, available to these children throughout their young lives? Are these children provided special support during the volatile period of adolescence? Can they look forward to socially acceptable employment opportunities in the public or private sector? The problem is rarely created upon the first contact with juvenile justice system, and it will not be solved there.

References

Austin, J., Dimas, J., & Steinhart, D. (1992). *The over-representation of minority youth in the California juvenile justice system.* San Francisco: National Council on Crime and Delinquency.

Mason, M. A., & Gibbs, J. T. (1992). Patterns of adolescent psychiatric hospitalization: Implications for social policy. *American Journal of Orthopsychiatry, 62,* 447-457.

Schwartz, I. M. (1989). *(In)justice for juveniles.* Lexington, MA: Lexington.

MARY ANN MASON and EILEEN GAMBRILL RESPOND

Professor Gibbs focuses almost entirely on the adult criminal justice system, rather than the juvenile justice system. Many of her observations, however, are similar to those made by the National Council on Crime and Delinquency regarding the California juvenile justice system. In both systems, black males are greatly overrepresented in prison populations. Both Professor Gibbs and the NCCD report attribute a great deal of this overrepresentation to racial policies.

Professor Gibbs notes that there are two hypotheses that attempt to explain the racial disparities in the criminal justice system. The first is differential involvement—"that blacks commit more crimes and more serious offenses (in proportion to their population) than do whites"—and the second is differential processing—"that differential rates of incarceration reflect selective law enforcement at every stage of the juvenile and criminal justice systems, from the police, to the prosecutors, to the juries and judges." Professor Gibbs states that "dozens of studies have been conducted to produce supporting evidence for both of these theories." She presents studies, however, to support only differential processing. Following a review of these studies, she states that "a fair assessment of these studies is that 'there is convincing evidence of racial disparity at the sentencing stage, which contributes to the disproportionate incarcerations of minorities in several states' (Dehais, 1987)."

This assessment hardly proves that differential processing is responsible for the overwhelming racial disparities found in the criminal justice system. Moreover, she does not deal at all with the many studies utilizing victims' reports and other methods rather than official reports, which support differential involvement. One such study of victims using data produced by the National Crime Survey for 1973-1977 reveals that "the victims' reports of offenders' sex, race and age are strongly related to incidence rates of offending" (Hindelang, 1981). Another study that reviewed research concerning the extent to which studies of delinquency using official records produce results compatible with studies of delinquency that use self-reports found that although there is no serious racial disparity in the case of minor offenses, "both self-report and victimization data suggest an overinvolvement of Blacks in more serious offenses" (Hindelang, Hirschi, & Weis, 1979).

Professor Gibbs does not permit her support of the differential processing position to restrict her focus to the problems of the juvenile justice system. In her policy recommendations she argues for reforms that would attack the roots of crime beginning in early childhood. With these recommendations she is implicitly recognizing that racism in the juvenile justice system is not the cause of minority youth involvement in the criminal justice system but only one factor in a far more complex network of society's failures.

References

Dehais, R. J. (1987). *Racial discrimination in the criminal justice system: An assessment of the empirical evidence.* Albany: State University of New York, New York African American Institute.

Hindelang, M. (1981). Variations in rates of offending. *American Sociological Review, 44,* 461-475.

Hindelang, M., Hirschi, T., & Weis, G. (1979). Correlates of delinquency. *American Sociological Review, 40,* 99-1015.

JEWELLE TAYLOR GIBBS RESPONDS

Mason and Gambrill cite the recent report from the National Council on Crime and Delinquency (Austin, Dimas, & Steinhart, 1992) to support their position that the juvenile justice system does not discriminate against African American youth because they do, in fact, have much higher arrest rates than white or Latino youth for violent felony and drug offenses, and their incarceration rates nearly doubled between 1985 and 1989. Moreover, Mason and Gambrill suggest that critics of the juvenile justice system should really focus on the underlying issues of poverty, inadequate education, and lack of employment opportunities that combine to create incentives to black youth to engage in criminal activities.

Although they have correctly noted that black youth have high arrest and incarceration rates, Mason and Gambrill have failed to address some of the factors that have been advanced to explain the initial disparity in arrest rates, which is the first major event in a sequence of decisions that leads to different outcomes for blacks and whites in the juvenile justice system. First, black youth are more likely than white youth to be stopped and searched by police, partly because they live in inner-city neighborhoods with higher crime rates and partly because they have fewer private recreational facilities to keep them off the streets in the evenings. Second, police more often harass black youth and provoke them into verbal confrontations because of their antiauthority demeanor, so these youth become identified as troublemakers and are often arrested for minor offenses that would not result in arrests for white youth. Several large-scale studies have found that black and other minority youth are more likely than whites to be arrested, even when all other offense and demographic factors are controlled (Huizinga & Elliott, 1986; Tracy, Wolfgang, & Figlio, 1985). Moreover, surveys of self-reported delinquent behaviors show few differences between black and white youth, particularly when social class differences are controlled, but white youth consistently report higher levels of hard drug use than blacks (Dembo, 1988; Elliot & Huizinga, 1983; Tucker, 1985).

The fact that black youth are detained more frequently in juvenile hall and disproportionally committed to the California Youth Authority, even when the frequency and severity of their offenses are similar to those of white youth, cannot be lightly dismissed or attributed to good intentions of the sentencing judges. In fact, these decisions to incarcerate black youth rather than place them in alternative community programs or on supervised probation status are not only discriminatory but also extremely detrimental to their well-being. Once they have been incarcerated, they will be stigmatized, labeled as "jailbirds"; moreover, their education is interrupted and their occupational options are severely diminished.

California, for example, shows clear patterns of differential treatment in four of its largest counties in the overrepresentation of black youth at every stage of the juvenile justice system, and the disparities between white and black youth are even greater than in the nation as a whole, although this trend of disproportional commitment of African American youth to juvenile detention centers has been increasing throughout the country (Krisberg, Schwartz, Fishman, Eiskovitz, & Guttman, 1986). Whereas it is reasonable to expect a correlation between violent felony offenses and postarrest incarceration rates, it is also reasonable to question the consistently high initial arrest rates of black youth in counties with different demographic characteristics and overall rates of juvenile delinquency. As the authors of the NCCD report conclude after a careful analysis of the data and interviews with juvenile justice professionals from the four counties surveyed in the study: "In broad terms, this analysis unveils a picture of persistent, differential treatment for some minority groups after having accounted for pre-referral factors such as offenses and prior record. This leads us to the observation that some ethnic disparities in detention and sentencing outcomes arise sometime after arrest, possibly as an artifact of bias which is inherent in the juvenile justice decision-making process" (Austin et al., 1992, p. 20). Given this conclusion, enlightened public policy suggests that racial bias in the juvenile justice system must be identified and eliminated so that African American and other minority youth will not be triply penalized—first by their race, second by their poverty, and third by their involvement in the only system that offers them "equal opportunity."

References

Austin, J., Dimas, J., & Steinhart, D. (1992). *The over-representation of minority youth in the California juvenile justice system.* San Francisco: National Council on Crime and Delinquency.

Dembo, R. (1988). Delinquency among black youth. In J. T. Gibbs (Ed.), *Young, black and male in America: An endangered species.* Westport, CT: Auburn House.

Elliott, D. S., & Huizinga, D. (1983). Social class and delinquent behavior in a national youth panel: 1976-1980. *Criminology, 21,* 149-177.

Huizinga, D., & Elliott, D. S. (1986). *Juvenile offenders: Prevalence, offender incidence and arrest rates by race.* Boulder, CO: Institute of Behavioral Science.

Krisberg, B., Schwartz, I., Fishman, G., Eiskovitz, Z., & Guttman, E. (1986). *The incarceration of minority youth.* Minneapolis: University of Minnesota, Humphrey Institute of Public Affairs.

Tracy, P. W., Wolfgang, M. E., & Figlio, R. N. (1985). *Delinquency in two birth cohorts.* Washington, DC: U.S. Department of Justice.

Tucker, M. B. (1985). U.S. ethnic minorities and drug abuse: An assessment of a science and practice period. *International Journal of the Addictions, 20,* 1021-1047.

DEBATE 15

DUE PROCESS FOR ADOLESCENTS

> *Should adolescents have the same due process rights as adults when they are involuntarily committed to psychiatric hospitals?*

EDITORS' NOTE: There has been a recent rise in adolescent admissions to private psychiatric hospitals, prompting a closer look at the admissions standards pertaining to children and adolescents. All states, in the past 20 years or so, have passed stringent civil commitment laws restricting the involuntary commitment of adults to those who are judged by a court to be dangerous to themselves or others. These laws were passed in large part to protect the rights of individuals from inappropriate commitment, often by close relatives. In addition, there was a widespread belief that most mental institutions were merely warehousing patients, rather than providing effective treatment. Lawmakers have been divided, however, on what standard to apply to children and adolescents. Most state laws are silent on the subject, or allow commitment by parents with no judicial review if the admitting medical staff affirms there is a need for treatment. The U.S. Supreme Court, in *Parham v. J.R.,* affirmed this "need for treatment" standard, adding that parents will act to protect the best interests of their children and therefore judicial review is not necessary. Critics say parents may choose hospitalization for the wrong reasons: They may have no viable alternative in dealing with a troubled child, and their insurance may cover hospitalization. Although it is the reverse situation from the abortion issue, where adolescents may seek medical treatment without their parents' consent, this problem presents the same question: Who makes the medical decisions for an adolescent? Although our two authors agree on several issues, they disagree on the role of parents in the commitment process.

Mary Ann Mason says YES. She is an Associate Professor of Law and Social Welfare in the School of Social Welfare, University of California, Berkeley. She is the coauthor of "Patterns of Adolescent Psychiatric Hospitalization" (*American Journal of Orthopsychiatry*, 1992) and coeditor of this volume.

James W. Ellis argues NO. He is a Professor of Law at the University of New Mexico Law School and the coauthor of "Treating Children Under the New Mexico Mental Health and Developmental Disabilities Code" (*New Mexico Law Review*, 1980).

YES　　　　　　　　　　　　　　　　　　　　MARY ANN MASON

Who should have the power to admit children to psychiatric facilities, and what standards should govern those decisions? These two issues remain unsettled in nearly all states, but most states allow parents almost unlimited authority to commit their children to psychiatric hospitals if the admitting staff certify that there is a need for treatment. Meanwhile, the rate of admissions of juveniles, particularly older adolescents, to psychiatric hospitals has skyrocketed in the past two decades. Increasingly these admissions are to private, rather than public, hospitals. The increased numbers of hospitalized adolescents and the lack of clear-cut admission standards have raised the concern in the mental health community that some of these admissions may be inappropriate.

Take, for example, the hypothetical case of Myra. Myra was a rebellious 16-year-old who at first frequently skipped school and then began to disappear for days at a time. Her frantic parents notified the police upon her first disappearance. The police found Myra at a friend's house and returned her to her parents. The second time, Myra escaped to another state. The police in that state telephoned her parents, but claimed that Myra refused to return home. The police informed Myra's parents that they were unable to detain Myra any longer because she had committed no crime. A week later, Myra finally returned home on her own. Her parents, acting upon the advice of her high school counselor, immediately committed her to a private psychiatric hospital in a nearby city that specialized in working with troubled adolescents. The family's medical insurance covered a psychiatric stay of up to 60 days. Myra was released on the sixtieth day.

Let us examine Myra's hospital experience from the point of view of all the parties involved. First, Myra's parents: What options do they have in dealing with their incorrigible daughter? They have found that the police can provide little support. In their state, as in most, status offenders (juveniles who have broken no adult law but fail to conform to the rules for juveniles, such as school attendance, or who run away from home) are no longer controlled by the juvenile justice system. In a nationwide effort to decriminalize status offenses, most states will not detain a status offender overnight. Although police and school officials will often work diligently with the adolescents and their parents to correct unacceptable behavior, they do not have the power to threaten or to impose a jail stay.

What other choices do Myra's parents have? In their community, as in most, there is a dearth of community mental health centers that could provide intensive counseling and outpatient care on a daily basis. Their only real choices, short of hospitalization, are whatever counseling is available at Myra's high school (probably minimal) or the hourly services of a private psychotherapist. Their medical insurance, provided through Myra's father's employer, allows them 10 hours per year of outpatient psychotherapy. These hours were quickly exhausted. However, this same insurance policy allows up to 60 days each year for psychiatric hospitalization. It is not difficult to understand why Myra's parents chose this option.

What about the hospital? What is that institution's legal constraint in accepting or rejecting Myra? The U.S. Supreme Court addressed this issue in *Parham v. J.R.* (1979). In this case the Court agreed with Georgia law that when parents commit a minor they are acting in the child's best interests. The admitting physician must only agree that the minor has need for treatment. The willingness, or unwillingness, of the minor is irrelevant.

States can and sometimes do set higher standards. The legal standard regulating the involuntary civil commitment of minors varies widely among the states. A few states require the same standards for adolescents and children as they require for adults. The commitment threshold under this standard is that the individual constitutes a danger to self or others. Frequent judicial review upholding the same strict standard is required for longer stays. Most states, however, have lesser standards for adolescents and children, and they may or may not require judicial review. California, the pioneer in civil commitment laws relating to adults, currently holds three different standards for adolescents. Following recent changes in California law, minors 14 or older, like Myra, committed by their parents to a private hospital will be told by a patient's rights advocate upon admission that they have an opportunity for a second medical review if they object to their commitment. The second examiner —a doctor, not a judge—must only certify that there is a need for treatment, not that the adolescent is a danger to self or others. However, if a minor 14 or older is committed to a public hospital by his or her parents, the adolescent can request a judicial review. The judge (or hearing officer) must be convinced only that there is a "need for treatment." If the minor is a ward of the court, on the other hand, he or she is subject to the strict adult standard of "danger to self or others," and a judicial review must take place within 72 hours.

What about Myra? In most states the hospital would probably accept her for treatment following the Supreme Court ruling that parents and doctors are the appropriate decision makers. In California she would have the opportunity to request a second medical review that would determine whether she has "need for treatment," and whether the hospital is the "least restrictive alternative." Given the lack of alternative facilities and the vague standard of "need for treatment," the commitment would probably be upheld. In fact, it is unlikely that Myra would request this review. Most teenagers are too stunned by the experience of commitment to a psychiatric hospital with restraining rooms and locked wards to demand their rights.

Myra may or may not be helped by her 60 days in the psychiatric hospital. She may return home a chastened teenager with insight into her bad behavior and a will to adhere to authority, or she may return home even more defiant. She may or may not receive psychiatric treatment that is beneficial to her. What she definitely will gain from her experience is the stigma of psychiatric hospitalization. Her friends, her family, and the people at her school will look at her differently, and she will see herself, possibly for her whole life, as someone who is the victim of mental illness. Unless she is lucky or exceptionally strong, a victim mentality could overtake the proper development of her sense of individual responsibility. Her normal adolescent development may be arrested.

What if Myra is, in fact, mentally ill and not simply an incorrigible teenager? I would argue that the adult standard of "danger to self or others" would cover most serious manifestations of mental illness that would merit hospitalization. These would include suicide attempts, schizophrenic breaks that would render a minor out of touch with reality, and violent acts toward others. In the statutory scheme for adults in virtually all states, involuntary hospitalization is usually considered a temporary measure, with continuing judicial review. Usually only the most severe and chronic conditions would allow hospitalization for 60 days or more.

What if there are some forms of adolescent mental illness that would benefit from hospitalization, but will not meet the adult standards of civil commitment? Conceding that there may be some cases in this category, the risk of refusing these cases must be weighed against the greater risk of unnecessary hospitalization. The risk must also be balanced against the denial to adolescents of all the due process rights accorded to adults when their physical liberty is taken from them.

A study that I conducted with Jewelle Taylor Gibbs of psychiatric hospitalization of adolescents in California suggests that the presence or absence of private medical insurance plays the greatest role in determining which adolescents are hospitalized, and for how long (Mason & Gibbs, 1992). The typical patient is white, 15 or 16 years old, and privately insured, and is being treated in a private psychiatric hospital. Patients' lengths of stay are determined by the coverage allowed by their medical insurance. Many of these private hospitals advertise aggressively in medical and social work journals, and some extend their promotional reach to television. Minority adolescents, on the other hand, are far less likely to have private insurance and are far less likely to be found in psychiatric hospitals. If they are hospitalized, it is usually in one of the few public hospitals that offers beds for adolescents. Although our study does not prove that adolescents are being inappropriately hospitalized, it does suggest that the psychiatric commitment of adolescents is being inappropriately driven by insurance coverage.

What, then, are Myra's parents to do? They have insurance and they have run out of other options. They do not want to see their daughter fending for herself on the street, possibly victimized by adults or other adolescents. The problem is serious and widespread, but the solution is not psychiatric hospitalization. More facilities for troubled adolescents, including residential facilities, shelters for runaways, community mental health centers that offer comprehensive outpatient treatment, and school-based mental health clinics, can be part of the solution. Insurance coverage should be radically revised to include more emphasis on extensive outpatient therapy rather than its current support of hospitalization. As for all complex problems, the solutions are not easy, and they are not quickly forthcoming. The law, however, can take the lead by banning the inappropriate solution of psychiatric hospitalization of an adolescent who is no danger to self or others.

Reference

Mason, M. A., & Gibbs, J. T. (1992). Patterns of adolescent psychiatric hospitalization: Implications for social policy. *American Journal of Orthopsychiatry, 62,* 447-458.

NO JAMES W. ELLIS

In most states, parents may commit their children to mental institutions without a hearing or any other form of judicial scrutiny. If a parent wants a child committed, and a hospital will accept the child as a patient, no legal authority will hear the child's protest. Moreover, the child-patient has no standing to petition for release from the institution until he or she reaches the statutory age of majority. Until that time any request for discharge must be made by the parent. Thus the minor admitted to a mental hospital on application of a parent is denied access to virtually all procedural protections—notice, hearing, appellate review, and habeas corpus—rights afforded all other patients institutionalized against their will.

The Decision to Commit

The significance of the role parents play in the commitment of children is difficult to overstate: The parent alone may seek hospitalization and release of the child. Currently the only limitation on parental discretion is the requirement of concurrence by the committing authority, usually the administrator of the hospital or the admitting physician. These officials frequently fail to exercise independent judgment, however, generally deferring to the wishes of the parents. Many institutions may investigate a proposed commitment no further than the information supplied by the family of the proposed patient.

Probably, few parents are guilty of railroading their children into asylums in the manner that spurred nineteenth-century reform movements. Still, the emergence of a countercultural lifestyle among young people and the troubled reaction of some parents lends support to the suggestion that some parents have resorted to voluntary commitment procedures in order to sanction behavior of which they disapproved. Parents may be confused, bewildered, and saddened by what they perceive as their children's "crazy" behavior. In individual cases there may be some validity to the parents' belief in a connection between acceptance of countercultural styles and emotional difficulties, but parents' own visceral reaction to the different lifestyle may color their diagnosis. Where parental action does result in unjustified commitment, it is probably not out of malevolence or filial hatred but out of a feeling more akin to irritation or embarrassment over the child's unconventional behavior.

The level of irritation or embarrassment can become acute and reach a level at which parents become desperate.

Given that parents make the decision to commit their child at a time of great emotional stress, the decision may be made without a careful consideration of possible alternatives. The availability of alternatives is in large part determined by the socioeconomic status of the family. Although no studies have been found that focus on the relationship of social class to early or late hospitalization, it has been observed that upper-middle-class families have access to alternatives short of hospitalization—such as special schools, long vacations, and private psychiatric treatment—that are not available to families from lower socioeconomic groups. The poor, when faced with acute family problems, do not have recourse to these facilities; they also have the least access to informed assistance in making decisions involving their children's illness and possible commitment.

Parental Authority and Family Privacy

Thomas Szasz (1973) argues that a source of parental power is the law's interest in shoring up the institution of the family, and that hospitalization serves this interest by reducing family tensions "without disrupting the moral integrity of the family as an institution" (p. 120). Thus, unlike the social institutions of divorce and separation, commitment maintains the legal structure of the family, and promotes the illusion that nothing is irremediably wrong with the relationships involved. Szasz concludes:

> Thus, for the individual, involuntary hospitalization ensures the maintenance of the family as a good institution. For society, it ensures the maintenance of family relationships, loyalties, and responsibilities as positive moral values. Our whole social system needs the safety valve that commitment laws provide. Without it, our traditional ideas about the duties and rights of family members would have to be reexamined, reassessed, and changed. (p. 122)

One does not have to share Szasz's ideology to agree that commitment laws, and juvenile commitment provisions in particular, have as their paramount objective the maintenance of family autonomy in dealing with aberrant behavior within the family. As a result, the authority granted to parents in the area of commitment to mental hospitals is extremely broad. Can such a broad grant of power be justified? To justify such an extensive grant of power, supporters of broad parental prerogatives point to analogous areas of the law and argue that the state should continue to decline to intrude into the parent-child relationship.

An Appropriate Role for Parents in the Commitment Process

What should be the parents' role in a new legal framework for the hospitalization of mentally ill children? The first parental function will continue to be diagnostic. Parents (and to a certain extent schoolteachers) will be the persons most likely to observe disturbed behavior at an early stage, and will continue to be the persons most likely to refer the child for professional diagnosis and treatment. However, the advantage of proximity to the child does not necessarily give parents the expertise or objectivity required to make a determination of the precise nature of the problem or to decide whether hospitalization is a necessary or desirable response. Thus the parent may remain the initiator of the inquiry into the child's situation, but should not retain the power to conduct that inquiry alone or to decide on the final disposition.

A second parental function may, in some cases, include personal involvement in the treatment process. This may take the form of individual counseling or therapy for one or both parents, work with a psychiatric social worker, conjoint family therapy involving both the child and the parents, or a combination of these and other treatment approaches. Depending upon the kind of treatment that the child, and perhaps other family members, are to undergo, parents may also be asked or required to contribute financially to the cost of the hospitalization. Depending upon the child's age and the family situation at the time of his or her release from the hospital, the family may also be called upon to take the child back into the home when treatment is completed. But none of these admittedly important functions requires that parents decide whether the child should be hospitalized. They are often ill equipped to make that decision by themselves. A legal framework must be devised that will infuse expertise, and objectivity, into a function that the parents now exercise alone.

Alternative System for Juvenile Commitment

An acceptable juvenile commitment system will take into account the developmental differences between adults and children, the child's family situation, and procedural safeguards designed to protect the child's interests.

One way to ensure that every child has an impartial determination of his or her need for hospitalization is to require a judicial hearing whenever hospitalization is sought. There are, however, disadvantages to such a system. A stressful and superfluous legal proceeding could not be avoided even if the child agreed to hospitalization. The child could be allowed to waive a formal hearing and consent to the hospitalization after consultation with an attorney. Safeguards, such as retaining the right to seek release in a later hearing, should be provided to prevent this system from camouflaging a return to unbridled parental discretion. Therefore, an appointed attorney should certify to the court having jurisdiction in juvenile commitment cases that he or she has (a) consulted with the child about the proposed commitment, (b) explained to the child both the right to contest the commitment and the possible alternatives to commitment, and (c) ascertained that it is the true wish of the child to enter the hospital and forgo a judicial proceeding.

If a child waives the commitment hearing and later wants to be released from the hospital, a hearing should be mandatory if the release is contested. Just as a juvenile should not be allowed to waive the right to counsel prior to commitment, so hospitalization of a child should not go unreviewed for a long period of time, nor should judicial scrutiny depend on the child's uncounseled initiative in submitting a notice of intent to seek release. The system should contain a provision for mandatory periodic review of all cases of committed children, regardless of whether the commitment was initially contested.

The Standard for Commitment

Children could be committed under the "in need of treatment" standard, but no child committed under that standard should have treatment continued involuntarily for more than six months. By comparison, under a dangerousness standard a child might be hospitalized beyond that time limit if necessary. This compromise recognizes that although the state and the parents have a strong interest in providing involuntary treatment for a child who needs it, this rationale loses force if the child is still unwilling after a period of months, because treatment is unlikely to be successful when the patient strongly and consistently opposes it.

Reference

Szasz, T. (1973). *The age of madness: The history of involuntary mental hospitalization.* New York: Anchor.

JAMES W. ELLIS RESPONDS

The civil commitment standards for adults are a poor match to the legal situation and therapeutic needs of children and adolescents. Limiting commitment to minors who are dangerous to themselves or to others creates a dilemma that is not present in the adult system.

Limiting adult commitment to cases of dangerousness allows nondangerous individuals whose mental disability would benefit from treatment to seek that treatment as voluntary patients. The analogy to minors is strained on this point: They may be unable, because of their youth, to seek and obtain treatment as voluntary patients. A better solution is a child commitment standard that focuses on the child's therapeutic needs and avoids the harm caused by unnecessary institutionalization. For example, New Mexico's statute requires "(1) that as a result of mental disorder or developmental disability the minor needs and is likely to benefit from the treatment or habilitation services proposed; and (2) that the proposed commitment is consistent with the treatment needs of the minor and with the least drastic means principle" (Ellis & Carter, 1980, p. 281).

But far more important than the precise formulation of the standard is that hearings be held at all. In the years since the U.S. Supreme Court decided *Parham,* the discussion about the desirability of hearings has focused largely on the rights of older adolescents who have expressed their objections to hospitalization. In my view, our attention needs to be directed to children who remain unprotected by all but the most liberal statutes. In particular, I believe we need to provide hearings for younger children and children with mental retardation. The purpose of such hearings is not so much to provide a forum for the child's articulated objections as it is to prevent unnecessary institutionalization of those children most likely to be harmed by it. We need hearings for these younger children not because we want to hear what they have to say, but because we recognize the potential damage they may suffer if institutionalized inappropriately.

More than a decade has passed since *Parham,* and over that time, our ability to develop beneficial and effective alternatives to hospitalization has grown. Simultaneously, the threat that children will be institutionalized inappropriately has grown, largely because of the aggressive marketing of private psychiatric hospitals. The time may have come to revisit this issue.

Reference

Ellis, J. W., & Carter, M. (1980). Treating children under the New Mexico Mental Health and Developmental Disabilities Code. *New Mexico Law Review, 10*, 279-309.

MARY ANN MASON RESPONDS

Professor Ellis and I are in agreement about many aspects of this troubling issue. We both agree that poor children have less access to mental health treatment than children with money (or, more likely, insurance). We also agree that the cause of the adolescent's troublesome behavior may not be mental illness, but rather social dysfunction, or "acting-out" behavior. We part company, on two counts, however, with regard to our recommendations for commitment standards.

Professor Ellis advocates a "need for treatment" standard, with a modified judicial review. I insist upon the adult standard of "danger to self or others" with full judicial review, as provided for adults. It may be that our disagreement stems from Professor Ellis's confidence in the efficacy of hospital treatment and mine stems from a serious lack of confidence in such treatment. As I note in my initial argument, insurance plays a determining role in adolescent hospitalization; for the most part, it determines the incidence of admission as well as the length of stay. This fact does not inspire confidence in the appropriateness of hospital treatment.

Professor Ellis is also far more sanguine than I about the positive role of parents in the diagnosis and continuing involvement in adolescents' treatment. This factor sways him toward a paternalistic model of commitment for adolescents. Although positive parental involvement is certainly an ideal, I believe it is often not the reality. With the retreat of the juvenile justice system from the regulation of status offenders, parents are forced to deal with incorrigible and often hostile children on their own. Sometimes the only way parents can keep a child off the streets is to hospitalize that child. But hospitals cannot serve the role of the police. Adolescents deserve the same protection as adults from punitive and unfair curtailment of their liberty, and that includes inappropriate hospitalization.

DEBATE 16

LIMITING ABUSE REPORTING LAWS

➤ *Should current reporting laws regarding sexual and physical abuse of children be sharply limited to discourage overreporting?*

EDITORS' NOTE: Mandatory reporting laws were introduced in 1974 with the passage of the federal Child Abuse Prevention and Treatment Act. This act offered funds to states that developed laws requiring medical, education, social work, child-care, and law enforcement professionals to report suspected physical abuse, sexual abuse and exploitation, physical neglect, and emotional maltreatment of children. Failure to report triggered civil or criminal penalties. The general public was encouraged, but not required, to report suspicion of child abuse as well. Many states had such laws already in place and nearly all others followed suit. These reporting acts produced immediate and dramatic effects. In 1963 approximately 150,000 children were brought to the attention of public authorities; in 1982 the number had soared to 1.3 million. Following thorough screening of reports by child protective agencies, more than 400,000 American families were placed under home supervision. Responding to this rapid rise of state intervention into private homes, advocates for parents' rights and critics of child protection philosophy questioned several aspects of the state's procedures. How were protective agencies defining abuse and neglect? Were their definitions based on an ethnocentric vision of middle-class family life? Was the postremoval solution of foster care placement in the best interests of the children? Were mothers on AFDC, who were under continual supervision in order to receive benefits, placed under unfair scrutiny while richer families never came to the attention of child protection agencies? And finally, was the basic right of parenthood being terminated without due process? Our authors attempt to ascertain the delicate balance between the state's right to protect children from abuse and neglect and parents' right to privacy and equal treatment.

Douglas J. Besharov says YES. He is a Resident Scholar at the American Enterprise Institute for Public Policy Research and the author of many articles and books on abuse and neglect, including *Protecting Children from Abuse and Neglect: Policy and Practice* (1988). His contribution to this debate is reprinted with the permission of The Free Press, a Division of Macmillan, Inc., from *Recognizing Child Abuse: A Guide for the Concerned,* by Douglas J. Besharov. Copyright © 1990 by Douglas J. Besharov.

Richard P. Barth argues NO. He is the Hutto-Patterson Professor, School of Social Welfare, University of California at Berkeley. He is also Co-Principal Investigator at UC Berkeley's National Child Welfare Research Center.

Limiting Abuse Reporting Laws

YES   DOUGLAS J. BESHAROV

At the same time that many seriously abused children go unreported, there is an equally serious problem that further undercuts efforts to prevent the maltreatment of children: The nation's child protective agencies are being inundated by "unfounded" reports. Although rules, procedures, and even terminology vary (some states use the term "unfounded," whereas others use "unsubstantiated" or "not indicated"), in essence, an "unfounded" report is one that is dismissed after an investigation finds insufficient evidence on which to proceed.

The emotionally charged desire to "do something" about child abuse, fanned by repeated and often sensational media coverage, has led to an understandable but counterproductive overreaction by professionals and citizens who report suspected child abuse. Depending on the community, as many as 65% of all reports are closed after an initial investigation reveals no evidence of maltreatment. This situation is in sharp contrast to that found in 1975, when only about 35% of all reports were unfounded.

New York State has one of the highest rates of unfounded reports in the nation, and its experience illustrates how severe the problem has become. Between 1979 and 1983, although the number of reports received by the Department of Social Services increased by about 50% (from 51,836 to 74,120), the percentage of substantiated reports fell about 16% (from 42.8% to 35.8%). In fact, the *absolute number* of substantiated reports actually fell by about 100. Thus almost 23,000 additional families were investigated, but fewer children were aided (Root, 1984).

These statistics should not be surprising. Potential reporters are frequently told to "take no chances" and to report any child for whom they have the slightest concern. There is a recent tendency to tell people to report children whose behavior suggests that they may have been abused—even in the absence of any other evidence of maltreatment. These "behavioral indicators" include, for example, children who are unusually withdrawn or shy, as well as children who are unusually friendly to strangers. However, only a small minority of children who exhibit such behaviors have actually been maltreated.

Ten years ago, when professionals were narrowly construing their reporting obligations to avoid taking action to protect endangered children, this approach may have been needed. Now, however, all it does is ensure that child abuse hot lines will be flooded with inappropriate and unfounded reports. For example, a child with a minor bruise, whether or not there is evidence of parental assault, is often reported as abused.

Many hot lines accept reports even when callers cannot give reasons for suspecting that a child's condition is caused by the parent's behavior. I observed one hot-line operator accepting a report about a 17-year-old boy found in a drunken stupor. That the boy, and perhaps his family, might benefit from counseling is not disputable. But that hardly justifies the initiation of an involuntary child protective investigation. As Chris Mouzakitis (1984), a professor of social work, concludes: "Much of what is reported is not worthy of follow up" (pp. 71, 75).

There is a deeper problem. Across the nation, child protective agencies are being pressed to accept categories of cases that traditionally have not been considered their responsibility and for which their skills do not seem appropriate. In community after community, the dearth of family-oriented social services is pushing child protective agencies to broaden their role from that of highly focused services for children in serious danger to that of all-encompassing child welfare services.

In essence, child protective agencies are paying the price for their past successes. People know that a report of possible maltreatment will result in action. As a result, child abuse hot lines are being barraged by reports that, at base, really involve the truancy, delinquency, school problems, and sexual acting out of adolescents—not abuse or neglect. Other inappropriate reports involve children who need specialized education or residential placement; parent-child conflicts with no indication of abuse or neglect; and chronic problems involving property, unemployment, inadequate housing, or poor money management. Many of these reports result in families receiving much-needed services, but many do not. Either way, these additional, inappropriate calls to child abuse hot lines significantly increase the number of unsubstantiated cases, misdirect scarce investigative resources, and are an unjustified violation of parental rights.

Laws against child abuse are an implicit recognition that family privacy must give way to the need to protect helpless children. But in seeking to protect children, it is all too easy to ignore the legitimate rights of parents. Each year, about 700,000 families are put through investigations of unfounded reports. This is a massive and unjustified violation of parental rights. In response, a national group of parents and professionals has been formed to represent those who have been falsely accused of abusing their children. Calling itself VOCAL, for Victims of Child Abuse Laws, the group publishes a national newsletter and has about 5,000 members in more than 100 chapters. Every state except Rhode Island has at least 1 chapter; California has 10. Canada has 9 chapters. In Minnesota, members of VOCAL collected 2,000 signatures on a petition asking the governor to remove Scott County prosecutor Kathleen Morris from office because of her alleged misconduct in bringing charges, subsequently dismissed, against 24 adults in Jordan, Minnesota. In Arizona, VOCAL members were able to sidetrack temporarily a $5.4 million budgetary supplement that would have added 77 investigators to local child protective agencies.

Few unfounded reports are made maliciously. Studies of sexual abuse reports, for example, suggest that, at most, 4-10% are knowingly false (Berliner, 1988; Jones & McGraw, 1987; Pearson & Thoennes, 1988, pp. 91, 93). Many involve situations in which the person reporting, in a well-intentioned effort to protect a child, overreacts to a vague and often misleading possibility that the child may have been or is being maltreated. Others involve situations of poor child care that, although of legitimate concern, simply do not amount to child abuse or neglect. In fact, a substantial proportion of unfounded cases are referred to other agencies to provide needed services for the families.

Moreover, an unfounded report does not necessarily mean that the child was not actually abused or neglected. Evidence of child maltreatment is hard to obtain and may not be uncovered when agencies lack the time and resources to complete thorough investigations, or when inaccurate information is given to investigators. Other cases are labeled unfounded when no services are available to help the families involved. Some cases must be closed because the children or families cannot be located.

A certain proportion of unfounded reports, therefore, is an inherent—and legitimate—aspect of reporting *suspected* child abuse or neglect and is necessary to ensure the adequate protection of children. Hundreds of thousands of strangers report their suspicions; they cannot all be right. But current rates of unfounded reports go beyond anything that is reasonably needed. Worse, they endanger children who are really abused.

Inappropriate Reporting Endangers Abused Children

The flood of unfounded reports is overwhelming the limited resources of child protective agencies. For fear of missing even one abused child, workers perform extensive investigations of vague and apparently unsupported reports. Even when a home visit in response to an anonymous report turns up no evidence of maltreatment, workers usually interview neighbors, schoolteachers, and day-care personnel to make sure that the child is not abused. Even repeated anonymous and unfounded reports do not prevent further investigation. All this takes time.

As a result, children who are in real danger are getting lost in the press of inappropriate cases. Forced to allocate a substantial portion of their limited resources to unfounded reports, child protective agencies are less able to respond promptly and effectively when children are in serious danger. Some reports are left uninvestigated for a week or even two weeks after they are received. Investigations often miss key facts as workers rush to clear cases, and dangerous home situations receive inadequate supervision, as workers ignore pending cases to investigate the new reports that arrive daily on their desks. Decision making also suffers. With so many cases of insubstantial or unproved risk to children, caseworkers are desensitized to the obvious warning signals of immediate and serious danger.

These nationwide conditions help explain why 25-50% of deaths from child abuse involve children who were previously known to the authorities. Tens of thousands of others children suffer serious injuries short of death while under the supervision of child protective agencies. In one Iowa case, for example, the noncustodial father reported to the local department of social services that his 34-month-old daughter had bruises on her buttocks; he also told the agency that he believed that the bruises were caused by the mother's live-in boyfriend. The agency investigated and substantiated the abuse. (The boyfriend was not interviewed, however.) At an agency staff meeting the next day (two days after the initial report), it was decided *not* to remove the child from the mother's custody, and, instead, to make follow-up visits, coupled with day-care, counseling, and other appropriate services. *But no follow-up visit was made.* Eight days later, the child was hospitalized in a comatose state, with bruises, both old and new, over most of her body. The child died after three days of unsuccessful treatment. The boyfriend was convicted of second-degree murder. The father's lawsuit against the agency for its negligent handling of his report was settled for $82,500 (see *Buege v. Iowa,* 1980).

Ironically, by weakening the system's ability to respond, unfounded reports actually discourage appropriate ones. The sad fact is that many responsible individuals are not reporting endangered children because they believe that the system's response will be so weak that reporting will do no good or may even make things worse. In 1984, a study of the impediments to reporting conducted by Jose Alfaro, who was then coordinator of the New York City Mayor's Task Force on Child Abuse and Neglect, concluded: "Professionals who emphasize their professional judgment have experienced problems in dealing with the child protective agency, and are more likely to doubt the efficacy of protective service intervention and are more likely not to report in some situations, especially when they believe they can do a better job helping the family" (p. 66).

All communities have had their share of news stories about children who have been "allowed" to die. Newspapers, television, and radio reports all focus on the sensational details of unproved charges and follow up with editorials about helpless children and the need for more reporting. The *New Republic*'s

TRB complained: "A lot of the graphic horror stories in the press are little more than child porn, published or broadcast because editors and producers want to titillate. And when they're not being salacious, the media [are] being mawkish, which sells almost as well." The result? More media spots calling on people to report suspected abuse; another brochure or conference for professionals describing their legal responsibility to report; and, perhaps, a small increase in agency staffing. But the main result of these periodic flurries of activity is an increased number of unfounded reports.

Professionals and private citizens need to do a much better job of identifying and reporting suspected cases of child abuse, while also guarding against inappropriate reporting. Recognizing appropriately reportable situations is difficult, but the current high rates of simultaneously under- and overreporting are unfair to the children and parents involved and threaten to undo much of the progress that has been made in building child protective programs. A proper balance must be struck.

If child protective agencies are to function effectively, they must be relieved of the heavy burden of unfounded reports. To call for more careful reporting of child abuse is not to be coldly indifferent to the plight of endangered children. Rather, it is to be realistic about the limits to our ability to operate child protective systems.

References

Alfaro, J. (1984). *Impediments to mandated reporting of suspected child abuse and neglect in New York City.* New York: Mayor's Task Force on Child Abuse and Neglect.

Berliner, L. (1988). Deciding whether a child has been sexually abused. In B. Nicholson (Ed.), *Sexual abuse allegations in custody and visitation cases* (pp. 48-69). Washington, DC: American Bar Association.

Buege v. Iowa, No. 20521 (Allamakee, Iowa, July 30, 1980).

Jones, D., & McGraw, J. M. (1987). Reliable and fictitious accounts of sexual abuse in children. *Journal of Interpersonal Violence, 2,* 27-45.

Mouzakitis, C. (1984). Investigation and initial assessment in child protective services. In W. Holder & K. Hayes (Eds.), *Malpractice and liability in child protective services.* Longmont, CO: Bookmakers Guild.

Pearson, J., & Thoennes, N. (1988). Difficult dilemma: Responding to sexual abuse allegations in custody and visitation disputes. In D. Besharov (Ed.), *Protecting children from abuse and neglect: Policy and practice* (pp. 91-112). Springfield, IL: Charles C Thomas.

Root, C. (1984, September 14). [Memorandum to Sandy Berman from Charles Root, New York State Department of Social Services].

TRB. (1985, May 13). Greasy kid stuff. *New Republic,* p. 4.

NO RICHARD P. BARTH

A child abuse report has become the passport to services delivered by the public child welfare services system. Although many have argued that we need to provide family-centered, community-based services to families who are in trouble but have not yet become entangled in child abuse, the fiscal realities are that public child welfare services are focused on clients in the gravest danger. These are children who have been seriously endangered or harmed by child abuse and neglect. The vast majority of children who have been abused or neglected but have not been *seriously* endangered or abused will receive little more than a child abuse report, a brief telephone or face-to-face assessment of their needs, and a referral to existing community-based agencies for services. Reports such as these that are not followed by ongoing services are often called "unfounded" or "unsubstantiated" reports. Much—indeed, too much—has been made of the apparent inefficiencies of such reports. Many of these "unfounded" reports result in children and families getting needed assistance. Indeed, Fryer, Bross, Krugman, Benson, and Baird (1990) found very high client satisfaction among families who received child protective services attention, even though their cases were "unfounded."

The de facto definitions of *child abuse* and *child neglect* have been sharply narrowed over the past few years to reduce overly intrusive agency responses and to save scarce dollars. In California, legislation was passed in 1988 to limit the definitions of physical abuse and neglect. There was no apparent direct impact on the number of child abuse reports or investigations. Fewer children received services after those investigations, but the steady increase in investigations that characterized previous years did not waiver. Apparently, social workers had gradually narrowed the category of child abuse to such an extent—as a response to fiscal and judicial pressures to spend less and intrude less—that a change in the law had virtually no impact on their practice.

Arguing against further limiting the definitions of child abuse risks two important charges: first, that the flood of unfounded reports is stretching the child welfare system so thin that truly abused children are harmed by the lack of services; and second, that unsubstantiated child abuse reports lead to harsh intrusions into the lives of families that do more harm than good. The notion that resources devoted to child protective services investigations and referrals diminish the overall effectiveness of ongoing child welfare service provision is often argued (e.g., Kamerman & Kahn, 1990; Pelton, 1989), but it remains undocumented. This assumes that child welfare services have fixed resources and that a unit increase in child abuse reporting results in a unit decrease in ongoing services. This assumption is not founded, as increased child abuse reports are generally met with increases (albeit not always one-to-one increases) in resources needed to serve child abuse victims. That is, the public is squarely behind the need to reduce the harms of child abuse and its aftermath and is willing to increase services to protect children. This argument also assumes that long-term services to the most abused children are more effective than assessment and referral to families at the brink of crisis. There is no compelling evidence to indicate that the benefits that accrue from child welfare "investigations" are any more or less than those that accrue from ongoing services. Indeed, it is quite plausible that social workers achieve good results when they go out and talk with families in crisis, indicate the community's concern, and steer them to resources that reduce the risk of subsequent harm. We know that this cannot help all families, and that as many as 40% of reports will be followed by subsequent child abuse reports. Nonetheless, at least some subsequent reports are preempted by social workers' visits and referral to other services.

Unsubstantiated child abuse reports have information value. Many unsubstantiated reports are later followed by substantiated reports. An unsubstantiated report provides information to social workers who must make future decisions about substantiation. These reports may also provide information that helps some parents avoid substantiated child abuse reports. Fryer et al. (1990) report that the clients in their study were satisfied with the way social workers treated them and, more significantly, that the clients found the social workers generally helpful. Some cases are determined to be unsubstantiated if the social worker and the parent can agree on an informal supervision plan; it is plausible that these plans have value to the children involved.

The concern about intrusion into people's lives that may result from improper child abuse reports and investigations is very important. This intrusion certainly does occur and has sometimes led to tragic consequences. More and better-trained social workers are needed to reduce erroneous and unnecessarily intrusive investigations. Yet, as Finkelhor (1990) points out, the police, the Internal Revenue Service, border guards, and airport security personnel all intrude on millions of innocent and nonoffending citizens each year. Americans' tolerance for these intrusions is in proportion to the value of the negative outcome they are trying to prevent and to the fairness of the identification and investigation process. Most sexual and physical abuse investigations do not involve the threat of any criminal sanctions against parents. They do, of course, often involve the threat of loss of care and custody of one's child. That is certainly a grave concern. Yet, the likelihood that a child abuse report would result in removal of a child from the home was less than 5% in 1990.

(This ratio has declined precipitously over the past 15 years.) The risk of an unfair removal is probably considerably smaller. Such an error rate can still be reduced, but not without significant cost in training and salaries. The public is, on the whole, accepting of this error rate. The National Committee for the Prevention of Child Abuse sponsors an annual poll each year that asks the public if child abuse should be investigated if there is a suspicion of abuse and, separately, if child abuse should be investigated only if there is clear evidence of serious harm or injury to the child. Public support is always much stronger for reporting "regardless of the seriousness of the crime."

Child abuse reports can be conceptualized as "SOSs for children and families in trouble," and child abuse investigations can be reframed as "family assessments." In this way, the current standard that encourages reporting whenever there is suspicion that a family is in serious trouble can be used to continue to promote outreach to very vulnerable families who can benefit from an expert assessment and referral process. Child abuse reports provide opportunities for children to be protected and for families to be supported. Probably only a small fraction of the families considered in serious trouble by professionals, relatives, and neighbors who report them get the help they need. For some of those children, the help they get will be lifesaving. For some of those parents, the help will be family preserving. Child abuse reports are a signal that a family needs help. There could and should be other mechanisms to initiate the helping process. The mechanism we now have is, however, in place in every state and has resulted in an infrastructure of training and research that promises still better "assessment and referral" services. Now it is critical that we build a supportive web of family-, school-, and neighborhood-centered services that will offer assistance to families that need something other than child protective services. Such readily accessible services would do still more to enhance the value of child abuse reports.

References

Finkelhor, D. (1990). Is child abuse overreported? *Public Welfare, 69,* 23-29.

Fryer, G. E., Bross, D. C., Krugman, R. D., Benson, D. B., & Baird, D. (1990). Good news for CPS workers. *Public Welfare, 69,* 38-41, 47.

Kamerman, S. B., & Kahn, A. J. (1990). Social services for children, youth and families in the United States. *Children and Youth Services Review, 12,* 1-185.

Pelton, H. (1989). *For reasons of poverty: A critical analysis of the public child welfare system in the United States.* New York: Praeger.

RICHARD P. BARTH RESPONDS

Mr. Besharov makes an evocative but flawed argument in his crafty mixture of anecdotes, media reports, and statistics. Although Besharov and I are both in agreement that child abuse reports must lead to helpful and protective responses that fall well within the families' right to privacy, we disagree on the likelihood that investigations not resulting in substantiated child abuse reports are harmful or useless. Indeed, he presents no data to support his premise that the vast majority of child abuse reports do not result in some benefit. Indeed, he seems to ignore the very plausible possibility that a visit from a social worker communicates to a family that the community is concerned about families and children, assists families in getting connected to services that they may not know about or may not know how to access, and encourages adoption of less harmful and more effective parenting methods. We do not know how often this occurs, but Fryer, Bross, Krugman, Benson, and Baird's (1990) study and at least as much anecdotal evidence as Besharov can muster indicates that "investigations" are helpful. We know, for example, that many child abuse reports come from family members who are concerned about their very young kin and need the support of social services to protect beloved children from relatives who are heavy substance abusers. These callers often come from neighborhoods with considerable experience with child protective services; the calls continue to be made because caring citizens have not otherwise been able to engage informal helping systems and community-based agencies to achieve the necessary protection.

Besharov and I agree that more careful reporting and investigating of child abuse reports are needed and that a careful balance between child protection and family privacy must be struck. I believe, and I can only surmise that he does too, that, when in doubt, the balance should be on the child protection side. Child abuse is a community problem, and the community must be involved in reporting, providing assistance to abusive families, and providing foster and adoptive families when all else fails. Professionals must be trained to assist the community in this response. Curtailing of unprofessional responses to child abuse is certainly needed and can be achieved with greater education and training resources.

Reference

Fryer, G. E., Bross, D. C., Krugman, R. D., Benson, D. B., & Baird, D. (1990). Good news for CPS workers. *Public Welfare, 69,* 38-41, 47.

DOUGLAS J. BESHAROV RESPONDS

In his thoughtful piece, Professor Barth makes a number of important points, some with which I agree and some with which I disagree. I would like to take this opportunity to comment on three of his points.

As Professor Barth rightly observes, "a child abuse report has become a *passport* to services delivered by the public child welfare services system" (emphasis added). The problem is that, to receive the benefits of this "passport," the family must first undergo an unavoidably intrusive investigation, be listed in a county- or statewide register of reported cases, and tolerate the sometimes unreasonable demands of one or more child protective workers and the bureaucracy that employs them. If the result were really quality child- or family-oriented services, all this might be worthwhile. But too often a child protective investigation is followed with only a paper promise of help.

Most of those families investigated for suspected child abuse and neglect are economically disadvantaged and often are members of racial and ethnic minorities. Surely, if we wish to provide supportive services to families, we should do so directly—without putting them through a process that middle-class families would not abide.

Second, Professor Barth says that "child abuse reports are a signal that a family needs help." I am afraid that this is only partially true. Of course, the mere fact that a report is determined to be "unfounded" or "unsubstantiated" does not mean that the child was not abused or neglected. As I explain in my initial argument, important evidence may have been missed or the investigator simply may have made the wrong decision. But it is equally true that many of the reports that are dismissed (remember, 60-65% are closed with no action being taken) involve totally innocent parents.

Finally, Professor Barth also argues that "de facto definitions of *child abuse* and *child neglect* have been sharply narrowed over the past few years to reduce overly intrusive agency responses and to save scarce dollars." In support of this point, he cites the fact that reports in California did not decline even after the 1988 passage of a law limiting definitions of physical abuse and neglect. But there is another explanation: The law was ineffective. We need both more precise reporting laws and better public and professional education.

In 1987, at Airlie House in Warrenton, Virginia, a national group of 38 child protective professionals from 19 states adopted a policy statement titled *Child Abuse and Neglect Reporting and Investigation: Policy Guidelines For Decision Making* (Besharov, 1988, chap. 13). Meeting for three days under the auspices of the American Bar Association's National Legal Resource Center for Child Advocacy and Protection in association with the American Public Welfare Association and the American Enterprise Institute, the "Airlie House group," as it has come to be called, developed policy guidelines for reporting and investigative decisions. (I was the "rapporteur" for the effort.)

As the Airlie House group concludes, "Better public and professional materials are needed to obtain more appropriate reporting" (Besharov, 1988, p. 346). The group specifically recommends that "educational materials and programs should: (1) clarify the legal definitions of child abuse and neglect, (2) give general descriptions of reportable situations (including specific examples), and (3) explain what to expect when a report is made. Brochures and other materials for laypersons, including public service announcements, should give specific information about what to report—and what not to report" (p. 346).

Reference

Besharov, D. J. (Ed.). (1988). *Protecting children from abuse and neglect: Policy and practice.* Springfield, IL: Charles C Thomas.

DEBATE 17

PUTTING JUVENILES IN ADULT JAILS

➤ *Should there be an absolute prohibition against the placement of children and adolescents in adult jails and correctional facilities?*

EDITORS' NOTE: It is not uncommon for children to be placed in adult jails and lockups. Is this a harmless practice that is required by overcrowding, or is this harmful to the children and youth so confined and thus unacceptable? If it is harmful, don't children and youth have a right to be protected from such harm? Some argue that there is no other choice but to confine children and youth in adult jails and lockups. They argue that sometimes no other place is available. Is this an acceptable argument? If so, under what circumstances? Our two authors discuss the issue of whether there should be an absolute prohibition against the practice of placing children in adult jails.

Rosemary C. Sarri says YES. She is a Professor of Social Work and Faculty Associate in the Institute of Social Research at the University of Michigan, Ann Arbor. She has long been interested in child welfare and juvenile justice policy, having served as codirector of a national study of juvenile corrections in the United States. She has completed cross-national research on child welfare and juvenile justice in Australia and Canada. She recently completed a study of alternative programs for urban juvenile offenders in Michigan. She is the author of *Brought to Justice: Juveniles, the Courts and the Law, New Directions for Youth* and *Community Education for Substance Abuse Prevention.*

William H. McCready argues NO. He has been Judge of Probate for Iosco County, Michigan, since January 1, 1965.

YES   ROSEMARY C. SARRI

The placement of juveniles in adult jails and lockups is the darkest side of the criminal justice system in the United States, as far as children are concerned. Nearly 75 years ago, Joseph Fishman, a jail inspector, referred to jails as "giant crucibles of crime." Removal of children from this environment has been a matter of public concern for at least two centuries, but only since the 1960s has there been concerted action to eliminate this practice. It has been universally condemned by the American Bar Association, the Children's Defense Fund, the National Association of Counties, two Presidential Commissions on Crime, the National Sheriff's Association, and the National Council on Crime and Delinquency, to name but a few. In 1974 the Juvenile Justice and Delinquency Prevention Act (P.L. 93-415) stipulated that the jailing of children and youth should stop and that states should begin an orderly transition to that end. It provided grants to the states so that they could develop alternative facilities, thereby eliminating the need for jailing. A number of states have passed statutes prohibiting the placement of juveniles in adult jails and police lockups, but the practice continues today because of the lack of effective enforcement mechanisms. Local police departments and juvenile courts retain much discretion in the United States, and as a result effecting national changes in the juvenile justice system has been difficult.

This essay examines the issues surrounding the placement of juveniles in adult jails and lockups, not those who are waived to adult courts and are tried as adults. More than 2,000 youth are incarcerated in adult prisons today, sentenced there as adults. However, the issues surrounding the placement of juveniles in adult prisons are so varied that space prohibits my dealing with issues pertaining to prisons as well as jails. My primary concern in this debate is with those juveniles who are held in adult jails and lockups prior to adjudication by the juvenile court.

On an average day in 1991, there were approximately 2,333 juveniles held in adult jails and thousands more in police lockups, but we lack information about the latter. Over the period of a year, that means that approximately 60,000 juveniles (53,257 males and 6,924 females) spent time in adult jails where there were both convicted and unconvicted adult offenders (U.S. Department of Justice, 1992a). The number of juveniles held in jail declined during the 1970s, from a high point of 7,800 in 1970 to 1,611 in 1978, but then the trend was reversed and the numbers have increased ever since. This change occurred during a period in which the total number of juveniles in the society declined significantly, so the rate of placement has increased even more than the actual numbers suggest. For all these reasons it is clear that there must be strong legislation with tough penalties and a commitment to enforcement if these practices are to be discontinued.

Why is the placement of juveniles in jail so damaging that an absolute prohibition against this practice is necessary? In the following, I discuss 10 specific reasons.

Placing juveniles in adult facilities is physically and psychologically damaging. Numerous studies have shown that juveniles are often raped, otherwise abused, and physically beaten by other inmates or by guards. Standards presented by the National Council on Crime and Delinquency (1981) state:

> The case against the use of jails for children rests upon the fact that youngsters of juvenile court age are still in the process of development and are still subject to change, however large they may be physically or however sophisticated their behavior. To place them behind bars at a time when the whole world seems to turn against them, and belief in themselves is shattered or distorted merely confirms the criminal role in which they see themselves. (p. 2)

In communities where the separation of juveniles from adult inmates is enforced to protect juveniles, the juveniles often have little contact with staff, or anyone at all. Incarceration becomes very dangerous because youth may panic in such situations, and suicide or attempted suicide is the result. Juveniles in adult jails are eight times more likely to commit suicide than are juveniles held in juvenile facilities. A youth found hanging in a cell in one state left a penciled note nearby that read, "I don't belong anywhere!" Conditions in jail are overcrowded, unsanitary, and often unconstitutional for all offenders. Most lack any type of medical care and have deplorable conditions for bathing and toilets, as well as poor food, heating, and light. Children in such facilities have no access to education or physical exercise, because jails are established for adults. In *Hamilton v. Love* (1971) the court ruled that the conditions of confinement are often so cruel and inhumane that they constitute a violation of the Eighth Amendment. Judge Hammerman in Baltimore ruled that children could not be held in jails or even some detention facilities, because "there is absolutely no question in my mind that even the more limited exposure by young people to some of the deleterious conditions which presently exist in these [detention] places can have very damaging effects and impact on them" (*In re* Baltimore Detention Center, 1971). Further, juveniles who survive these conditions are likely to be even more embittered and are at risk for the commission of serious crimes after they leave.

The jailing of children and youth is wholly unnecessary. There are juvenile detention centers in all states, and policies such as home detention and intensive community detention have been shown to be effective in many jurisdictions. Of the juveniles held, only about 15% are held because of serious or violent felonies, whereas the overwhelming majority are charged with misdemeanors, noncriminal and status offenses, or even are allowed to stay there by child protective workers who argue that they have no other place to go. It is probable that the abuse experienced in jail will be worse than any abused child may have otherwise experienced up to that time. One community volunteer told about a 12-year-old boy: "He had been found by a motel owner asleep behind the ice machine where he went to keep warm. The owner called the police who put him in a cell for lack of an alternative, they said. He then experienced abuse by both adult inmates and staff" (U.S. Department of Justice, 1981, p. 4).

Probation violators are often placed in jail by juvenile court judges to "teach them a lesson" when many more humane and effective alternatives exist. All too often the convenience of staff prevents the use of these latter alternatives when juveniles are picked up or apprehended. It is easy to place a juvenile in jail in many jurisdictions, whereas securing an appropriate alternative may take much more time and effort.

The Juvenile Justice Act of 1974 was aimed at the removal of all juveniles from adult jails through the provision of grants to states that would take such action and develop alternatives. Since the act was passed, nearly all of the 50 states have been awarded millions of dollars to reduce and then eliminate jailing of juveniles. Each time the act has been amended the provisions against the jailing of juveniles have been strengthened or maintained without change. Particularly targeted has been the elimination of all status offenders from jail. Although the majority of youth found in jail are male, females have a far greater likelihood of being jailed for status offenses such as running away from home, promiscuity, or curfew violations. Most states that have laws against jailing of juveniles have not been explicit about implementation of the prohibition or about enforcement mechanisms. Pennsylvania is one exception. After much public outcry about conditions for juveniles in adult jails, Pennsylvania passed a law strictly prohibiting jailing of juveniles. It has been very effective because it is unlawful for a jail employee or director to receive any person he or she has reason to believe is a child.

Adult jails do not meet the minimum recommended standards for the pretrial detention of juveniles. Two presidential commissions, the National Council of Juvenile Court Judges, the National Council on Crime and Delinquency, and the American Correctional Association all have approved policies that require any facility holding juveniles to provide (a) education, recreation, counseling, and health services to juveniles who are detained; (b) separation of juveniles, in both sight and sound, from adults; and (c) adequate supervision of juveniles by appropriately trained staff. In sharp contrast to these standards are court decisions that testify to the atrocious physical conditions in jails. Part of the decision by Don J. Young in *Jones v. Wittenberg* (1971) aptly describes the situation faced in many jails:

> When the total picture of confinement in the Lucas County Jail is examined, what appears is confinement in cramped and overcrowded quarters, lightless, airless, damp and filthy with leaking water and human wastes, slow starvation, deprivation of most human contacts except with others in the same human state, no exercise or recreation, little if any medical attention, no attempt at rehabilitation, and for those who in despair or frustration lash out at their surroundings, confinement, stripped of clothing and every last vestige of humanity, in a sort of oubliette....
>
> If the constitutional provision against cruel and unusual punishment has any meaning, the evidence in this case shows, it is much more comparable to the Chinese water torture than to such crudities as breaking on the wheel. The evidence also shows that, in this case at least, the punishment is unusual. (p. 99)

In another situation, a teenage boy said:

> I think that I have a little claustrophobia, or something, but I couldn't stand to be locked in a room, as much as I was when I was in solitary confinement several times. I didn't control my temper, I mean, I deserved it, but I think, I don't know. I don't think that it's right to lock kids away like animals out there. I think it makes them worse; I think it makes them resentful and hateful. I don't see any purpose in it. (quoted in Sarri, 1974, pp. 22-23)

The jailing of juveniles is concentrated in a few states. More than 50% are held in the states of Indiana, Florida, Virginia, and New York. The largest number, 563, were held in Florida; Indiana was second, with 132 juveniles (U.S. Department of Justice, 1992b, p. 613). In contrast, Connecticut, Delaware, Georgia, Hawaii, Massachusetts, Oregon, Pennsylvania, Rhode Island, Utah, Vermont, and West Virginia held no juveniles in jail in 1990. There are no common sociodemographic characteristics of these two groups of states that would explain the differences in their policies and practices. These figures do, however, indicate that the jailing of juveniles can be effectively prohibited, with no obvious negative consequences.

There are serious legal and liability problems associated with the jailing of juveniles. There have been lawsuits against sheriffs' departments, jail staff, county commissioners, juvenile judges, and probation officers because of various violations of the rights of juveniles or the lack of maintenance of proper conditions for holding youth. These lawsuits have often resulted in significant damage awards, costly attorneys' fees, and related court expenses. More than a dozen states have had such lawsuits, and in most instances law enforcement officials have been found at fault. As a result, local governments have had to pay hundreds of thousands of dollars in damages.

Jailing of juveniles does not protect the public. As noted above, the overwhelming majority of juveniles are held for minor or nonoffenses. Thus the issue of public safety is inappropriate in this instance because the juveniles held in jail are not persons who threaten the public's safety in any real way. Nonetheless, it must be recognized that the symbolic function of jailing to control delinquency is important to many citizens. Many believe that if juveniles can be punished immediately when they break the law (or are suspected of breaking the law), the community will be safer and local norms will be thereby reinforced because of the deterrent effect of the jailing of some youth.

The placement of juveniles in adult jails and lockups can be prevented through the use of alternatives such as nonsecure holdover sites with trained staff to supervise youth, juvenile detention centers, intensive community supervision, home detention, and tethers that allow juveniles to remain at home pending action on their cases. Other alternatives include shelters, runaway facilities, evening report centers, community aide programs, family crisis counseling, and proctor homes in which juveniles reside with adults who provide supervision and work with the youths in an orderly, disciplined way to demonstrate the safe and constructive use of one's time. Also important are 24-hour assessment and referral services for juveniles; otherwise, they may be held in police lockups or jails for "convenience" when they are picked up by police.

The public and the news media need to be informed regarding the truth about adult jailing. Concerned citizens, acting cooperatively with community organizations, can become powerful forces to stop the indiscriminate jailing of youth. Citizen groups need to visit their local jails to observe who is being held and the conditions of their incarceration. When systematic information has been obtained, advocacy groups need to make that information available to the public. They then need to secure the support of other organizations, such as service clubs (Jaycees, Rotary, Kiwanis, League of Women

Voters, Junior League, and YM/YWCA). With strong community support, local advisory groups can put pressure on judges, sheriffs, and police departments to change their behavior, but that alone is insufficient. In addition, public interest groups need to develop and secure the passage of legislation that truly prohibits all placement of juveniles in jails and lockups with adults. Such a goal will not be achieved easily, so a campaign will have to be substantial and will probably need to be active for an extended period of time. Following passage of effective legislation, there must be strict enforcement, monitoring, and evaluation to be certain the jailing of juveniles is eliminated. The experience since 1974 with the Juvenile Justice and Delinquency Prevention Act indicates that legislation can have an effect, but only when there is effective evaluation.

Last, but not least, youth who are placed in jail disproportionally represent poor and minority populations who are already disadvantaged. They also lack legal counsel to ensure that they receive full acknowledgment of their rights. The solution to this problem is complex because of institutionalized racism and classism in U.S. society. However, a total prohibition against all jailing of juveniles will have particularly positive impact on minority youth, who already experience a great deal of discrimination. In addition, there is a need for more thorough monitoring of who is held in jail, for how long, and for what reasons, followed by systematic efforts to see that fairness, humaneness, and justice prevail.

The issue of juvenile jailing deserves immediate attention. The United States has the dubious distinction of having the highest incarceration rate in the world. Elimination of the jailing of juveniles would send an important message to young people and also to the rest of the world that the United States plans to implement more humane criminal justice practices.

References

Hamilton v. Love, 328 F. Supp. 1182 (E.D. Ark. 1971).
In re Baltimore Detention Center, 5 Clearinghouse Rev. 550 (Baltimore City Court, 1971) (subsequent amendments 15 June 1973).
Jones v. Wittenberg, F. Supp. 93 (N.D. Ohio 1971), aff'd. sub nom. *Jones v. Metzger,* 456 F. 2d 854 (6th Cir. 1972).
National Council on Crime and Delinquency. (1981). *Standards and guides for the detention of children and youth* (2nd ed.). New York.
Sarri, R. (1974). *Under lock and key: Juveniles in jails and detention.* Ann Arbor: University of Michigan, Institute of Social Research.

U.S. Department of Justice, Bureau of Justice Statistics. (1992a). *Jail inmates, 1991* (Bulletin No. NCJ-129756). Washington, DC: Government Printing Office.

U.S. Department of Justice, Bureau of Justice Statistics. (1992b). *Sourcebook of criminal justice statistics, 1991*. Washington, DC: Government Printing Office.

U.S. Department of Justice, Office of Juvenile Justice and Delinquency Prevention. (1981). *It's your move: The un-jailing of juveniles in America.* Washington, DC: Government Printing Office.

NO WILLIAM H. McCREADY

It is my position as a juvenile court judge that placing juveniles in adult jails and lockups should be avoided whenever possible, but it should not be prohibited. There are circumstances in which juveniles should be placed in jail because their behavior threatens public safety and no appropriate alternative exists. My position reflects my current role as a juvenile court judge in a rural county in Michigan.

Iosco County, Michigan, a county of approximately 31,000 population, is located in the northeastern section of Michigan's lower peninsula. It is but 1 of the 27 counties in the northern section of the lower peninsula and the 14 counties in the upper peninsula that do not have juvenile detention facilities within the county. Until 1990, the court operated with a staff of three persons: the judge, a juvenile officer, and the probate register, who also served as juvenile register and court recorder. In 1990 we added a juvenile register, who shares the duties of court recorder, and in 1991, through a federal grant, we added a juvenile probation officer. Although we have a Michigan State Police Post, the Iosco County Sheriff, East Tawas-Tawas City Police, and the Oscoda-AuSable Township Police agencies in our county, financial difficulty within the county and budgetary constraints cause the State Police Post to close at midnight and have left the sheriff without a road patrol. The two other enforcement agencies have limited jurisdiction, and so are not available to the entire county. Prior to becoming judge of probate on January 1, 1965, I had served four years as Iosco County prosecuting attorney and have now served almost 28 continuous years as judge of probate and juvenile court in Iosco County.

When a petition is filed or a complaint is made involving delinquency by a juvenile and there is a determination made that for the safety of the juvenile or other persons in the community, or because of the heinous nature of the offense committed, that it is necessary to detain the juvenile in custody, our normal procedure requires the juvenile officer to attempt by long-distance telephone to arrange with a court in a nearby county that has a detention facility to provide bed space for our juvenile. On occasion, she has telephoned 10 or more facilities to attempt those arrangements. On some occasions, she has telephoned all facilities in the state without luck in finding available space. When that occurs, we are forced to utilize the Iosco County Jail or to resort to nonsecure facilities and trust the juvenile will not escape or run from placement until other arrangements are made. Depending upon the seriousness of the risk that is posed, I decide whether or not to use the jail.

When our juvenile officer is successful in locating a facility willing to accept our ward, that facility does so with the understanding that, if at any time during the juvenile's detention that bed space is needed for detention of a juvenile resident of the county in which the facility is located, upon notification of that fact, we will again take custody of the ward and seek to make other arrangements.

Further, when the juvenile officer is successful in locating a facility with space available for our ward, she then must also locate "volunteer transporters" to transport him or her to the facility. A round trip for our volunteers is not less than 140 miles and sometimes is more than 400 miles. We have a limited number of volunteer transporters, and most of them are retirees. In many instances, additional hearings are necessary, and this works a real hardship on our limited staff and volunteers.

In addition to time lost and expenses incurred in locating available bed space, and for transportation of our juveniles, our procedure does involve a certain element of risk. Although so far none of our volunteer transporters has been attacked, on at least two occasions wards being transported have bolted and fled when the volunteers made a comfort stop or stopped for gasoline en route to their destination. I also recall one instance when a caseworker for the Department of Social Services skidded on icy roads and rolled a state car while transporting two juveniles to placement on the western side of the state. Fortunately, injuries were slight and no litigation resulted, but the accident did serve to demonstrate some of the risks involved when we are forced to transport juveniles all over the state, sometimes in adverse weather conditions and never under the very best conditions, when some cells in the Iosco County Jail, separate and apart from adult prisoners, are available right next door to the court.

Juvenile detention facilities cost the county no less than $110 per day, whereas it costs the county approximately $30 per day to house a person in the jail. We are acquainted with the sheriff and members of the jail staff and know from previous experience that the care and attention afforded juveniles detained in the jail exceed that given them while in detention facilities. In any instance where extended visitation is required, visitation of the juvenile by his or her parents is much simpler than if the juvenile is detained many miles from home. In the past, comparisons of the recidivism rate of juveniles detained in jail with those detained in a secure detention facility have convinced me that a short stay of two or three days in jail has been much more effective than a similar or longer stay in regular juvenile detention. Some of that result could probably be attributed to the fact that while in jail, the juvenile is alone in a cell with plenty of time to think, whereas those detained in a detention facility far from home encounter juveniles from all walks of life, more sophisticated and streetwise than youth from our northern counties, where they are subject to the influence of family and friends in the community. In at least four instances, I have had juveniles who had been detained in jail come to my office to say they had not enjoyed the experience and would certainly not do anything again to warrant additional confinement, whereas those detained in detention facilities have only reported they did not like being there.

For the foregoing reasons, I firmly believe discretionary use of jail as a possible detention facility for our juveniles should be permitted and should be used on a limited basis.

WILLIAM H. McCREADY RESPONDS

Although I agree in principle with Dr. Sarri that the United States must develop a more humane system of treating juvenile problems, until adequate juvenile facilities are provided, I will maintain my position that when it is necessary to protect a juvenile from him- or herself or to protect other juveniles in the community, or when it is necessary to protect the property rights of others in the community, and convenient and suitable juvenile facilities are not available, juvenile courts should have the right to confine juveniles in adult jails separate and apart from adult prisoners.

In stating her position against jailing of juveniles, Dr. Sarri apparently presumes that all adult jails are unkempt, unsanitary, filthy dens of iniquity where juveniles are admitted for the gratification of adult perverts. If that has been her experience, I can understand the vehemence of her feelings and would urge her to make those facts publicly known to inspire the public to develop building projects to correct defective jails and to bring about proper supervision of existing jails. Notwithstanding the fact that we are considering a problem created by jailing of juveniles, matters such as those observed by Dr. Sarri should be brought to the attention of the public or federal authorities. Even adult prisoners should not be subjected to such inhumane conditions or treatment.

Fortunately, my experience with county jails has been much different from Dr. Sarri's. Our local county jail is clean and the sheriff and staff are not cruel or vicious but have great concern for our youth and for adult prisoners. Additional precautions for protection of juveniles in a jail located nearby include availability to visit by their parents; further, the juvenile caseworker or court juvenile officer may visit and interview jailed juveniles each day.

In the past, Michigan legislators have seemingly recognized the lack of adequate juvenile treatment and detention facilities and have authorized limited jailing of juveniles when the juvenile is over 15 years of age and cannot be safely lodged elsewhere or where it is for the safety of other juveniles in the community. Another statute affords the county prosecuting attorney discretionary power to charge a 15-year-old juvenile as an adult when certain offenses have been committed. Still another statute permits the prosecuting attorney to seek waiver of a juvenile from probate court for trial as an adult in courts of general criminal jurisdiction when the juvenile is at least 15 years of age and where treatment facilities available to probate court for treatment of that individual have been exhausted and further use of those facilities for treatment of that juvenile would not be productive. Once a juvenile is charged as an adult or has been waived by probate court to a court of general criminal jurisdiction, that juvenile may be held in jail or subject to release on bond just like any adult.

In order to present properly my position favoring limited jailing of juveniles, I must reiterate the inadequacy of juvenile care or treatment facilities and the lack of juvenile detention homes in northern Michigan. Although Iosco County does have a holdover room for juveniles located near the sheriff's office, the room is totally without locks or bars. Use of the holdover room is restricted not to exceed 16 hours of continuous use in holding any juvenile. Even though the room is equipped to hold either male or female juveniles, both cannot be held simultaneously. When juveniles are being held, they are supervised for the most part by retirees who have been trained to avoid any confrontation or physical contact with the juveniles; so if a juvenile is prone to run from being held, he or she may do so without physical intervention by the holdover attendants. Restriction to no more than 16 hours of continuous use does not provide a long enough period to save the court the time and expense of finding other housing for a juvenile apprehended for some offense committed on a weekend.

Currently there are 19 juvenile detention homes located in the entire state of Michigan, 4 of which will not accept commitment of a juvenile from any other county. The remaining 15 homes, located from 65 miles to more than 200 miles from Iosco County, will accept juveniles from other counties (if bed space is available) with the understanding that if bed space is needed for one of their own county's juveniles, the committing court of a nonresident juvenile will again take custody of the juvenile at any time, day or night. These arrangements present a real hardship to a county without a juvenile detention home and expose our juvenile population and transporters to unnecessary risk of spending hours on busy highways even in adverse winter weather conditions.

It is difficult to understand or to justify the unnecessary expenditure of so much time and effort to secure housing for a juvenile when we have a perfectly adequate, safe, clean jail nearby where juveniles might be kept separate and apart from adult prisoners, where they would be convenient for visits by their parents, where the court juvenile officer would have access for supervision, and where trained officers are present to monitor their activities over closed-circuit television to prevent them from harm, whether from themselves or others. I realize that jailing of juveniles is not acceptable under all conditions, but I do believe that juvenile court judges are conscientious enough to use jail only when it is advisable or necessary and where there are built-in security measures to prevent abuse to the juveniles.

Under the conditions set forth above, I still maintain the position that limited jailing of juveniles should be authorized until such time as proper and adequate facilities are otherwise available.

ROSEMARY C. SARRI RESPONDS

The most compelling argument made by Judge McCready is that, lacking alternative local resources, judges place juveniles in adult jails. He expresses a legitimate concern of the court, because it is responsible for both the protection of the public and the safety of the individual youth. Unfortunately, placement of a juvenile in an adult jail very often exposes him or her to serious abuse and danger that all too often is life-threatening, such as assaults by adults or attempted suicide, because many jails try to isolate such youth. Seldom, if ever, is any official action taken by the juvenile court when a juvenile commits suicide or is raped in jail. It is merely considered an unfortunate and unintended event.

The question then remains: Does protection of the public safety require that juveniles be placed in adult jails? Having completed a study of jailing practices in one state in 1992, I have learned that the juveniles who are placed in jail are primarily minor offenders, and sometimes nonoffenders, such as abused and neglected children. Only rarely does one find a youth who has been charged with a felony against a person. I found cases of youths who were placed in jails because judges reported not having an alternative rather than because the juveniles had been charged with serious crimes. The majority of these juveniles were charged with status offenses, minor misdemeanor offenses such as shoplifting or fraud, or probation violation. In all of the latter instances the juveniles could be released to their parents' supervision or to supervision by a local resident, and not threaten public safety. But it is often far easier for the police and courts to take juveniles to jails or lockups than to investigate alternatives.

The state departments of social services are responsible for the care and supervision of all children who are delinquent or abused/neglected, under state as well as federal law. They must ensure that there are alternative placements available that are readily accessible to all communities in the country. There are now many alternatives that have been tested and found to be more effective than the practice of secure holding of youth in jails. These alternatives include in-home detention with close supervision or tethering, group homes with both secure and nonsecure rooms, and detention in the homes of trained local residents. The cost of all of these alternatives is well below that of placement in jail, if costs are objectively calculated. The long-term cost in terms of damage to the lives of many youth is incalculable.

The federal statute, P.L. 96-415, passed in 1974 stipulated that juveniles should not be placed in adult jails or prisons because there is no evidence that it is necessary to protect the public, whereas the potential damage to youth is great. Rather than focus only on the juvenile who is at risk and in trouble, the juvenile courts must charge the departments of social services with their responsibility to provide safe alternatives and enjoin them when they do not fulfill that responsibility. The United States currently punitively incarcerates more youth than does any other Western industrialized country. It is time to prohibit at least the placement of juveniles in adult jails.

PART V

Work and Family Issues

DEBATE 18

AFDC MOTHERS AND WORK

> *Should AFDC mothers be required to work in order to receive benefits?*

EDITORS' NOTE: The question of whether recipients of Aid to Families with Dependent Children (AFDC), or welfare, should be required to work is a hotly debated one. Some argue that work requirements would help families to get off of welfare. Others argue that they would only add to the abuse already heaped on poor children and their parents. We contacted a number of individuals to write the yes argument in this debate, but those favoring that view seemed to be so busy preparing book chapters and articles arguing their position that they did not have time to write something for our book. We therefore reprint here one of the two yes arguments that appeared in an earlier volume edited by Eileen Gambrill and Robert Pruger, *Controversial Issues in Social Work,* the contribution of Ailee Moon. Some other recent publications that have appeared regarding this question include Lawrence Mead's *The New Politics of Poverty: The New Working Poor in America* (Basic Books, 1992) and Isabel V. Sawhill's "The New Paternalism: Earned Welfare" (*The Responsive Community,* Spring 1992).

Ailee Moon, Ph.D., says YES. She is Assistant Professor in the School of Social Welfare at the University of California at Los Angeles, where she teaches social policy and research methods. Her interests include the political economy of welfare states, fiscal welfare systems, and tax expenditures, and ethnic minority older populations. Her current research activities include studies of the determinants of individual charitable contributions to voluntary human service organizations and the politics of catastrophic health insurance. Her contribution to this debate appeared originally as "Should Welfare Clients Be Required to Work?" in *Controversial Issues in Social Work,* edited by Eileen Gambrill and Robert Pruger, copyright © 1992 by Allyn and Bacon. Reprinted by permission of Allyn and Bacon.

Martha N. Ozawa, Ph.D., argues NO. She is Bettie Bofinger Brown Professor of Social Policy at Washington University in St. Louis, Missouri. She is the author of *Income Maintenance and Work Incentives: Toward a Synthesis* and editor of *Women's Life Cycle and Economic Insecurity: Problems and Proposals*.

YES   AILEE MOON

Whereas the popular use of the term *workfare* is a relatively recent phenomenon, the notion that "employable" public assistance recipients be required to work or to participate in work-related activities in exchange for their benefits is neither a new nor a radical departure. If one defines workfare so as to encompass any form of mandatory work-related obligation, workfare was already at work when participation in the Work Incentive (WIN) program became mandatory in 1971. That is, in order to receive AFDC benefits, all able-bodied adults without preschool children or special circumstances that prevented them from participating would have to be engaged in job search or job training activities, and would have to accept employment offers. Similarly, the Carter and Reagan administrations had included in their welfare reform proposals some form of mandatory work requirements, although there were important differences in their designs of workfare. Nine states already operate statewide mandatory workfare programs.

The Family Security Act of 1988 enacted a new nationwide workfare scheme in the Job Opportunities and Basic Skills (JOBS) program. Most long-term AFDC recipients with children under age 3 (or, at state option, age 1) or those at highest risk of becoming long-term recipients, such as teenage mothers, are required to "work off" their benefits by participating in the JOBS program. The nature of work activities includes job search, community work experience or other unpaid work, and subsidized employment or on-the-job training. Child-care, transportation, and other work-related expenses needed for a recipient to participate in the program are assured.

Whether welfare recipients should be required to work is a question of pragmatism, values, and politics. Workfare in theory may not be identical to workfare in practice. Thus it is important to be pragmatic and judge the merits of workfare in the light of the practical feasibility of making workfare work. Can workfare be constructed in a way that helps break the cycle of welfare dependency, restores individuals to self-sufficiency, and leads to welfare savings? What are the preconditions for workfare to work? The answers to these questions provide a strong rationale for or against workfare.

Although the pragmatic approach is essential, it is nevertheless insufficient to determine the appropriateness of workfare. In fact, the issue of workfare cannot be dealt with in isolation of prevailing social values and political reality. Even in the absence of a strong economic rationale, workfare may be preferred if it better fits with the nation's social values and improves equity or perceived fairness of the welfare system. Further, any proposals that claim to serve the best interests of welfare recipients but ignore political reality are doomed to failure. Thus, before saying yes or no to workfare, one must further consider the following questions: What are the likely consequences of opposing workfare for recipients themselves? What are the trade-offs involved in workfare? In short, the question is, Workfare in exchange for what?

Facing Economic and Social Realities

When Aid to Dependent Children (now AFDC) was enacted as part of the original Social Security Act of 1935, the initial assumption was that only a small number of poor families with children would receive benefits, and that enabling mothers to stay home and care for their children was better than compelling them to go to work. It was also expected that the need for the program would diminish as more and more of the typical ADC beneficiaries—widows and wives of disabled workers with children—would become eligible for social security benefits. Strong support for the program prevailed. Issues of possible work disincentives and long-term dependency did not arise. The focus was on the welfare of financially needy children.

More than 55 years later, the AFDC program has become the least popular and the most problematic social welfare program. Political controversy has focused on the able-bodied adult beneficiaries. In fact, every major welfare reform proposal since the mid-1960s has called for a redefinition of welfare entitlement and restoration of the work ethic by weaving work incentives together with financial assistance. What happened?

Clearly, the modern reality of AFDC is quite different from what the advocates of its original ADC program could imagine. At the same time, other social, economic, and political realities of the country have undergone considerable changes. Conceived during the New Deal as a program for children of widows, today the children in most AFDC families have fathers who are absent through divorce or desertion; many of them were born out of wedlock, and many of their parents never married. The program did not diminish as expected, but instead evolved over time into a major welfare program. Both the number of AFDC families and the program's total costs have risen rapidly, especially during the 1960s and 1970s. The number of AFDC families increased from about 490,000 in 1940 to more than 4.1 million in 1990, and the costs from $133 million in 1940 to $19.1 billion in 1990 (Social Security Administration, 1992; U.S. Bureau of the Census, 1992).

The continued rise in the number of nontraditional AFDC cases has weakened public support for and sympathy toward AFDC recipients. It also has provoked public suspicions that the program sends wrong signals. AFDC has come to be regarded by some as a cause, not a cure, of many social problems—erosion of the very foundations of sexual morality and parental responsibility, family breakdowns, teenage pregnancy, illegitimate birth, poverty, and dependency (see, e.g., Murray, 1984). The consensus has been reached that something must be done to reverse the trends and to restore a strong sense of personal responsibility among AFDC recipients. In this context, workfare emerges as an expression of public insistence upon fulfillment of parental obligations by all parents, including the poor, in one way or another.

It is also important to assess the appropriateness of workfare in the broader context of social and economic realities of contemporary American families. At a time when few mothers worked outside the home, in the 1940s, 1950s, and even 1960s, forcing mothers on welfare to work would have been considered punitive and inappropriate, as it would have been inconsistent with the prevailing norms of family life. In the past two decades, however, the situation has changed dramatically. For many two-parent families, one income is no longer adequate to maintain a reasonable standard of living, and most mothers, including single parents with very young children, work outside the home to make ends meet. Today, less than 10% of all families are families with the father at work and the mother at home taking care of the children. Almost two-thirds of all mothers with children younger than 14 are in the workforce. The proportion of working women with children under the age of 14 rose sharply, from 12% in 1950 to 57% in 1987 ("Child Care Legislation," 1988). Most strikingly, today more than 50% of working mothers have children under age 1 ("Child Care Legislation," 1988).

The trend of the increasing employment rates of all women may be comforting or disturbing, depending on one's point of view. What is evident, however, is that the trend is irreversible. From the above figures it is also evident that most women with children, including single parents, take their financial responsibility seriously. Of course, financial responsibility is only one of many parental responsibilities. Nonetheless, it is a critical one. Thus, at a time like today, when most women with young children work outside the home, the idea of asking welfare recipients to work is in itself neither considered inhumane nor inconsistent with social norms. Rather, it is only fair to expect welfare recipients to contribute to their own support by working or participating in training to help them become self-sufficient. This is the reality of the 1990s. Being on the welfare rolls is no shame, but it is not a privilege, either.

Long-Term Dependency Is the Target

Although receiving AFDC is a short-term, transitional phenomenon for most recipients, it is also a long-term source of income support for some. Approximately 32% of recipients are on AFDC for one year or less, but 26% receive AFDC for five years or more, and 15% for eight years or more (Danziger & Weinberg, 1986; DiNitto, 1993, pp. 123-124). In fact, the 15% of 3.7 million families dependent on AFDC, approximately 555,000, is a large enough number to lead to "the new consensus" that "the problem of the late 1980s is no longer poverty but rather dependency and that the problem of dependency is primarily a moral problem" (Novak, 1987, p. 26). Consistent with this diagnosis, the target of welfare reform efforts of the 1980s was long-term welfare dependency.

The shift in the focus of the problem raises a new set of AFDC policy questions. Who are the long-term recipients? What causes and perpetuates their condition? Does AFDC promote a "culture of poverty"—for example, intergenerational dependency, teenage pregnancy, and social isolation—among the poor? What are the barriers to independence? Finally, what is to be done to break the cycle of welfare dependency and facilitate work and independence?

As people persistently disagree on the causes of poverty and dependency, there is no agreed-upon single cure for the problem. Is the lack of jobs the only cause of dependency? If so, workfare will not be fruitful. Is the inability of AFDC recipients to afford medical care and day care for their children after they leave welfare rolls the barrier to work and independence? If so, the government ought to remove the barrier by providing or subsidizing these services for needy families. What about the lack of incentives to work, social isolation, and lack of education, skills, and work experience? Are they not part of the cause of dependency and barriers to self-sufficiency? The point is that there is no single cause of dependency that explains it all. It is undeniable that workfare, as a solution to welfare dependency, is far from perfect. However, considering the components of workfare and a variety of services attached to it, is it not worth pursuing?

Can Workfare Work?

Many argue that workfare does not work, sometimes with reference to the unsuccessful story of the WIN program—its failure to establish "meaningful" work-related obligations for recipients. Because WIN was never fully funded or properly implemented, however, its failure still leaves much room for imagination: What would have been the outcome if WIN had been adequately funded and properly implemented? Some argue further that workfare does not work simply because there are no jobs. No one disagrees that the lack of jobs is the primary barrier to self-sufficiency and that even workfare, to be successful, must rely on the existing market for the supply of jobs. The "jobs only" explanation is an oversimplification of the complexity involved in the problem of poverty and dependency, however. For example, between 1960 and 1985, the number of AFDC recipients grew constantly and at a fast rate regardless of the unemployment rate, so that it continued to grow even when the unemployment rate fell. Between 1968 and 1978, the number of AFDC families doubled. Although the increase was attributed in part to changes in eligibility criteria and increases in the number of children who do not receive financial support from their absent parents, the labor market condition alone seems to leave a substantial portion of the increase unexplained. After all, it must be remembered that workfare targets long-term recipients who tend to remain on welfare regardless of the labor market condition.

Focusing on the findings from experiments with workfare in five states, using control groups, a study by Gueron (1987) indicates the following:

1. The programs led to increases, though relatively modest, in employment, except in West Virginia.
2. The programs had a stronger impact on recipients who had some obstacles to employment, as opposed to the more job-ready recipients.
3. Within a relatively short time, program savings offset costs.
4. Most of the participants regarded a work requirement as fair and responded positively to the work assignments.

Although the workfare programs did not move substantial numbers of people out of poverty, and although in the state that then had the nation's highest unemployment rate (West Virginia) the program did not lead to employment gains, this study suggests that workfare had its intended impacts in four states—that is, cost-effective employment gains, not to mention possibly greater welfare savings in the long run and intangible gains such as felt sense of dignity and responsibility among the participants. Thus, although it remains unclear whether the gains come from the services provided or the mandatory aspect of the programs and whether a comprehensive universal workfare would lead to more or less employment gains, the outlook for the feasibility and effectiveness of these programs is not quite as bleak as some believe (see Training Research Corporation, 1988; Weidman, White, & Swartz, 1988; Wilcox, 1988). Rather, the overall findings are encouraging.

Facing Political Realities

Considering that workfare was only one of several major components of the 1988 welfare reform bill, it raises a question as to whether a strong opponent of workfare would still oppose the entire bill on behalf of welfare recipients because of the workfare component ("Should the 'Family Welfare Reform Act,' " 1988). How would social workers have voted? When the political reality dictates that to kill workfare would also be to kill some or all other provisions in the bill, including establishment of AFDC-UP and child support enforcement in all states and extended child-care and medical benefits for AFDC recipients who leave the rolls, which would lead to significant improvement in the lives of poor families with children, the question becomes, Is workfare too high a price for passing such a bill? Those who still insist that it is are reminiscent of those liberals who opposed the Family Assistance Plan almost three decades ago.

Those who oppose workfare call it "slavefare." Those who support it call it "workfair." Whatever terminology one prefers, workfare is not a bad idea because of what it reflects and what it brings in exchange in the context of political, social, and economic realities of the 1990s.

References

Child care legislation. (1988). *Congressional Digest, 67*(1), 261.
Danziger, S., & Weinberg, D. (1986). *Fighting poverty: What works and what doesn't*. Cambridge, MA: Oxford University Press.
DiNitto, D. (1993). *Social welfare: Politics and public policy* (3rd ed.). Englewood Cliffs, NJ: Prentice Hall.
Gueron, J. M. (1987). Reforming welfare with work. *Public Welfare, 45,* 13-25.
Murray, C. (1984). *Losing ground: American social policy, 1950-1980*. New York: Basic Books.
Novak, M. (1987). Sending the right signal. *Public Interest, 89,* 26-50.
Should the "Family Welfare Reform Act of 1987" be enacted? (1988). *Congressional Digest, 67*(2), 40-64.
Social Security Administration. (1992). *Social Security Bulletin: Annual statistical supplement.* Washington, DC: Government Printing Office.
Training Research Corporation. (1988). *Training for change: An analysis of the outcomes of California employment training panel programs.* Santa Monica, CA: Author.
U.S. Bureau of the Census. (1992). *Statistical abstract of the United States 1992.* Washington, DC: Government Printing Office.
Weidman, J., White, R., & Swartz, B. (1988). Training women on welfare for "high-tech" jobs: Results from a demonstration program. *Evaluation and Program Planning, 11,* 105-114.
Wilcox, L. (1988). Reworking welfare: Creating jobs in Maine. *Public Welfare, 46,* 13-18.

NO   MARTHA N. OZAWA

The American economy is going downhill. Since the mid-1970s, American workers' wages have stopped growing in real terms. The median wage of full-year full-time workers now is below the 1973 level. Federal, state, and local governments are facing growing deficits. Many savings and loan institutions, one of the financial foundations of the real estate industry, are bankrupt, and the federal government is obligated, under the law, to bail them out, which is fueling the federal deficit even further. The nation's infrastructures need repair. Many industries—the auto, electronic, apparel, steel, and banking industries—are threatened by international competition. Thus, now more than ever, the American people are being told to work harder for less money. They are also being told that they will have to pay more taxes in the future to finance the growing national debt.

Under such an economic predicament, American families are struggling. They are trying to maintain their living standards by sending not just husbands but wives into the labor market. They no longer are able to save as much as previous generations could; many of them are buying goods and services on credit, which is resulting in greater personal financial debt. If ordinary American families are struggling this much financially, can mothers who receive Aid to Families with Dependent Children be exempt from work? The answer seems to be no.

The requirement that mothers must work to receive AFDC reflects public sentiment. The 1981 Omnibus Budget Reconciliation Act (P.L. 97-35) introduced the explicit work requirement. This policy was a clear departure from the policy of work incentives implemented in the 1960s and 1970s by the now-defunct Work Incentive (WIN) program. The 1988 Family Support Act (P.L. 100-485), which established the Job Opportunities and Basic Skills (JOBS) training program, provided various types of transitional support, so that the work requirement could be enforced more effectively.

The work requirement is at the center of various proposals for welfare reform presented by various groups and individual academics. Gilder (1981) and Murray (1984) want to eliminate AFDC. Mead (1986) wants to make AFDC mothers work for their payments, and Ellwood (1988) wants to ensure that all AFDC mothers work at least half-time, even if the federal government has to guarantee public works jobs at the minimum wage. The National Commission on Children (1991) has envisioned that AFDC mothers' earnings plus a new refundable tax credit for children, the expanded earned-income tax credit, stronger enforcement of child support, and universal health insurance coverage for children and pregnant women should enable AFDC mothers to become working mothers with enough income to pull their families out of poverty without relying on AFDC.

All these economic and legislative developments notwithstanding, I argue against mandating work for all AFDC mothers. At issue here is the work requirement for AFDC mothers with preschool children aged 3 or older, as I assume that AFDC mothers with children under age 3 will not be required to work, as stipulated by the 1988 Family Support Act. Further, I assume that AFDC mothers with school-age children could be expected to work at least part-time without much controversy. I argue against mandating work for AFDC mothers with preschool children on several grounds: economic, demographic, ideological, and moral.

Economic Reasons

AFDC mothers are a diverse group. Those who rely on AFDC for a relatively short period are typically well educated, have relatively small numbers of children, and tend to enroll in AFDC as a result of divorce. These mothers quickly move off of AFDC either by remarrying or by earning more (U.S. House of Representatives, 1991, pp. 640-641). They have no problem in finding jobs and working, if jobs are available. Their earnings, plus child support from absent fathers, dependent-care credit, and earned-income tax credit, all of which are currently in operation, will make them self-sufficient.

But the mothers who stay on AFDC for a long period are different. They tend to bear children out of wedlock in their teenage years, have dropped out of school, and have more children than short-term AFDC mothers (Moore & Burt, 1982). Ellwood (1988) estimates that in 1986 AFDC mothers in states with median payment levels had to earn $5 per hour or more and work full-time year-round just to come out even with AFDC payments. Furthermore, they were unlikely to find jobs with health insurance coverage. Thus it would not make economic sense for them to work and pay for child care. Instead, it would be more beneficial for these mothers and children, as well as for taxpayers, if these mothers were given the opportunity to stay at home and concentrate on caring for their children.

Indeed, there is reason to believe that AFDC mothers naturally will sort themselves out and voluntarily choose to work outside their homes or to stay at home and care for their children to maximize their economic well-being. Economists have long theorized that well-educated mothers tend to work more, so they will not lose their opportunity to earn (Cain, 1966; Gronau,

1973; Hill & Stafford, 1980; Leiborwitz, 1974). For them, the forgone earnings and financial incentives (tax credits), if they did not work, would be just too great to ignore. On the other hand, less-educated mothers tend to stay at home and take care of their children because their opportunity to earn good wages is too slim and, therefore, staying at home becomes an economically viable option. Moreover, less-educated mothers tend to have more children than do well-educated mothers. In short, letting AFDC mothers make their own decisions will result in the most economically efficient mobilization of AFDC mothers.

Demographic Reasons

The need to care for AFDC children is increasingly important in this rapidly changing demographic environment. While the elderly population is increasing rapidly, the population of children is shrinking. By the year 2040, the proportion of elderly people will have surpassed that of children (U.S. Bureau of the Census, 1984, p. 8, Table F). Underneath this demographic shift are the changing patterns of marriage and fertility. Fewer women are choosing to marry; if they do, they tend to marry late (Bloom, 1982; Bloom & Trussell, 1984). (Even unwed mothers are having fewer children than in earlier years; U.S. National Center for Health Statistics, 1990.) As a result, the total fertility rate among all American women has been declining. However, the disparity in fertility rates between nonwhite and white women has stayed relatively constant. In 1975, the ratio was 1.34 to 1; in 1987, 1.33 to 1 (U.S. Bureau of the Census, 1990, pp. 84, 86, Tables 126, 128).

These demographic trends indicate that a greater proportion of children will be born to nonwhite women, who are overrepresented among AFDC mothers. Put another way, the shrinking population of children will include an increasingly larger proportion of children born to nonwhite families— particularly nonwhite low-income families. These children will carry the greater burden of supporting the growing elderly population and will face stiffer competition in the global economy.

Thus the challenge to these children will be enormous. Not only will they have to be more productive than their earlier counterparts, but the educational achievement of the nonwhite low-income children will have to improve greatly. Because children from such families (who tend to lag behind other children in educational achievement) will constitute an increasing proportion of the population of children, the improvement in their scholastic achievement at a rate that is equal to that of white middle-class children can result in a decline in the overall average score for all children. This is exactly what is happening to the scores on the Scholastic Aptitude Test among all American children. Each racial group has improved in its own average scores, but the overall average for all American children has declined (Putka, 1989).

The implication of the demographic shifts is clear. Unless the policy makers in Washington concentrate on the development of human capital among nonwhite low-income children, the American economy will suffer from slow growth in productivity. Therefore, special attention should be paid to AFDC children because nonwhite low-income children are overrepresented among AFDC children. Although the general thrust of policy development has been to mobilize AFDC mothers to enter the labor force, the policy makers cannot ignore the importance of developing human capital among AFDC children. Thus allowing AFDC mothers the opportunity to care for their preschool children should be considered a vital part of the policy strategy of nurturing these children to reach their potential. Given proper supervision and training, these mothers will be more effective in nurturing their children than will be paid, untrained caregivers. Training these mothers to become effective caregivers may be costly in the short run, but it will be cost-effective in the long run.

Ideological Reasons

The work requirement for AFDC mothers stems, in part, from the well-entrenched American work ethic. But does such a requirement really enhance the ideology of work in America? I doubt it; rather, I believe that such a requirement will backfire.

The value attached to work has certainly been a uniting force from the inception of the United States. Through work, the American people were given the opportunity to be part of the young, developing country. Through work—rather than through other means, such as a caste system or religious affiliations—waves of immigrants could be given relatively equal opportunities to pursue their dreams. Thus the value attached to work is vital for a racially and ethnically diverse country such as the United States in integrating its people and developing a common identity as a nation (Ozawa, 1982, 1991b).

But the dynamics involved in work occur only if people work voluntarily. If everyone is forced to work, there will be no individual hunger for work, no individual curiosity to pursue certain types of jobs, no motivation to work harder. Requiring American citizens to work is no different from prohibiting them from earning an unlimited amount of money.

In an important way, the absence of the work requirement differentiates an essentially free enterprise economy, such as that of the United States, from a planned economy, such as that of the now-collapsed Soviet Union. The generation of energy and ambition through work occurs only when people are left alone to decide whether or not to work and what kind of work to pursue.

Of course, American society gives higher status to workers than to nonworkers and has established a whole array of fringe benefits for workers, just to make sure that most people prefer the world of work to the world of nonwork. All sorts of employer-provided benefits, such as pensions and health insurance, and government provisions for social security, unemployment insurance, and workers' compensation are good examples.

The establishment of various incentives is fine, but requiring people to work crosses the line of the norm expected of a free enterprise system. In a free enterprise society, no one can force anyone else to work. In a viable and strong free enterprise system, people can genuinely see the world of work as an arena in which to pursue their life goals and dreams. For such a society to become a reality, the economy must be strong and run fairly, and the people must be given opportunities to develop their human capital through good education so they can participate in the world of work with confidence and pride.

Moral Reasons

Over the years, the federal government has gained a great deal of power to direct the lives of individuals, as well as organizations, through the passage of laws and the establishment of rules and regulations. But one has to question whether the federal government has a moral legitimacy to require AFDC mothers to work.

Although the federal government has been directly involved in AFDC through the development of rules and regulations regarding the benefit formula, eligibility requirements, and so on, in one crucial area it has been only a passive participant: financing AFDC and setting its payment levels. Faced with a constitutional issue involved in the direct financing of AFDC (then Aid to Dependent Children—ADC), President Franklin D. Roosevelt chose the grant-in-aid approach to assisting the states to finance ADC (Altmeyer, 1968). The result of this grant-in-aid approach has been the unequal distribution of federal subsidies among states. The federal government has been channeling more subsidies, in absolute terms, to recipients in states with smaller percentages of blacks, in rich states, and in states with high tax rates than to recipients in states with the opposite characteristics (Ozawa, 1991c). Thus, for example, in 1990, each AFDC child in Alabama received only $29 per month from the federal government and $11 from the state of Alabama, or a total of $40. In contrast, in the same year, each AFDC child in Alaska received as much as $123 per month from the federal government and $123 from the state of Alaska, or a total of $246 (U.S. House of Representatives, 1991, pp. 609, 617).

If the federal government has provided for the nation's AFDC children in such a glaringly unequal fashion over the years, how can it have a moral legitimacy to force all AFDC mothers across the country to work, so the American economy can be strengthened? How can it face, with good conscience, the children who have been receiving such meager AFDC subsidies from the federal government and thus have been ill fed, ill housed, and ill clothed, just because they were born in the wrong places, and now require their mothers to go out and work at minimum-wage jobs? These AFDC children reside in states with large percentages of blacks, in poor states, and in states with low tax rates (Ozawa, 1991c). In the final analysis, a viable social contract between the federal government and AFDC mothers can be established only if these two parties deal with each other on a level playing field. The federal government has not done its part to ensure a uniform, minimum level of economic well-being to all AFDC families across the country; therefore, it does not have the moral legitimacy to require AFDC mothers to work.

Where Do We Go From Here?

To make it possible for AFDC mothers with preschool children to choose whether or not to work, AFDC must be replaced with another set of programs. AFDC embodies too much ideological and moral confusion to be a vehicle for accomplishing the task of letting AFDC mothers make their own decisions. Although the public wants to assist low-income female-headed families through AFDC, it suspects that AFDC traps them in long-term dependence because it believes that AFDC causes work disincentives (Ellwood, 1988). Moreover, the American public generally is not interested in helping families just because they are poor, because it is widely believed that poverty is self-inflicted. On the other hand, the American public can be quite generous if tax dollars are spent for some specific purpose (Ozawa, 1986, 1992).

The way to go, then, is to develop a package of income-support programs, each with a specific purpose. I recommend that the following programs be considered: refundable income tax credit for children, earned-income tax credit, dependent-care credit, enforcement of child support from absent fathers, financial compensation for mothers who choose to stay at home and care for their children, and guaranteed health insurance coverage. All of these, except financial compensation, have either been implemented or proposed. A refundable tax credit of $1,000 per child has been proposed by the National Commission on Children (1991). The Senate Finance Committee, led by

Senator Lloyd Bentsen (D-Texas), is considering the adoption of another version of a refundable tax credit for children that provides a smaller amount.

The earned-income tax credit is designed to subsidize the earnings of low-income taxpayers with children. It is refundable. This program helps AFDC mothers who decide to work. The Omnibus Budget Reconciliation Act of 1990 introduced an adjusted credit according to family size, providing a higher rate of subsidy to working families with two or more children. The act also provided a supplemental credit for children under the age of 1 year. It could be further improved to include more refined adjustment for family size. The rate of the earnings subsidy, which was, as of 1991, 16.7% for families with one child and 17.3% for those with two or more children, could be made higher.

The dependent-care credit is designed to assist taxpayers in paying for the care of qualified dependents. Thus AFDC mothers who decide to work could use it to pay for child care; however, because it is not refundable, AFDC mothers are unlikely to benefit from it. The credit is equal to a proportion of expenses up to $2,400 if there is one dependent, or $4,800 if there are two or more. The credit rate varies inversely with the level of adjusted gross income. Refundability should be introduced in this program so that working mothers whose incomes are too low to claim credit can also benefit from it.

The Child Support Enforcement Program, created by the 1975 amendments to the Social Security Act, has been strengthened over the years. In 1984, automatic income withholding for child support was introduced. The Family Support Act of 1988 (P.L. 100-485) brought an additional rigor to enforcing child support. The act requires that states establish paternity in at least half the out-of-wedlock cases, obtain the social security numbers of both parents when issuing birth certificates, and use genetic tests in disputed cases, when any party requests such a test (U.S. House of Representatives, 1991, pp. 656-724).

The idea of providing financial compensation for nonworking mothers is new. This proposal draws on a Japanese income-support program for single mothers. Under this program, the Japanese government acknowledges that nonworking mothers are contributing to society by raising their children on their own and thus deserve to receive compensation for the daily expenses incurred in caring for their children. Income support for single mothers is provided independent of children's allowances, which in essence are similar to the refundable income tax credits for children proposed in the United States (Ozawa, 1991a).

Assurance of health insurance coverage, whether mothers work or not, is an important part of the whole package. This item has been proposed by the National Commission on Children (1991). Universal health insurance coverage soon will be a major political issue.

The package of programs described here signifies the idea that single mothers with children will no longer be considered idle users of tax dollars. Instead, they will be cast as another type of service providers who will be encouraged, supported, and appreciated for giving good care for their children, in whom the public increasingly will have greater stake, given the rapidly changing demographics. Unless these children grow to their full potential, the entire society will suffer.

To ensure that nonworking mothers with preschool children engage in good parenting, they should be given supervision, guidance, and counseling. Along with parenting, they may be encouraged to join job training programs to prepare themselves to join the labor force when their children become old enough to go to school.

Summary

Because of the mounting public sentiment that all able-bodied persons should work to make the American economy more competitive, AFDC mothers are under increasing pressure to become self-sufficient through work. However, when one looks at the little economic payoff deriving from work by uneducated AFDC mothers with preschool children, and when one realizes how important it is to develop human capital in each child in the shrinking population of children, coupled with the increasingly racially diverse U.S. population, one has to question the viability of mandating all AFDC mothers to work. One must also be concerned with the backfiring effect of such an mandate on the ideology of the work ethic. Finally, the federal government has no moral legitimacy to require work by AFDC mothers because it has subsidized the payments for AFDC families unequally, depending on where those families live.

For all these reasons, it would make more sense to substitute for AFDC a package of income-support programs, so that AFDC mothers can choose whether or not to work. Letting these mothers decide would result in a more economically efficient mobilization of AFDC mothers, as well as in the greater development of human capital among their children.

References

Altmeyer, A. J. (1968). *The formative years of social security.* Madison: University of Wisconsin Press.
Bloom, D. E. (1982). What's happening to the age at first birth in the United States? A study of recent cohorts. *Demography, 19,* 351-370.

Bloom, D. E., & Trussell, J. (1984). What are the determinants of delayed childbearing and permanent childlessness in the United States? *Demography, 21,* 591-612.
Cain, G. G. (1966). *Married women in the labor force: An economic analysis.* Chicago: University of Chicago Press.
Ellwood, D. T. (1988). *Poor support: Poverty in the American family.* New York: Basic Books.
Gilder, G. (1981). *Wealth and poverty.* New York: Basic Books.
Gronau, R. (1973). The effect of children on housewife's value of time. *Journal of Political Economy, 81,* S168-S199.
Hill, C., & Stafford, F. P. (1980). Parental care of children: Time diary estimates of quantity, predictability and variety. *Journal of Human Resources, 15,* 219-239.
Leiborwitz, A. (1974). Education and the allocation of women's time. In F. T. Jester (Ed.), *Education, income and human behavior.* New York: McGraw-Hill.
Mead, L. M. (1986). *Beyond entitlement: The social obligation of citizenship.* New York: Free Press.
Moore, K. A., & Burt, M. R. (1982). *Private crisis, public cost: Policy perspectives on teenage childbearing.* Washington, DC: Urban Institute.
Murray, C. (1984). *Losing ground: American social policy, 1950-1980.* New York: Basic Books.
National Commission on Children. (1991). *Beyond rhetoric: A new American agenda for children and families.* Washington, DC: Author.
Ozawa, M. N. (1982). Work and social policy. In S. H. Akabas & P. A. Kurzman (Eds.), *Work, workers, and work organizations: A view from social work.* Englewood Cliffs, NJ: Prentice Hall.
Ozawa, M. N. (1986). The nation's children: Key to a secure retirement. *New England Journal of Human Services, 6*(3), 12-19.
Ozawa, M. N. (1991a). Child welfare programs in Japan. *Social Service Review, 65,* 1-21.
Ozawa, M. N. (1991b). Income support for children: A time for change. *Children and Youth Services Review, 13,* 7-27.
Ozawa, M. N. (1991c). Unequal treatment of children on AFDC by the federal government. *Children and Youth Services Review, 13,* 257-269.
Ozawa, M. N. (1992). The nation's children: Key to a secure retirement. In M. Bloom (Ed.), *Changing lives: Studies in human development and professional helping* (pp. 293-302). Columbia: University of South Carolina Press.
Putka, G. (1989, September 12). Scores on college entrance tests fall, adding to concern about U.S. schools. *Wall Street Journal,* p. A28.
U.S. Bureau of the Census. (1984). *Projection of the population of the United States, by age, sex, and race: 1983 to 2080.* Washington, DC: Government Printing Office.
U.S. Bureau of the Census. (1990). *Statistical abstract of the United States: 1990.* Washington, DC: Government Printing Office.
U.S. House of Representatives, Committee on Ways and Means. (1991). *1991 green book: Background materials and data on programs within the jurisdiction of the Committee on Ways and Means.* Washington, DC: Government Printing Office.
U.S. National Center for Health Statistics. (1990). *Vital statistics of the United States, 1988: Vol. 1. Natality* (DHHS Publication No. 90-110). Washington, DC: Government Printing Office.

MARTHA N. OZAWA RESPONDS

Dr. Moon has done a good job in writing a political commentary on the subject at hand. One of the characteristics of political writing is the alteration of reality through the incorrect or inappropriate use of data. A few examples follow.

First, citing the number of AFDC families and the total AFDC payments, Moon suggests that the taxpayer dollars spent and the number of families receiving AFDC are getting out of control. To be more accurate in presenting data, one needs to make adjustments to the data Moon cites. Regarding the number of families: One needs to adjust for the increase in the population and for the downsizing of families over the years. Thus a more reasonable indicator is the percentage of children (under age 19) who were on AFDC in 1940 and 1990: 2% of children were on AFDC in 1940, compared with 10% in 1987 (Social Security Administration, 1941, p. 69; U.S. Bureau of the Census, 1975, p. 15; 1984, p. 47; U.S. House of Representatives, 1992, p. 660). These figures give quite a different impression from that projected by Moon's figures of 490,000 families in 1940 versus 4.1 million families in 1990. Next, regarding aggregate AFDC payments: To compare the AFDC payments in two different years, one needs to adjust for inflation to arrive at the figure for 1940. Thus, in 1987 dollars, the 1940 aggregate AFDC payments were $1.08 billion, compared with $16.3 billion for 1987 (Darnay, 1992, pp. 224-225; Social Security Administration, 1941, p. 67; U.S. House of Representatives, 1992, p. 654).[1]

Second, Moon also implies that the government has become too generous in its payments to AFDC recipients. Such concern is unwarranted. In 1987 dollars, the average annual AFDC payment per recipient was $1,214 in 1940, compared with $1,475 in 1987—or a 21% increase.[2] During the same period, the U.S. per capita income increased by 221% in real terms (Darnay, 1992, pp. 224-225; U.S. Bureau of the Census, 1975, p. 225; 1990, p. 437). Thus, on the basis of the nation's ability to pay, AFDC payments were less generous in 1987 than in 1940.

Third, Moon says that the number of AFDC families doubled between 1968 and 1978. This statement is unreasonable. First, the comparison years are too old to argue, even politically. Second, because the size of families has become smaller over the years, the number of recipients is a more appropriate indicator of the change in AFDC clientele. From 1983 to 1992, the number of recipients increased by 27% (U.S. House of Representatives, 1992, p. 660). The U.S. population increased by 8% during the same period (U.S. Bureau of the Census, 1984, pp. 41, 57). Therefore, taking the increase in the population into account, the net increase in AFDC recipients is construed as 19%. To bring even more sense to these figures, the number of poor persons living in female-headed families increased from 8.8 million in 1978 to 11.7 million in 1986, or 33% (Ozawa, 1990). These data show that the number of persons on AFDC today is not at all out of line compared with a decade ago.

On substantive issues, I stand by my argument. Moon says that "in the absence of a strong economic rationale, . . . workfare may be preferred." There is ample economic reason AFDC mothers should have the option to work or not to work. AFDC mothers who think they can maximize their families' well-being by working will choose to work, whereas those who think they can maximize their families' well-being by caring for their children at home will choose not to work. The society as a whole will be ahead. Even based on the data Moon cites, 44% of mothers with children younger than 14 are choosing not to work—presumably to maximize their families' well-being. The situation of AFDC mothers is no different.

Showing the findings from experiments with workfare in five states (Gueron, 1987), Moon justifies the mandatory work requirement of all AFDC mothers. As the researcher notes, and as Moon agrees, none of the experiments has resulted in large reductions in AFDC payments (see also Gueron & Pauly, 1991). Furthermore, the enrollment of AFDC mothers in the JOBS program will be limited for a long time: States are mandated to enroll at least 20% nonexempt AFDC mothers in the program by the end of 1995 (U.S. House of Representatives, 1992, p. 614). Thus the question is how best to deploy all the AFDC mothers in the meantime to ensure the healthy development of children, regardless of the work status of the mothers.

In the final analysis, the debate depends on whether one is concerned about the development of children or about the work behavior of AFDC mothers. Given the current political climate, Moon's concern with work behavior of AFDC mothers may be more sensible. However, given the long-range agenda of the nation—that is, steady economic growth—my concern with the development of children is more sensible.

Notes

1. This response was written before Moon adjusted and updated some of the figures in her originally published argument.

2. In 1940, mothers of AFDC children did not receive assistance payments. Thus, in that year, the number of children on AFDC equaled the number of recipients.

References

Darnay, A. J. (Eds.). (1992). *Economic indicators handbook*. Detroit, MI: Gale Research.

Gueron, J. M. (1987). Reforming welfare with work. *Public Welfare, 45,* 13-25.

Gueron, J. M., & Pauly, E. (1991). *From welfare to work*. New York: Russell Sage Foundation.

Ozawa, M. N. (1990). The feminization of poverty in the United States. *Quarterly of Social Security Research, 26,* 228-242.

Social Security Administration. (1941). [Program data]. *Social Security Bulletin, 4*(2).

U.S. Bureau of the Census. (1975). *Historical statistics of the United States: Colonial times to 1970* (Part I). Washington, DC: Government Printing Office.

U.S. Bureau of the Census. (1984). *Projection of the population of the United States, by age, sex, and race: 1983 to 2080*. Washington, DC: Government Printing Office.

U.S. Bureau of the Census. (1990). *Statistical abstract of the United States, 1990*. Washington, DC: Government Printing Office.

U.S. House of Representatives, Committee on Ways and Means. (1992). *1992 green book: Background materials and data on programs within the jurisdiction of the Committee on Ways and Means*. Washington, DC: Government Printing Office.

AILEE MOON RESPONDS

Dr. Ozawa's position against mandating work for AFDC parents is well intended, but it fails to recognize the true needs of poor families and the changing social realities surrounding them. As Dr. Ozawa points out, most long-term AFDC parents tend to be teenage mothers and high-school dropouts, many of whom have never worked. However, I disagree with Dr. Ozawa's argument that it is "more beneficial for these mothers and children, as well as for the taxpayers, if these mothers were given the opportunity to stay at home and concentrate on caring for their children." This opportunity to stay at home often leads to the perpetuation of dependency on AFDC, which never pays enough for sufficient care of the children; for many of these families, poverty becomes a way of life, with little hope for the future. What these parents really need is not the opportunity to stay at home, but the opportunity to gain education, work experience, job training, and child care that will prepare them to become self-sufficient when employment opportunities arise. This is a more realistic and desirable avenue toward hope and improved quality of life for both AFDC parents and their children. For this reason, workfare is more beneficial for both AFDC families and the taxpayers in the long run, although it costs more to the taxpayers in the short term as it provides additional benefits (e.g., child care, transportation, work experience, job training and referral) to AFDC parents.

Although I agree with Dr. Ozawa's view on the importance of developing human capital among AFDC and low-income children, I am skeptical about the impact that allowing AFDC mothers to stay at home to care for their children will have on the "development of human capital." As long as society is unwilling to ensure a uniform, national, and adequate standard for the economic well-being of all children, and as long as the majority of AFDC children are ill fed, ill housed, ill clothed, and ill educated, staying with their parents for 24 hours a day each day will add little mileage to their journey on the tough road of human capital development. This difference in viewpoints suggests the need for empirical research investigating whether the AFDC children whose parents stay at home demonstrate significantly greater academic performance than those whose parents participate in work or job training programs, after controlling for relevant intervening variables such as race, age, AFDC benefit levels, and other available nonmonetary support.

Dr. Ozawa's ideological reason for opposing workfare troubles me the most, as it seems to fantasize about the American "free enterprise economy" and the reasons people work. According to her, no one should be forced to work in a free enterprise economy. If so, is it not logical and equally fair to say that in such an economy, no one should be forced to support others who choose not to work, and yet who cannot be forced to work? The point is that the virtue of a free enterprise economy is far from being "free" from having to work, and opposing workfare on the ground of freedom not to work is neither convincing nor desirable for AFDC families who have become the burden of most working individuals and families. Let us not mystify the work reality of many working fathers and mothers, including single parents; they work not because they "hunger for work" or have "curiosity to pursue certain types of jobs," but because they are in a sense "forced" to work in order to be responsible and self-sufficient, for themselves and for their children. Are they somewhat lesser parents than those who stay at home with their children? I do not think so.

Dr. Ozawa further argues that the federal government has no moral legitimacy to require AFDC mothers to work because it fails to provide a uniform, minimum level of economic well-being to all AFDC families across the country. Whether it is morally legitimate or not for the federal government to impose work requirements is a question of what society's prevailing norms and expectations for parents with dependent children are. As social norms and values change over time, the definitional standard of moral legitimacy also changes. Thus when mothers were expected to stay at home and only few mothers worked outside the home, it was morally illegitimate to *require* AFDC mothers to work outside the home. However, today, when the majority of mothers with young children work, it appears to be morally illegitimate to *exempt* AFDC mothers from work. For this reason, I disagree with Dr. Ozawa's belief that the work requirement for AFDC mothers will backfire. Rather, I believe that insisting on "no strings attached" to AFDC benefits is more likely to backfire.

Finally, although I support the idea of requiring AFDC parents to participate in work or job training programs, it must be emphasized that workfare is no solution to a more fundamental problem of the AFDC program—that is, the absence of a uniform national standard for the eligibility criteria and benefit levels, which has resulted in differential and inequitable treatment of poor dependent children. I strongly believe that the current 50 states' AFDC programs can and should be federalized into a single program (even as a budget-neutral program), as has been done for the poor elderly, blind, and disabled through Supplemental Security Income. The budget neutrality that assures no additional cost to the federal government will result in increased benefits for AFDC families in most poor states while reducing the benefit levels for those in the most affluent states. However, adopting a budget-neutral federalized AFDC program is still a better policy choice than the current AFDC system, because by ensuring a uniform, minimum economic well-being to all AFDC families, it will help the most needy families most.

DEBATE 19

PARENTAL LEAVE POLICY

> *Should paid parental leave for family issues such as birth of children or elder care be government mandated?*

EDITORS' NOTE: We contacted many people both in and outside of academia to write the negative response to this question, but we were unsuccessful. So we have prepared that statement ourselves, even though it does not reflect our position. We believe that being informed on a controversial issue should prepare one to argue either side. Arguing one side well usually requires a knowledge of arguments that the other side will present. One of the best ways to arrive at a well-reasoned position on an issue is to take both sides of the question and make the best argument one can. We do not know if we offer the best argument possible on the negative side, but it is one argument. We have drawn from some of the statements by U.S. legislators and President Bush as a family leave bill was winding its way through the legislature to be vetoed by Bush in September 1992.

Sheila B. Kamerman says YES. She is Professor of Social Policy and Social Planning at the Columbia University School of Social Work, where she chairs the school's Doctoral Program. She is also Codirector of the Cross-National Studies Research Program. Her current research activities include studies in comparative social policy (child and family policies) and a comparative study of social policies affecting very young children and their families. She is the author or coauthor of many books and monographs and has published more than 100 articles and chapters. She is coauthor, with Alfred J. Kahn, of *Mothers Alone: Strategies for a Time of Change* (1988), and coeditor, with Alfred J. Kahn, of *Privatization and the Welfare State* (1989) and *Child Care, Parental Leaves, and the Under 3s: Policy Innovation in Europe* (1991).

Eileen Gambrill and **Mary Ann Mason** argue NO. Gambrill is a Professor of Social Welfare at the University of California, Berkeley, and coeditor of this volume. Mason is an Associate Professor of Social Welfare at the University of California, Berkeley, and coeditor of this volume.

YES　　　　　　　　　　　　　　SHEILA B. KAMERMAN

In what follows, I focus specifically on the need for government-mandated paid parental leave following childbirth.

The high proportion of women who are now in the labor force when they are pregnant and shortly after they give birth reflects a major social change in women's life experience that warrants a public policy response. If a woman's health is to be protected at the time of childbirth, she needs adequate time to recover physically and to adapt to a new role and a new baby. Moreover, if children are to develop well, they too need some opportunity to get to know their parents. Furthermore, taking time off at childbirth without paid leave could seriously overburden family income at a point in time when financial demands are increasing. A paid parental leave following childbirth or adoption is essential.

Almost two-thirds (63.5%) of all women who had their first child between 1981 and 1984 (the most recent birth cohort for which such data are available) worked while pregnant (O'Connell, 1990). This is about 50% more than did so 20 years earlier. Working while pregnant has become the norm for American women, and three-quarters of those who are in the labor force remain there until the last month of their pregnancies. Moreover, they return to work very soon after childbirth. In 1990, 51% of women with children *under* the age of 1 year, and 54% of those with children aged 1 and under were in the labor force. Indeed, of those who had their first children between 1981 and 1984, 44% had already returned to work six months after childbirth; the proportion is likely to be higher now.

Working wives raise the income of husband-wife one-earner families by about 54% and contribute more than 35% to the income of husband-wife two-earner families. Families increasingly find that they cannot afford to do without this income, especially when there is a new baby in the household. Thus the pressure on women to return to work soon after giving birth is very strong.

The United States is the only major industrialized country that does not provide a paid and job-protected maternity or parental leave on the basis of national legislation (Kamerman, 1991; Kamerman & Kahn, 1991). More than 100 countries around the world, including many developing and newly industrializing countries, provide such leave at the time of childbirth, and most of the industrialized countries cover adoption as well. For example, Singapore provides an 8-week leave, Japan provides a 14-week leave (and up to one year of unpaid, job-protected leave following childbirth), Italy gives a 5-month leave, Canada and Denmark mandate 6-month leaves, Sweden provides an 18-month leave, Germany offers 14 weeks at full pay and two years with a modest flat rate cash benefit—and the list continues.

Employers are unlikely to provide such a benefit voluntarily. A 1981 Columbia University survey found that only about 40% of working women were entitled to paid leave that would cover the six to eight weeks that most physicians believe is the minimum time women need to recover from childbirth (Kamerman, Kahn, & Kingston, 1983). A 1990 study carried out by the Institute for Women's Policy Research concluded that about 44% of working women had such coverage a decade later, only a 10% increase in coverage despite a 40% increase in the labor force participation rates of women with children under the age of 1 during these years (Spalter-Roth & Hartmann, 1990).

There is no indication that mandating such a policy would have negative consequences for U.S. employers. There is no country with which we compete economically that does not provide such a benefit, and almost all are enhancing and expanding their policies while we do nothing. Furthermore, comparable policies already exist in the United States without any evidence of negative impact on business. Thus, for example, five states (California, Hawaii, New Jersey, New York, Rhode Island) have temporary disability insurance (TDI) laws mandating a "pay or play" approach to TDI benefits that provide cash benefits at the time of non-job-related disabilities including pregnancy and maternity. These laws cover very small firms (with fewer than 10 employees) and have not created problems for either these or larger firms in the states involved.

The benefit is inexpensive when the costs are shared by all employers and employees, rather than by a small group who voluntarily decide to provide the benefit. The U.S. General Accounting Office has carried out several studies of the potential economic costs of unpaid leave requiring continuation of health insurance benefits. A 1989 GAO report concluded that the cost of a 10-week unpaid leave for the birth or adoption of a child or to care for the serious health condition of a child, spouse, or parent and 15 weeks of medical leave per year for the worker's own serious health condition would be only $7.10 per covered worker per year. Those states that have TDI, which provides the equivalent of an unemployment insurance benefit for the 10-12 weeks (4 weeks before birth and 6-8 weeks after) of maternity disability leave for a normal birth find that 0.5% (one-half of 1%) in the form of a payroll tax covers *all* disabilities, and there has often been a surplus, even during the 1980s. Indeed, the TDI tax in some states is paid completely by the employee, thus employers experience no burden at all.

Such leaves are an essential component of national child-care policy. Without them, parents may be forced to place infants in out-of-home child care at a very young age. Not only is there some debate about the consequences of such a choice, but high-quality infant care is very expensive, leaving most parents in the position of having to settle for less than adequate care or suffer an economic penalty by withdrawing from work. It is of some interest that many European countries have elected to enact longer parental leaves as an alternative—or a supplement—to an inadequate supply of infant care (Kamerman & Kahn, 1991).

Maternity and parenting a newborn infant constitute a normal "social" risk for working mothers and fathers. Women need to recover physically from childbirth and from the variety of new demands that are placed on new parents. If we want children to develop well and parents to be responsible and sensitive to their children's needs, we must become more responsive to the social and family changes that are occurring. Enacting legislation that provides for paid and job-protected leave at the time of childbirth or adoption is a modest action, but it is an essential first step.

References

Kamerman, S. B. (1991). Child care policies and programs: An international overview. In S. L. Hofferth & D. A. Phillips (Eds.), Child care policy research [Special issue]. *Journal of Social Issues, 47,* 179-196.

Kamerman, S. B., & Kahn, A. J. (Eds.). (1991). *Child care, parental leaves, and the under 3s: Policy innovations in Europe.* Westport, CT: Auburn House-Greenwood Group.

Kamerman, S. B., Kahn, A. J., & Kingston, P. (1983). *Maternity policies and working women.* New York: Columbia University Press.

O'Connell, M. (1990). Maternity leave arrangements: 1961-1985. In U.S. Bureau of the Census, *Current population reports: Work and family patterns of American women* (Series P-23, No. 165). Washington, DC: Government Printing Office.

Spalter-Roth, R., & Hartmann, H. (1990). *Unnecessary losses: Costs to Americans of the lack of family and medical leave.* Washington, DC: Institute for Women's Policy Research.

NO EILEEN GAMBRILL and MARY ANN MASON

A concern for family issues on the part of employers is not only an ethical matter, it is a practical concern. Who wants unhappy employees? Who wants employees who are so worried about unattended family concerns that they cannot attend to their jobs? Unhappy employees are likely to be less productive employees. Therefore, employers must be concerned with responsibilities that employees have as family members—as mothers, fathers, and siblings. As our population ages, we hear more about the "sandwich" generation, the group in the middle that has responsibilities not only for small children but for the care of elderly relatives. With 50% of mothers working full-time and with many employees single parents, how can employees fulfill family responsibilities without paid and job-protected leave for family issues?

The answer is not straightforward. The recently passed Family Leave Act mandates *unpaid* leave for 12 weeks. The effects of this act have yet to be evaluated, and yet there is a growing chorus advocating *paid* leave. There are problems with both paid and unpaid leave. Government-mandated job-protected unpaid family leave for birth or illness of children or elder care may have serious negative consequences; paid family leave would be even more problematic. First of all, these regulations would place excessive economic strain on businesses, especially small ones. Second, employers may be less likely to hire women it they know it may result in costly obligations if the women become pregnant. Third, government interference in this arena undermines individual initiative and employer responsibility, the hallmarks of our free enterprise system.

Who Pays?

The first concern is largely fiscal, but that does not render it less compelling. Where is the money to come from for paid leave? If it comes from businesses, how many can afford it? Where is the money to come from to train and hire replacement workers? Who will do the jobs of people whose training requires many months? It is obviously impractical to hire and train someone to fill the position of an employee who will be returning to work before the training period is up. Many businesses already have voluntarily assumed unpaid leave policies but cannot afford to provide paid leave. Other businesses cannot afford to have even unpaid leave policies—how can they afford to offer paid leave? Mandated paid leave coupled with job protection (that is, a guarantee that employees' jobs will be waiting when they return) may strain businesses to the point where they will have to close, leaving all the employees without jobs. If the government is supposed to pay for such leave (perhaps under some reimbursement policy), where is this money to come from? The budget deficit is already at a level impossible for the average person to imagine, and no one wants to assume new taxes.

Increased Job Discrimination Against Women

In choosing between a young man and a young woman, an employer would be forced to consider the possibility that the young woman could become pregnant and not only drop out of the workplace for several months, but force the employer to hold her job for her. This could cause problems in productivity or service, resulting in economic loss. In addition, the employer would be forced to pay the employee while she is at home. Even though the legislation would apply equally to men and women, experience has shown that it is women who are far more likely than men to make use of family leave. A 1991 Gallup Poll of small businesses found that 45% would be less likely to hire young women if the law were passed.

President Bush considered this negative consequence for women when he vetoed the Family Leave Act (which provided *unpaid* leave). "Think of the impact mandated family leave has on hiring decisions," he told a meeting of AT&T employees and women's service organizations. "I know it's not supposed to happen, but how many employers will think, why not hire a man instead of a women? He won't leave to care for a child. He won't leave to care for his family. And this is illegal, but we must enforce the law. But mandated family leave could encourage this subtle kind of discrimination" (quoted in Wines, 1992).

Government Interference
With Fundamental Freedoms

The third objection is more philosophical and rests upon our conception of what constitutes fundamental freedom in the United States. We have been told frequently that we are out of step with European nations—all of which offer some form of paid maternity leave and various accommodations for family illness. The fact that many countries now offer paid job-protected leaves of at least five months is not a good reason in and of itself for us to do so in the United States. Not all observers feel that this country needs to follow Europe's lead. For instance, Burton Y. Pines, director of the National Center for Public Policy Research, said recently, "I'm not sure if I like the European model for America. If you say we're being different from Europe, I'd say, 'Good.' We've always had a looser employee system here in America. A conservative would say family leave is between employer and employee" (quoted in Barringer, 1992, p. A13).

Many Americans would probably agree that the American way of life is superior to that of European countries because it offers more freedom and more opportunity. Indeed, most of our ancestors came to this country to escape authoritarian forms of government that regulated their everyday lives and impeded their chances for raising their station in life. Individual freedom is more highly prized in the United States than in any other country. A core element of this freedom is the ability to build and expand a business without excessive government interference. Property is placed alongside life and liberty in both the Fifth and Fourteenth Amendments to the Constitution as a primary individual right that must be protected from undue government influence. A government that prohibits an employer from replacing an employee who is not working is infringing on that central right.

Family leave also cuts into another freedom that Americans hold dear: the privacy of a family. This includes both the right and the obligation of families to work out their own family arrangements, including arrangements for childbirth and child care.

Alternatives

There are alternatives to mandated leave, both paid and unpaid, that involve government encouragement and practical incentives, rather than force and punitive controls. As a voluntary measure, many businesses that can afford it are already offering paid family leave. These businesses believe that they will be better able to attract the best employees if they offer this job benefit. The *New York Times* reported this voluntary trend on September 11, 1992:

> Eleven of the nation's leading corporations are joining with more than 100 smaller businesses and private organizations to collaborate on a $25.4 million project to help provide their employees care for their children and aging relatives. The money will be used to finance 300 local programs in 44 cities. The local programs include new day care centers, in-home care for the elderly, vacation programs for school-age children and training for women who care for children in their own homes. (Lewin, 1992; see also Haase, 1988)

Many businesses are already taking additional steps to help employees manage family needs, such as providing day care for children at the business site. Sometimes these day-care programs are part of a collective bargaining package with unions. The same *New York Times* article quoted above noted that "A.T. & T. in 1989 agreed to give $25 million for six years to a Family Care Development Fund that would make grants to projects in the communities serving the company's workers. A year later, I.B.M. created a similar fund, setting aside $25 million over five years" (Lewin, 1992).

Tax credits to employers who voluntarily develop family leave programs are another positive alternative to mandatory legislation. Tax credits that would allow employers to receive special tax benefits if they voluntarily assume family leave plans would offer an incentive, rather than a bludgeon, to achieve the same end. Such incentives would allow employers to decide whether their businesses can handle the burden of family leave, and would provide economic relief if they choose to do so. Tax relief alone could not save some businesses from financial disaster if they attempted to provide paid childbirth leave, but tax incentives would likely do the job for businesses with larger, more flexible personnel bases.

Summary

Government-mandated paid leave is not the answer for helping families to cope with such family events as childbirth or elder care. There are other options, some of which are already in place; others, especially tax incentives, could be quickly implemented. Businesses, family advocacy groups, and government officials should work together to forward options that help both businesses and families and do not impinge upon the privacy and responsibilities of families and businesses.

References

Barringer, F. (1992, October 7). In family-leave debate: A profound ambivalence. *New York Times*, pp. A2, A13.

Haase, D. K. (1988). Evaluating the desirability of federally mandated parental leave. *Family Law Quarterly, 22*, 341-365.

Lewin, T. (1992, September 11). 11 companies join on family project. *New York Times*, p. A10.

Wines, M. (1992, September 24). Senate vote is set today on Bush's veto of family-leave measures. *New York Times*, p. A14.

EILEEN GAMBRILL and MARY ANN MASON RESPOND

Professor Kamerman raises several points in favor of mandated *paid* parental leave following childbirth. The original question referred to unpaid leave and included reasons such as illness of a family member and elder care. However, most of Kamerman's observations pertain to unpaid leave as well.

Professor Kamerman argues that women must return to work shortly after birth because they need the money that a second income provides. How do we know they need the money? Surely many women have husbands who could support them for longer leaves. Why should other employees or the public be expected to pay for leave that could be supported by the family income? The same objection could be made for unpaid leaves that unfairly burden employers by requiring them to leave positions open.

Kamerman suggests the importance of protecting the mother's health and the need for adequate time to recover from childbirth. What amount of time is needed? What data are available that would help us to decide how much time is needed to adapt to a new role? What individual differences exist? Won't some people take longer than others? The length of leave provided in different countries varies greatly, from eight weeks to one year. Why such variation? If physicians recommend six to eight weeks, why would anyone offer a full year of leave time? Doesn't this variation reflect different values rather than data describing what is medically or psychologically best for children and families?

Kamerman claims that "if children are to develop well, they too need some opportunity to get to know their parents." We need further clarification and data to support these assertions. For example, what does "get to know" mean? What do we know about the future development of children whose mothers took a leave following childbirth compared with those whose mothers did not? Does this make any difference 20 years later?

The fact that other industrialized countries provide paid and job-protected leave does not in itself support the assertion that we should provide this in the United States. What can be done with success in other countries may differ in substantial ways from what can be done with success in the United States. In relation to Professor Kamerman's third point, we note in our initial argument that many employers already make some provision for leave, thus calling into question the need for government intervention. Is lack of day-care arrangements for infants a sound reason for mandating parental leave?

Shouldn't other alternatives be explored for providing adequate day care for children?

The cost of a leave policy could be less expensive for any one individual or business if shared, as Kamerman suggests. However, this would mean that employees on marginal incomes as well as those with plentiful incomes would share this cost via a payroll tax. Aren't marginal employees already taxed enough? Don't the temporary disability insurance laws also depend on contributions from individuals with marginal incomes? We have argued that the cost would be excessive for many small businesses. Cost estimates of the 1989 GAO report cited by Kamerman do not appear to consider costs to employers of loss of skilled employees and the effects of this on production. How can a leave policy allow flexibility for the family to select different lengths of leave without harming businesses through removal of skilled workers for different time periods?

SHEILA B. KAMERMAN RESPONDS

It is true that the effects of the Family and Medical Leave Act of 1993 have yet to be evaluated. Nonetheless, the experiences of several states that enacted unpaid parental leave policies have been evaluated, and the conclusion is that the employers in these states have experienced no difficulties or any particular costs in implementing the policy (Bond, Galinsky, Lourd, Staines, & Brown, 1991). Further, employees have experienced significantly better health outcomes. My responses to the subsequent arguments against paid parental leave follow.

First, mandating a paid parental leave would not place excessive economic strain on small employers or on firms regardless of size. To begin with, really small employers are excluded from the federal legislation, which covers only those firms employing 50 or more employees. This limitation should be changed, however, to include at least employees in all firms now covered by Title VII of the Civil Rights Act of 1964 and its subsequent amendments, namely, firms with 15 or more employees.

With regard to the issue of the economic burden on small employers, there is strong evidence that a parental leave cash benefit, providing partial wage replacement to a qualified employee while on leave, would not add to the employer's burden. There is now a 15-year history in five states (California, Hawaii, New Jersey, New York, and Rhode Island) that have temporary disability insurance programs in place that, since 1978, are required to cover pregnancy and maternity as disabilities. State TDI programs cover all employees in firms with one or more employees who are at home as a consequence of a non-work-related disability and provide a benefit somewhat similar to that provided under unemployment insurance. The costs are very modest (about 0.5-1% of payroll) and are paid largely by employees (California, Hawaii, and Rhode Island). In New Jersey and New York, employers contribute a modest amount as well, but less than that paid by employees. In some states there has even been a surplus in the fund during the past two decades, and in no state has the program proved expensive or burdensome. Certainly, there is no evidence, for example, that small businesses have left these states for adjacent states that do not have TDI programs.

Second, there is extensive evidence from existing research that in most firms, the work of the employee home on leave is covered by the efforts of other employees, picking up what is urgent, on a temporary basis (Kamerman & Kahn, 1987). Moreover, permitting employees a phased-in return to work following childbirth would further ensure that the most urgent work would be picked up by the employee when she or he returns, albeit part-time initially.

Third, more than 100 countries around the world now provide paid as well as job-protected leaves, for at least 12 weeks at the time of childbirth. Our major competitors, Japan and Germany, provide more than this. Certainly, if they can provide such benefits, we can as well.

Fourth, if such a policy were in place, employers would not be any more likely to be biased against young female workers than they are now. If it were a gender-neutral policy, as it is now, targeted on "parents" and not just "mothers," some men would participate and take at least a part of the leave. Although more women would take advantage of the policy, and certainly use it for longer periods of time, the fact that men could—and increasingly would—take the leave would mitigate employers' penalizing of women. The only way to avoid hiring an individual who may need to take a leave would be to avoid hiring men as well, and that seems extremely unrealistic.

Fifth, there is no reason employers would find this form of government regulation any more onerous than such other existing forms as minimum-wage laws, occupational health and safety laws, and mandatory social security contributions. In general, employers find all government regulations onerous and antithetical to their preferences. Nonetheless, when those laws are enacted, employers conform. Our neighbor to the north, Canada, now has in place a mandatory six-month leave at the time of childbirth that is, in fact, delivered and paid for through the nation's unemployment insurance fund, under a policy that was first established in 1971.

Sixth, to argue that employers will provide this benefit voluntarily is nonsense. Employers did not provide job-protected unpaid leaves voluntarily, despite the increasingly feminized workforce and workplace. Paid parental leaves are even less likely to be provided voluntarily. In January 1993, the *Monthly Labor Review* reported that paid parental leave was "rare" as a family-related benefit in 1991 even in medium and large firms, let alone in small firms (with fewer than 100 employees).

Tax credits creating incentives for employers to provide more in the way of family-related policies have been in place for almost two decades and have had extraordinarily little impact. Furthermore, most of what the small number of "family-friendly" employers now provide is very modest at best—child-care information and referral services, salary reduction plans, and occasional lunchtime seminars.

We have a long history in this and other countries that documents how limited employers' voluntary responses are to social change and changes in the workforce, the workplace, and society at large. Women now constitute more than 45% of the workforce and husbands constitute most of the rest.

Their work and family lifestyle patterns have changed, and society must become more responsive to those changes. Paid parental leaves are an essential if modest policy if adults are to become parents while remaining in the labor force, and if they and their children are not to suffer severe economic penalties as a consequence.

References

Bond, J. T., Galinsky, E., Lourd, M., Staines, G. L., & Brown, K. R. (1991). *Beyond the parental leave debate: The impact of laws in four states.* New York: Families and Work Institute.

Kamerman, S. B., & Kahn, A. J. (1987). *The responsive workplace.* New York: Columbia University Press.

ABOUT THE EDITORS

Mary Ann Mason is Associate Professor of Social Welfare at the University of California, Berkeley. She has been a family law practitioner and has written on issues concerning women and children and the law. She is the author of *The Equality Trap* (1989), and *From Fathers' Property to Childern's Rights: A History of Child Custody in America* (1994)..

Eileen Gambrill, Ph.D., is Professor of Social Welfare at the University of California, Berkeley. She has been interested in the field of child welfare for many years and has published articles, chapters, and books in this area, including *Supervision: A Decision Making Approach* (with T. J. Stein). She is also interested in the area of clinical decision making, as reflected in her recent book, *Critical Thinking in Clinical Practice* (1990).